Who Pays for Bank Insolvency?

Also by David G. Mayes and Aarno Liuksila

IMPROVING BANKING SUPERVISION (*with Liisa Halme*)

Also by David G. Mayes

PUBLIC INTEREST AND MARKET PRESSURES (*with W. Hager, A. Knight and W. Streeck*)

MODERN PORTFOLIO THEORY AND FINANCIAL INSTITUTIONS (*with D. C. Corner*)

SOCIAL EXCLUSION IN EUROPEAN WELFARE STATES (*with R. Muffels and P. Tsakloglou*)

SOCIAL EXCLUSION AND EUROPEAN POLICY (*with J. Berghman and R. Salais*)

THE EVOLUTION OF THE SINGLE EUROPEAN MARKET

SOURCES OF PRODUCTIVITY GROWTH

THE SINGLE MARKET PROGRAMME AS A STIMULUS TO CHANGE (*with P. E. Hart*)

INEFFICIENCY IN INDUSTRY (*with C. Harris and M. Lansbury*)

THE EVOLUTION OF RULES FOR A SINGLE EUROPEAN MARKET (*editor*)
1 Industry and Finance
2 Rules, Democracy and the Environment
3 Social and International Issues

FOREIGN DIRECT INVESTMENT AND TRANSITION (*editor with G. Csaki and G. Foti*)

THE EXTERNAL IMPLICATIONS OF EUROPEAN INTEGRATION (*with others*)

ACHIEVING MONETARY UNION (*with A. Britton*)

A NEW STRATEGY FOR SOCIAL AND ECONOMIC COHESION AFTER 1992 (*with I. Begg*)

THE EUROPEAN CHALLENGE

A STRATEGY FOR THE ECU (*with A. Britton and Ernst & Young*)

SHARPBENDERS (*with P. Grinyer and P. McKiernan*)

INTEGRATION AND EUROPEAN INDUSTRY (*with M. Macmillen and P. van Veen*)

THE EXCHANGE RATE ENVIRONMENT (*with S. Brooks and K. Cuthbertson*)

APPLICATIONS OF ECONOMETRICS

THE PROPERTY BOOM

INTRODUCTORY ECONOMIC STATISTICS (*with A. C. Mayes*)

Who Pays for Bank Insolvency?

David G. Mayes

and

Aarno Liuksila

with

Thorsten Beck, Bethany Blowers, Henk Brouwer, Peik Granlund, Christos Hadjiemmanuil, Gerbert Hebbink, Eva H. G. Hüpkes, Eigil Mølgaard, Jón Sigurðsson, Gary H. Stern, Sandra Wesseling and Garry Young

palgrave macmillan

SUOMEN PANKKI · FINLANDS BANK

The views expressed in this publication are those of the authors and are not necessarily those of the Bank of Finland.

First published 2004 by
PALGRAVE MACMILLAN
Houndmills, Basingstoke, Hampshire RG21 6XS and
175 Fifth Avenue, New York, N.Y. 10010
Companies and representatives throughout the world

PALGRAVE MACMILLAN is the global academic imprint of the Palgrave Macmillan division of St. Martin's Press, LLC and of Palgrave Macmillan Ltd. Macmillan® is a registered trademark in the United States, United Kingdom and other countries. Palgrave is a registered trademark in the European Union and other countries.

ISBN 1–4039–1740–X

This book is printed on paper suitable for recycling and made from fully managed and sustained forest sources.

A catalogue record for this book is available from the British Library.

Library of Congress Cataloging-in-Publication Data
Who pays for bank insolvency?/[edited by] David G. Mayes, Aarno Liuksila.
p. cm.
Includes bibliographical references and index.
ISBN 1–4039–1740–X
1. Bank failures – Government policy. 2. Banks and banking – State supervision. 3. Banking law. 4. Intervention (Federal government).
I. Mayes, David G. II. Liuksila, Aarno.
HG1725.W47 2004
332.1—dc21 2003056404

10 9 8 7 6 5 4 3 2 1
13 12 11 10 09 08 07 06 05 04

Printed and bound in Great Britain by
Antony Rowe Ltd, Chippenham and Eastbourne

Contents

List of Tables

List of Figures

Preface

This book addresses two concerns. The first is that, should large and complex banks operating in more than one country get into difficulty, adequate systems are not in place for organizing their orderly resolution. The second consequential concern is that, if suitable exit mechanisms do not exist, such banks will be tempted to run themselves on the basis that they will be bailed out by the authorities, using taxpayers' money, if difficulty arises – a typical example of reciprocal 'moral hazard'. This could also have adverse consequences for the rest of the economy and smaller banks in particular.

The problem occurs where banks operate as a grouping under centralized management yet their parts are subject to resolution as separate legal entities. This is particularly acute for the smaller countries of Europe, where there is an important mismatch between bearing the economic consequences of bank failures and adequate sharing of the legal powers to resolve such groupings in the public interest of the countries involved. The recent Winding-up Directive only addresses that part of these problems which relate to the exit liquidation and reorganization of branches of an EEA bank located in other EEA countries. The Directive relates to the exercise of concurrent jurisdiction by 'host' and 'home' countries in the case of a single legal entity. With the coming expansion of the EEA this concerns at least 20 countries.

There are two consequences in these circumstances. First, despite the increased peer pressure at intergovernmental level in the form of the Basel Committee discussions for improved management of risks by banks themselves, an important challenge to the stability of the economic system may remain. There are already worries that the Basel proposals themselves may increase the overall volatility of the financial system. If the authorities are not in a position to organize bank exits in the event of substantial problems then there will be an incentive for banks to take on 'correlated risks'. This is the problem of herding – if too many banks get into difficulty at the same time then the taxpayer will bail the banks out because too many simultaneous failures would threaten the stability of the financial system as a whole. The second consequence is that the bailing out of large banks by the taxpayer inherently results in substantial issues of competition and equity. The consequences of realized risks may be shifted from those who have been paid for taking them to those who have not and the playing field for fair and efficient competition among banks may be tilted.

A key problem that emerges is delay. Delay tends to permit increasing losses. If handling a large problem bank is difficult, there are strong incentives for the supervisory authorities to delay action in the hope that the problem will right itself, particularly that the private sector will be able to come up with a solution. Unfortunately that optimistic outcome only occurs some of the time and forbearance is likely to encourage risk-taking and increase losses. Management in difficulty may already be facing their maximum loss in the sense of their jobs and share options. When the problem is relatively small, several approaches to its solution are possible; as it grows over time, only the taxpayer has the resources to cover the eventual losses and the problem acquires the label 'systemic'.

Although provisions for the orderly exit of banks that have ceased to comply with the conduct-related conditions for registration are in place, they have been impossible to apply in practice to close larger banks that are failing or have failed in the economic sense. Sanctions other than withdrawal of authorization appropriately apply to all banks for disobeying instructions or breaching their own undertakings *vis-à-vis* regulators. The principal difficulty is one of law which is based on a demonstrated disruption of payments rather than the economics of intervention based on valuation.

The main business of the failed bank needs to continue uninterrupted even if the legal ownership and management of the bank are changed in the process. An efficient coordinated system of managing this transition under rules that are known in advance needs to be in place. Such a system exists in the United States where a single authority is required to act promptly under public law to liquidate the assets and liabilities of insured depository institutions in a way that minimizes the losses incurred by the deposit insurer. Other possibilities exist and are discussed in the Introduction. Chapters 6 and 11 argue strongly in favour of the 'London Approach' in which the authorities rely on the equity courts for case administration (judicial liquidations and reorganizations).

We, however, offer a simple transparent system based on a version of the US public law approach, which could be widely adopted, particularly by small countries that are home or host to large geographically dispersed banking groups. The authorities are required to act quickly to effect an exit of the failed bank under a scheme that restructures its assets, liabilities and equity as if it had been liquidated up-front, helping to transform it without liquidation into a solid bank that can continue the main business without interruption. This scheme of reorganization measures was originally proposed in a companion book, *Improving*

Banking Supervision (David Mayes, Liisa Halme and Aarno Liuksila, Palgrave, 2001). Here we offer more detail and answers to common questions about the scheme, and augment that with discussion and appraisal of the issues it raises by experts in the field who come from a variety of backgrounds. However, the point remains the same – to have a structure where the incentives for all those involved – shareholders, supervisors, depositors alike – are directed towards having both prudently run banks and an efficient and smoothly running system in which the public has confidence, innovative and competitive banks are born and grow and the weak decline, are acquired or close.

Fortunately, many of the risks highlighted in this book have yet to be realized and it is our hope in writing it that action will be taken sufficiently quickly that they remain theoretical possibilities rather than reality. However, the substantial rash of banking crises over the last 20 years suggests that problems remain. The threats are particularly clear from a Finnish perspective. It is only a decade since Finland suffered an economic crisis, which was by most measures more severe in its impact than the Great Crash of 1929. Excessive risk-taking by banks, weak regulation and supervision and destabilizing macroeconomic management were major contributors to the difficulties, even if the collapse of the former Soviet Union may have been the final straw that precipitated the crisis. While the severe problems might have been avoided by running a more prudent system, as existed nearby in Denmark at the time, the key outcome was that taxpayers' funds were used in large measure to bail out the banks and an unconditional guarantee of the availability of reserves for banks was issued to bank creditors and depositors. The financial consequences are likely to persist for another decade. The expectation of a future bailout, should there be another crisis, will also remain, whatever the rhetoric to the contrary, unless a credible framework for avoiding it is put in place.

Furthermore since the crisis, the banking system in Finland has become both highly concentrated and international. The Finnish authorities can no longer act on their own to resolve the problem. They have to act with the authorities of the surrounding countries which are also affected. This is a daunting prospect as it is frequently necessary to act rapidly. The problem is by no means unique to Finland. As the book explores, the largest Swiss banks are so big compared with their home country that they are in a very real sense too big for the authorities to save, as opposed to the continuing traditional concern of also being too important to the stability of the financial system to be allowed to fail.

David G. Mayes

Acknowledgements

We are particularly grateful to the contributors to this volume who provided a vigorous opportunity to debate and therefore refine the ideas we have proposed. While they are in no way implicated in our views their role has been crucial. The views expressed here and in the continuing discussions are, of course, personal and do not necessarily reflect those of the organizations for which they work. We were keen to get the best international team of experts in this field, mixing both economists and lawyers, academics and practitioners drawn from the different regulatory traditions across the world, particularly the USA, UK, continental European and Nordic countries. They were helpful, not just in commenting on our chapters, but on each others'.

The Bank of Finland too has been instrumental in encouraging and providing the resources for this work, particularly in organizing the workshop in November 2002, at which first versions of the chapters were discussed. Helsinki produced some unseasonably cold weather to encourage a focus on the scholarship. We owe a debt to numerous colleagues in the Bank, including Karlo Kauko, Tuomas Takalo and Juha Tarkka, and to Kaarlo Jännäri, Director General of the Finnish Supervision Authority who participated in the whole workshop. Other colleagues from the FSA, particularly Paula Launiainen and Oili Wuolle were very helpful in providing advice and material for our work. Heli Tikkunen at the Bank helped with some of our technical difficulties and Mia Erkko, Kaisa-Liisa Nordman and Marjut Salovuori with the logistical support.

David Mayes organized the project, the workshop and edited this book.

DAVID G. MAYES
AARNO LIUKSILA

Notes on the Contributors

The editor(s)

David G. Mayes is Advisor to the Board at the Bank of Finland, Professor of Economics at London South Bank University, and Honorary Professor of Banking and Financial Institutions at the University of Stirling.

Aarno Liuksila is Managing Director of the International Arbitration Management Corporation in Washington, DC.

Thorsten Beck is with World Bank in Washington, DC.

Bethany Blowers is an analyst in the Domestic Finance Division, Bank of England.

Henk Brouwer is Executive Director of De Nederlandsche Bank.

Peik Granlund is a lawyer in the Finnish Financial Supervision Authority.

Christos Hadjiemmanuil is Senior Lecturer in Law at the London School of Economics.

Gerbert Hebbink is Senior Economist at the Financial Stability Department of De Nederlandsche Bank.

Eva H. G. Hüpkes is Head of Regulation in the Legal Department of the Swiss Federal Banking Commission.

Eigil Mølgaard is a legal and financial adviser, and former Director General of the Danish Financial Supervisory Authority.

Jón Sigurðsson is President and Chief Executive Officer of the Nordic Investment Bank.

Gary H. Stern is President of the Federal Reserve Bank of Minneapolis.

Sandra Wesseling is Senior Economist at the Directorate Supervision of De Nederlandsche Bank.

Garry Young is Senior Research Manager in the Domestic Finance Division, Bank of England.

Introduction

Aarno Liuksila

This book stems from the papers contributed to the workshop organized by the Bank of Finland in November 2002, on the topic, 'Who Will Pay for Bank Insolvency?'

The lightning rod for the discussion was an invitation to comment on a 'Proposed Bank Reorganisation and Liquidation Scheme' (the 'Proposed Scheme') which had been published in *Improving Banking Supervision*, by David Mayes, Liisa Halme and Aarno Liuksila in 2001. The 'who' that will pay for bank insolvency under the Proposed Scheme are the pre-existing shareholders and unsecured creditors that can absorb their own losses – in all cases including individual banks of some size and, in the systemic cases, subject to the adoption of a robust exit policy that will eliminate delays in the initiation of the process of distribution of losses, and a requisite legal reform of case administration that will eliminate delays in the completion of the process. Were bailouts to occur, nevertheless, the Scheme would eliminate the incidental benefits for the pre-existing shareholders and unsecured creditors. Moreover, the substitution of concessions by the risk-takers for contributions by taxpayers would re-establish the prudential incentives, defeating the well-embedded expectations of solvency support from public resources. The Scheme marshals the resources for meeting the loss (negative net worth); by logical necessity, the prescribed concessions from the pre-existing shareholders and unsecured creditors suffices to restore the failed bank in a (marginally) solvent condition.

Hence, in its operation the Proposed Scheme is the very opposite of many flexible case-by-case approaches that categorically deny, *ex ante*, any 'special treatment' of failed or failing banks, except bailouts that deny the 'general treatment' on a case-by-case basis. It applies in all cases, including bailouts that might be carried out on a case-by-case basis.

For their lack of perfect foresight the national legislators tend to limit the exercise of legislative jurisdiction to the resolution of failed banks to a core of 'normal cases', which are, in effect, small banks. Because legislators do not want to address unforeseeable or remote contingencies such as 'national defaults', they do not want to take a categorical position against undertaking bailouts on a case-by-case basis if there were a systemic threat. Their denial of special treatment is founded on a conviction that the public treasury is the 'who' that bears the residual liability for the net expected social costs and benefits under, say, an (emergency) universal deposit guarantee.

The denial of special treatment for any failed bank has great appeal where banks show an extreme diversity in their size, functions or other characteristics. The legislators easily see that failed banks should share the 'normal' fate of other failed businesses, withholding, however, any judgement on bailouts on a case-by-case basis.

The first approach throws out a safety net that precludes the closure of any bank for the potential systemic effects and consequences of the closure. By not achieving the same degree of preclusion, the second approach risks a panic as the (inadvertent) judicial closure of a single failed bank might bring about the failure of other banks. Indeed, the natural consequences of any bank closure include the dumping of assets and collateral, freezing of bank balances, imposing of undue delays in transfers of funds in settlement of commitments, and disruptions of credit supply in the community that the bank serves. *Ex ante* any bank closure risks systemic effects and consequences because the systemic case is not obvious *ex ante*, and can only be proven *ex post*. Indeed, both approaches have an element of official moral hazard that amplifies private moral hazard on the side of failing banks.

The systemic case has come to serve as an *ex post* rationalization of all bailouts. Therefore, the authors' criticism was that the differentiation between the so-called systemic and non-systemic cases, that is at the heart of the aforementioned flexible approaches, only works by way of 20/20 hindsight (*ex post*) and not *ex ante*, almost invariably starting from a single bank failure. However, although it applies in all cases, the Proposed Scheme does not preclude differentiation between banks at the margin, a local definitional issue. The stipulated generality of the Proposed Scheme simply means that it covers the systemic case, subject to up-front exclusions. In terms of the Winding-up and Reorganization Directive, the systemic case comprises (i) the authorized banks at home and their branches abroad under the single legal entity approach; and (ii) the local branches of banks authorized abroad where the directive authorizes their reorganization as separate entities. It neither presupposes any consolidation of case administration in respect of an affiliation of separate bank or non-bank legal entities under centralized management, nor any other access to the Scheme for separate non-bank legal entities. At the bottom line, subject to the law of the EU (for example, Deposit Guarantee Directive), it imposes no residual liability or other responsibility on the part of the Public Treasury for losses incurred by banks or other third parties.

This introduction has four parts:

1. *Antecedents* pertain to the preparatory work for the workshop, reviewing first, in broad outline, the case for the enactment of a '*lex specialis*' in support of a robust exit policy in the field of bank insolvency law, and giving an illustration of how the Proposed Scheme works.
2. The ensuing *Discussion* pertains to the diversity of 'principled' answers to a question of who are the third parties who may be 'bailed in' as contributors to 'bail out' a failed bank, and who are the intended or incidental beneficiaries of that bailout of the bank.
3. *Findings and Conclusions* summarize the conclusions of the Workshop on the need for possible policy and legal reform.
4. The *Resumé* is a current assessment of world-wide legislative trends, and the divergent directions taken by national legislators, governments and other authorities who drive the process of exit policy formulation, and the design and drafting of bank insolvency laws.

0.1 Antecedents

The Proposed Scheme is a market-based solution to the problem of bank failure, which is consistent with the notion that banking is a private industry, albeit a heavily regulated one. By a market-based solution we mean that it is for an individual bank to resolve the problem of business failure itself proactively through workouts against the backdrop of a threat of failure, and that the authorities intervene only when the bank has insufficient assets to cover liabilities. Here experience shows that there are not only two separate and distinct phases – private workouts and their opposite, public intervention – but also a third phase, which includes a period of delay caused by affirmative inaction on the part of bank supervisors, between the two proactive phases.

We believe that the solution to the problem at hand is the elimination of the undue delay in intervention, which in itself causes the bunching of the officially unrecognized bank failures, transforming what was a bad situation into a case of systemic dimensions in the face of adverse developments in the market. The systemic case has been one where the losses shift from the banking sector to the public sector, in the interest of avoiding the prescribed form of intervention, which is the opening of judicial reorganization and liquidation proceedings in respect of an insolvent bank. This course of action, indeed, can be avoided, as general banking laws typically authorize and direct the administrative authorities to exercise administrative discretion in guessing whether or not the competent court might determine that a failed or failing bank, that is, nevertheless, kept open and operating, is legally insolvent, too. It is true that, as long as the bank in question keeps encashing its assets in order to discharge its obligations and liabilities on a first-come-first-served basis, it is not insolvent.

0.1.1 Working definitions

The legal term of 'insolvency' where used in reference to a debtor bank means, paraphrasing statutory language, a state in which the debtor for want of liquid assets, not merely a temporary short fall, is unable to discharge all of his or her debts as they mature. Therefore, there is a distinction between the economic state of 'silent' bank failure, the determination of which typically vests in the administrative authorities, on the one hand, and the legal state of a 'loud' bank insolvency, the determination of which typically vests in the judicial authorities on the demonstration supplied by the petitioner of a default in payments or a 'run', on the other. To simplify the following presentation, where the discussion pertains to 'failure' or 'default' on the part of a subject bank, the text has to be construed accordingly. In law, if opposed by the subject bank, the economic test of failure and the legal test of default are demanding tests; however, were the bank to assert in good faith any failure or default on its own part, it would be unusual for the authorities to oppose the submission.

0.1.2 The public interest

Perhaps the only non-market-based feature of the Proposed Scheme is a re-interpretation of the 'public interest' of the kind that drives the (public) decision-making by which the process functions thereunder, or any like process of intervention ultimately functions. Over the years, the public interest at stake has become defined in a way that implies both:

(i) affirmative action in the form of banking supervision that represents the devotion of public-sector human resources in the intense process

by which a failed or failing subject bank may engage in the above mentioned 'workouts' on its own account, and
(ii) as a corollary, 'affirmative inaction' on the part of the competent administrative or judicial authorities.

The proposed reinterpretation of the public interest would work in a manner that mandated a take-over of the bank, and other specified actions, upon finding the earlier of failure or default on the part of the subject bank.

The above specification of purposes that are within the 'public interest' involved is, indeed, the critical feature of the scheme, which distinguishes it from any antecedent schemes. By combining administrative tests of bank failure with judicial insolvency tests (default) these schemes are eventually triggered only by the more demanding judicial determination of insolvency in the case of a failed or failing bank. As opposed to the prevalence of a range of informal and '*ad hoc*' measures pertaining to individual and systemic bank restructuring, the opening of judicial bank insolvency proceedings has not been a recurring event. Hence, the Proposed Scheme is informed of a diversity of administrative frameworks that exist for the purpose of 'out of court' administration of a failed or failing bank that continues in legal entity and personality.

0.1.3 The threshold case

The threshold case of a failed or failing bank is one in which the subject bank keeps open and operating, as it is apparently 'not insolvent' on the prescribed legal criteria, although it may well be critically undercapitalized. Here the public support typically takes the form of 'affirmative inaction', a purpose within the public interest. If it does not constitute a compelling case for the opening of judicial proceedings, it may, nevertheless, make a case for a bailout in aid of corporate restructuring (as opposed to reorganization under supervision of the competent court). An alternative pre-insolvency 'restructuring scheme' may be readily activated in order to pre-empt the forthcoming automatic stay both on the making of payments by the subject bank, as well as on the institution of the prescribed judicial reorganization and liquidation proceedings against the bank. Ordinarily, the restructuring scheme is a special vehicle that meets the net cumulative loss incurred by the subject bank, having been adequately capitalized or guaranteed for that purpose by the Public Treasury. In that event, the problem has been resolved. However, the question of the appropriate treatment of the above mentioned threshold case raises a number of concerns regarding principles.

0.1.4 The 'common pool' approach

By its very purpose, the common pool approach avoids inter-creditor wars as well as shareholder–creditor wars. The principle is, therefore, the foundation of any market-based economy.

How does it work?

Pure bargaining drives bank rescues of the kind that take the form of corporate restructuring such as the merger of a solid bank with what may be, in truth, a failed bank, or of the latter's division into parts that become parts of existing solid banks, or new banks.

The characteristic feature of a merger or division is the requisite 'succession' that takes place, by the operation of law 'without liquidation'. Hence, the valuation at which the assets and liabilities, of which the ownership changes hands, is a matter of pure bargaining. Losses can be carried on through a series of mergers and divisions without overstating assets or understating liabilities. Hence, at the receiving end of a merger or division we may find

(i) the very bank that has been 'invited' to participate in the 'assisted' transaction; or
(ii) more likely, a publicly pre-funded, or guaranteed special purpose entity which will pay for bank insolvency.

The same is true of any sales of 'assets and liabilities', or of the so-called 'purchase and assumption' transactions.

Arguably, a corporate restructuring is an expeditious, economic and efficient way to merge or divide the 'problem pool'. However, there is always tension with the applicable bankruptcy and general insolvency laws that operate retroactively in respect of transactions carried out during a prescribed 'pre-insolvency' period. Where the successor entity fails, the transactions may be reopened. Hence, we find the common pool approach superior to the alternative restructuring schemes that entail the financing of losses by the public treasury.

Indeed, the US approach to corporate restructuring is the 'common pool' approach. There is a limitation on the liability of the FDIC that operates so as to bar the assumption by the FDIC of any uninsured losses incurred by the depository institution. Therefore, all 'purchase and assumption' transactions are carried out on a realistic market-related valuation.

The potential for transferring losses through overvaluation of assets, and under valuation of liabilities is the pathology of any approach other than the common pool approach. Namely, corporate reorganizations are unlikely to extinguish all bad debt, permitting any failed or failing bank to continue in fresh legal entity and personality. Unless corporate mergers, divisions and 'sales of assets and liabilities' are carried out on a realistic valuation, they generate failed or failing successor legal entities. The same is also true of so-called 'publicly assisted' mergers, divisions and 'sales of assets and liabilities' that are not carried out on a realistic official valuation, and of any generic 'reorganization measures' that consolidate, deconsolidate or otherwise confuse separate legal or economic entities.

0.1.5 Advantages and disadvantages of the common pool approach

In the field of banking, an outright bankruptcy is the superior legal technique from the vantage point of minimizing any unequal treatment of creditors (that is, protecting creditors against each other), but, in the general perception, it is certainly an inferior legal technique for maximizing the total available for them all in bank insolvency. There is an obvious trade-off between how much is available to all, and how much is available to each relative to all others under a hypothetical liquidation valuation carried out up-front, and an actual liquidation of the assets of the debtor. We believe that any discrepancies in shares are tolerable against much larger discrepancies in the respective total amounts. The 'who' that will pay for bank insolvency depends on the applicable rules and standards that govern the distribution of losses in relative terms, and, conversely, the allocation of cash or other entitlements in relative terms.

The characteristic feature of the approach in all EEA countries is the theory of the eventual application of the common pool principle vesting all property, assets and income of the debtor in a receiver charged with their liquidation, and the eventual distribution of proceeds thereof according to the ranking of claims and interest listed on the liability side. The problem is, however, the application of the various 'pre-insolvency' schemes to a failed or failing bank pending its legal insolvency. Such schemes work on a basis *prima facie* inconsistent with the traditional common pool approach. Mergers and divisions create successor pools of assets, as well as new pools of assets.

Indeed, retroactive in their legal nature, the general bankruptcy and other general insolvency laws recapture property, assets and income of the debtor in transactions conducted during the prescribed suspect period. They work retroactively in time for the two purposes which are

(i) to swell the 'estate' in the interest of maximizing the liquidation value of the debtor's assets; and
(ii) to realize the objectives of uniformity, equality and symmetry both:

in the treatment of creditors (*pari passu* principle), and
in the treatment of owners relative to the creditors (the absolute priority principle).

In refraining from having a court to determine that, in truth, a particular failed or failing bank is a legally insolvent bank, the administrative authorities cite formal grounds; for example, that the subject bank is apparently 'not insolvent' because they themselves extended official liquidity to it, or in the light of a forthcoming package of solvency assistance. For the same reason, the administrative authorities differentiate in their treatment of what are, in truth, insolvent banks. This may give rise to the treatment of creditors in potential violation of the *pari passu* principle, on the one hand, and to the treatment of owners relative to conditions in breach of the absolute priority principle, in the interest of permitting a failed or failing bank continue in legal entity and personality.

0.1.6 Advantages and disadvantages of the 'compartmentalized' approach

The highly 'compartmentalized' approach to the resolution of failed or failing banks supplies multiple 'bins' according to the size and the systemic importance of each particular case, based on a free characterization of the case up-front on administrative discretion alone, in effect something like a royal prerogative to defer the operation of general laws in a particular case. As a result, what obtains is 'ad hockery'.

There is no uniform distributional or allocational key to control the execution of exit policy, and the case administration in respect of any bank insolvency. Indeed, exit policy treats the choice of a framework as a matter of choice between competing 'models' without regard to the special distributional key that then determines the eventual effects and consequences of the particular bank insolvency.

Therefore, the compartmentalization overrides, on extralegal criteria, the 'common pool' principle, indeed, the overriding principle through a substitution of what the administrative authorities believe as appropriate 'in this case', for the common pool technique of distribution of losses and the allocation of cash and other remaining entitlements.

Generally, the uniformity of treatment that must obtain in any allocation of public resources as specified in any policy for their use, and the doctrine equality of treatment that governs the distribution of losses under law, are determined under the mutable policy predicated on an *ad hoc* characterization of each case.

Indeed, the discretion pertaining to the making of well-founded choices between available actions, taking into account any compelling grounds for inaction, has been vested in administrative discretion as a matter of policy, not law.

Salutary as the basic principle of bankruptcy undoubtedly is, one of its aspects in particular – the automatic stay – is an extraordinarily dangerous instrument of dismemberment. In the historically long period that ended upon the advent of modern exit policies and bank insolvency laws – indeed, pursuant to the legal reforms that arose from the experience of a series of world-wide crisis that ended in the USA in the late 1930s – it was demonstrated that, in their use of the sledgehammer remedy of bank closure, the legislators have become alert to the danger that the judicial extension of bankruptcy by mere logical processes of manipulation in the field of banking might produce results that were destructive to national and international prosperity.

In the USA, the competent courts themselves moved away from the outright application of general bankruptcy laws to insolvent banks as early as in the 1830s by way of appointing 'administrative receivers' for case administration. Finally, debtors that were banks in distress were exempted from exit and case administration under Federal bankruptcy laws through the substitution of Section 11 of the FDI Act for Federal bankruptcy laws in respect of debtors that were insured depository institutions.

Section 11 of the FDI Act is predicated on:

(i) the substitution of principles and methods of official valuation for the judicial bankruptcy tests that had deferred any such valuation until the completion of the process of asset liquidation;
(ii) the elimination of an 'automatic stay' by appointing a bank regulatory agency to step into the shoes of a failed or failing bank;
(iii) the liquidation of the assets and liabilities of a seized bank forthwith; and
(iv) carrying out the liquidation of liabilities on their official valuation (under (i)) through a settlement of claims without awaiting the completion of asset dispositions.

Section 11 of the FDI Act and other statutes authorized and directed the bank regulatory agencies to adopt a robust exit policy in conjunction with the new bank insolvency law. Now, the recently amended Section 11 of the FDI Act, which mandates 'haircuts' of uninsured depositors and other creditors, precluding bailouts of pre-existing shareholders and uninsured creditors.

0.1.7 Legislative trends

The trends of the evolution of bank insolvency laws are yet to converge, however. Indeed, in EEA countries (European Economic Area), it would appear that unless the authorities judge the case to be the isolated instance of:

(i) a small bank of little consequence to the system (for example, a thrift, a savings and loan, credit cooperative or other specialized institution operating outside the inter-bank clearing and settlements system operated by the central bank); or
(ii) an empty shell of what used to be a bank of some size,

there is a chance that all other banks will not be declared 'insolvent', either upon its own voluntary petition, or upon an involuntary petition filed by an individual depositor or other creditor, or any other third party that may be authorized and directed to file such a petition. The cumulative delay in bank case administration that is the consequence of the long period of initiation and judicial reorganization (including forbearance) is, indeed, the characteristic feature of bank insolvency regimes of the kind that exist in the EEA countries.

As a corollary of the applicable policy and law in EEA countries, bank insolvencies do not, therefore, trigger the general rules and standards of creditor protection, of which the characteristic feature is the unrestricted ability of an individual depositor or other creditor to avail itself of recourse to the courts for the determination, recognition and enforcement of private rights and obligations. In effect, the current framework for case administration is predicated both on policy-based informal and *ad hoc* bailouts of failed and failing banks (the case for individual bank 'restructuring'), and on the existence of the requisite restrictions on the ability of the competent courts to resolve them.

Therefore, it would appear to be hard to fault the Proposed Scheme on the grounds that it would, if enacted, constitute an allegedly intolerable exemption for insolvent banks from general bankruptcy and insolvency laws, and short-circuit the stable operation of the legal system. We are already beyond that point.

The actual cases seldom fit the functions performed by the general bankruptcy and insolvency law regime operated by the competent general courts of first instance, and, indeed, the administrative authorities may remove the case from the competent court to the competent administrative authorities. More generally, the discretionary characterization of up-coming cases leads to compartmentalization, with each compartment providing a different answer in what might well be an identical case, or an identical answer in different cases, leading increasingly to an individualized and highly non-uniform treatment of each insolvent bank, ultimately the answer to the question of who will pay for bank insolvency, is the casuistic 'according to the case'.

We drafted the question of 'who will pay for bank insolvency' in terms of making payments on, or in connection with a single bank insolvency, and had in mind involuntary contributions required of the 'who' by the operation of law.

The phrase 'will pay' referred to the making payments 'for bank insolvencies'. The drafting carried some constructive or studied ambiguity because the recipient of 'payments' was not necessarily an insolvent bank as the intended beneficiary.

The word 'for' included situations in which the insolvent bank would be the incidental beneficiary of payments made to a third party on, or in connection with, its insolvency. In the systemic case, which is predicated on a bunching of bank insolvencies, the issue may be stated in the form of 'who will bail out the failed bank'. The subject 'who' may be paying a third party, with the insolvent bank serving as an intended beneficiary, having in mind the case in which a third party (for example, new, bad, or a bridge bank) is employed as a bailout vehicle, making non-transparent payments with the insolvent bank, or its pre-existing shareholders, or unsecured third parties, serving as incidental beneficiaries. For example, the deposit guarantor may not have any direct relationship with the insolvent bank.

More specifically, the question was fashioned to prompt discussion of the possible substitution of less costly and risky alternatives for bailouts that involve the public treasury as the ultimate lender and investor of last resort, in the light of a range of different approaches to the control of costs and risks that the public treasury may incur on its own account on, or in connection with, bank failures occurring in the future. In recent bank failures, both in cases of individual banks of some size and in the so called 'systemic' cases, a large part of the massive losses registered by subject banks had shifted to the public sector away from the intended or incidental beneficiaries of bailouts that have meant diverse transactions undertaken for the purpose of shifting the losses of failed banks. The beneficiaries of bailouts may include the failed bank itself, or its pre-existing shareholders, or the unsecured creditors. It would appear that the losses shifted, one way or another, to the respective states, their central banks, other state agencies, the general governments and to diverse private and official entities, generally referred to as 'special vehicles'.

0.1.8 The case for a *lex specialis*

In *Improving Banking Supervision* (Mayes, Halme and Liuksila, 2001), recommendations for a robust exit policy were made in Chapter 8 and for a proposed bank insolvency law (the 'new scheme') in Chapter 9 (included in this book as Appendix 1). They pertain to the resolution of a bank that has failed, or is failing, in economic terms as determined by a resolution agency, for example a back-up agency for the deposit guarantee system, or deposit insurer.

The intervention point under the Proposed Scheme is determined in economic terms on a revaluation of the assets and liabilities of the failed, or failing, bank and not necessarily in overt legal terms. In the case of involuntary petitions, the task assigned to the competent courts in EEA countries is to determine legal insolvency on the basis of a demonstrated default on the part of the subject bank (bankruptcy test). The task assigned to the supervisory authorities or banking commissions is to determine regulatory solvency in terms of its observance or non-observance of the applicable regulatory capital requirement– a regulatory accounting issue.

Whether or not a bank has failed, or is failing, is determined administratively, on an observed ratio of assets over liabilities, with the excess of liabilities constituting 'negative net worth', a dangerous condition. The bank might have failed in economic terms some time ago although it may be, in legal terms, apparently not insolvent. The standard judicial test of insolvency is predicated on the demonstration of a default on the part of the bank in repaying deposits, or in making other payments as they fall due and payable. The test of regulatory solvency is ambiguous; the bank may not have failed yet although it is now critically undercapitalized, or, conversely, it may have failed and still be well capitalized.

We argued that the threshold point of time at which the execution of exit policy and case administration shifts from the administrative authorities to the judicial authorities was ambiguous in the EEA countries because the execution of exit policy was subject to the concurrent action of the administrative and judicial authorities. The coordination of positions gave rise to delays in intervention shifting the threshold point to the point at which all agree. Similarly, the period of judicial reorganization of liquidation could not be fixed beforehand with certainty in terms of any beginning or ending date.

Bankruptcy and other general insolvency laws have been modified in their operation in respect of banks since banking became a regulated industry in the late nineteenth century. In the EEA area, starting as late as the 1930s, banks have been protected against any bankruptcy petitions in that the statutes vest discretion in the administrative authorities regarding the institution of judicial reorganization and liquidation proceedings. The restriction, an innovation in the 1930s, was imposed for an apparently good reason, in order to avoid possible closures by courts of individual banks, and the closure by the competent court of all banks in systemic cases.

Now, it is not by any means excluded that the disjointed and convoluted state of arrangements for the execution of exit policy and case administration in the EEA countries defeated other solutions than the carrying out *ad hoc* bailouts of individual banks and entire banking systems, eventually taxing generations of taxpayers for the compounded losses. The BCCI alone was not bailed out and was put through a decade-long judicial liquidation proceeding in London, Luxembourg, and many other places, for the simple reason that no country volunteered to bail it out. It is not by any means excluded that the experience of bailouts may be repeated 'out of court', unless the systemic crises (resulting from bunching bank failures), are avoided by way of the faithful execution of a robust exit policy, with recourse to speedy resolution techniques.

Indeed, a 'resolution track' may be created, managed by a specialized body charged with the identification of any failed, and failing, banks which operates alongside the 'supervision track' managed by bank supervisors occupied with the avoidance of bank failures, and the 'central bank track' managed by the modern central bank occupied with the effective functioning of payments systems. These three specialized functions are independent functions.

More specifically, the authors of *Improving Banking Supervision* made the case for an institutional reform that consolidated the execution of exit policy and case administration into one single body. The proposed consolidation of the various tasks previously shared between the administrative and judicial authorities would remove the restrictions on their respective abilities to intervene at the earliest possible point in time. Acting on its own motion, the above-mentioned resolution agency would not be restricted by any need to obtain the concurrence of others for filing a petition with the competent court.

Indeed, an intervention in the case of a failed, or failing, bank would be based on a valuation by the agency of the assets and liabilities of the subject bank and its own ultimate finding of bank failure, a question of fact rather than law. It is, of course, true that the existing system eventually identifies the failed, or failing, bank in a roundabout way: that is, upon the later of its non-observance of the applicable regulatory capital requirement as the subject bank becomes critically undercapitalized, or the event of default on the part of the bank. Neither of the last-mentioned two tests is conclusive proof of the occurrence or non-occurrence of a bank failure, however, except in conjunction with the performance of the critical net worth test upon a revaluation of the subject bank's assets and liabilities on the basis of prices in the market, excluding intangible equity. The net worth test should suffice.

A cumulative test may be preferable for the certainty of determination, but as a prerequisite for intervention such a test would delay, by logical necessity, any intervention from the earliest to the latest point of time. The delay might be indeterminate for the sole reason that there is unlikely to be any default on the part of the bank, nor is there any certainty, that it became critically undercapitalised when it failed. For a determination of 'legal insolvency', it is necessary that the administrative authorities file a petition to the competent court which then goes ahead and applies the legal test. The test of 'regulatory insolvency' only refers to the critical undercapitalization of a subject bank which finding is not germane to the ratio of assets over liabilities. Its use as grounds for reorganization or liquidation might well expose the authorities to pre-existing shareholders claims for the payment of compensation due to a wrongful expropriation of the subject bank's positive net worth that belongs to shareholders as the 'real value' of outstanding shares.

The question of 'how' to apply the principle, and to select the appropriate methods for its application, belongs to technical experts. It is noteworthy that the FDI Act in the US allows no deferral of the seizure of a critically undercapitalized bank 'unless it has positive net worth'. Indeed, this is the ultimate test for the subject bank to avoid its own termination in legal entity and personality, and the liquidation of its assets and liabilities.

0.1.9 Modalities of the proposed new scheme

The expedition, economy and efficiency required of the execution of a robust exit policy, and the carrying out of case administration in case of a failed or failing bank, presupposes an enactment of a special bank insolvency law (here '*lex specialis*'). In order to cut losses to what may be absorbed by the market, the law would:

(i) exempt banks from judicial reorganization and liquidation proceedings under the supervision of the competent general courts of first instance; and
(ii) consolidate the decision-making by which the entire process of resolution functions – from the execution of exit policy to the completion of case administration in each case – into a specialized administrative body charged with the resolution of banks.

Necessary and sufficient legal safeguards would be in place, including a requirement of the government's prior approval of the takeover, triggering the activation of the statutory scheme. The Scheme authorizes and directs the designated body to proceed immediately with reorganization measures, indeed, a range of prescribed measures that comprehend compulsory debt and equity restructuring; the disposition of the resulting newly solvent bank in legal entity and personality; and the liquidation of those assets and liabilities for which no buyers can be found. Transactions would be carried out on the account of the bank on prices agreed for each transaction on the basis of prices in the market.

To combat delays that increase losses, and undue delays in particular, the intervention would take place early on a net worth test in case of a failed or failing bank. An official valuation of a subject bank's assets and liabilities, to be carried out on the basis of prices in the market (hypothetical liquidation valuation), would substitute for the regulatory valuation. Regulatory valuation is not appropriate since it is carried out on the basis of stable prices on the assumption of continuity of business ('going concern valuation'), a presumption that fails in the face of adverse developments. Equally, the period of reorganization should be short: subject to an equalization of its assets and liabilities up-front, the point is to keep the bank open and operating without liquidation, continuing it in legal entity and personality.

The key for the determination of absolute amount of the total loss, and for the distribution of the relative shares, must be non-negotiable. Indeed, fixing the formulae in advance is the only way to combat strategic behaviour by banks themselves, their shareholders and creditors, a source of great delay in judicial reorganization proceedings. Here, the use of principles and methods of hypothetical liquidation valuation also means that the concurrent restructuring is carried out by the operation of law. The relative share of each holder of claims and interests is determined pursuant to the so called 'absolute priority principle' which applies, in conjunction with the *pari passu* principle, in judicial bank liquidations to a distribution of the proceeds of liquidation, but it does not apply in judicial bank reorganizations that are carried out without liquidation in EEA countries.

Then, the question of who will pay for bank insolvency, or bail out a failed bank permits a comparison of all possible bailouts omitting, for the time being, any 'indirect bailouts' of which a failed bank is but an incidental beneficiary. Then, with the above qualifications and reservations, the answers would appear to be:

- The failed bank cannot bail itself out. Liquidating assets surely does not restore the bank to a solvent condition: instead of improving its position, any liquidation of its assets is likely to increase the excess of its liabilities over assets (negative net worth), dismemberment would involve deep discounts relative to book values. Unless the assets can be overvalued, compulsory sales of assets and liabilities do not count as a valid technique of restructuring either. It is also futile to seek to resolve the problem by taking deposits or borrowing at premium rates, and making loans at relative discounts.
- Any third party can volunteer to bail it out, of course, including the public treasury. Non-repayable receipts of property, assets and income generate net assets. This may take the form of receipt of non-repayable cash, or cash-equivalent obligations issued by third parties. There are only voluntary contributions in this category of bailout.

Pre-existing shareholders and creditors can either volunteer concessions in a 'workout', or be required to bail it out in so-called compulsory reorganization proceedings. Concessions by pre-existing shareholders through the cancellation of outstanding shares which enables the bank to issue new shares, and concessions by unsecured creditors in the form of debt and debt service reduction generate net assets. Involuntary contributions belong to this category of bailout.

No doubt the pre-existing shareholders and unsecured creditors are the only real prospects as concessions (as opposed to any real resources) can be exacted by the authorities from them for zero compensation. The making of a case for voluntary contributions from the public treasury (taxpayers) might well encounter taxpayer resistance. At least any future bailouts are unlikely to follow the pattern of a bailout first, rationalization to follow. They will be subjected to intense public scrutiny reducing the size and incidence of compelling cases.

Pre-existing shareholders and unsecured creditors are likely to become hold-outs and free-riders. Hence, the only private-sector resources are the pre-existing shareholders that hold worthless shares, and the unsecured creditors who, for no loss of their own, may well surrender their worthless holdings in debt and equity restructuring. Equally, the imposition by the authorities of a requirement that they surrender any such claims and interests for cancellation, does not give rise to any payment of compensation under the law of expropriation.

However, the same does not apply to the question of who will bail out a 'failing' bank. A failing bank may have positive net worth. The imposition by the authorities of a surrender of such claims or interests for cancellation may well give rise to the payment of compensation under the law of expropriation. The protected property rights and interests of pre-existing shareholders is equal in value to the positive net worth involved, calculated as an excess of assets over liabilities. However small in amount, any positive value that may reveal itself, is compensable to the pre-existing shareholders.

0.2 Discussion of policy and law

In general, the case for reform arises from existing conditions that create the need for *ad hoc* bailouts of all shapes and sizes. From the vantage point of resolution of bank failures at a reasonable cost and risk to the public treasury, effects of past bailouts linger on as economic incentives for excessive risk-taking in the field of banking, and, as a corollary, disincentives for desirable prudent behaviour, over time. They distort prices (for example, interest rates and cost of equity). This resolves the normative issues about the 'goodness' of any new framework, as stipulated, on its economic efficiency in minimizing the size, and reducing the incidence of bank failures and bailouts over time. This may work through the announcement of a robust exit policy and the consolidation of the execution of policy and case administration in one place, with the purpose of the reorganization and liquidation of failed banks without bailouts. Having a new scheme in place would defeat expectations arising from any series of past bailouts which form the incentives for risky behaviours, and disincentives for prudent behaviours, maximizing the size, and increasing the incidence of bank failures over time.

The case for reform is the elimination of underlying conditions that give rise to a revealed or perceived need for bailouts. Reform was necessary given the inherent weakness of any future case against 'necessary' bailouts. As the practice of the EU Commission on the prior approval of state aids to the banking sector shows, it is hard to talk a member state out of the necessary bailout as and when the occasion arises, or in systemic cases. Arguably, the deeply embedded expectations of bailouts could be reduced by an announcement by the authorities of a robust exit policy, coupled with a recommendation for an appropriate legislative change to consolidate the resolution of failed and failing banks into one institution, would be in order to ensure that the decision-making by which the execution of the robust exit policy and case administration functions, is longer disjointed and convoluted.

0.2.1 Discussion of feasible solutions

Traditional solutions do not work. A key problem that emerges, of course, is the delay that increases losses, and the undue delays in particular. If handling a large problem bank is difficult, it may be because there are strong incentives for the supervisory authorities to delay action in the hope that the problem will right itself, particularly that the private sector will be able to come up with a solution. Unfortunately that optimistic outcome only occurs some of the time and forbearance is likely to encourage risk-taking and increase losses. Management in difficulty may already be facing their maximum loss in the sense of their jobs and share options. When the problem is relatively small, several approaches to its solution are possible, as it grows over time only the taxpayer has the resources to cover the eventual losses.

Withdrawal of authorization is not realistic in the case of a failed bank of some size or in systemic cases. Although provisions for the orderly exit of banks that have ceased to comply with the conduct-related conditions for registration have been in place in many countries for a number of years, they may be impossible to apply in practice for larger banks that are failing, or have failed, in the economic sense only, as opposed to disobeying injunctions and breaching their own undertakings. The principal difficulty is one of law rather than economics. First, traditional insolvency proceedings under corporate insolvency law take too long to commence as they are predicated on the demonstrated occurrence of a default on repayments of deposits or on other payments, and the filing of a petition. Runs do not happen as long as the bank repays deposits in currency, at par and on demand, and makes other payments, which generally obtains even where a failed bank keeps liquidating its own or borrowed reserves, and distributes proceeds thereof, on a first-come-first-served basis. Second, the eventual judicial reorganization and liquidation proceedings are too protracted to be feasible for a large bank.

The realistic solution has to allow the bank to continue in legal entity and personality without liquidation of its assets. The main business of the failed bank needs to continue uninterrupted even if the legal ownership and management of the bank are changed in the process. In the United States, the FDIC liquidates the assets and liabilities of insured depository institutions in a way that minimizes the losses incurred by the deposit insurer that enjoys a liquidation ('depositor') preference upon subrogation to the rights of insured depositors and other creditors. There is no reorganization option, however, as the insured depository institution is terminated in legal entity and personality upon seizure. However, the main business of the failed bank may continue uninterrupted through the process of its termination in legal entity and personality, and the liquidation of its assets and liabilities. The so-called 'purchase and assumption transactions' which, unlike 'assisted mergers', are not carried out at book values (modified by the agreed exchange ratio for shares), but on a payment (assumption) by the purchaser at a price agreed for each transaction on the basis of asset prices in the market. The FDIC may establish a new bank to acquire the assets and liabilities of a failed bank.

0.2.2 Legislative options

Other possibilities are also available for the legislature, including:

(i) the option to liquidate forthwith the assets and liabilities of a subject bank, or to continue the subject bank in legal entity and personality without dismemberment and interruption (this reorganization option does not exist in the USA);
(ii) the option to apply the absolute priority principle that wipes out the pre-existing shareholders in the distribution of cash proceeds of liquidations, also to the distribution of the non-cash proceeds of reorganizations (the proceeds of reorganization are the good balance of claims and interests);
(iii) the option to arrange for case administration to take place under the supervision of administrative or judicial authorities; and
(iv) the option to have permanent staff to run case administration.

0.3 Conclusions and findings

In contradistinction to the bank insolvency law of the kind that prevails in the USA today, which is mandatory law, most EEA legislators have retained a virtually unfettered option to defer the opening of the prescribed judicial reorganization or liquidation proceedings. In effect, they have avoided the surrender of their own competence and jurisdiction over apparently insolvent banks for a compulsory reorganization or liquidation by Courts, and have, in the meantime, stood ready to entertain *ad hoc* legislation for bailouts from the public treasury, that is, the taxpayer. Here the Proposed Scheme serves as an illustrative example of a limitation placed by a legislature on any liability of the public sector for losses associated with bank insolvencies, and the authors argue, in principle, against the use of public resources for bailing out any pre existing equity- and debt-holders that may be 'under water'.

Improving Banking Supervision recognized that banking supervision is but one very limited instrument of early warning to avert defaults and failures in the field of banking. Here, the prospects of banking supervision as the principal technique were somewhat clouded. Liisa Halme had studied the experience of Finnish savings banks from her position as Deputy Director of the Government Guarantee Fund that had to handle the crisis of the early 1990s. The recommendations she made, having studied the elements that had unfolded in the crisis, pointed to a need for formal, institutional and legal changes. Ultimately, banking supervisors could not profitably operate banks but the task of general management was one for bankers themselves under an appropriate new structure of incentive and sanctions.

In making their case against constructive ambiguity, the authors argued that banking crises, individual and systemic, have become common in world-wide terms. Great advances had indeed been made in the techniques of bank restructuring outside the field of bank insolvency law proper. The time had come to take stock of bad memories and incorporate the lessons into appropriate amendments of national bank insolvency laws that had failed, as taxpayers had to intervene in lieu of courts and tribunals. It was generally believed that the whole point of having bank insolvency law was to quash expectations of bailouts and to enact appropriate legislation to give prior written notice to bank shareholders and uninsured creditors of the consequences of bank insolvency.

There was no point in trying to fashion a consensus view. Any compromise in the form of having 'flexible bank insolvency laws', would have been a contradiction in terms, and result in precisely the kind of unconstructive ambiguity about outcomes that prevails today. Should the legislature tie the government to the mast to avoid having the government entertain any temptation to give in to pressure from interest groups, and, by so doing effectively close the political option for the government to propose, and the legislature enact, *ad hoc* solutions to a banking crisis?

The *ad hoc* measures enacted by different countries over time, follow the same pattern, which is to prop up the capital of a remaining bank directly through capital increases to meet its losses; to guarantee the maintenance of the value of its assets or liabilities; or indirectly, by way of the establishment of a bad bank against payment to the insolvent bank for the purpose of the purchase of assets. The nature and medium of the requisite payments vary depending on the sources of funds; typically, the central bank provides cash, and the public treasury provides government bonds. The necessary *ad hoc* law that enables the public treasury to disburse may take the form of a delegation of legislative authority to government or designated administrative authorities, to take place in conjunction with the grant of commensurate authority to borrow on the account of government or designated official entities, for the purpose of unconditionally bailing out banks or the banking system as a whole.

The possibility of the enactment of any *ad hoc* legislation to avoid the withdrawal of authorizations, and the surrender of subject banks to the jurisdiction of competent courts, never appeals to those who want to give precise legal form and content to bank reorganization and liquidation proceedings ahead of any crisis. An enactment of this kind is motivated precisely to avoid the applicability of bank insolvency laws in the event of bank insolvency. Ultimately, any general answer to the question of 'who will pay for bank insolvency', will be a political one because legislatures may enact *ad hoc* legislation to set aside pre-existing laws.

Of course, at the point of crisis, where the legislature intervenes on a government proposal to avert rapidly spreading bank insolvency, there are hardly any conditions that may be imposed through *ad hoc* legislation. Conditions cannot be of the kind that could have been enacted years before when there was no specific crisis or problem bank in mind. At that point the crisis must be resolved by creating financial cash and tax incentives for banks themselves, as well as for bank shareholders and creditors, to do something that they did not do before then, for the simple reason that there previously was nothing in it for them. At this point, there is no way to override collective action clauses by way of an administrative decision, for example, for decreasing and increasing capital without convening shareholders meetings, or for disposing of the need to obtain the individual assent of each creditor to debt or debt service reduction.

In casu, governments are always tempted by any option they may have to resort to an 'open bank policy', and announcing that they so do on an 'exceptional basis', without creating any 'precedent'. This is the policy of studied or constructive ambiguity, as the public sees the policy. Here the concept of law and the concept of policy are very different in nature in that any breach of an announced policy becomes part of the policy itself and there is nothing illegal to it, whereas any breach of law can be cured only by way of an amnesty.

The option between the resolution of insolvent banks and keeping them open and operating works one way only, where government looks towards winning the next election by suppressing bad news. Any democratic government in resolving bank insolvencies, if unguided by any legislatively fixed criteria that required it, will have a concern for their electoral future. There would be a political backlash for failing banks by lifting their authorizations and surrendering them to the jurisdiction of competent courts, notwithstanding any case that the government could reasonably make for having saved the taxpayer massive costs and risks by biting the bullet, instead of keeping insolvent banks open and operating at whatever costs and risks to the taxpayer.

Economists see the problem in the same way as lawyers but couch it in different terms. Governments face a problem of time consistency. When there is no looming crisis a government can see that the greatest long-term benefit to the economy will come from setting up a framework which precludes bailing out and forces an early reorganization without the use of taxpayers' money. When it comes to a crisis shorter-run pressures argue for overturning the framework and bailing out. Banks and society at large can see that inconsistency coming and will act on what they expect to happen not on what the prior rules state. A credible scheme, therefore, not only has to mandate what should happen from the vantage point of calm foresight but frame it in such a way that future revision in the heat of the crisis seems unlikely.

The Proposed Scheme mandates a burden-sharing between government, at least in its capacity as the main 'private' creditor of the insolvent bank upon subrogation to the rights of insured creditors, on the one hand, and the bank shareholders and uninsured creditors, on the other. The proposed solution takes into account, and resolves, the conflicts of interests in the event of a bank's insolvency by assigning the losses to shareholders and uninsured creditors, including the subordinated creditors, subject to a liquidation preference that it grants to depositors (equivalent to the depositor preference that was enacted into the federal banking laws in the USA in 1993). Moreover, the Proposed Scheme exempts the resolution of insolvent banks from the jurisdiction of general courts, and assigns to government the task of stepping into the shoes of an insolvent bank carrying out an asset, debt, and equity restructuring concurrent with the take-over, to avoid any successor liability that it may incur otherwise.

0.4 Resumé

The Proposed Scheme was presented in *Improving Banking Supervision* to attract comment on what should be the criteria, fixed in advance, to prevent the government shifting the costs and risks of bank insolvency to the public treasury over and above its liability for unfunded deposit insurance schemes. In all cases, the losses would be attributed first to bank shareholders, and, then, to uninsured depositors and other creditors, in compliance with the absolute priority and *pari passu* principles that applied in bank liquidation.

Adjusted to the circumstances of countries where there are only a few banks and the danger of closing down a major portion of the banking sector along with one bank, the Proposed Scheme offers a reorganization option of the kind that does not exist in the USA.

The two characteristic features of the Proposed Scheme are

- government steps into the shoes of pre-existing shareholders, and
- government carries out a concurrent asset and debt restructuring of each and every bank that comes under its provisions.

The result would be a marginally solvent bank, which, operating under a government guarantee, would be able to discharge its obligations and liabilities in full to insured depositors and the remaining claims of uninsured creditors. That would keep the subject bank (in reorganization) open and operating for the time-being, subject to a possible voluntary liquidation if it is not viable even in the reorganized form and cannot find acquirers for the bank as a whole or for its business in the private sector. Here, the Proposed Scheme differs radically from the US scheme, which terminates each and every bank upon its take-over, in legal entity and personality, and leads to the liquidation of its assets and liabilities, subject to the systemic exception that waives, in the case of a bank that may be too large to fail, the limitation on any liability of the deposit insurer for the uninsured losses of insured banks.

From the vantage point of the public treasury that may be responsible for the underfunding of deposit insurance funds, the economics of the EEA and US banking systems approximate each other. The EC deposit guarantee directive requires the granting of guarantees to depositors, as opposed to bestowing the intended benefits *also* on the banks themselves, say, under an open bank policy predicated on the notion that it may be cheaper to save the bank than its depositors. The directive does not exclude the use of deposit guarantee funds for bailouts, but, nevertheless does not create any expectation or grant any entitlement on the part of banks for recourse on their own account to the deposit guarantee in the event that, on a least-cost approach from the vantage point of the taxpayer, the bailing out of the bank itself would be more efficient than closing it down and carrying out a depositor payout. Indeed, the directive presupposes that the beneficiaries of deposit insurance are 'insured depositors', not 'insured banks', prohibiting the banks from calling themselves insured depositary institutions.

Here we have an assimilation of the economics of the two polar systems of legislation and other regulation of bank insolvency; that is, between the US system of bank regulation and supervision, which is predicated on protecting deposit insurance funds, on the one hand, and the operation of the EEA system which is predicated on the Public Treasury keeping an eye on the funded and unfunded deposit guarantee liabilities of the Public Treasury, on the other.

However, on the EEA side, the implications of the deposit insurance directive for the resolution of insolvent banks in the EEA countries may have been underestimated notwithstanding the fact that any non-implementation of the Directive might, indeed, give rise to a residual liability on the part of the Public Treasury.

This may be said with the exception of Norway. Norway insures bank deposits up to €250,000, the highest level of deposit insurance in the world, mandating a regime for prompt corrective action in the event of threat of insolvency and a separate legal regime for haircuts. That is to say, a regime for wiping out pre-existing shareholders and carrying out, by way of an administrative decision, a debt and equity restructuring to restore the solvency of the subject bank and resume its compliance with regulatory capital requirements.

There is a chance of reform in the offing in Norway for the reason that it would appear that the above legislation sets aside the legal effect of certain provisions of the Second Capital Directive which concern the exclusive power that has been conferred on shareholders' meetings to decide upon capital decreases and increases. The Directive is the nucleus of national company law in EEA countries.

Part I

The Problem and the Proposed Solution

1
An Overview of the Issues*

David G. Mayes

It is well known that the economic impact of the insolvency of banks poses different problems for society from the insolvency of non-financial companies and indeed from many other financial companies. These differences stem primarily from two causes: the holding of deposits and the spill-over from a problem in one bank to others and to the rest of the economy.[1] The laws relating to insolvency try to provide a balance between the various groups exposed to the loss in the case of company failure – creditors, shareholders, customers, employees, and so on – and some equality of treatment of those within each group. In the latter respect this often involves measures to coordinate the interests of large numbers of people with individually small exposures and little power and information. Views differ across societies about the appropriate balance but it is normally only those directly involved who have a say. Courts can determine that the rules for sharing the cost are properly applied in each case. While it is only natural that those about to make losses would like to shift the burden onto others, the case for external assistance from taxpayers through the government is usually weak. The authorities are thus not normally directly involved unless they are exposed to the direct loss in the normal course of business.[2] Having an efficient competitive economy involves entry, growth *and exit* of enterprises in a framework that gives confidence to the participants.[3] This includes the orderly exit of insolvent banks.[4]

In the case of non-financial companies, fully secured creditors may escape any losses. Insolvency may impose losses on the unsecured creditors, such as suppliers who have not been paid for their deliveries and customers who have paid in advance. Customers who have already purchased and received delivery will face relatively little loss or inconvenience. (Indeed, where there is substantial advance payment involved there are frequently insurance schemes available, as in the travel industry. Commercial law and practice address these possibilities.) In the case of bank insolvency all existing depositors are unsecured and hence at risk. For some people those deposits may represent a large portion of their savings. The insurance therefore needs to relate not just to the customers involved in transactions at the time but to the balances of all customers. The scale and nature of what is involved is thus much greater. It has to relate to the stock of deposits and not just to the flow of current transactions.[5] Banks cannot seek temporary protection from their creditors to restructure their business and obligations like commercial companies, as that would involve interfering with the business of banking itself.[6]

Although ultimately the payout to creditors in the case of insolvency may be a substantial proportion of what they are owed, that process of payout can be slow, even if there are interim payments. If in the meantime customers cannot access their deposits the consequences for their other transactions and indeed livelihood may be severe, leading to knock-on failures to pay and drastic reductions in spending. This knock-on will also occur through the banking system as banks have substantial exposures to each other. Failure of one bank will therefore pose problems for others. Worse than that, depositors in other banks may simply fear that their bank also has a problem and try to withdraw their deposits. Such a run on other 'sound' banks could tip them, too, into insolvency, as they cannot realize their assets in a hurry at prices that reflect their longer-term value and hence may not be able to meet their obligations. Even if the other banks can succeed in meeting their obligations, this will tend to involve cutbacks to new lending and refusal to roll over loans. That will cause a consequential reduction in economic activity and a spiral of commercial failures. Borrowers as well as depositors face potential losses in the face of bank failures. For these reasons, schemes exist in many countries to insure deposits and central banks stand ready to supply liquidity to the banking system to head off any consequential run on other banks that are otherwise solvent. Furthermore, the whole system of banking regulation is designed to try to get banks to behave in a manner that makes insolvency relatively unlikely. In many countries, it also leads to the use of special laws, rather than a general law that applies equally to all institutions, to handle insolvency in banks, so that these special circumstances can be taken into account.[7]

As De Bandt and Hartmann (2000) show, the extent of the knock-on to other banks from the initial failure through their transactions with each other has been relatively limited in the past.[8] Moreover, simulations, particularly for the USA, show that the implications in both the interbank market and the payments system would be relatively limited in most scenarios, even where the failing bank is large.[9] There is, however, a limit and at some point the insolvency of a single bank or of several banks at the same time is likely to have such a big knock-on effect to the rest of the economy – the cases of 'too big to fail' and 'too many to fail' – that the authorities intervene.[10] Once intervention takes place there is a reallocation of the losses from those who would have lost under insolvency to those who are providing the new funds to keep the bank(s) in business. Normally those providers are current and future taxpayers, although it is possible that they may ultimately be repaid if there is a strong recovery in the bank or the economy fares sufficiently better as a consequence.

However, as soon as a system of actual or expected bailout or insurance exists, this will tend to affect people's actions. Depositors who are insured may no longer take such trouble to check that the bank holding their deposits is being managed prudently. Banks and their shareholders will be less concerned if they think the bank will be bailed out.[11] This 'moral hazard' will then increase the chance of banks reaching the point of insolvency.[12] As explained in Mayes, Halme and Liuksila (2001) (hereinafter MHL), in many countries the fears about the consequences of bank failures and the costly nature of the insolvency legislation means that most banks can expect to be bailed out. According to the Fitch IBCA assessment of which banks are 'thought to be supported' over 60 per cent of banking assets were supported in ten OECD countries (out of a sample of 14) in 1999 (Soussa, 2000, p. 11).[13] The greatest proportion was in Finland, 96 per cent.[14] It may well be that the actual costs of bailing out are higher than the costs of permitting insolvency, if some of the more unattractive consequences, such as delay, can be avoided.[15]

The existence of deposit insurance *per se* does not mean that the problem of being too big to fail disappears. Deposit insurance funds may themselves be too small to meet the losses as in the USA with the savings and loan problems in the 1980s and in some states in the 1920s (Wheelock and Kumbhakar, 1994, 1995). The state then has to decide whether to bail out the deposit insurer or let it fold. Even if the deposit insurance is state-provided, funding may be inadequate and the fund may have to call on the taxpayer until it can be replenished by new premiums or the sale of assets of the failed institutions.

As explained by Eisenbeis and Wall (2002), although failure prevention and minimizing losses in the case of failure are related, they have very different implications for the conduct of policy and for the size and distribution of losses. If the aim is failure avoidance then the responsibility for its achievement lies with the supervisor and consequentially the burden falls on the taxpayer should failure occur or seem likely. If the aim is loss minimization (in the US case for the deposit insurance fund) then the incentive lies with bank shareholders and managers to limit their own exposure to losses, as the authorities' objective offers them nothing in the case of failure.

There is thus a complex network of actual and potential costs and their distribution involved in the occurrence, discouragement and avoidance of bank failures. In MHL we put forward a scheme for the regulation of the prudential management of banks that sought to discourage the occurrence of bank failures, at a low cost to society as a whole. (The two key chapters in MHL dealing with this scheme are reprinted as Appendix 1 to this book for ease of reference.) An integral part of that scheme was the proposal of a credible scheme for handling such failures as did occur. For credibility, the scheme needed to convince owners and managers in particular, and the market in general, that a resolution would be achieved, in most likely circumstances, that did not involve bailing out the owners or uninsured depositors. The threat of insolvency thus needed to be real to reduce the moral hazard. To achieve this the process needed to proceed in a manner that:

- was rapid enough to allow the business to continue,
- respected the ranking of claims on the bank,
- made none of the parties worse off than they would have been under a traditional insolvency and, in particular,
- did not require the use of taxpayer funds, except to guarantee the new organization until it could become adequately capitalized from normal private sector sources.

Achieving such a rapid resolution required the authorities to be able to intervene at prescribed benchmarks, such as zero economic capital (zero net worth), appoint an administrator who would take over the running of the firm from the shareholders and existing management. The immediate task would be to value the assets and claims on the bank up-front and apply a haircut to the claims in priority sufficient to enable the bank to continue in operation. While acting at speed will necessarily involve some inaccuracy and may require some financial redress at a later date, this reorganization will not be worse for the creditors than would be achieved by the normal drawn-out process of insolvency. Indeed, if the option of normal insolvency appeared to be a lower-cost outcome, that option would be open to the administrator.

It is the purpose of our research to provide a wider reconsideration of these proposals in the light of analysis from a variety of legal and economic points of view and from experience in a number of countries and regimes. This set of experiences is chosen to encompass both severe problems and considerable success in resolving insolvent and problem banks. Initial versions of the various contributions were presented at a workshop at the Bank of Finland in November 2002.

The rest of this chapter seeks to lay out the main issues that have been raised. We begin with a brief recapitulation of our proposed scheme for resolving insolvent banks. The next two sections then deal briefly with the issue of who bears the costs of seeking to avoid insolvency through the use of the regulatory/supervisory system and through the operation of markets. Section 1.4 provides an outline survey of some of the problems involved in assessing the costs of discouraging, avoiding and incurring insolvency. The final section offers a summary of the issues raised in the other chapters of this book, highlighting the way they contribute to the discussion of the MHL proposals.

1.1 The MHL approach to bank insolvency

The point of our scheme is to offer a credible way of handling the insolvency of large (and complex) banks that are currently thought to be individually 'too big to fail' (TBTF) or of a number of banks at one time that are currently thought to be 'too many too fail' (TMTF) that does not entail the use of public money to bail out the existing shareholders and unsecured debtors.[16] The MHL scheme can of course apply to all banks irrelevant of size. However, even though closure of any bank may be unusual in some countries, most jurisdictions have credible means of closing banks where there are no systemic consequences. Since TBTF is a judgement call, some countries may set the maximum size for permitting insolvency very low.

Our suggestions rest on two main premises. The first is that in circumstances judged TBTF or TMTF, the real requirement is that any 'solution' has to allow the institutions involved to continue trading with only a trivial break in business.[17] However, allowing the business of the bank to continue does not imply that current ownership continues nor that unsecured creditors avoid losses.[18] Figure 1.1, drawn from Hoggarth *et al.* (2002), provides a picture of the theoretical options open in resolving an insolvent bank and the article itself runs through each of the options (legal structures may prevent the realisation of some of them in practice). (Government solutions in this context do not necessarily involve

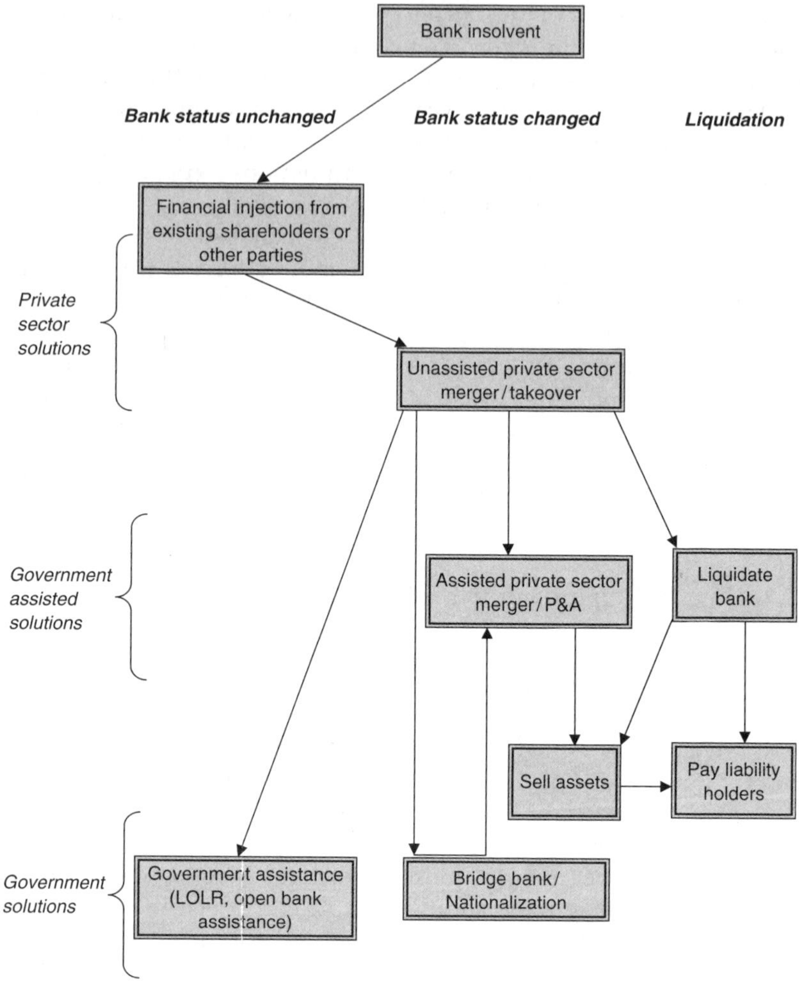

Figure 1.1 Decision tree in crisis resolution (drawn from Hoggarth *et al.*, 2002)

financial assistance.) The second premise is that the balance of costs from allowing the losses to shareholders and unsecured creditors on the hopefully rare occasions that this occurs is more favourable than often thought compared to the consequences of continuing expectation of bailout and actual bailout when insolvency occurs.

The MHL approach to insolvency is part of a wider scheme, set out in Chapters 4 to 7 of that book, which involves:

- improved supervisory procedures,
- improved corporate governance of banks – including transparent structures,
- improved disclosure by banks to enable better market discipline,
- prompt corrective action requirements for undercapitalized banks to seek market solutions rapidly before insolvency looms,
- increased incentives, including gaol terms for regulatory infractions, to more prudent behaviour by bank directors,
- actions by the authorities to reduce the knock-on effects of the closure of a bank to the rest of the system by features such as netting arrangements and the reduction of systemic risks through the payment and settlement systems.

The combination of the above, the expectation that the authorities will in fact wipe out the shareholders and write down creditors claims, that the managers will lose their jobs in the event of insolvency, and ready means of voluntary market solutions, should mean that:

- problems occur less frequently,
- they are more likely to be handled by the banks themselves before insolvency is reached,
- they are less serious if they do occur.

Thus in many respects our scheme is intended to be deterrent. Its existence will help reduce the chance of its being needed. However, that deterrence is applied in a non-distortionary manner, unlike schemes that seek to limit failures by supervisory controls on the actions of banks. If the authorities seek to minimize losses, then forbearance is generally going to be discouraged.

Step 1: The authorities are required to take over control of the bank according to prescribed benchmarks

The fundamental requirement for being able to move rapidly in the case of difficulty is that the authorities have the power to intervene, assume control of the problem bank without having to consult the existing shareholders (whose shares are in any case valueless in the case of insolvency) and apply a sufficient haircut to the claims of the creditors that the insolvency is ended (assets are no longer less than liabilities). This means in practice that bank insolvency has to be dealt with by a *lex specialis* under public law rather than by a *lex generalis* under private law. The United States is probably the best example of this regime. But our scheme differs in one crucial respect from the US counterpart, namely, that the scheme is not necessarily implemented on behalf of the deposit insurance fund. In some countries deposit insurance schemes do not exist, while in others they are funded by the state or co-funded.[19]

Like the US arrangements, the MHL scheme requires the authorities to act at certain points and is structured to restrict the opportunity for forbearance. Ambiguity is not constructive if banks interpret it to mean that there will probably be forbearance and ultimately a bail out. The scope for official discretion is limited in the scheme not just by prescribed published rules for prompt action[20] but by requirements for transparency/disclosure on the part both of banks and of the supervisory authorities. Thus not only will it be impossible to keep the existence and extent of a bank's problems confidential for long but the authorities will be publicly accountable for their actions after the event. In any case information tends to leak out and the well-informed professional investors have an advantage.[21]

Defining the prescribed intervention point is a problem. If the bank were thought to be technically solvent under normal private law definitions then closure could be thought to deprive the shareholders, managers and indeed possibly some of the employees of rights. However, enforced bank closure of solvent banks is already possible under certain circumstances (in addition to cases of criminal behaviour or failure of a 'fit and proper persons' test). For example, it is normal to insist on the meeting of at least the Basel criteria for permission to operate as a bank. Rescinding a banking licence in the event of undue delay in recapitalization is a normal feature of most prompt corrective action regimes.[22] If such a bank is not insolvent then it should be possible to achieve an orderly winding up where depositors do not lose access to their funds and there is no systemic fall out from the closure. Unfortunately, however, the capital adequacy ratios as computed under the Basel criteria do not equate with measures of solvency. The Basel criteria relate to risk-weighted capital on a book-value basis not to the concept of economic capital relevant to measuring insolvency. Capital as measured under the Basel criteria can be clearly positive when net worth is negative and the changes proposed under Basel2 will not alter this. The US regulations address this by requiring that a bank must be closed if its capital ratio falls below 2 per cent.[23] The chances are that such a bank is already insolvent in the sense that the sale of its assets will not meet the total of the claims.[24] The Tier 1 capital of a bank does not represent an unencumbered pile of cash that can be used to pay out depositors and creditors but an obligation that ceases on the insolvency of the bank, in the case of shareholder capital. Tier 2 capital is simply junior debt.[25] In any case the size of these measures of 'regulatory' capital depends on the degree to which the bank chooses to recognize the extent of its problems and the degree to which the authorities impose that recognition (Evanoff and Wall, 2002).[26]

In MHL we suggested that an appropriate benchmark for intervention might be a concept of 'economic insolvency' or net worth. At this point the current value of the liabilities just exceeds the market value of the assets. The rationale is simple: this is the point at which creditors and depositors could not expect to be paid back sufficiently rapidly and hence the point at which a run on the bank would be a sensible strategy. 'Economic insolvency' differs from legal insolvency in that, in the legal insolvency case, the circumstances can only be determined after the event when the assets are eventually sold and the expenses deducted, which may take a period of many years. Net worth is normally on a 'present value' basis. Legal insolvency is triggered either by failure to pay due liabilities or the expectation of failure to pay in the view of the courts.[27]

A different way of looking at economic insolvency would be the point at which the central bank could no longer continue to lend against available collateral, because that collateral was exhausted.[28] The two would not be the same because the central bank is prepared to take a longer-term view of asset valuation than the market. In any case the fact that the distressed bank had been unable to find a market solution for its problems might imply that even taking the value of 'goodwill' into account it could not come up with a positive net value. Our concern was to try to find a benchmark where the information could be readily available and where it would be difficult for shareholders or creditors to complain that they were being worse treated than under insolvency.[29]

Step 2: The administrator of the insolvent bank values the assets and liabilities up front and writes down the claims so as to return to operational solvency[30]

The authorities need to make a rapid assessment of the value of assets and liabilities in order to make an appropriate write-down. This entails that normal supervisory requirements ensure that both bank structures and reporting are adequate to make this feasible. (In the same way, bank structures have to be such as to make seizure feasible. This requirement is particularly difficult in the case of complex multinational institutions, to which we return in Section 1.1.1.) Such an assessment will no doubt be inaccurate. Hence, while creditors and shareholders will not have the right to challenge the actions of the authorities in resolving the bank, as delay could effectively kill the scheme, they would have the right to seek compensation after the event, should the assessment be more unfavourable than they would have received under insolvency.

In writing down the claims the administrator will need to respect the priority of claims. One of the 'neat' features of the US system is that the state moves itself to the front of the queue because the FDIC becomes decision-maker in succession to the claims of the insured depositors. This is not a feature of some European systems, where despite the liability for paying out on deposit insurance the state does not get to control the decision over how to resolve the bank.

Having got the bank back from insolvency the authorities would have to find a means of recapitalizing the bank.[31] In the interim, however, to give confidence to depositors and all those involved in future transactions the authorities would no doubt have to issue a guarantee against loss by the new, resolved institution. A variety of methods have been advanced for recapitalization (and the initial write-down), including a suggestion by the Reserve Bank of New Zealand that the creditors should in effect swap debt for equity and become the new owners of the bank. The proposals by Aghion *et al.* (1992) are a related approach whereby each group of creditors can effectively auction off their claims in increasing order of priority. It is of course always open to the state to recapitalize the bank and then sell it at some later date. MHL do not make a choice between the methods, as the particular choice is not crucial to the principle of the reorganization scheme.

There are, however, some important issues about who should be responsible that need to be resolved. The structure will depend very much on the nature of the regulatory system, with roles for the central bank, as provider of liquidity to the market or individual institutions in the traditional lender of last resort framework (that is, collateralized lending to institutions thought solvent in the sense of having adequate collateral), the supervisors of the relevant financial sectors, the bank licensing authority, the deposit insurance fund and the ministry of finance. MHL largely describe this in the simplest framework, where the central bank is also responsible for supervision and licensing. A key issue however is that to preserve incentives it is important to separate the responsibility for instituting and managing the insolvency resolution from the authority with access to public funds. Even where it is the central bank, it is essential not mix the lender of last resort function with responsibility for the closure of individual banks. It would be easy to use lender of last resort as a means of advancing the public sector up the priority of claimants on an insolvent institution.

Step 3: The bank reopens for business under new control/ownership with no material break in operation

We anticipate that such a reorganization would normally take place over a weekend. More than a working day or so of closure would be likely to start generating the systemic consequences that the scheme is intended to avoid. Unless the government wishes to get into the business of banking, we anticipate that it would wish to return the bank to normal private sector ownership and recapitalization as soon as possible, whether by merger, acquisition, flotation or other means of disposal. Where there are no systemic concerns then orderly closure still remains possible and the choice of solution would presumably depend on the public cost.

It is of course always open to the authorities to decide that they wish to use public funds to compensate the losers, at whole or in part, presumably only if they could show that the alternative involved a larger net present value of the loss to the taxpayer.[32] This issue is picked up again in Section 1.4.

1.1.1 Cross-border complications

The discussion thus far in this section treats the problem of handling bank insolvency as if it were an issue for a single jurisdiction. Indeed it does not even address the issue of complex national financial firms in more than a few words. Both regards are considered more important and more intractable by MHL than the foregoing. The largest bank in Finland is spread over Finland, Sweden, Norway, Denmark and indeed the Baltic States (with branches in Poland and Russia). The second largest bank is not only operating in more than one country but is also the second largest insurance company. In general the EU is not well organized for handling problems with cross-border institutions. Although the responsibility for consolidated supervision and deposit insurance may be clear and Memoranda of Understanding exist for the sharing of information among supervisors, it is not at all clear how the failure of a major cross-border bank would be handled (as discussed by Brouwer, Hebbink and Wesseling in Chapter 8).

Whereas in the case of very large national institutions the expectation is currently that they will be bailed out in the face of insolvency (that is, that the authorities will provide emergency funds to keep the business trading, even if they are in the form of purchase and assumption), the position for cross-border banks is much more difficult. The position is very clear for Switzerland, where both UBS and Credit Suisse have the majority of their operations outside Switzerland. The new Swiss legislation, which is very similar to the MHL proposals and is described by Hüpkes in Chapter 10 of this book, explicitly places a ceiling of 4 bnCHF on the payout for any one institution. Otherwise the liabilities for deposit insurance funds and taxpayers in small countries could become unsustainably large.[33] (As suggested by Sigurðsson in Chapter 5, such banks can be 'Too Big to Save', for a small country.) Since many of the losses will accrue to people in other countries from operations in those countries it is not likely that the authorities in the headquarters' country will be willing to make very extensive payments. In the case of the USA it is possible to discriminate against foreign depositors but not in the EEA, where equal treatment is required, especially with respect to depositors in other EEA countries. In order to stop a grab for local assets, the winding up directive requires the treatment of insolvency on a group basis, although frequently administrators would want to sell off viable subsidiaries early on in a liquidation process in order to maximize the realizable value of the assets (Moss *et al.*, 2002).[34]

MHL argue that the same process described at the national level should also apply at the cross-border level in the EEA. This would require making one authority responsible for decision-making regarding the international banking group. While in the longer term it may appear sensible to create a European level organization for the purpose, at present it would be necessary at least to have a panel of acceptable people who can be called upon to act in the event of the failure of a multinational bank. Such administrators might very well face considerably greater problems over obtaining the information to value claims up front. The national supervisors would have to be collating information on a continuing basis to make this possible. Secondly they may well face a *conflict of interest*. A bank with systemic implications for one country in which it operates may not be regarded as systemic by the authorities in the headquarter (home) country, where the decisions will be taken.[35] It is thus necessary to know in advance the attitude of the participants.

In contrast with the national position it is not clear what the fall back will be in the case of difficulty. One clear possibility is insolvency, if the home country does not feel it has adequate resources for a rescue and other parties cannot be got round the table in time. If this were the case then the incentives for prudent management and early private sector resolution might be sharper than in the national case and the moral hazard smaller. However, such a 'disorderly' outcome for unfortunate practical reasons would not represent responsible regulation. Some form of credible system needs to be in place by the time of the first crisis. The inhibiting factor in achieving this is that it is a 'small country' problem in a forum where decision-making is dominated by larger countries that do not necessarily face such a pressing need.

All of the other issues raised for national banks are writ large for complex cross-border institutions – clarity of corporate structure, availability of adequate information produced according to coherent accounting standards and reputable audit. Although the issues may have been adumbrated (see Brouwer *et al.* in Chapter 8) it is by no means clear that they are well on the way to being addressed.

1.2 Regulatory encouragement and supervisory action

As mentioned above, although we focus on what to do in the event of actual or imminent insolvency, the point of the arrangements is to ensure a competitive, efficient and smoothly running system, in which the normal birth, growth and death of enterprises can take place in a framework in which society has confidence. The system of regulation and banking supervision therefore needs to provide a network of incentives to all those involved with the financial system to encourage prudent behaviour. For banks to add value as financial intermediaries, this process inherently involves the taking of risks. The normal requirements are that these risks should be managed carefully and their nature be transparent to all those who are exposed to them.

There are generally accepted principles for such schemes of regulation (see Llewellyn, 1999, for example) but in the present context the principal requirements are that the regulations be effective and that those imposing the regulatory system should be aware of the costs the measures impose. As in other industries, regulation is applied not for its own sake but to reduce social costs. Detailed supervision, for example, imposes direct costs on banks that will in the main be passed on to their own customers. However, much of the pressures of recent years, now bound up in the Basel2 proposals, have been to get banks to apply the sorts of risk-management procedures that the better-managed banks have already put in place. This will not impose any significant cost on the bank if the regulatory methodology closely resembles the sort of techniques the bank would itself have applied and should convey considerable benefits to all the stakeholders in the bank.[36] In New Zealand, for example, the extra cost of applying and reporting on the risk management methods for the benefit of the authorities was calculated by the banks as being very small (MHL, Chapter 7). It is the wider cost of the regulation that is both more difficult to calculate and likely to be much larger. One of the main explanations of the different shares of bank finance in the financing of industry stems from differences in the regulatory system (La Porta *et al.*, 1997, 1998). The actual costs of disclosure are likely to be limited. The information to be disclosed normally has to be collected in much more detail and higher frequency in the course of running the bank. The question of whether the disclosure affects banks' profitability and ability to compete could be much more significant.

In so far as regulations and supervisory interventions restrict lending opportunities, they may inhibit the process of economic development and thereby lead to lower income and wealth per head than is otherwise possible. With a positive link between risk and return, reducing the risks that may be run may reduce the returns that can be earned. This of course is completely different from trying to insist that banks manage their risks well and improve their information. Particularly, trying to get banks to reduce the risks that stem from the way they operate will tend to be a benefit. Prudence and risk aversion are not one and the same thing. Edwards and Scott (1976) provide an early and comprehensive review of the ways in which different regulatory interventions designed to address the problems of solvency might affect risk-taking, costs and the incidence of insolvency. Their conclusion (pp. 52–3) is striking: 'most... solvency regulations have ambiguous effects on bank solvency... of all the detailed solvency regulations, capital and liquidity requirements seem to be the most effective devices to increase bank soundness.' Some well-known measures such as entry and activity restrictions can have perverse results.

The Basel2 proposals are intended to get a better balance among the incentives to banks for prudential behaviour through their three pillars. While the first pillar aims at changing the capital buffer against unexpected risks, not merely to remove anomalies but to encourage better risk assessment systems, the second seeks to supplement this with a supervisory review of each bank to consider its specific problems. The third seeks to ensure sufficient disclosure that market discipline can be more effective. It is worth noting in passing that the Basel2 capital proposals have themselves come in for criticism as being likely to lead to greater instability in the system rather than less (Jokivuolle and Peura, 2001, 2003). Valuations of capital and corporate ratings are procyclical. So also are defaults and the loss given default. Hence requiring a given capital backing that takes no account of these cyclical movements will tend to exacerbate the chance of failure in an economic downturn. This is currently being addressed both by changes in the rules for the holding of capital and by suggestions that supervisory requirements should be counter-cyclical – by measures such as dynamic provisioning (Fernandez de Lis *et al.*, 2000). However, the point of the present remarks is not to offer a specific solution but to illustrate the two-way relationship between the regulation of normal times and crises and the regulation of crises and behaviour in more normal times.[37] The herding behaviour in upturns partly in response to the actual or perceived protection that can exist in downturns is an obvious case in point.

A large element of prudential supervision hangs on this first pillar of banks insuring themselves against risk by holding a minimum level of capital against contingencies, weighted by the risks being undertaken. There is a cost to holding that capital and indeed some perversities encountered when extra capital is required. If a bank in trouble needs to raise more capital it will have to pay a premium to do so. This presents one of the big dilemmas for the handling of difficulties. There is little point in taking action against the bank at that time unless of course it is a case of fraud or other breaches of the regulations. The emphasis is on trying to find a way for the bank to get back to a safe buffer as soon as possible. Such prompt corrective action normally focuses on the bank finding its own routes to acquiring more capital quickly while restraining it from taking actions that would worsen the position (on both sides of the balance sheet).[38] It makes no sense to fine a bank that has become undercapitalized, as that merely worsens the capital position (although it could be a cynical move by the authorities to improve their ranking among the creditors in the face of an imminent failure). If a bank cannot or will not undertake the necessary recapitalization within the prescribed time limits then the process of withdrawal of the banking licence and probable liquidation would be triggered. The threat of withdrawing a licence is in any case likely to push a bank into insolvency. (An alternative route can be the threat of withdrawing deposit protection.)

Much of the intention in the regulatory framework is to discourage banks from ever getting into difficulties. It also encourages the finding of a market solution that does not involve the intervention of the authorities and a turn-round in the performance well before failure. There is thus a dilemma, the costs to the banks of going too close to insolvency need to be high enough encourage prior action but they need to avoid being so high that they encourage even higher risk-taking in a last ditch attempt to keep away from insolvency. Indeed one of the problems is that the costs of insolvency are so high to those running the banks in terms of loss of jobs and future earnings that these high-risk actions are thought to be worth it.

The authorities themselves face some problems from the nature of their involvement with the banks. The very fact of supervision can be taken as some sort of guarantee that the banks are run well. Implicitly, if they were not, the expectation would be that they would lose their licences. In some people's minds therefore bank failure could be taken as a regulatory failure. The real danger of course is that a supervisor would make this connection and therefore be keen to avoid any such bank failures if at all possible. The transparency of the system therefore has to be such as to try to minimize the conveyance of this notion to outsiders. Similarly the transparency in the process of action when a bank gets into difficulty has to be such as to ensure that the regulator is not facing similar incentives as bank managements – to keep in business if possible with little regard to the potential cost to others.

There are some difficulties here as most supervisors and indeed banks argue that there is some merit in secrecy about the existence of problems at least for a short period of time while solutions are being worked out. This poses a real dilemma for the authorities, as they could be thought liable for any consequential loss from failing to reveal the existence of problems they knew about. These issues point to having clear obligations on the supervisors in the event of difficulty.[39] Knowing that information will become public is one of the important incentives for banks to get on with recapitalization very rapidly before they have to face the enhanced costs in the market. Supervisors themselves need to know that the sequence of their actions or inaction will be scrutinised after the event. It is particularly important in setting incentives to make sure that successful actions are just as much open to public scrutiny as 'failures'.[40]

Not all of the regulatory questions relate directly to prudential supervision. However, the creation of barriers to entry may permit higher profits, that is, higher costs to borrowers and lower returns to lenders. Such barriers are created in part by the qualifications necessary to get a banking licence. However, the process used in resolving problems can also lead in the same direction by creating very considerable concentration in the banking system. If a bank is in difficulty then the only possible changes in ownership are likely to come from a merger with an existing bank. (It would certainly be difficult to pass the 'fit and proper' tests for having a banking licence in the hurry of a banking crisis.) It is those that can gain competitively who may be keenest to take on the task. Being able to serve a wider client base from a smaller number of outlets is an incentive. Being able to acquire entry to a new market through a bank in difficulty may not look so attractive. This problem of concentration is likely to become greater the deeper the crisis or the more crises that have occurred in the past.

This process of resolution through merger, coupled with the ability of larger banks to run more sophisticated risk management systems may make it more difficult for smaller banks to compete. However, these days, in the larger markets this is a less likely route for significant new entry. Entrants are more likely to be large institutions either in other countries or in a different but related area of finance.

Competition rules can also be challenged in the process of the resolution of banks in a 'conduct of business' sense. If the government steps in to support a large bank that gets into difficulty, this could be thought to constitute an unfair subsidy. The extent of subsidization could be even greater if the bank is taken into public ownership. However, in that case the recipients of the subsidy are no longer the previous owners. In these circumstances, saving one bank can be contributing to putting pressure on the others that have been prudently managed. It is clear from cases such as Credit Lyonnais that authorities have pushed the EU rules very close to the limits. Since the government as owner has access to funds on conditions much more favourable than the private sector it is difficult to decide at what stage the injection of funds becomes unfair competition, an issue that the Commission has addressed specifically in the case of the German Landesbanken.

1.3 Market discipline

Trying to ensure a strong measure of market discipline forms the second of the main features of supervisory regimes both in normal operation and in the resolution of problems. The key feature of market discipline is that it should provide incentives to all of the stakeholders in the bank, whether shareholders, managers, depositors, creditors or supervisors, to see that the bank is prudently managed. This discipline exists because the market players can act on the basis of the information that is available on the bank, not just in absolute terms but relative to its competitors in the sector.

While the recommendations in the Basel2 proposals for the amount of information to be publicly disclosed by banks meets much of the argument we set out in MHL for efficient market discipline, its timeliness does not. If the information available is six months or more out of date, the actual position of a bank has been able to change markedly from that published. Market players will then try to rely on more informal information, which may not only be less accurate and comparable but will not be equally available to all the stakeholders. The ability to put off knowledge of the true circumstances and the size of any revelations that may then occur can on the one hand contribute to the instability of the market and on the other make it more difficult for the process of trying to take over the bank as a going concern to succeed.

Banks that are not performing as well as the rest of the sector tend to be subject to takeover bids. Such bids will occur when the bank is still readily meeting the regulatory criteria. If the market can react to these more marginal signals then the chance of getting into severe difficulty will be reduced. The problem comes for banks whose governance structures do not permit the ready exercise of market discipline. Obvious examples are where the bank is privately owned, say as part of an industrial group, or its shares are not directly quoted, where it is state-owned or where it is a more mutual organisation, as in the case of a cooperative or savings bank. In these circumstances, not only is it difficult for the signals to be observed but there is much less pressure that those who are affected can place on the back to see change. For this reason it is often suggested that all banks should be forced to face significant exposure to the market, say, by being required to have a significant amount of subordinated debt, which has to be rolled over in the market in the short run, so it is actively priced (Calomiris, 1999). Even though this finance may in some sense be superfluous it results in signals to which others, including the authorities, react (Evanoff and Wall, 2002).

On the whole the nature of the incentive structures from market discipline is relatively clear. The employees of the bank clearly have something at stake, in terms of income in the short run. It is, however, more difficult to say whether the failure of the bank they work for harms or advances their careers in the longer term. When it comes to the managers or directors who can in some way be thought responsible, then it may harm their career prospects and those who have suffered losses as a result of those actions will no doubt think that is only appropriate. Once one is dealing with the higher echelons of management where part of their remuneration is linked to the performance of the bank then the potential losses from failure will be greater and hence the incentive to avoid it and have a less ignominious exit also greater. Thus the incentive to avoid or take excess risks will have an extra facet when problems occur, depending upon the likely action of the authorities. If senior managers think the authorities may keep the institution in being and allow them to retain their jobs if they respond in a risk-averse manner (as was arguably the case for some US thrifts in the 1980s) then they will do so. But if the only real hope of retaining their jobs is through taking a large gamble then that too is likely to be the choice they will make.[41]

The position for depositors is complicated when their deposits are insured. In the first place, to the extent their deposits are insured, particularly if they can access them rapidly after a failure, they will have little incentive to monitor the bank. In any case it is normally thought that the general run of depositors are not sufficiently well informed to either process or act on the information available. Only the larger depositors are likely to be in that position. The deposit insurance organization therefore tends to act on behalf of the depositors it insures. While it may rely on the supervisors to look after its interests when the bank is performing normally it can have a much greater role in the event of difficulty, ending up as the lead organization in a reorganization in the case of the US FDIC, for example. However, having the authorities take the lead on behalf of depositors is not the same as having them take account of both those who are directly exposed as taxpayers and those who are indirectly exposed as the customers of other banks or as taxpayers. It is therefore important to recognize that borrowers and their customers, creditors, and so on are also exposed. If a bank has to retrench it may not roll over some loans and prefer to remain in liquid assets. Some of their clients may themselves then go out of business or shrink if this experience is fairly widespread in the banking sector. MHL therefore argue that it is this wider public interest that should be taken into account in deciding how to act.

It was noted in Section 1.2 that valuations of assets can be decidedly procyclical, as can assessments of risk, particularly those like KMV that make use of equity prices. The market can therefore be a very harsh judge of the valuation of a bank, as the valuation reflects not just the underlying position of the bank under consideration but also the position of the potential purchasers. This double valuation approach is the appropriate way to value a problem bank from the point of view of the stability of the system as a whole, as the problem does not disappear, but is merely acquired by another bank in the system. The weakness applies to the system as a whole and not just to the problem bank in these circumstances. However, this valuation implies that the risks are borne by the shareholder side of the market. It is a valuation based on the full extent of creditor claims. If the bank were declared insolvent and the creditor claims written down then the valuation to an acquiring bank would be different. Similarly the valuation would be different again if the acquirer were only acquiring various of the assets and liabilities of the troubled bank and not the business as such.[42] Acquiring access to the customer base is likely to have a clear value and indeed it is normally argued that despite the 'fire sale' element in market valuations, the valuation of the bank as a going concern tends to exceed that under insolvency (Hoggarth *et al.*, 2002; James, 1991). Guttentag and Herring (1983) suggest that 'banks usually are worth more alive than dead even when their value alive is negative'. This in itself helps to explain the authorities' enthusiasm for finding market solutions prior to failure.

The most important aspect in this regard in the event of insolvency is that the time horizon of the parties involved differs. If the assets of the bank are to be sold off under insolvency proceedings and maximum discounted value extracted from the non-performing loans then a rather longer time horizon will be adopted than would be the case in a more rapid sale with the aim of staying in business. This dilemma is reflected in the accounting standards for valuation and in the internal methods of valuation used by the bank. In general, US practice under GAAP tends to result in a valuation closer to the immediate market prices than the IFAS approach (although the two are coming close to a generalized agreement). This poses both problems of international comparability and of rapid valuation in the case of a resolution. Typically a regulator would not be able to get an immediate valuation on the ideal basis for taking a decision about how to proceed. However, it is arguable that this is precisely the information that the supervisors should insist on obtaining, rather than simply regulatory capital measures, which will be increasingly less relevant as failure approaches. Problems are of course much worse if accounting and auditing standards are not up to international best practice in Halme *et al.* (2000, p. 58) points out that 'Skopbank was apparently one of the most solvent banks in Finland at the start of the 1990s. However the bank was taken over by the Finnish central bank in September 1991.'[43] The fact that the authorities can take a longer-term view than markets for the assets of a bank in difficulty means that there can be a role for a lender of last resort. The major question then becomes how far down the list of collateral the authorities are prepared to go, particularly when the discussion extends, say, to the mortgage portfolio.

In so far as the authorities step in, even in the form of liquidity assistance, problems can emerge from altering the ranking of creditors. The central bank, for example, can indulge in collateralized lending earlier to reduce the chance of uncollateralized or weakly collateralized lending later. Actions within what can be described as the market framework can nevertheless have implications if insolvency actually materializes.[44]

As Edwards and Scott (1976) point out, the value of the capital buffer varies very considerably depending on the routes used and available to an undercapitalized bank in tackling its problems. If a bank can raise new capital, albeit at relatively high cost, then it does not have to sell assets, merely write down the value of impaired assets according to the prevailing rules. If a bank has to realize assets in order to handle losses then it faces a much more difficult downward spiral, as many such assets will have to be sold at a discount while liabilities are met at par.[45]

1.4 Problems in assessing the potential costs to society of insolvency

A problem for the authorities in assessing the potential costs of insolvency is that there is concern not just for the expected value but for the upper limit of the cost. Mis-estimation matters whether it is under- or over-estimation but it is normally easier to live with the economic and political costs of finding that the problem is smaller than anticipated. The time path of actions matters. Once a decision on closure or continuation is taken it cannot readily be unwound (delay is itself a decision). A range of outcomes has to be considered dependent upon a number of unknowns. The full extent of the problems of the bank is something that can only be estimated. The willingness of other parties to step in can only be judged and since they will want to negotiate favourable terms it is also necessary to estimate what the final outcomes are likely to be. Thirdly the extent of bad loans and the likely valuation of assets will depend upon external economic events as well as on the factors affecting the particular bank. Values in asset markets are strongly driven by expectations, which themselves may hinge, particularly in the short run, on rather intangible factors. The actions of the authorities are themselves factors affecting expectations.

1.4.1 Assessing the social cost of banking crises

Although this is a discussion of what may happen in the future, the obvious first step in forming these assessments is to look backwards and to try to unpick the costs of previous failures and rescues. These costs involve more than the size of the public funds employed or the losses actually incurred by the parties to the insolvency. The question is 'what was the wider impact on the economy?'. This in itself, however, is only half the question, because it explores what the alternative costs are given that the point of failure is reached. A principal purpose of the MHL scheme is to avoid reaching the point of failure. Hence much of the relevant arithmetic lies in assessing the net costs of the operation of the economy with an MHL scheme in place compared to under an alternative regime.[46] However, let us restrict ourselves to the narrow question for the time being as this will always be the relevant one in the event of a crisis.

Answering this question involves comparing the actual outcome with a hypothetical, what-would-have-happened-otherwise, scenario. The norm is to follow one of two routes. One is to look at how long it took for the economy to get back on its previous track (Hoggarth and Saporta, 2001; Jonung and Hagberg, 2002). The other is to try to model the alternative path. The problem with the first of these routes is that it involves two hypotheses: first that without the crisis the economy would have continued on the same track over the medium term, and second that it is possible to identify what proportion of the departure from that longer-term trend is due to the banking problem and what to other contributions. The impact on GDP or the assessment of financial costs as proportions of GDP are not the only ways of looking at the cost in social or economy-wide terms. Other indicators of the wider impact, such as unemployment, participation or net migration, can also be used.

Most of these computations relate to banking difficulties that involve a number of banks rather than the failure of a single 'systemic' bank. In part this is because the occurrence of such single failures is relatively rare. Banking problems tend to be cyclically related, so when a large bank is in trouble the chances are that the banking system as a whole is also in difficulty. Hence the options for a market-led resolution are much more limited. When other banks are in reasonable condition mergers are much more achievable (as Mølgaard points out in Chapter 9). Such computations of the consequences of 'too big to fail' hence tend to get bound up in the analysis of 'too many to fail'.

The problematic nature of this sort of analysis is illustrated vividly by the Finnish banking crisis of the early 1990s. Jonung and Hagberg (2002) suggest that the cost of the crisis was around 25 per cent of GDP (Table 1.1). These estimates are obtained by asking how much GDP was 'lost' in the period before GDP got back to its previous growth rate. It is thus a measure of the size of the downturn in the economy. The authors try to avoid over-estimation by subtracting the 'excess' growth that occurred in the period immediately prior to the crisis. Not only could 'permitting' that extra growth be regarded as part of the cause of the crisis but it is itself a gain to economic welfare that should be taken into account.[47] There are various means of comparing these losses to an extrapolation of previous trends as discussed in Hoggarth and Saporta

Table 1.1 Alternative calculations of the costs of the 1990's crisis in Finland (percentage points)

Measure of trend	Loss of real income	Loss of industrial production	Loss of employment
4-year trend	27.3	21.4	24.2
All years	23.3	25.7	26.3
Monetary regime	21.1	20.4	not computable

Note: The costs are calculated by summing the differences between the trend growth rate and actual growth rate between the first year of recession until the growth of the series returns to trend.

Source: Jonung and Hagberg (2002).

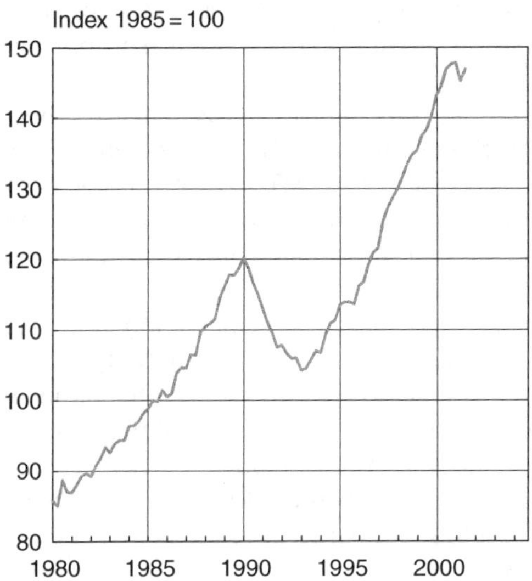

Figure 1.2 Finland's GDP

Source: Statistics Finland, Statfin database.

(2001). However if one uses *levels* of GDP, as opposed to growth rates, it is clear from Figure 1.2 that it took until around 2000 for Finland to recover the level of GDP it would have had on the basis of extrapolating previous trends.[48] The cost would then be at least double that estimated by Jonung and Hagberg. These numbers are, however, largely valueless as the crisis was due to a combination of factors, only some of which were related to the inadequate performance of banks (MHL,

Chapter 2). The only relevant calculations relate to the outcome for the economy if (a) banking regulation and financial supervision had been better in the period before the crisis and (b) different treatments had been offered to insolvent banks during the crisis. Given the experience of the Danish economy over the same time period the benefits from better regulation and supervision could have been considerable but the relative costs of different approaches to insolvency would have been very difficult to estimate. An orderly resolution without the use of public money, along the lines we recommend, might have had fairly similar results. But letting the banks become insolvent with no other actions would have had very serious implications indeed. The deviation approach thus has a string of disadvantages. It makes a very simplified assumption about the nature of the counter-factual against which to judge what has happened. It combines in the calculation any other sources of deviation, including the random and not just the choice of exit regime.

It is clear therefore that the only reasonable method of making an assessment after the event would be the modelling route, with a comparison of two scenarios of bank resolution rather than the computations of the loss of GDP or indeed employment caused by the deviation from trend. Even so the probability of default under different regimes and the loss given default would require some strong assumptions, which could be hotly contested. The deviation approach is likely to be a heavily upward-biased indicator of the potential costs of not bailing banks out. Not only is it likely to blame other unavoidable costs of an economic downturn on the behaviour of banks and their regulators but it takes 'no crisis' as the outcome of alternative feasible actions. Unfortunately, it nevertheless provides the basis on which much of the enthusiasm for bailing out banks is based, namely large estimated costs from banking crises.

This comparison of scenarios route could be applied to investigation of the speed of reaction. It is inherent in the US approach, for example, that there should be Prompt Corrective Action, where progressive intervention by the authorities and reaction by the banks is prescribed as regulatory capital falls below the required levels. In other systems, such as Japan's, more forbearance is possible. One could contrast the impact on the total cost of a sharp but deeper problem with a shallower but more prolonged one.

The problem is easier to assess when it is applied to a single bank, as in stress-testing exercises, without the need to consider the wider implications for other institutions. Once wider contagion is considered it is not realistic to employ models that treat other features of policy as fixed. If a systemic bank becomes insolvent the central bank would provide liquidity to the rest of the financial system to offset the problem. Such a general provision under normal lending terms could be followed in specific cases by the exercise of the lender of last resort function, offering loans at penal rates of interest against less marketable collateral. Similarly in these circumstances asset prices will themselves also be affected. Again the central bank is likely to intervene as part of its monetary policy and wider stability obligations. Interest rates will be cut and asset prices may be supported by central bank purchases on its own account. As a central bank can take a longer view, because it could ultimately call on the taxpayer to fund its operations, it can purchase assets to hold to maturity or until the market recovers in a way in which commercial banks that have to meet regulatory capital requirements cannot. Such comprehensive exercises are not common in the literature.

It is equally important in the comparison of scenarios to make sure that the analysis has not been too narrow. A bank that has been able to improve its position by rapidly reducing the size of its loan book may have caused a consequential cycle of losses elsewhere for the creditors and suppliers of its customers and a second-round set of reductions in their spending, which will in turn reduce economic activity of yet another group. One must look at the consequences for all of the stakeholders and not just for depositors, shareholders, other creditors and the direct impact on the public sector budget.

The modelling route can also be used in trying to assess in advance what will happen, as that is the context of the actual decision that has to be taken. This approach is used in the case of the Bank of Finland. As part of the regular assessment of financial stability, banking sector models are run in combination with the economy-wide models. In the case of Finland such an exercise is simplified because it would be reasonable to assume that there would be no response by the single euro area monetary policy to a purely Finnish banking sector problem, caused, say, by a company specific shock in the telecommunications sector.

1.4.2 Assessing the cost of public intervention

As noted above, it is necessary in assessing the costs of the bank exit regime to consider the costs that are incurred in preventing failures and not just the cost of bailouts. Nevertheless, in forming the overall picture an accurate assessment of the costs of different forms of intervention is needed. Over the years the IMF has worked on how official assistance to banks should be computed, in the narrow sense of the funds actually provided. It is easy to take too narrow a view of the funds disbursed. Daniel *et al.* (1997), for example, have pointed out that governments tend to understate the cost; interest subsidies may not be clear. Guarantees that are not drawn upon at the time are not recorded, nor are other contingent liabilities. Impaired loans that are acquired need to have a value reflecting the time to their ultimate repayment and not just the extent of that repayment. The same arguments need to apply to any cost benefit analysis that is applied in advance to the assessment of the merits of a particular bailout or reorganization. Daniel (1997) records a whole range of devices where governments have avoided recording the extent of subsidies on their accounts. One way of course is to let the central bank or some other agency acquire the impaired assets or make the favourable loans and hence keep them off the government's balance sheet. Finland's accounting for the crisis in the 1990s is included under more than one heading of questionable practice, although it accorded with the convention of the time and was not undertaken with deception in mind.

It is rather more straightforward to try to tease out the counterfactual in response to some of these more direct measures. Daniel suggests that one can observe reductions in interest spreads for banks after the restructuring. With a large banking sector a reduction in spread can be significant in terms of GDP. Secondly, if there is not full Ricardian equivalence, a switch of wealth from the public sector to the private sector may actually stimulate demand and ease the crisis, even though people are aware that future taxpayers will have to pay. Recent experience in Japan might suggest that this mechanism does not always work and that people can indeed be relatively Ricardian in their actions. The outcome will no doubt be affected by issues such as the age structure of the population and the nature of existing public and private pension provisions. What is likely to be more effective is the existence of guarantees for the new bank, which will help instil confidence even though they may not be drawn on. (Daniel does not, however, suggest how that effect might be measured.) Alternative scenarios will remain speculative – avoiding a bailout in the short run may merely mean an even worse circumstance later on that generates a larger government intervention.

Frydl and Quintyn (2000) offer one of the most comprehensive attempts to value the costs and benefits of different crisis interventions from an economic point of view. Unfortunately many of the items remain largely speculative even with respect to the direct costs that will or should enter the public sector's balance sheet. While it is possible to discuss the direction of change of moral hazard, quantifying its impact is another matter. Initial estimates of ten crises studied by the authors were reassessed by more than a factor of two in some cases, as more information emerged. In the case of Indonesia in 1997–9 the reassessment by the IMF amounted to 20 per cent of GDP in a period of about six months.

They use their methodology to estimate the ex-post cost of the Swedish crisis of 1991–3. In terms of simple discounted direct costs the government recouped half of its outlays through the rise in the value of the shares in the banks that it acquired at the outset. This helps to emphasize the importance of taking a longer-term view and valuing the franchise of the bank. The survey of evidence in Hoggarth *et al.* (2002) shows that it is difficult to come up with a hard and fast view of what features of bank resolution techniques lead to higher or lower costs. It is clearly essential to try to differentiate crises by type. Twin exchange-rate and banking crises typically have higher costs than crises just in banking. Bordo *et al.* (2001), for example, find that GDP losses are larger when there is open-ended liquidity support (on the basis of crises in 29 countries over 1973–97). Honohan and Klingebiel (2000) find the same applies to fiscal costs. However, it is the very last sentence of Hoggarth *et al.* which underlines our contention: 'although the *types* of techniques used can reduce the net costs of crises, the costs in any case are still likely to be large suggesting that crisis *prevention* should be a key objective of financial stability' (Hoggarth *et al.*, p. 37, emphasis in original). Indeed their survey offers a straightforward answer to the question in the title of this book: 'Shareholders have usually lost their capital and senior managers their jobs, but creditors have rarely made losses. Liquidations have been used only occasionally and typically for smaller institutions' (p. 37). Taxpayers have indeed paid, often handsomely through the direct fiscal costs, but society at large has also paid through the subsequent impact on economic activity.

1.4.3 The costs in insolvency and alternative arrangements

The process of insolvency is itself costly, with the need to establish claims, concert claimants, value and realize assets etc. However, the alternative processes are not without direct costs (ignoring any moral hazard involved). The costs of merging one bank with another are usually substantial unless they can be run as standalone operations, which is relatively unlikely in the case of virtual failure. While the process of discovery of the nature of the problem may be less expensive it is likely that the management and IT systems will have to be changed, considerable redundancies and property sales and relocation undertaken and so on.

The major difference lies in where the costs fall. In the case of insolvency proceedings the costs fall on the creditors. In the case of a merger/acquisition the costs fall on the new owners and on the customers of both the acquiring and the troubled bank. Failure by some borrowers to service their loans properly may very well be partly financed by other borrowers who repay throughout, in the form of increased spreads. Chapter 7 by Granlund gives an idea of how big the impact on spreads might be of a regime that offers less protection to creditors. Variations across markets can be as much as 50 basis points but variations within markets tend to be rather smaller. However, the more likely the bailout of any bank then obviously the less the importance of any concept of TBTF. Stern and Feldman (2003, Table 3.1) offer an assessment of the effect of TBTF on rating as assessed by FitchRatings. The difference in the rating, with and without the 'implicit' government guarantee, can be as much as two rating classes.[49]

The consequences of this could be substantial for the banking sector and the economy at large. As Soussa (2000, p. 23) argues 'TBTF does appear to lower the funding cost for larger banks and thus creates an uneven playing field in banking. TBTF therefore reduces competition and thus efficiency, exemplifying the general trade-off official intervention in the financial sector presents between efficiency and financial stability.'

Of course such an assessment does not reveal what would apply if the system were to change because bank behaviour would change along with the regime. More capital would be held against contingencies and risk-taking might also change thereby resulting in a much smaller change in ratings or spreads from current levels. Soussa (2000) suggests that, despite the scope for moral hazard, the evidence that large banks actually respond and run greater risks is rather thin. Transparency and increased disclosure requirements similarly tend to result in banks voluntarily holding more capital against risks (Baumann and Nier, 2002). While holding such capital should reduce the probability of failure, the net cost is more moot, since the response to increased prudence may be an increased willingness to lend to banks.

While shifting repayment from those who cannot pay to those who can may maximise the revenue for the bank there is no guarantee that this is for the benefit of the economy as a whole. Such a process may allow uncompetitive firms to remain in business while inhibiting the profitability of those that are profitable. In this way the shift of assets from the inefficient to the efficient may be restricted with customers getting both less attractive products and less favourable prices.

The main question in the case of 'too big to fail' is how far the losses will go in the process of resolution. In the USA, for example, the practice since 1988 has been to allow the bank holding company to fail and hence to wipe out the shareholders (Kaufman, 2002). The question then relates to the extent of losses for the non-insured depositors that will be accepted. In one sense the system in the USA has not been tested in that there have been no cases large enough to contemplate using the 'too big to fail' clause, as defined by the systemic risk exemption (SRE), since it was introduced in 1993.

There is thus a framework available within which costs and benefits of different treatments of insolvency could be sketched out by the authorities. The process is well documented in the USA, as the 1991 FDIC Improvement Act (FDICIA), requires the FDIC to resolve the problem bank 'at the least possible long-term loss to the deposit insurance fund'. The means of computation of those losses is also described, thereby limiting the scope for the FDIC to take wider factors into account. Nevertheless the method is likely to be decidedly inaccurate and only useful in indicating the appropriate directions when the differences between proposals are substantial and robust to changes in specification. The key feature will then be the prescribed action in the event of a lack of evidence for a contrary decision.

In the MHL proposals the authorities responsible for bank resolution under insolvency would have a prescribed route of action. It would be a separate issue for the fiscal authority and the central bank to decide, on the grounds of social costs and systemic stability, whether, on the basis of the analysis of the costs involved, any public funds should be injected into the banking system rather than simply into more macroeconomic measures. The bank resolution can proceed rapidly in all cases, whether or not the fiscal authorities decide to provide any funds.

It is a difficult question to decide how well minimizing the cost to the deposit insurance fund equates to minimizing the social cost. It assumes that the social consequences for losses by non-insured creditors and any spill-over impact into the rest of the economy will also be minimized. One obvious way in which this may not be true would be if the impact were highly concentrated – the total cost even in fiscal terms of the consequent collapse of the key employer on a 'company town' may be greater than the extra widely distributed impact of losses to the deposit insurance company. It would also might not be true if it simply increased the size of the general direct loss to creditors. The insurance fund only loses when those below it in priority have nothing more to lose.[50] If priorities are altered, as in the US case, then it might be possible that minimizing the insurance fund loss is not coterminous with minimizing the general loss.

1.5 Structure of the book

The chapters in the book cover the issues we have outlined from a variety of perspectives. Chapter 2, by Liuksila, begins by developing the issues that have been raised in more detail. It is structured in the form of a series of questions and answers about the MHL approach. While the present chapter has a predominantly 'economic' slant to the problem, Chapter 2 balances this with a predominantly 'legal' perspective. The two need to be taken together for an understanding of the scope of the issues in the book. Liuksila starts by contrasting the *lex specialis* approach we advocate with the *lex generalis* context for insolvency, which characterizes insolvency in much of Europe, before going on to consider the detailed provisions of the proposal. In particular, he contrasts the proposal with the approach that is currently applied in the USA, as that is probably the closest current regime. Although, as described by Hüpkes in Chapter 10, the new regime to be introduced in Switzerland also has much in common with our framework. By using this 'question and answer' framework, Liuksila is able to expose both why the problem over the treatment of bank insolvency has arisen – particularly in the cross-border context – and why most existing regimes have difficulties in facing up to the challenge. Key to his approach is the recognition that a new legal framework has to handle the political realities that have helped form the current frameworks and impair their operation.

The remainder of the book is divided in two, with the first, Part II, containing five chapters related to assessing the size of the problem we are addressing. The four chapters in Part III then go on to explore different ideas and experiences in solving the problem that complement or contrast with our own.

Chapter 3 by Stern and Chapter 4 by Beck are concerned with how to design systems of regulation and bank resolution that provide appropriate incentives for the running of the banking system both in normal times and in the face of stress. They are concerned that all parties to the financial system should find that the regulatory framework encourages them to pursue their own interests in a way that is to the benefit of the good running of the financial system and the economy as a whole. The system should thus reward good risk management and penalize the bad. It should encourage the stability of the system as a whole while permitting normal competitive adjustment within it. Key requirements for this to happen are that information should be good, both about risks and about the future actions of the authorities, particularly in times of stress, and market mechanisms should function well, not just for the banking business but also for corporate control. Stern sets out the case for better disclosure so that the market can be well enough informed to act. Stern's approach is developed in much more detail in a companion piece (Stern and Feldman, 2003). Of course, as he also suggests, being able to act does not imply necessarily that the action takes place. As Bliss and Flannery (2001) point out, the next step in the argument is also not a necessity. Just because market signals are clear it does not mean that the bank management necessarily responds to them. The key message of Stern's contribution is 'Disclosure is not Enough' but it is an important step forward.

A major problem of balance comes in how the system protects itself from the adverse consequences of extreme events. Beck is concerned that the design of the deposit insurance system should remove neither the incentives for bank managements to avoid undue risk, especially when difficulties start, nor the incentives for larger depositors and shareholders to 'discipline' managements.[51] In Chapter 10, Hüpkes, in setting out the new system for handling bank insolvency in Switzerland, includes a description of the deposit protection scheme, where the incentive issues are addressed but some of the choice over course of action is still left open in the legislation.

Stern is concerned more widely that the arrangements for handling difficulty should not create moral hazard by encouraging the stakeholders in banks to believe that, despite what may be said in advance, they will come through the difficulty satisfactorily. They need to have enough at stake that they fear the consequences and hence seek to avoid the difficulties in the first place. Nevertheless, an adequate safety net has to exist for the hopefully rare cases of distress, so as to limit the impact on individuals to socially tolerable levels and to ensure that the impact on society as a whole is managed to the general benefit. There is some dispute about how that balance may be achieved as it is widely argued that 'constructive ambiguity' about what may happen in the case of difficulty may encourage people to be prudent. We repeat our argument that the chances are that the reverse may occur, particularly in European and other countries with a history of bailing out banks. If the authorities are ambiguous then people will continue to expect a bailout. Indeed even if the authorities try to say that, despite the past, there will be no such bailouts in the future, they may not be believed. As Soussa (2000, p. 22) phrases it, 'constructive ambiguity does not appear to work – markets still believe that support would be forthcoming for certain large banks should they encounter difficulties.'[52] The results of Gropp and Vesala (2001) show that the introduction of explicit, capped deposit insurance appears to lead to lower risk-taking and moral hazard, when the starting point is an assumed blanket guarantee. However, it may only be by observing examples of the authorities applying the harsher treatment that the new system can gain substantial credibility (Mishkin, 2000).

Chapter 5 by Sigurðsson gives a very clear picture of the extent of the exposure of the Nordic and Baltic countries to an unclear system of responsibility in the light of the rapid pace of merger both within the countries and across the borders. He emphasizes that the regime of blanket support in the past is no longer available under current EU rules and that the participants need to know what the future position will be. His chapter expands the concerns by focusing on the degree to which systemic risks are increasing with the development of new layers and depth of transactions among the banks in the region. The remark in his conclusion that '[c]urrent accounting, auditing and regulatory regimes may, unfortunately, not be well equipped to deal with the explosion of financial engineering that has taken place in recent years' suggests that the problems of being able to detect and handle the looming and actual insolvency in the main banks in the region may in some respects be getting worse and not better.

Chapter 6 by Blowers and Young complements the findings on the possible extent of exposures to insolvency problems by outlining what the impact of differences in insolvency regimes can actually be. They show that the incidence of insolvency is affected by the costs and difficulty of the recovery for the creditor and that business decisions are affected by the balance of shareholder and creditor rights. Thus in US states where the costs to owners of businesses from bankruptcy are greater, households are less likely to start a business. On the other hand it is easier for such businesses to get loans and the costs of those loans are lower. There is thus a balance to be struck. In assessing the costs of a framework for insolvency it is not just a matter of determining the probability of insolvency and the costs and their distribution given insolvency but also one of assessing how the business system functions. A small reduction in the rate of growth every year from a system that discourages entrepreneurial activity may be a high price to pay for an expensive systemic event once every 20 or 40 years.

Chapter 7 by Granlund seeks to explore how differences in the regulatory framework for the treatment of insolvency actually affect the decisions of the stakeholders in banks. He shows that there appears to be a clear relationship between market prices and the degree of protection that the system offers. By contrasting regulation of bank exit in the largest financial markets – USA, Japan, UK and Germany – he gives a picture of the range of choice currently available, using a scorecard rating system with respect to both shareholders and creditors. His results suggest that a system that is more favourable to creditors in the event of bank failure has smaller spreads for borrowing by banks. Thus these banks have an international competitive advantage all the time as the result of a greater safety net. The overall impact is then determined by who pays for this greater safety net (as explained by Beck in Chapter 4). The costs will still be borne by the banks to the extent that it is funded by a general *ex ante* charge on all banks, largely irrelevant of their individual risk of failure, and *ex post* by a charge on the survivors to replenish the funds. However, if some or all of the contingent liability is borne by the taxpayer, then this will effectively be a subsidy to the banks.

What is more difficult to understand is Granlund's finding that greater shareholder rights in the event of distress are associated with slower growth in the size of banks. One might have expected that this would encourage banks to be more aggressive. Perhaps the cost of capital is more important. However, given the constraints that data impose on the analysis, the difference could simply be the effect of a third factor that is not captured by the model. Nevertheless his division of the regulatory differences into probability of support, power of the stakeholder in the event of insolvency and likely speed of resolution provide some helpful dimensionality to assessing how those affected may react.

Both Granlund and Blowers and Young argue that it is not just the rules that matter but also the culture in which they are operated. While most regimes tend to argue that individual institutions will be allowed to fail and it is only where the system is threatened that the authorities will step in, if in fact there have been almost no failures then banks will believe that one way or another it will be possible to work out a solution that does not involve failure, if they get into difficulty. The same applies to creditors. The London Approach of voluntary restructuring can work if the parties are convinced that that is the most likely source of gain and that the other creditors will play. The typical rush to insolvency occurs when some creditors realize that there is a problem and seek to unwind their own position to get better than equal treatment. Those who are less informed will consequently receive less than equal treatment. This is not quite the traditional prisoner's dilemma, as a creditor who emerges unscathed by getting out first cannot normally do better by cooperating. However, if by organizing an orderly work-out everybody gets paid in full but with a delay, there is a clear net benefit and only a loss of liquidity. Creditors will be much more likely to play this game if there is a clear history of fairness in its operation and a high success rate – as suggested by evidence mentioned by Blowers and Young for the London Approach. This same argument applies to discretion for the authorities. If the authorities use their discretion predictably and in a manner that both sides to the action find fair both individually and across cases then discretion is likely to offer a flexibility that all parties find advantageous. If exactly the same discretion shows partiality then it may well be that there is a net benefit in having a system that follows much more rigid rules. The benefits of a rule system vary with the environment in which it operates.[53]

The book also considers how the difficulties can be revealed and resolved in practice, although there are many other examples, which are not covered, but are of value. The case of Argentina is extreme, with pressures on both sides of bank balance sheets leading to closures. Economic circumstances push loans into default, the costs of borrowing rise dramatically and depositors rush for the door, a classic example of a severe banking crisis. As with the case of the Finnish crisis at the beginning of the 1990s, much of the problem lies outside the banking system and with the pursuit of other unsustainable macroeconomic policies and an external shock. Nevertheless, given the choice of supporting policies, the authorities responsible for handling banks in distress still have to act. The Danish (Chapter 9) and Japanese experiences show contrasting approaches. In the Japanese experience the approach has been to try to work through the problems and soften both the external pressure on the banks and allow them to continue to operate rather than fall into insolvency or 'forced' reorganization. The Japanese crisis has, as a consequence, been very drawn out and much of the potential and actual losses have remained unallocated. As a result there has been a general build-up of savings in the economy to try to offset the potential losses, contributing to a failure for the economy to resume its growth path on the back of a recovery in demand. Since the allocation (or indeed extent) of losses has not been decided all parties are reluctant to take decisions that might worsen their future exposures: banks are reluctant to make new loans, firms are reluctant to borrow more to invest.

The Danish experience on the other hand, as discussed by Mølgaard in Chapter 9, illustrates how problems can be resolved when the banks are pushed into early resolution, with strong encouragement for solutions that involve merging the satisfactory operations of banks in difficulty with those of other banks. However, even there a point was reached where the extent of the difficulties was such that the banks with adequate capitalization found acquiring further problem banks unattractive – at the prices the authorities could orchestrate. Two key messages emerge. The first is simply that having well capitalized banks in the first place makes a substantial difference in the face of a crisis. The second is that the recipe for reducing the chance of crises in the first place and improving the ability to solve them in the second involves quite a long list of ingredients, only some of which are under the control of the banking supervisors. The list of 15 points is well worth noting:

- a package of up-to-date legislation covering the banking system and the resolution of problems;
- a well-trained, well-informed and well-resourced supervisory authority;
- substantial capital buffers in each bank;
- rules for provisioning that adapt to the external environment;
- stable and adequate earnings from banking operations (an avoidance of increasing business on the back of transient windfall gains);
- reliable, independent external auditors;
- a responsive government;
- a willingness to let insolvent firms fail, avoid politically directed loans and permit early intervention;
- a safety net through Lender of Last Resort, a deposit insurance fund and ultimately government guarantees and loans;
- a banking sector prepared to participate in restructuring at realistic prices;
- good corporate governance of banks;
- good business ethics;
- no strong expansionary strategy;
- universal (diversified) banks;
- international competition among banks.

An important ingredient of the list is that it is the coordination of supervisors, governments and other banks that matters in the resolution of problems in an adequate legal framework. The picture thus far has been spelt out very much in terms of individual countries that have an ability to bring all the relevant aspects within their own jurisdiction. This plainly does not apply in Europe, whether in individual countries such as Switzerland, as considered by Hüpkes in Chapter 10, the EU/EEA or the euro area, as addressed by Brouwer *et al.* in Chapter 8. Substantial parts of the operations of banks being supervised lie in other countries while substantial operations in the jurisdictions of the individual member states are actually run by financial institutions that are supervised in other member states. Brouwer *et al.*'s numbers for Finland make the problem look smaller than it is as they relate to the euro area whereas the overlaps are very considerable and lie with EEA members outside the euro area, as is clear from the tables in Chapter 5. While this may present problems for the coordination of supervision it presents even greater problems for the management of banks in difficulty. Resolution of a bank would require international action by other banks and government guarantees would need to be coordinated across borders. Such undertakings would be very difficult to carry out in the usual sorts of emergency circumstances that surround bank failures.[54]

Chapter 10 by Hüpkes sets out in some detail the issues that have had to be addressed in designing a new system for the treatment of bank insolvency in Switzerland. The characteristics of the new regime that has been proposed has a great deal in common with our own proposals:

- a *lex specialis* to handle the problems of resolution that need to be effected quickly, with sole competence for the banking supervisor to act in these circumstances – in particular the ability to act without the need for meetings of creditors/shareholders, haircuts can be imposed;
- a presumption that market forces will prevail and there will be no taxpayer money available;
- a system of required and publicly known prompt corrective action with only limited scope for discretion;
- clear closeout arrangements to limit direct contagion to the rest of the financial system;
- judicial review opportunities for affected parties after the event but no options to block the reorganization;
- an approach to handling the problems of multiple jurisdictions for international banks.

The proposals also include a mandatory deposit protection system up to a limit (per depositor) for all accounts, with prompt pay-out with the deposit protection agency then being subrogated to the depositors' claims against the bank. While our own proposals are consistent with this approach it is not essential to them.

Chapter 11 by Hadjiemmanuil complements Hüpkes work by focusing on some of the key features of the way in which the process of initiating and managing insolvency proceedings are organized.[55] Our proposals argue for the appointment of an administrator to implement insolvency and restructuring on the initiative of the authorities. This is based largely on the judgement that decisions have to be taken so rapidly, normally over the course of a weekend, if a legal closure of the bank is not to result automatically in the 'economic closure' of the enterprise by default, that this is unlikely to be achieved by a court administered process.[56] Hadjiemmanuil rightly raises a series of concerns about whether all the parties affected by the proceedings will be properly treated if they do not have access to the courts at the time. In large part he bases his judgement on the effective way that the English system appears to have worked, although his case studies highlight some problems. There are natural conflicts of interest over how to proceed when a bank gets into difficulty and any scheme has to find a means of providing what is viewed as a fair balance among them. To some extent the discussion relates to whether the legal system or the authorities operating within in it are too debtor or creditor 'friendly'. If one believes that regulatory capture is as likely in banking as in many other industries then regulators need to be constrained in the opposite direction by the system of rules. This is clearly a motive behind our own proposals for a clear programme of prompt corrective action and efforts to get private sector solutions for banks in difficulty before the reach the point of insolvency or the withdrawal of a licence.[57] An essential element of 'fairness' in any system is that the nature of the outcome and the process for achieving it should be clear in advance. In that way people can work out how to bear the risks involved in advance. Surprise outcomes are costly, not just *ex post* to the disadvantaged, but *ex ante* as the risks to be covered are greater.

As Hadjiemmanuil also points out, these conflicts of interest also extend to the European level. His chapter includes a review of the current EU law that governs insolvency in banks. Although the Winding up Directive may have sorted out which authorities and jurisdiction should apply when a bank facing insolvency has operations in a number of member states, it does not eliminate the conflicts. It is not clear that moving responsibility to the EU level would operate readily unless the member states were operating a much more harmonized system of banking regulation and supervision. In any case many of the international banks that are operating in the EU have significant operations (including their headquarters) outside the EU's jurisdiction and a purely European agreement would not address the full problem.

It is clear, therefore, that the outstanding problems for the orderly exit of large complex international banks may well prove too great to address both because they are too large to fail and *inter alia* too large for some of the authorities to 'save'. Progress on national exit policies is mixed, sufficient progress on international policies, even within the EEA, may unfortunately have to await the next crisis.

Notes

* I am grateful for comments and suggestions to Bob Eisenbeis, Glenn Hoggarth, William C. Hunter, Tuomas Takalo, Larry Wall, David Wheelock, Geoffrey Wood and the other participants in this book.

1. In most industries the spill-over from the failure of one firm to its competitors is positive – they pick up its customers and do not have any liability to pay for its losses, as is the case with deposit insurance.
2. The role is of course different if fraud or some other criminal activity is involved.
3. Carletti and Hartmann (2002) dismiss one of the reasons often advanced for protecting banks. They conclude (p. 32), 'On the basis of the theoretical and empirical survey [in their article], the idea that competition is something dangerous in the banking sector, since it generally causes instability can be dismissed. In the light of the importance of the market mechanism for allocational efficiency and growth, competition aspects need to be carefully considered in industrial countries, also in banking.'
4. In recent years there has been quite a substantial development of texts setting out what the laws handling bank insolvency are and should be, including Oditah (1996), Ramsey and Head (2000), Asser (2001) and Campbell and Cartwright (2002).
5. It is difficult to think of other instances where people are prepared to hold such important unsecured claims – banks are certainly not prepared to do this in transactions with each other. Collateral is normally required.
6. A limited degree of protection is available for building societies and other institutions where a delay can be imposed on access to deposits.
7. Wood (2003) points out that it is easy to exaggerate the possibility of bank runs. While the existence of central banks and regulatory restraints make more recent data difficult to interpret, early evidence from the United States in the nineteenth and early twentieth centuries suggest that it was rare to have to suspend payments. Furthermore, customers appeared to be able to distinguish between fragile and sound banks and runs on sound banks were unusual (Gorton, 1988; Kaufman, 1986; Rolnick and Weber, 1986). To some extent the concern in the literature over the potential susceptibility to bank runs in a less regulated system may stem from focusing on models such as Diamond and Dybvig (1983), where there is no required capital cushion. Similarly, the extent of the contagion in the Great Crash in the USA is thought to have been substantially aided by the decision of the Federal Reserve not to make very active use of its lender-of-last-resort function in providing liquidity to both illiquid but otherwise solvent banks and the financial market as a whole (Schwartz, 1994).
8. Even in the case of Continental Illinois, which is the largest recent failure in the US (see also Chapter 3 by Stern), although uninsured balances of other banks in Continental exceeded 100 per cent of capital in 65 cases and 50 per cent in

166 cases the recovery rate was around 96 per cent (Wall, 1993). Normal alternative sources of liquidity through the market and the Federal Reserve discount window therefore could suffice.

9. One problem, which was re-emphasized in the 11 September 2001 experience, is that there is some concentration in the derivatives markets, particularly among market makers in the OTC market. The consequences of a failure of one of the main players, while probably not very large in terms of direct losses could cause considerable exposures in the short run as those whose contracts have failed seek to re-hedge their positions. As Wall (1993) points out this could be exacerbated if the shock that causes the bank failure also affects the price of the underlying securities at the same time. The problem can be reduced by lowering the concentration and facilitating unwinding and recontracting. Of course if the failure of the bank in question is in large part due to unfortunate derivatives trading the exposures could be considerable. The problem is complicated because derivatives markets are themselves trying to arrange contracts in such a form that they do not get caught up in insolvencies.
10. Even in the case of the very largest and most complicated banks, it is difficult to envisage how really large insolvencies could emerge. They would require the failure of markets, supervisors, auditors and the bank's control systems to observe a problem large enough not merely to erode the entire capital cushion without prior warning but to result in substantial negative net worth. It tends to be simultaneous problems across a range of banks that generate the largest losses. Large proportionate losses tend to occur in small banks where the absolute size of the problem is less likely to be big enough for outsiders to spot.
11. Conversely, if the authorities make it clear that failing banks will be merged with solvent institutions, Perotti and Suarez (2002) show that this will tend to encourage more prudent behaviour in order to be the survivor that benefits from greater concentration in the market.
12. This poses a real dilemma for those like the IMF who want to set out clearly how actions to resolve banks that are in distress should be structured (Asser, 2001). The very fact that there are prepared and respected legal frameworks that involve the use of public money in the resolution process will strengthen the prior belief for any bank that should it get into difficulty it will be assisted. Yet it would appear irresponsible not to set out what should be done if, despite all attempts to the contrary, a large bank or a banking system reaches the point at which the use of public money appears less costly to society than allowing exit without it.
13. The countries included were Australia, Canada, Germany, Denmark, Spain, Finland, France, Ireland, Italy, Japan, The Netherlands, Norway, Sweden and the UK.
14. Sweden was also over 90 per cent.
15. The extent of the distortions and costs to the economy will be more than this simple description of moral hazard, as the cost advantage that TBTF conveys on large banks will have a number of consequences. It will make it more difficult for small banks to compete and for new innovative institutions to emerge. Secondly, it will encourage bank mergers and acquisition to increase the proportion of the banking system that is regarded as TBTF. Similarly, in

the case of TMTF, it will encourage banks to participate in the same risky activities and to be less concerned about their own risks if others are already under pressure, thus compounding difficulties.

16. Despite the enactment of FDICIA (Federal Deposit Insurance Corporation Improvement Act) in 1991, there has been long-standing pressure to resolve the problem of TBTF: 'Regulators would be well advised to look for ways to close a large failing bank without protecting uninsured creditors' (Wall, 1993).
17. In US terminology this would usually imply the establishment of a 'bridge bank', because a 'purchase and assumption' option would normally need some period to put in place and would probably have been under negotiation before the point of insolvency was reached.
18. Wall (1993, p. 11) suggests TBTF implies 'thought to be too large to close in a way that imposes losses on uninsured depositors and certain other creditors.' Our interpretation is that the extent of the losses imposed by the available means of closure on those directly and indirectly exposed are thought to be too large.
19. One point we return to later is that the US scheme has an important logic to it that is missing from many other deposit insurance schemes. Namely, in the USA the FDIC not only succeeds to the claims of the depositors under insolvency but it then has priority in the resolution of the problem and can direct the solution towards the interests of the fund. In other countries, including Finland, the deposit insurer becomes liable to pay out depositors to the full extent of their insurance but has to take its place with the other claimants in a court-directed insolvency process. In so far as such funds are inadequate or state provided there will be an extra exposure of the taxpayer to losses, at least temporarily, compared to the US system. Under MHL the loss to be minimized by the authorities in resolving the problem is the loss to society as a whole in so far as it has not taken on a specific risk through deliberate exposure to the bank in trouble, largely in the sense of the taxpayer.
20. The MHL scheme is complementary to the normal proposals for Prompt Corrective Action (Basel Committee on Banking Supervision (2002), for example) but it will normally shorten the process of seeking solutions to an undercapitalized bank's problems by commencing the 'exit' procedure earlier.
21. In a careful survey of experience since FDICIA, Eisenbeis and Wall (2002, p. 39) note that even in the USA there has been a drift away from trying to minimize the insurance losses: 'Recent supervisory efforts appear to be directed towards the long-standing goal of minimizing the probability of bank failure.' They see Basel2 in particular as a move away from trying to minimize the social costs of bank failure and eliminate moral hazard.
22. Basel Committee on Banking Supervision (2002) provides a comprehensive exposition of the recommended types of prompt corrective action.
23. Capital ratio is defined as tangible equity capital to total assets ratio.
24. Berger *et al.* (1991) provide an early exposition of the accounting valuation problems involved.
25. While meeting the Basel requirements probably involves simultaneous solvency in the MHL sense, the authorities would be well advised to switch to focusing on solvency if the minimum Basel conditions are breached, in deciding upon the appropriate course of action. As discussed in Section 1.3, market views of the riskiness of the bank, as expressed in the spreads on

subordinated debt, will also provide useful information to the supervisor on the need for action.

26. As Evanoff and Wall (2002) point out the Basel2 proposals are largely aimed at improving the measurement of the denominator of the capital adequacy ratio. Many problems remain with the measurement of 'capital' in the numerator. Since recognizing losses automatically reduces the ratio and encourages supervisory intervention there is bound to be a tendency for the acknowledged ratios to overstate the real position even if accounting is on an economic value rather than an historic cost basis.
27. It is important to call a halt as early as possible in the process of declining net worth, because otherwise a bank can continue to liquidate its unencumbered assets at a discount to pay out those depositors and creditors who request it at the expense of the uninsured depositors or creditors who are not aware of the problem. Non-financial companies cannot usually realize their assets in a similar way as they are normally collateral for loans although there have been some notorious examples of gaining access to the employee pension fund. If the problem can be caught early then the loss and its systemic implications will be smaller and the chances of arranging a solution without recourse to the taxpayer greater.
28. This is effectively the concept of 'liquidity-based insolvency' described by Ramsey and Head (2000).
29. An inherent part of any resolution process is that it should take due account of the 'franchise' value of the bank. This helps explain the keenness among regulators to keep the business of the bank going and the relative rarity of solutions that do not at least involve separating the failed institution into a 'good' and a 'bad' bank.
30. We use the generic term 'administrator' to embrace the possible regimes of receivers, conservators and so on and cases where the authority involved may be an organization or an individual.
31. This temporary organization is usually labelled a bridge bank in the USA.
32. MHL refer to the 'taxpayer' as the body with respect to whom the loss is minimized. This is a representation of some form of social loss minimization, i.e. that it is the cost to society as whole that should be minimized in dealing with actual and potential bank failure.
33. Many deposit insurance 'funds' are not really funded as such but as in the USA can draw on public funds. Premiums paid in advance are similar to hypothecated taxation. Similarly, increases in premiums after depletion of the 'fund' are levied on surviving banks to replenish the notional balance.
34. Other than the EU Winding-up directive for credit institutions (2001/24/EC) there are few rules governing international insolvency, other than the UNCITRAL Model Law on Cross-Border Insolvency of 1997 and the International Bar Association Concordat on Cross-Border Insolvency of 1995 (see Contact Group (2002) for a discussion).
35. When the EEA expands in 2004, with the addition of what is expected to be ten new members, the chance of a bank being viewed as systemic in a second country but not in the headquarter country will rise noticeably, given the degree of foreign ownership of banks in the accession countries.
36. Some are less sanguine about the likely impact of Basel2 on the social costs of banking regulation (Eisenbeis and Wall, 2002).

37. Liisa Halme argues in Halme *et al.* (2000, pp. 57–8) that the tax rules limiting tax-deductible provisions for loan losses to 0.6 per cent of lending in Finland were one of the main causes of the Finnish banking crisis at the beginning of the 1990s. It led the banks to mask their potential losses from the supervisors. Had the problems been clear then the authorities could have acted vigorously in the late 1980s perhaps heading the crisis off altogether, as was achieved in Denmark, where the disclosure rules were much stricter and on a mark-to-market basis, see Chapter 9.
38. Basel Committee on Banking Supervision (2002).
39. Supervisors need to have requirements to disclose promptly problems that will have a material impact on uninsured depositors and creditors just as companies have such an obligation to their shareholders.
40. When actions are not disclosed, not only can the cards appear to be stacked against the authorities because successes are not observed but there is no effective way in forming an external judgement to assess the authorities' assertions that such successes exist.
41. I am grateful to Larry Wall for this point.
42. In effect therefore there are three valuation bases none of which are totally transparent.

    - valuing the entire bank (or its parts) as a going concern
    - market valuation of the assets/liabilities of the bank – including off-balance sheet items
    - valuation of the bank under insolvency.

    Until a bid for part or whole of the bank is completed, the price can only be estimated not known. Marking some parts of the bank's balance sheet to market is very difficult, although the position has improved in recent years as markets have deepened and valuation techniques improved and been standardized, and many off-balance sheet items such as guarantees and contingent liabilities can be even harder. Similarly, valuation under insolvency is only something which can be known at the end of the process and can only be estimated along the way.
43. Halme cites similar problems in the savings and loans crisis in the USA where regulatory accounting rules (RAP) were less strict than US GAAP.
44. In the US case the roles of the FDIC in triggering and managing insolvency and of the Federal Reserve in exercising the Lender of Last Resort are clearly distinguished. Not only are there limitations to the length of Federal Reserve lending according to the CAMELS rating (five days for a critically undercapitalized bank) but the FDIC can claim restitution if the Federal Reserve's actions have materially increased the costs to the FDIC.
45. They argue that this discriminates against small banks as they will find it more difficult to raise capital on the market.
46. This means that the consideration of the costs of different options under insolvency on a case by case basis, as in the IMF approach of Asser (2001), for example, will always veer more towards the use of public money, as the implications for future behaviour by other banks in and avoiding other crises are not considered.
47. Strictly speaking both subsequent losses and prior gains should be estimated in present value terms.

48. As Boyd *et al.* (2002) show, the effects of a banking crisis can be quite persistent, lasting long after the banking system has recovered. Their estimate of the cost of the Finnish crisis has a present value of over 400 per cent of GDP as they assume that the previous growth path is never regained.
49. Soussa (2000) suggests that the difference is nearer to three rating categories.
50. As Nivorozhkin (2003) points out, there are steps in the loss functions of the parties. The signalling value of subordinated debt will change once insolvency costs are expected to wipe out junior debt entirely. This could occur above the point of economic insolvency if the uninsured credits were small and the costs of insolvency large.
51. Cordella and Yeyati (2002) show that if deposit insurance premia are related to the riskiness of the bank then there is an incentive for banks to reduce risk, thus offsetting much of the moral hazard and indeed reducing the cost of finance.
52. He also argues in the following sentence that constructive ambiguity is 'unnecessary' as large banks do not appear to be taking on excessive risk.
53. As Campbell and Cartwright (2002, pp. 209–11) remark, there is little pressure for change in bank insolvency legislation in the UK.
54. Many of these problems were clearly identified in Group of Thirty (1998) in response to issues posed by the Barings crisis.
55. His chapter also provides a survey of many of the issues involved.
56. In the UK it appears possible to get very rapid action through the courts, if they respond to the requests of the authorities – formerly the Bank of England, now the FSA – and give them the authority to act.
57. The Bank of England was criticized in its handling of Barings for not having adequate systems in place to forestall the crisis (Wilkinson and Turing, 1996).

2

The New Approach to Orderly Bank Exit: Questions and Answers

Aarno Liuksila

These 'Questions and Answers' pertain to a number of institutional issues concerning the 'new approach', in particular some formal and legal issues that arise in seeking an appropriate fit between the new scheme and national legal systems.

In the main this 'new approach' does not challenge the current theory or practice of banking regulation or supervision. Efforts to limit the residual liability of the public treasury to financial accidents are consistent with the concept of a regulated financially autonomous banking industry, with the banks being liable for each other's losses to the extent covered by the deposit guarantee or insurance system.

Ideally there is a level playing field occupied by a good number of more or less specialized private entities, authorized to take deposits (receive repayable funds from the public) and make loans and invest their reserves.

2.0.1 What is the fundamental 'why' to the new approach?

The focal point of the new approach is at the last stage before the default takes place. That is to say, on the question of what is the appropriate treatment of an apparently solvent, critically undercapitalized bank that has no positive net worth. Why exit it?

Assuming that the power to exit has been vested in the administrative authorities, as is almost invariably the case, there may be three and more valid reasons for the bank described above, forthwith, including the following:

- First, the designated authorities, who may, in their discretion, acting for a purpose that is in the public interest, exit the bank for one valid (good) reason, which is that the bank has now come to a point at which it is bound to expose not only the public treasury and the other banks under deposit guarantee arrangements, to a residual liability for a loss upon default on the part of the bank, but wipe out the pre-existing shareholders and impose losses on its unguaranteed or uninsured depositors and other creditors.

- Second the delegation of legislative authority for a programme of prompt corrective action may make the exit mandatory at the point at which the above described bank is bound to expose the public treasury to a residual liability for a loss upon default on the part of the bank, without a further review of the subject bank's position, policies and prospects, or any further deferral of the prescribed or required action, that is, the law may authorize and direct the designated authorities to exit the bank at that point without delay (as in the USA).
- Third, in a broader sense, a delegation of legislative authority for a comprehensive programme of bank regulation and supervision charges the authorities with the maintenance of a level playing field, which presupposes the adoption of a robust exit to remove the unevenness.

Once the questions of why and when to exit the subject bank have been resolved, there comes the critical question of how to do it in an efficient, economic and expeditious manner. Despite a universal consensus on the desirability of each country adopting an exit policy that spelled out 'why' and 'when', there is no consensus on 'how' and 'by whom'.

The EEA countries have set up banking commissions and the like as primary regulators or supervisors charged with the formulation, announcement and implementation of exit policy, but have not consolidated the resolution of banks into an administrative agency, a move that would require, in all cases, an exemption of the banks, for the purpose of their reorganization and liquidation, from the supervision of general courts of first instance (but not any derogation from their jurisdiction to settle disputes).

The problem in the EEA countries from the institutional vantage point is the division of delegated legislative authority for bank reorganization and liquidation between the government (central bank, banking commission and the deposit guarantee agency) on the one hand and the general bankruptcy courts (the courts of first instance) on the other. Exit is necessarily a two-ended thing that requires extensive coordination as long as those countries do not consolidate all functions into one, say, the national deposit guarantee back-up fund or agency which operates to minimize the residual liability of the public treasury and other banks.

In the EEA countries, the national bank regulatory systems have become needlessly disjointed and convoluted as the functions of the resolution of insolvent banks have been divided up between the administrative and judicial authorities. The side-by-side existence of central banks, banking commissions and deposit guarantee agencies presupposes either:

(i) a system of coordination between the administrative authorities charged with the decision-making by which the process functions and the judicial authorities charged with the actual work, which is the takeover, reorganization or liquidation of the subject bank (as in the EEA countries), or
(ii) the consolidation of both the decision-making and the actual work into one administrative agency that carried it through the respective departments of the agency (as in the USA).

2.0.2 The case

Under the current state of law in the EEA countries, the above-mentioned bank would move on along the supervisory track under the national bank regulatory scheme until the eventual intervention by the competent court upon a 'default' on the part of the failed bank. The opening by the court of reorganization or liquidation proceedings depends, however, on supervisors filing an involuntary petition with the competent court or other showing by the supervisors of a green light to such a petition by a third party.

Awaiting a bailout by the public treasury, the above bank may continue to move on along the supervisory track until the event of a 'default'. No administrative finding of negative net worth (the event of 'failure') would derail it in the meantime. In comparison, under the prompt corrective action programme under the US banking and bankruptcy laws, the takeover of a critically undercapitalized bank that does not have positive net worth cannot be deferred by the supervisors.

The task in *Improving Banking Supervision* (Mayes, Halme and Liuksila, 2001; henceforth MHL) was to analyse the problem of improving it 'upwards' from the stylized concrete case which was, indeed, what to do with a critically undercapitalized bank that has no positive net worth. This is the critical dimension of any robust exit policy which is to separate the wheat from the chaff. In economic terms, such a bank has failed and should be divested of any charter, licence or authorization of the kind that permitted it to move along on the supervisory track for ever. By that point, its shareholders will have little or no incentive to observe the conduct-related injunctions laid down in general banking laws and the exhortations of supervisors thereunder. Their incentives to make any (further) concessions to restore the bank to a solvent condition evaporate, as there would be nothing in it for them. Shareholders of such banks may become 'free-riders' and 'holdouts', as they are called in economics and the bank faces 'moral hazard', yet another relevant term of art in economics.

Alert depositors and other creditors vote with their feet. A bank is not in 'default' as long as it makes payments and transfers funds in settlement of its commitments, on a first-come-first-served basis, that is, in law, the state of not being in default means being legally solvent or being at least 'not insolvent'. Hence, until declared legally insolvent by the competent court in the event of default, the bank may keep reducing its reserves in a manner that increases the losses of any remaining depositors and other creditors. For example, it might make distributions to shareholders to fend off unfriendly market forces.

In the meantime, however, it might also enjoy continuing access to the central bank, at least in the sense that the central bank does not call for a liquidation of its debtor position under the payments system (for example, by calling its loans made to the bank). To stabilize its liquidity position, as an alternative to its increasingly uncertain access to lender of last resort facilities, the bank may do other things that are harmful to its residual depositors and other creditors: it may keep calling its loans to customers (by liquidating collateral) and keep liquidating its other assets through the market, both at an accelerating pace. The process may go on until the bank has exhausted its unencumbered assets, giving rise to the event of default.

There is no final answer to the question of 'who will pay for bank insolvency'. Any political answer such as 'the government', 'shareholders' or 'depositors and other creditors', is subject to the 'constructive ambiguity' that is inherent in resolving the type of political tension that will flare up again the inevitable next time around. While it is, therefore, true that no national bank insolvency legislation can supply the final answer, it is equally clear that the legislature can settle the issues in a persuasive manner as a matter of firm policy, until a further review. Provided that it resolves the issues in a principled manner, the legislature may not have to resolve the burden-sharing issue, including the definition of the burden to be shared, on a case-by-case basis in an atmosphere of national default. By laying down the rules of burden-sharing beforehand, the legislature is likely to exercise legally significant control over the present expectations that the public may entertain about bank bailouts. Any lowering of such expectations will reduce political justification for access to the public treasury upon the next 'unforeseeable' event.

What has been done so far to reduce the incidence, costs and risks of bank insolvency? Here we have (1) the North Americans with the US banking system that is a national banking system and the Canadian banking system; (2) the EU banking system that comprises *inter alia* the French, German, Italian and the UK banking systems, an approximately equal number of banks as under (1) above (counting the EU as a banking system but not as a 'country' which it is not);[1] (3) the Japanese banking system, which is a national system with its own special features in respect of burden-sharing, and (4) a diverse residual group of 'other' banking systems, including the hybrids. The statistics are quite alarming, many of these countries having had banking crises over the past decade or so, and a total of some trillion US$ in terms of quantifiable fiscal and quasi-fiscal outlays was reportedly spent on bailouts, excluding the non-quantifiable and contingent liabilities.

Would the specific form, scope and content of the applicable bank insolvency law matter? More specifically, in the field of bank insolvency law, there are only two main systems of burden-sharing, one of which has abandoned the traditional bankruptcy rule, and the rest that have more or less modified it regarding its applicability to banks. Hence, from the vantage point of choice or law and jurisdiction, there are not four, or any higher number of, mutually exclusive choices, but only two basic choices among the G-7 which are (1), or (2–4). For historical reasons, the residual category of banking systems (under (4) above), follows the characteristic features of the European model (general bankruptcy laws apply *mutatis mutandis*), with a number of outliers, however.

Namely, the *lex generalis* approach of the kind that prevails, as a permanent regime, outside the US, and Canada, and (arguably) in New Zealand (that has the specific problem of dealing with branches and subsidiaries of foreign banks only), is based on a *mutatis mutandis* application by general courts of general insolvency laws in the event of bank insolvency. Indeed, this grouping includes the rest of the world which, in the main, shares the core feature of the *lex generalis* approach. The universal theory underlying the *lex generalis* approach is the withdrawal of the licence of an insolvent subject bank, and its treatment as a non-bank firm thereafter, like any other firm, upon the opening of bankruptcy proceedings.

However, the modern (modified) *lex generalis* approach, admits a range of legally significant permanent modifications and temporary exceptions, including the following:

- The very requirement of licence withdrawal as a prerequisite for the lodging of voluntary or involuntary petitions, does not apply as a prerequisite for the opening of judicial reorganization proceedings, now a tempting option under the 'collective action clauses' contained in modern, general corporation and insolvency laws in Europe (they masquerade as 'Chapter 11' clones but are not). Namely, the reorganization feature of general insolvency laws applies to banks in Finland, France, Germany, Switzerland, the UK and many other European countries, where it was initially thought to be inappropriate for banks. It stands to reason that banks in reorganization normally maintain their licences as they continue in legal entity and personality (and, indeed, even banks in liquidation might well retain a licence for the winding-up of their operations if not placed under 'public administration'); and
- Diverse forms of *ad hoc* emergency (*lex specialis*) legislation which set aside of the legal effects and consequences of the *lex generalis*, by way of exemptions or derogations of the kind that respectively may (a) preclude the opening of judicial insolvency proceedings (for example, by interrupting or staying them for the time being); and (b) substitute governmental measures for judicial actions (for example, through a governmental vesting order); or
- The universal (emergency) deposit guarantee that restores an insolvent bank to a solvent condition keeps it in play (mere 'assurances' regarding a future bailout may put sand in the wheels of courts);
- The modifications themselves that subordinate private rights and interests to public interests, with the 'public law of banking' overriding the traditional institution of bankruptcy, or deforming it.

The key distinction is that the *lex specialis* approach is predicated on delegated legislative authority, of the kind that may be conferred on a government, or even on an independent administrative agency, to lawfully affect, modify or annul private rights and obligations, as opposed to the *lex generalis* approach which is predicated on the vindication of private (vested) rights, and the enforcement of private obligations, by the judicial authorities. Both approaches are predicated on the exact performance of private financial obligations, and not on measures that are confiscatory, discriminatory or otherwise odious. The interests being served in the court are solely the realization of private property rights and interests, and do not include *in casu* the realization of any public interest.

Although both approaches address the central issue, which is the insufficiency of assets, no legal scheme can mix the advantages, and eliminate the disadvantages, of both. Ultimately, the legislature must decide upon the questions of 'succession' in respect of an insolvent bank, its assets and liabilities, including the question how this works in the liquidation as opposed to the reorganization of banks. A logical arrangement of these simple building blocks (who gets the bank, assets, liabilities, and the equity, how, where, and when) into some kind of reasonable order, is what the legislators have to do in crisis, if they have not done it before.

It should be added that all banking systems have developed in the same direction in the field of banking supervision (by way of voluntary compliance with the Basel standards, which aim at uniform supervisory practice), but this system of a uniform treatment for undercapitalized banks, implies no uniformity regarding the treatment of insolvent banks, including exit policies. It would appear that the underlying deposit insurance, bailout, and bank reorganization and liquidation regimes, exhibit extreme variation and diversity. In form, all these regimes may be combined into one run by an administrative agency (the USA), or they may exist as separate and distinct administrative and judicial regimes. It also follows from this diversity that bailout and exit policies vary from country to country, along with the legal rules and standards that govern the eventual resolution of insolvent banks.

Finally, *in ultima analisi*, legal safeguards for private parties do not necessarily vary depending on the question whether the resolution of an insolvent bank is carried out in a court or an administrative tribunal. True, the *lex generalis* approach is based on the application by general courts of general corporation and insolvency law to banks (*lex generalis*), in analogy to what applies to other firms, and the *lex specialis* approach is predicated on an exemption of banks from general corporation and insolvency laws, and on a corresponding derogation from the jurisdiction of general courts. However, the latter administrative proceedings may, and typically do, involve a review by a court, or other an independent and impartial body. However, if we look at all of the relevant characteristics from the vantage point of authority and resources for handling bank insolvencies, it is the US banking system that forms a great exception from all others, or the other way around (if you wish). This creates two mutually exclusive categories of bank insolvency law.

2.1 How does the new approach compare with the *lex generalis* approach?

2.1.1 Who will pay for bank insolvency under the new approach?

As for the background for this discussion, Chapters 8–10 of MHL provide a new scheme for national bank insolvency legislation. (Chapters 8 and 9 are reproduced in this book as Appendix 1.) It is submitted that Chapter 9 supplies one unambiguous answer to the topical question addressed to the other participants in this book which is 'who pays for bank insolvency'.[2]

2.1.2 General scheme

How did we arrive at a new general scheme for bank insolvency law? By way of collective intuition, of course. No need to apply the 'contingency theory' of legislation because the purpose of the scheme is not to address knowable, re-defined contingencies only. Typically amendments to bank insolvency laws outlaw the making of knowable mistakes, or the making of the same mistake twice. Instead, the scheme modifies the pre-existing capital structure of a subject bank. In that sense it is an open scheme like the classic bankruptcy scheme that is reflected in the current capital structure although it seldom, if ever, applies.

The new scheme would create a level playing field by applying, without any case-by-case modifications, to all banks coming under the scheme. Under the prescribed sequence of steps, the scheme authorizes the exclusion of any insolvent subject bank. Concurrently with the takeover, it will be automatically restructured, and placed under a regime of temporary public administration and ownership. The restructured bank would be a marginally solvent bank, and would be kept open and operating for the time being. This obviates any need to liquidate its assets and liabilities through sales of assets and liabilities to other institutions, subject to its sale or voluntary liquidation at a later date.

One objective of the scheme is the avoidance of bank bailouts, without excluding them for the purpose of meeting legal or regulatory capital requirements. Here, the point is the prescribed sequencing of steps, which is to schedule the receipt of proceeds of bailouts to take place after the comprehensive restructuring, or 'deeming provision' that automatically post-dates such receipts. This precludes any incidental benefits from accruing to the benefit of the pre-existing creditors and shareholders. A closer look at the modalities of the scheme in Section 2.2, will reveal that the scheme must be the least costly and risky option, if compared with (i) outright bank liquidations; (ii) judicial reorganizations; and (ii) bailouts of any sort or size.

Why did we not, instead, improve upon the traditional bankruptcy rules that, according to standard text books, had their first round of application in respect of bankers in Italy as early as the 1500s? At about that time, it would appear, bankruptcy rules were substituted for the previous law of nature that favoured the fastest of competing creditors in an involuntary case. The winner took all that remained of a banker; that is to say, without liquidation of the property, and without any sharing of proceeds with other creditors. For banks that had multiple creditors (and debtors), the previous scheme did not work.

The described new rule addressed the issue of competing claims, by providing for a collective proceeding, with a *pari passu* distribution of payments from the 'insufficient' fund that there was to satisfy creditors (the fund was likely to consist of gold and other cash, whether transferred from the banker's reserves, or derived from the auction sales of land and possessions). Presumably, from then on, the bankruptcy scheme generalized with the result that (i) a debtor's property would not pass on to creditors without a liquidation and the sharing of the proceeds; and (ii) that collateral could be realised only through a public sale of collateral (*lex comissoria*) unless otherwise agreed after the event of default or failure.

Why is the bankruptcy rule the superior rule, despite its many perceived and revealed shortcomings, which make it, on balance, the inferior rule in the field of banking? As a general rule, of course, bankruptcy works perfectly in comparison with other rules:

- In its corporate form, bankruptcy is a pure debt-collection device, and has no other functions that would impede the reaching of a result where there are no bad debts left (upon the eventual dissolution of the corporate debtor, an empty legal shell);
- It is highly efficient because it only applies to situations involving competing multiple creditors, and, conversely, does not deal with single defaults or failures *vis-à-vis* non-competing creditors which can be worked out, or settled in court in a cheaper manner; it also separates the wheat from the chaff under the rules governing case administration (for example, it separates disputed claims, and eliminates contingent claims, cancels burdensome contracts, and so forth);
- In effect, there are two insolvency tests; (i) one for involuntary petitions which does not involve any valuation by the individual

petitioner of the assets and liabilities, which applies to involuntary petitions, which test typically with reference to a debtor; 'insolvency' means a state in which the debtor for want of liquid assets, not merely temporarily, is unable to discharge all his debts (in plural!) as they mature; and (ii) another test for voluntary petitions which involves a valuation by the debtor of the assets and liabilities, and the showing of 'negative net worth'. For the former test that operates in the 'realm of freedom of commercial speech', a lawyer will suffice to explain the finding of non-payment; only for the latter test do you need an expensive accountant.

- There is a public auction for the liquidation of bank assets, no maintenance of value provisions for creditors' claims (there is a burden to be shared, which is the negative net worth, but no legal definition, or any up-front determination of that burden, which is revealed only years later through claims administration (and the actual liquidation of assets)), and any remaining creditors and shareholders are wiped out upon the corporate dissolution of the bank (no bad debts); and
- The non-judicial expenses of reorganization or liquidation are deducted first from the gross assets of the receivership, and then the indebtedness incurred for any winding-up or reorganization of the bank in liquidation. Judicial immunity serves as a limitation of liability of the court supervising the receivership. There is no intervention by the state, which makes it a superior debt-collection device from the vantage point of the public treasury.

In the field of banking, it is debatable what has, indeed, tilted the balance of arguments against the outright application of the bankruptcy rule in the USA since the early 1800s, and in Europe since the 1920s. However, on a closer inspection, the disadvantages of using the traditional bankruptcy regime in respect of banks are overwhelming from two viewpoints.

Regarding purchasers and sales of assets and liabilities, one technical reason must have been that debts owed to banks have never become freely tradable claims of the kind that could be auctioned off in the same way as any other assets in the event of bank insolvency, and the other reason certainly has had to do with the ease of the transfers of deposit and other liabilities.

- There are legal restrictions on the purchase of assets, and the assumption of liabilities by third parties, where, say, such sales of assets and liabilities would violate the rule of equal treatment of creditors. Legal restrictions typically apply to the making of transfers of debts owed to

the insolvent bank (valued at par, they are but overvalued assets) between the original creditor and the purchaser, and, therefore, on the assumption by third of parties of the liabilities of a subject bank; and,
- There no is other market than an official market such as an 'investor of last resort' (if any, the FDIC is one) for overdue debt (overvalued bank assets and liabilities). On the bank assets side, that market is limited, ultimately, to the respective private borrowers, unless there is such an artificial market (for example, for hive-offs) for the reason that the official seller ('administrative receivership') undertakes to cover costs and risks as a non-quantifiable fiscal or quasi-fiscal liability (contingent liability). [A borrower, including the original customer, may be able to buy back collateral at a discount (by simultaneously borrowing against it), but hardly any of his overdue debts at a discount reflecting his own inability or unwillingness to pay. Had the borrower any additional cash on hand, the bank would attach the cash in partial payment of the overdue debt.]

Regarding the legal insolvency test, which is applicable in cases in which the administrative authorities, or an individual depositor or other creditor, lodges an involuntary petition with the court, the traditional bankruptcy regime reveals a fundamental flaw. Namely, the applicable test is one that addresses the problem of non-payment (illiquidity) whereas the real problem of an insolvent bank is the opposite one: that is to say, the availability of liquidity, up to the point at which a bulk of its assets have been converted into cash to discharge or meet its obligations and liabilities on a first-come-first-served basis.

In the light of the *pari passu* principle, the administrative and judicial authorities' failure to test insolvency on the basis of a valuation of the assets and liabilities of the subject bank in the first place, and, their failure to restrict the making of payments and transfers by the insolvent bank, results in a highly unequal, and grossly unfair, treatment of the residual uninsured depositors and other creditors to the extent they will be subject to a haircut (loss of their own net worth), relative to those that got all of their money out after the bank became insolvent. Bankruptcy regimes typically omit the rule that would require the reversal of any payments and transfers made during the suspect period (normally some six months before the date of the finding of insolvency by the court).

In any event, where an insolvent bank is subject to general insolvency laws, and, correspondingly, to the general jurisdiction courts, the 'fine print' of the law is likely to reveal that an administrative finding of insolvency does not by any means 'automatically' subject it to involuntary petitions. The opening of bankruptcy proceedings by the court may be delayed for reasons that are beyond the control of the court. Indeed, any access to the court typically depends on the judgement of the competent administrative authorities. They are unlikely to pull the licence of their captive, and will relinquish their control over it to the court, 'as soon as possible'.

In the meantime, however, the insolvent bank may, as long as it satisfies the legal insolvency test, keep liquidating its assets at an accelerating pace, until it has exhausted the available resources. At that point, the legal test would apply and require action by the administrative authorities. The opening of bankruptcy proceedings would axiomatically inflict a loss upon the residual uninsured, unsecured, depositors and other creditors. In the absence of a depositor preference, the deposit insurer which has a right to subrogate to the rights of insured depositors, would also incur losses.

The dynamic is this: unlike other insolvent firms that cannot keep liquidating their liabilities on a first-come-first-served basis and keep trading, an insolvent bank can do so as long as it has freely tradable assets, or any assets that are acceptable to the central bank or lender of last resort as collateral for liquidity support. This process of an insolvent bank making payments and transfers can go on until the administrative authorities eventually stop it, or there are no more assets. The concern of the traditional bankruptcy regime is the opposite of this phenomenon, which is non-payment.

Whatever the problem, the supervisors are not called upon to act in the best interest of any creditors, including the remaining creditors who will get short-changed in the process. Had they made an effort to stop the subject bank making payments and transfers, the bank (like any other debtor) could have challenged the applicability of a negative net worth test. In effect, the bank is immune from involuntary bankruptcy petitions lodged by the authorities or individual creditors, notwithstanding the fact that its ratio of assets to liabilities is less than or equal to one.

Generally speaking, as long as a subject bank in fact makes payments and transfers, the typical judicial 'insolvency' test does not, cannot or even should not, apply. The way the court sees it, any legal 'insolvency' means a non-payment; that is, a state of illiquidity in which the debtor for want of liquid assets, not merely temporary, is unable to discharge all its debts as they mature. General insolvency laws do not authorize the court to restrict the making of payments and transfers, or interrupt any transfers of funds that it may undertake in settlement of commitments. Indeed, bankruptcy laws only work in the opposite case of nonpayment, default or other failure.

In credit economies, the supply of credit, and the orderly operation of a payments system, is a matter of national concern. In Europe, Italy was among the first to depart from the bankruptcy rule in respect of bank liquidation, although it continued to apply the rules *mutatis mutandis* subject to an overriding modern public law of banking. In Europe all countries have modified bankruptcy law to fit bank insolvencies, so the ideal does not apply. Outside the USA, Canada and New Zealand, which have a *lex specialis* public law regime for bank insolvencies (following the exclusive *lex specialis* approach), virtually all countries have a more or less modified original bankruptcy law regime for handling bank insolvency. There remains a critical difference, however, between the two systems that is not a mere quibble, a distinction without difference.

In reality, under the *lex generalis* approach, the actions by the competent courts are likely to get pre-empted, or unduly delayed by temporary measures such as moratoria, or by way of bailouts (for example, bringing into effect a universal (emergency) deposit guarantee), which come into play under the public law of banking. More specifically:

- There is a new trend to enact *ad hoc* legislation on bank restructuring, something that has occurred in many countries in recent banking crises. In Sweden in the early 1990s, banks that did not comply with the government rehabilitation programme were made subject to compulsory redemption by the government of their outstanding shares, and to compulsory (public) administration in the case of noncorporate banks. This was only natural because the universal (emergency) deposit guarantee allowed the beneficiaries to operate and transact at the expense of the taxpayer. This compulsory approach was needed because the permanent regime precluded, however, intervention by the state in the affairs of banks, relying solely on private initiative. Norway is yet another example, but a more interesting one as adopted the interim bank insolvency regime as a permanent one, with some modifications.
- There is also a new trend to extend the application of the reorganization provisions (collective action clauses) of modern general insolvency laws to banks, too. On paper the activation of those collective action clauses surely addresses the problem of obtaining debt and

debt service relief for banks, which is due to the lack of cohesion in depositor and other creditor groupings (classes). True, the dual-technique of (i) the imposition by the administrative or judicial authorities of an 'automatic stay' on the enforcement of claims, and (ii) the imposition of majority debt restructuring provisions, resolves the problem by deferring any asset liquidations for the time being. However, it does not make sense to have such multi-year debt restructuring procedures in place. The process will be prolonged due to the lack of any up-front official valuation of the assets and liabilities, and of any asset and equity restructuring for the bank. A modified judicial reorganization scheme of the kind that may successfully address these problem is before the parliament in Switzerland where the proposal is that the administrative authorities may impose the deal, subject to majority creditor veto only (see Chapter 10). The UK administration regime is described in Chapter 11.

Who is accountable where the regulators or supervisors defer the opening of insolvency proceedings in respect of insolvent banks for reasons connected with the public interest, and not in the best interest of depositors and other creditors? Nobody is, although the administrative authorities may not unlock access to the court. Here, they surely may restrict the ability of private parties to vindicate their rights in the court, a denial of justice that is a 'rule of law' issue which has been settled by giving the final say to courts (a review function) on the public law legality of the delay: a lawful failure to perform public duties does not give rise to damage actions by third parties.

While the corollary of any lawful conduct of their business by the authorities is not the imposition of any financial liability for the benefit of banks, their depositors and other creditors (or other liability); that of any unlawful conduct is a legal and financial sanction (for example, the annulment of decisions, and the payment of compensation for damage inflicted on banks, or on their owners or creditors). However, the latter liability does not cover legislative, regulatory or supervisory failures, as the regulation and supervision of banks takes place only in the public interest, not in any private interest. It is for each bank alone to discharge or meet its own obligations, liabilities and losses (except in certain cases of 'centralized management').

It surely follows that bailouts are in their legal nature but voluntary contributions by the required taxpayer majority that may have been indifferent to the state incurring fiscal, and quasi-fiscal deficits (for example, the central banks mortgaging their income for years to come), as a result of public generosity. Bailouts, especially the bailouts of those that are too large to fail, are motivated in a 'perceived' public interest for the maintenance or promotion of 'financial stability' of which a necessary (but not sufficient) condition is the safety and soundness of banking systems, and, that of each individual bank as a part of it.

The above theory has a flaw in it, however. Although bailouts are legal provided that they are carried out solely for purposes that are within the public interest, or meet the 'private investor principle', bailouts distort incentives, and especially do so as they deny a level playing field for banks themselves and their customers, a prerequisite for monetary stability. 'Specifically, a level playing field necessitates the exclusion of uneven, that is, insolvent, players'.[3] Bailouts are not the only way to skin the cat. The authors submit that a robust exit policy should do, instead.

There is a distinction between supervision and bank insolvency law. Regulation and supervision are 'soft' administrative law functions pertaining to the 'conduct' of those who are regulated or supervised, unless the regulatory or supervisory authority can do more through an appropriate delegation of legislative authority for taking more drastic measures, as opposed to the implementation of bank insolvency law which is, by definition, 'hard' law in that such law may affect, modify or annul private rights and obligations. There is a difference there, for the reason that latter functions are not invested in the supervisors, but either:

- in the courts acting in the best interest of private creditors and other stakeholders (not involving political accountability, or any delegated legislative authority for the use of public resources), or
- in the government acting for purposes that are within the public interest, or based on re-delegation of legislative authority in a 'crisis management agency' as has been proposed in Sweden. (SOU, 2000, p. 66)

Typically, as opposed to judicial measures, the undertaking by the state of governmental or administrative measures involves a degree of political accountability, on the one hand, and a potential for budgetary liability for statutory compensation (i) if things go badly wrong; for example, regarding both unlawful actions, errors and omissions of the kind that affect, modify or annul private rights and obligations; and (ii) in the case of lawful expropriations. Administrative or governmental actions, errors and omissions, are subject to a review, however, by the designated court or tribunal (if any).

2.2 Description of the new approach

2.2.1 How does it work?

MHL argue that closing and liquidating an insolvent bank through judicial insolvency proceedings is generally unrealistic, either in the financial sense because such a procedure fails to maximize the net present value of the bank's assets, or with regard to maintaining public confidence in the banking system as a whole. The almost universal practice of guaranteeing all creditors of an insolvent bank in order for it to continue in operation, hopefully with new owners, is clearly not the least costly to the public treasury of all possible forms of intervention, and suffers from well known moral hazard.

The authors propose, as the general approach to insolvent bank resolution, that the government succeed to the outstanding shares of an insolvent bank, subject to an up-front restructuring of its assets, liabilities and equity. With the reorganization 'haircut' being sufficient to raise its net worth to zero, the bank would continue in operation under temporary public ownership (if new owners cannot be found immediately, which is generally unlikely), and then sold to private investors who would meet the applicable regulatory capital standards. A government agency with financial powers would be designated to implement the scheme, probably the deposit insurance fund (DIF).

The subject bank's operations would not be interrupted by the intervention. Under a full guarantee of their remaining claims, the depositors and other creditors would have continuous access to the balance of their claims remaining after the reorganization haircut as those amounts become due and payable (according to original or modified terms). While the bank remains in operation, the agency would evaluate the long-term viability of the bank, resulting either in a decision to sell the bank to new private owners, or in a decision to liquidate its assets and liabilities in voluntary proceedings. (Because its remaining liabilities are fully guaranteed, the bank no longer comes under bank insolvency law.)

The reorganization haircut, even if it proves too small after the fact, reduces the cost and risks of insolvency to the public treasury (as guarantor), and underpins market discipline by distributing most of the loss to pre-existing shareholders and uninsured creditors. The public treasury's exposure is greatly limited because no creditor of an insolvent bank – except insured depositors – is entitled to receive more under the scheme than it would have received if the institution had been liquidated up-front (unless the bank incurs further losses under the full guarantee of remaining claims). Compare this outcome with the costs and risks that the public treasury incurs by extending an emergency universal deposit guarantee that covers the beneficiary bank's over-indebtedness.

The required legal provisions for the introduction of the above scheme are unfamiliar in many civil law countries which typically rely on administrative procedures for the withdrawal of bank authorizations (exit policy), and on judicial bank receiverships as vehicles for insolvent bank resolution. In many common law countries, the key to overcoming the legal hurdles that stood in the way of more efficient procedures were the judicial and statutory initiatives that led to the adoption of administrative (bank) receiverships. This had already occured in the USA in the nineteenth century.

Generally, judicial bank receivership is predicated on the appointment by the court of a private party as receiver upon the succession of creditors to the proceeds of liquidation of the assets of a subject bank, as opposed to administrative receivership which is predicated on the succession of government (or a resolution agency) to the shareholders' interests, or to assets, and, with limitations, to the liabilities of the subject bank. As government steps into the shoes of an insolvent bank, it acquires plenary legal powers to dispose of it (for example, to own and operate the bank (subject to solvency guarantee in some countries); to sell its shares through a bidding process; to dispose of its assets and liabilities through purchase and assumption transactions; and so forth).

A forthcoming legal treatise on comparative bank reorganization law will discuss the apparent legal constraints on the setting up of the contemplated new scheme for the seizure and restructuring of insolvent banks in different legal environments, and how to successfully design, formulate and draft requisite legislation in those countries that have not accepted the legal concept of administrative (bank) receivership. The treatise will focus on the three key modalities of the scheme which are (1) the legal techniques of debt restructuring that are necessary to eliminate negative net worth; (2) the legal principles of equity restructuring such as the succession of the government to the interests of pre-existing shareholders; and (3) the applicable principles and methods of valuation.

2.2.2 Underlying assumptions

The assumptions underlying the scheme, relate to the following:

- In keeping with the definition of a bank, which means an institution that takes deposits from the public and makes loans to customers, the assumption is that subject banks, indeed, make loans, and, therefore, do not invest all their assets (other than reserves), say, in freely tradable bonds, but in collateralized promissory notes and other debt instruments. An actual fire-sale of non-freely tradable debts and debt instruments would inflict undue losses on the insolvent subject bank, deepening its insolvency. Only now, and with considerable difficulty, are attempts made to create a secondary market for such debts and debt instruments. In that secondary market (if any), the discounts are reportedly remarkably large (a factor which original creditors *should* take into account in setting the original interest rates on such loans);

- In keeping with the prescribed purposes of banks (located, after all, at the core of the monetary system), which include the making of payments and transfers in currency, at par, and on demand, any uninsured depositor 'haircuts' should not benefit the pre-existing shareholders and non-depositor trade creditors of the bank. Accordingly, the case administration is predicated on an up-front equity restructuring and the imposition of a depositor preference. The scheme seeks to eliminate all incentives for participants in bank insolvency, as opposed to the European-style reorganization option which is to continue the bank in legal entity and personality subject to equal depositor and trade creditor haircuts (debt restructuring), without wiping out the holders of worthless shares (except by their own agreement), or any provision for the ranking of trade creditors as junior to depositors; and
- Similarly, any voluntary contributions (bailouts) by the government should not benefit the pre-existing creditors and shareholders of the bank. The scheme would eliminate, through the automatic debt and equity restructuring, any incidental benefits of bailouts for pre-existing creditors and shareholders (who, indeed, were 'under water' on the date of intervention, and should not complain). As a technical matter, the bank (as the intended beneficiary) would book any receipts only as of a date after the date of intervention, from voluntary contributions (if any) from the government.

2.2.3 Sharing of the burden and payments, and allocation of any other entitlements

The guiding principle in the design of the new scheme is to achieve the same result as would have obtained had the subject bank been liquidated up-front on the day of intervention. On the basis, which is upon the concurrent placement of the bank in public administration, and the transfer of its ownership to government, the scheme engages the rules of bankruptcy. The net benefit of the scheme is that the respective banking and credit facilities remain open and operating, which removes the incentive for bailouts to avoid a bank closure, with its spillover effects on other banks and the economy as a whole.

The applicable principles of burden-sharing, including the controlling definition of the burden which is the negative net worth as determined up-front upon the opening of the proceedings, are the following:

1. Omission in the scheme of any automatic stay, and of any liquidation preferences for post-intervention obligations, liabilities and losses (that is, the omission secures the equal treatment of pre-existing and new, depositors and other creditors, which is a *sine qua non* for re-opening the subject bank for business after restructuring);
2. Elimination under the scheme of all contingent claims as of the date of intervention (mimicking the operation of bankruptcy rules that eliminate claims based on contingent liabilities), and the repudiation of certain burdensome contracts;
3. Application of a modified absolute priority principle that wipes out the holders of worthless equity, as a condition of debt restructuring, and vests the temporary ownership in the government but would not re-vest the new shares in the hands of unpaid creditors (as happens under the famous Chapter 11 of the US Bankruptcy Code in those limited cases where it still applies the above referred to principle without modification);
4. Incorporation of the *pari passu* principle that determines the ranking of creditors in debt restructuring (the rule of rateable treatment);
5. Full recognition and legal effect for the special liquidation preferences that the scheme confers on the depositors (the depositor preference that *inter alia* reduces the burden on deposit insurer), on its net creditors under netting arrangements (unless events of default can be cured), on the deposit insurer (upon subrogation to the rights of insured depositors), and on the central bank (for unsecured liquidity assistance (if any);
6. The observance of subordination agreements (subordinated loans); and
7. Assumption of the extension by government of a guarantee of reserves to the (reorganized) bank while it remains in public ownership and administration, or, alternatively, a capital infusion of equity for the bank to observe legal and regulatory capital requirements.

The interim public administration and government ownership – a critical component of the robust exit policy – which the scheme authorizes (and which is analogous to the US rules), necessarily implies that the government may make a profit or loss on its own account either (1) upon a resale of the marginally solvent bank to the public, or (2) upon a voluntary liquidation of its assets and liabilities in case of a bank that proves non-viable after restructuring. True, there is nothing to prevent the government from incurring a loss due to its extension of a guarantee of reserves for the interim period while the bank remains in public ownership and administration (the public administration may fail). On the other hand, there is nothing to prevent the government from making a profit either, unless the scheme imposed a specific constraint on its ability to do so (for example, for policy reasons).

The above-mentioned guarantee of reserves (under point (7)) which will be extended by the government to the now marginally solvent 'restructured' bank, refers only to the last step in the process of 'claims administration'. In the investigation and determination of each individual claim, the public administrator would dispute doubtful claims, and disregard all contingent claims only (as would happen in liquidation), and, conversely, allow other kinds of claims following their verification. The pre-prescribed documentation requirements need to be detailed to facilitate a quick settlement. In terms of amount, each claim would be subject to the total of allowed claims which is based on a hypothetical liquidation valuation of assets, and the prescribed liquidation preferences.

The bottom line is that bank creditors and shareholders would be guaranteed to receive what they would have received had the insolvent bank' assets been liquidated as of the date of intervention. Hence, as opposed to the claims that would be allowed, confirmed, and guaranteed for the time being, the residual claims 'under water' on the day of intervention, would be redeemed or cancelled but for zero compensation only. No further contributions would be required of those who ended up with the worthless shares and valueless claims in their hands. Technically, the time required for the valuation of the assets and liabilities presupposes that unless the valuation has already been carried out before the takeover, the clock is stopped upon the date of intervention, for the valuation to be carried out as of that date. However, the clock would not stop for years (as it does in the courts) but for days only, pending the reopening of the bank.

The scheme lays down a level playing field. The requisite principle and method of valuation is of a uniform application, including the thresholds that trigger the operation of the robust exit policy, based on a takeover by the government of a subject bank at the point at which the liabilities of a bank exceed its assets on a hypothetical liquidation valuation. The scheme does not exclude voluntary contributions by taxpayers or other third parties, subject to the sequencing of bailouts to take place after restructuring. The subject bank then continues under new directors, a new management, and new shareholders.

2.2.4 Summary of key concepts

The keys to understanding the scheme are the underlying definitions that attach to, and specify, the seemingly universal 'off-the-shelf' banking law concepts which are ambiguous in themselves. Under the scheme:

- the term 'bank' means an institution that issues absolute and unconditional demand liabilities which are payable in currency, on demand, and at par;
- 'bank insolvency', of which the determination is generally subject to diverse ambiguous tests, means 'negative net worth', as determined by the administrative authorities;
- 'asset restructuring' means the repossession of net assets on diverse legal theories through administrative or judicial actions;
- 'debt restructuring' means debt or debt service reduction to the point at which the assets equal liabilities (as opposed to expropriation or confiscation of the private property in bank debt);
- 'equity restructuring' means the wiping out of worthless shares as government steps into the shoes of pre-existing shareholders (succession); or the reduction of bank (legal) capital to zero, and the concurrent issuance of new shares to the government or to its order, or the issuance of a vesting order by government in respect of outstanding shares;
- the obligations and other liabilities of a subject bank, and its losses are determined by the administrative authorities on a legal-entity-by-legal-entity basis, and not on a consolidated basis unless the centralized management of the bank grouping implies in law unlimited holding-company, head-office, or affiliate liability for members of the grouping and branches thereof.

2.2.5 Country-specific constraints on the application of the new scheme

There are yet a number of problems to be resolved in fitting the new approach to the legal environment.

On the European side, the legally significant constraints on bank insolvency law design include the following:

1. The EU Commission has declared that it will not grant its prior approval for the bailout by governments of any 'insolvent' banks, as

opposed to bailouts of 'non-insolvent' banks which may come with a 'systemic' exception of sorts (as opposed to the US system that allows them in all cases subject to the above least-cost criterion). Does this injunction include as state aid the promulgation of any compulsory burden-sharing rules with respect to an insolvent bank?;

2. The ECJ has declared that the reorganizations of banks, which now qualify for corporate reorganizations, may take place on the basis of the same rules and standards that are applicable to other firms, which rules sanction the ability of depositors and other creditors to carry out debt restructurings for the benefit of a subject bank in reorganization (wiping out the excess of liabilities over assets), and the ability of shareholders to reduce capital to zero (wiping out the owners of worthless shares), as opposed to the USA where there is no bank reorganization option available for creditors or shareholders of banks. Does this injunction preclude compulsory equity restructuring rules with respect to an insolvent bank? Proposals are under way to amend the Second Capital Directive, however; and
3. The European Court of Human Rights may well hold that shareholders and creditors cannot be wiped out in (corporate) bank reorganizations pursuant to an official finding of negative net worth, but only pursuant to appropriate resolutions of creditors' and shareholders' meetings, or, by the operation of law, in a termination (dissolution) of the corporate body itself. This constraint (if any exists) on comprehensive bank restructurings, therefore, requires the enactment by the legislature of any bank insolvency law in the form of an 'expropriation law', providing for the delegation of legislative authority to the government to carry out expropriations thereunder, and for a separate judicial review regarding actions by the government, consistent with the ECHR (in principle, expropriations may take place only (i) for purposes that are *in casu* within the public interest; (ii) subject to appropriate compensation (standards of compensation are different for foreign shareholders); and (iii) subject to an administrative or judicial review by an independent and impartial court or tribunal). Would the zero compensation standard be acceptable in respect of insolvent entities?

In comparison, on the US side, the legally significant constraints on bank insolvency law design, under the FDI Act, include the categorical exclusion of any bank reorganizations which would involve the preservation of an insolvent bank in legal entity and personality, and the operation of the bank in public administration and government ownership for the time being.

2.3 How does the new approach compare with the *lex specialis* approach?

The ultimate finding of 'negative net worth' in the case of a 'critically undercapitalized bank' requires, pursuant to the rules governing the 'prompt corrective action' programme, the immediate termination (dissolution) of the subject bank. Concurrently, the FDIC succeeds, by the operation of law, to the subject bank, its assets and liabilities, and to its equity. It would appear from a careful reading of the mandatory language of the statute that, in the case of negative net worth, the takeover by the authorities of the subject bank cannot be deferred either through the so-called 'open bank policy', or outright forbearance, except in the event of a threat to systemic stability when the bailing out of an insolvent bank is exempt from the 'least cost' criterion that limits the applicability of so called 'open bank policies'. The statute allows, pursuant to the so-called 'open bank policy', the bailout of any bank either subject to least cost criteria, or subject to the systemic exceptions thereof; and, in the opposite case, authorizes the FDIC to proceed to place the closed bank 'in receivership' on an official valuation of the subject bank's assets and liabilities as of the date of takeover, coupled with a legally significant 'cleansing' of the bank's liabilities in the context of the administrative determination of claims (claims administration).

There is no reorganization option there to continue the bank in legal entity and personality, as its charter is 'pulled'. The 'administrative receivership' is a legal technique that 'resolves' the subject bank in a manner that (i) dissolves it in legal entity and personality; (ii) wipes out automatically, by the operation of law, bank shareholders' interests upon a succession by the FDIC to the shareholders' interests in the subject bank; (iii) vests, again through a succession, the assets of a bank upon takeover in the FDIC; and, importantly, (iv) limits the successor liability of the FDIC upon its assumption of liabilities, which takes place by the operation of law.'

There is a body of US federal banking law that authorizes the federal government to charter banks; to insure these 'nationally chartered' banks; to seize them for a host of reasons including insolvency (negative net worth); to 'pull their charter', a euphemism for terminating them in legal entity and personality; and to liquidate their assets *and* liabilities. Depositors and other creditors of their foreign branches are excluded from any deposit insurance coverage, and from the scope of the 'depositor preference' (a liquidation preference).

The above regime applies to nationally chartered banks which are, therefore, exempted from the operation of state corporation laws, as well as from federal bankruptcy laws (that is, from the US Bankruptcy Code), and from the respective jurisdictions of any state courts, and the federal bankruptcy courts. Also all other 'insured' institutions that enjoy the privilege of federal deposit insurance, also come under the *lex specialis*, and under the corresponding jurisdiction of the FDIC as deposit insurer, in full derogation both from state banking, corporation, and insolvency laws, and the jurisdiction of state courts, and of the federal bankruptcy courts.

The FDIC is an independent federal administrative agency (indeed, it was listed in old text books as a 'federal administrative tribunal'), of a highly efficient operation that is fully capitalized in terms of its long experience as an executing agency. (Who teaches the cat to catch a mouse? The mice do!) However, it does not have a comprehensive set of legal instruments on hand to deal with crises, due to the severe political constraints that its statute placed on its operations and transactions from the beginning. Hence, neither the US banking nor bankruptcy laws are the controlling antecedent for the new approach.

For example, the statute does not incorporate the core modality of the new approach, which is the 'reorganization' of an insolvent bank, but take the opposite route by requiring that the assets and liabilities of all insolvent banks be liquidated forthwith. Nevertheless, the FDIC approach is highly instructive of an approach that is based on containing the costs and risks of bailouts, by laying financial parameters on the deposit insurer's, ability to bail out banks. True, it may use, subject to pervasive restrictions and limitations, deposit insurance and other funds for the bailout, and the 'resolution' of any non-compliant or insolvent banks, thus vesting in it a mandate for the performance of all the investor-of-last-resort functions under the US banking system.

By placing the mandate on the bailout and resolution of insolvent banks in the FDIC, the statute requires the FDIC to perform diverse functions through the designated departments which share, in their separate but coordinated capacities, the respective statutory functions of (i) deposit insurance, (ii) supervision, (iii) seizures (such as takeovers, receiverships and conservatorships), (iv) the 'investment banking' activities that it carries on its own account, and, in that context, may enter into transactions with itself acting through two or more departments for the disposition of receivership assets and liabilities, and (v) for (intensive, but generally fruitless) litigation.

The statute places a duty on the FDIC to 'resolve' banks, that is, to 'pull the charter' and dissolve any critically undercapitalized and insolvent bank that has negative net worth, and to do it forthwith, to avoid further losses to uninsured creditors down the line. Alternatively, it may also engage in bailouts in order to retain the legal entity and personality a problem bank, of under a so-called 'open bank policy' that, as required by the statute, makes two separate and distinct exceptions from mandatory insolvent bank resolution. These are the legislative authorizations for (a) a bailout on a 'least cost' basis, on the one hand, and (b) a 'systemic' bailout that exempts the subject bank from the requirement of the 'least cost' calculation.

Under the likelier 'post-reform' course of action, which is the resolution of the insolvent bank forthwith, the FDIC helps to 'resolve' the subject bank, which event is predicated on the chartering agency (for example, the Office of the Comptroller of Currency) appointing someone to 'pull back' its federal corporate charter, usually within a day or two of the FDIC takeover. This action by the chartering agency corresponds to the erasing that 'mark' that any corporation is in the Registrar's book, terminating or dissolving, thereby, the subject bank in any legal and regulatory entity, and personality.

The takeover (or seizure) by the FDIC of the bank, which divests the subject bank itself up-front out of the control of its directors, managers and shareholders, divests the shareholders of their property rights and interests, and the uninsured creditors of their rights. Acting pursuant to its other superpowers, it may lawfully affect, modify or annul the rights and obligations of any third parties having claims against the receivership account that it operates on its own account subject to a limitation of its liability to the value on the asset side of the account.

Having that way compulsorily 'purchased' the remaining assets of a subject bank, and 'assumed' the equivalent 'good' portion of its liabilities, the FDIC will, by the operation of law, discharge and meet *forthwith* the insured obligations, liabilities and losses of the dissolved bank placed 'in receivership', which is a misnomer, subject to numerous defences against the institution of judicial proceedings by that residual class of necessarily dissatisfied holders of claims and interests who would have hoped for a bailout of the subject bank in the first place or, after the event, for better terms in the settlement of individual claims by the FDIC.

In allowing any individual claims against itself on the account of its assumption of the subject bank's liabilities, the FDIC must apply 'haircuts' regarding the obligations and liabilities owed to the subject bank, calculated on the basis of the shortfall of the value of assets held in the receivership account (that may be augmented in value if the amounts of recovery exceed the base-line, 'up-front' estimates on recoveries), and in keeping with the prescribed ranking of claims (based on specific liquidation preferences such as the personal depositor preference, the transactional 'qualified financial contract' or close-out netting preference), and the prescribed rules that govern the determination of whether or not a claim is 'admissible' in the first place, and then what is the amount subject to a haircut.

In claims administration, the FDIC (i) must ignore any (alleged) oral contracts; (ii) it may repudiate 'burdensome' contracts (including financial, management and employment contracts, leases and so forth); and (iii) may continue any 'beneficial' contracts for the time-being as the seizure cures any prior defaults, or may even prolong their date of expiry (with the exception of those that are under mandatory close-out netting), without incurring damages for their breach, but may not apply the 'depositors preference' for the ranking, or the deposit insurance funds for the benefit, of claims excluding particular depositors or other creditors (including uninsured depositors and creditors that are shareholders), and shareholders, or do anything that benefits the pre-existing shareholders; or (iv) provide for deposit insurance coverage for transboundary deposits (made in foreign branches of banks) (the 'qualified exceptions for bailouts themselves').

Those who have, by now, received an uninsured depositor haircut already form, of course, a highly dissatisfied class of pre-existing bank shareholders and uninsured depositors and other creditors, which surely grows every day.

A depositor preference results in a separation of the obligations or liabilities and the losses that the subject bank has incurred as a result of using funds received from the public, from its other obligations, liabilities and losses. Effectively, the preference divides the subject banks into two separate departments; one department is there for the acceptance of deposits on its own account, subject to their withdrawal in currency, on demand and at par, and the other department exists to receive other funds that create obligations and liabilities that rank lower than deposits, with the latter business subsidizing the former on the hypothetical liquidation plan. By implication, there is also a separation of bank assets, with the other creditors having a claim only with respect to the residual assets.

For example, under the scope and content of the depositor preference incorporated into the US bank insolvency law, the preference pertains to insured and uninsured deposits that are booked in banks located in the USA, and the definition excludes any foreign deposits payable solely at foreign branches of US banks. It naturally follows that the requisite 'haircuts', that only get applied to any unsecured and uninsured general and subordinated creditors in the event of liquidation of assets and liabilities, hit foreign branch creditors, guarantees and so forth very hard. Now, the preference is also there in the interest of the central bank, deposit insurer or the public treasury that conduct their business in the form of local deposits.

2.4 How does the new approach compare, in three ways, with its antecedents, the two polar regimes?

The original *lex generalis* approach was one that elegantly resolved any simple incidence of bank default or failure. By withdrawing the licence of a subject bank, the subject instantly becomes a non-bank, which transformation removes the bank from the jurisdiction of the designated regulators or supervisors.

Once there is no 'bank' left for regulators or supervisors to regulate, supervise, or resolve, the remaining non-bank legal entity may be judicially reorganized, liquidated, and dissolved like any other commercial firm.

In case of judicial reorganization, the answer to the question of who pays for bank insolvency was predicated on the autonomous actions of prescribed creditor and shareholder majorities, pursuant to the so called 'collective action clauses' imbedded in general corporation and insolvency law.

In case of judicial liquidation, the assets of the bank are placed in judicial receivership (as opposed to 'administrative receivership'), and, eventually, the remaining legal (corporate) shell will be terminated. That is to say, by erasing the entry in the corporate registrar's book of living corporations (dissolution).

The intellectual elegance of the *lex generalis* approach is enhanced for the reason that the state incurs no costs or risks of bank insolvency thereunder. It certainly does not have to discharge or meet the obligations, liabilities and losses of the non-banks in reorganization or liquidation.

The *lex generalis* approach is, therefore, from the vantage point of state budget the least or 'zero' cost and risk option, indeed, the optimal solution for any state that cannot and, therefore, will not pay for bank insolvency.

Take here as an example the island of Nauru, the home of banks that will never be bailed out by the local taxpayer: as a non-member of the IMF, Nauru cannot even mortgage its balance of payments for bailouts.

Indeed, because banks are different from other firms, the *lex generalis* regime has been modified accordingly in many places. As a result, the *lex generalis* solution has become only a fall-back position for the authorities, especially where the administrative authorities can control an insolvent bank's access to the court, say, by delaying voluntary or involuntary petitions.

Furthermore, it appears, that banks' insolvency deepens as the authorities delay action. It is this undue delay that ultimately makes a compelling case for a political decision in favour of a bailout of the insolvent subject bank.

In contrast, the scheme is meant to supply a bottom-line answer of the kind that accords both with the legitimate expectations, rights and interests of those involved, provided of course that the scheme is in place in good time before the next episode of bank insolvencies, and that the bottom-line results are not distorted by bailouts allowing the participants to fare better than they expected.

If the above conditions are fulfilled, the pre-existing creditors and shareholder could expect to share in the negative net worth of a corporate-form subject bank. This can be done without actually liquidating the assets of an insolvent bank, closing it down, and dissolving each and every such bank in legal entity and personality, provided that certain other familiar legal techniques are employed.

The asset, debt and equity restructuring involved would be based on a hypothetical liquidation valuation carried out as of the day the bank is placed under public administration, ignoring the effects of any prior or concurrent bailouts (which are not excluded albeit unnecessary) to restore the bank to a marginally solvent condition (through the three-way restructuring, its assets, by definition, would exceed its liabilities).

On the above basis, which is an estimate of the value of assets and liabilities carried out ignoring the otherwise applicable legal and regulatory accounting rules, the burden would be distributed in four ways:

- By making an estimate of lost assets that may be recaptured (as under the hypothetically applicable bankruptcy rules regarding transactions at undervalue, and fraudulent transfers);
- By cancelling that portion of the indebtedness of the subject bank through adjustment of the nominal amount of each claim of pre-existing creditors, with the total of individual haircuts being equal to the negative net worth calculated as of the opening date of public administration (as would be the result under the hypothetically applicable bankruptcy rules);

- By cancelling the outstanding shares of the bank as 'worthless' for zero compensation for the pre-existing shareholders (like creditors 'under water', they could record a total loss on their tax returns); and
- In addition, the contingent claims would be cancelled, burdensome contract would be repudiated (as under the applicable bankruptcy rules), and claims would be verified against detailed documentation standards.

The benefits for the remaining uninsured depositors and other creditors would be that the bank would resume payments and transfers upon reopening under a public guarantee of reserves that would be there until the public administration is terminated. The fact that the guarantor would meet any losses of the bank which it may incur after takeover would prevent any runs on the bank for the time being. Importantly, the scheme would restore access to funds, and permit transfers of funds in settlement of commitments, not years but days later. It assumes the parallel existence of a deposit insurance system, which is a constraint that can be relaxed, however, by having the deposit insurer to guarantee all insured deposits, or to administer the scheme outright on a delegated legislative authority in the public interest.

2.4.1 Legal safeguards?

Having the scheme in place in good time before the next episode of bank insolvency or insolvencies, which are certain to occur although we do not know where or when in advance, disposes in itself of legal objections under 'higher norms'. The timing of the requisite legislation is important, therefore. In law, the prohibition of retroactivity, which is a higher norm of the kind that might preclude the application of the scheme to pre-existing situations in many legal systems, might subject any retrospective or *ad hoc* application of the scheme to challenge or review.

The scheme affords adequate legal safeguards for banks, pre-existing depositors and other creditors, and shareholders. In addition to the prohibition of retroactivity, they include that the administration of the scheme by a government, and not by the judicial authorities who are not accountable for their errors (judicial immunity). Typically, where governments engage in measures that affect, modify or annul private rights and obligations, their actions are subject to review by independent and impartial courts or tribunals.

Other legal safeguards would also apply. The scheme places a limitation on the liability of the government for damages, but includes, at the same time, a provision for compensation if, in truth, the bank was not insolvent as of the date of intervention (gross valuation error). This could be coupled with a provision for a distribution of payments to unpaid creditors in the event that the government made a profit out of the operation of the scheme in the case of a particular bank.

Because the payment of compensation to pre-existing shareholders would undo the benefits of the scheme, it does not apply to critically undercapitalized, or any other banks, unless they had developed negative net worth, a factor that makes their shares worthless on the hypothetical liquidation valuation of an insolvent bank.

Finally, the hypothetical liquidation valuation must be carried out up-front, as of the effective date of public administration, by way of an estimate which necessarily ignores non-bank bankruptcy, regulatory, accounting laws and rules. Ultimately, this is a question of judgement to be reached on the facts of each case. For instance, so called 'book insolvency' is not the basis, although a pre-emption (although it may burst on a revaluation). In the event of insolvency, a bank cannot benefit from any going concern values predicated on consolidation, the showing of intangible equity as part of its capital, or the booking of assets (amounts of principal and collateral) at pre-crisis values. The event also triggers close-out netting and eliminates contingent claims and items.

2.4.2 Financial safeguards?

The scheme answers the question of who will pay for insolvency by shifting the burden onto pre-existing bank shareholders, and, then, to depositors and other creditors by way of sequencing of any bailouts to occur only after the 'record' date, or, regarding bailouts that had in fact occurred before that date, by way of a deeming provision that postpones the date.

Hence, the rules require the elimination, on the first round, of any 'incidental' benefits that would normally accrue to pre-existing creditors and shareholders of a bank that is the intended beneficiary of the 'open bank policy'. By way of carrying out a comprehensive bank restructuring up-front, as the first step in the case of a subject bank coming for public ownership and administration under the scheme, the scheme approximates the economic results of a quick judicial liquidation of the same: in reality, of course, there are quick administrative bank resolutions, but no known cases of quick judicial bank resolutions.

As noted above, the required up-front restructuring would take place on a hypothetical liquidation valuation of its assets and liabilities as of the date of intervention by the government, that is, without the actual liquidation of assets (auction), or without the support of any collective action clauses in general corporation and insolvency laws. The economic result is that the pre-existing creditors and shareholders would receive what they would have received, had the bank been liquidated as of the date of intervention (which also is the US rule governing the valuation of bank assets and liabilities upon takeover).

2.5 Avoidance of bailouts

2.5.1 What gives rise to expectations of bank bailouts?

That the public does, indeed, entertain expectations about future bailouts, can be readily understood. Especially, in Europe, the public believes that countries will no longer observe the classic, textbook bankruptcy rules in respect of banks, but have modified them; bankruptcy law is a dead letter now in that field. Indeed, banking is no longer a free profession of the kind it was, say, in France as recently as the 1920s. True, in the main, banking now is a highly regulated and supervised private industry, having been a nationalized industry in many countries (banks in France were nationalized as recently as the early 1980s). The current trends point to a 'public good' industry, in which banks at least 'might' be eligible for bailouts, at least in 'systemic cases'.

In law, however, any prospect of a bailout would appear to be wholly inconsistent with the idea that there must be a level playing field for all banks to compete with equal advantage, and contrary to the EU competition policy that precludes the approval by the Commission of any bailouts of 'insolvent' banks (here I am citing that very constraint on the prior approval of bailouts from the Commission's 1994 policy statement). The ECJ has a role to play, as does the ECHR.

As a result, prudential supervision now reflects public concerns regarding the stable supply of credit, and the punctual operation of payments systems, in the private sector (the market). However, public worries regarding the individual position, policies, and prospects of a particular bank, have more to do with the position of each bank relative to other banks. In an excess of caution, however, the official investigations into the character, competence and capital, have been extended to the individuals involved. Now, diverse applicants have to qualify against conditions governing entry into the industry. Not only do the supervisors decide upon the legitimate question of who can become a bank, but they may also decide upon the selection of significant owners of the bank, or on the eligibility of directors, officers, or even of a critically positioned employee of the bank. This is a slippery slope.

From the vantage point of privately-owned banks, the general move to abandon the direct instruments of monetary and exchange policy, have provided no relief from the regulation and supervision of the conduct of banking business. True, there is little directed domestic lending now, but instead there are prudential capital requirements (conditions of licence), on the one hand, and prudential restrictions on selected operations and transactions. In effect, prudential banking supervision has substituted as 'a new thing' for the now generally abandoned, direct instruments of monetary and foreign exchange policy (exchange and transaction controls), within which whatever is not permitted is prohibited. In addition, banks have become virtual agents of the state in the field of 'preventive' law enforcement.

As traditional banking secrecy recedes, banks have to report data pertaining to their operations and transactions in such detail that the affairs of individuals and corporations may be disclosed. The legislative trend is to vest in the supervisors both the right to approve voluntary bankruptcy petitions, and, in some countries, the initiative to file involuntary petition, to the exclusion of individual depositors and other creditors (Germany). The question is only whether the legislators, regulators, and supervisors can go too far, and pre-empt actions by competent courts and tribunals.

Taken together, all these public concerns give rise to private expectations for public accountability. For example, in the case of bailouts, how unfounded are such hopes in policy or law: in fact they are not, as long as the existence of unannounced bailout policies can be demonstrated by reference to recent experience that is not yet the other way around. More specifically, even where the general bankruptcy law applies to banks, because bankruptcy applies *mutatis mutandis* only, and does not apply at all as long as bank regulators and supervisors may delay any individual claimant's access to the court, or refrain from filing a petition on his or her behalf, and as long as the opening of bank insolvency proceedings requires any 'green light' from the government, the central bank, or the competent administrative authorities, as the case may be.

2.5.2 Is there any legal foundation for expectations regarding bank bailouts?

We had to ask first who pays – in law – for bank insolvency, and found that there are no prior undertakings by governments or central banks to carry out bank bailouts. No entitlements exist in favour of banks, their depositors and other creditors, and shareholders. This universal result was found by posing the question with respect to each particular national legal system that came under investigation, identifying the applicable legal rules and standards, carrying out the standard legal analysis, and stating the negative advisory opinion.

In fact, in virtually all countries the applicable laws and regulations provide for the settlement of bank insolvencies along the lines of the above rules of distribution and allocation, which are contained in the proposed scheme.

Then we had to ask who has – in fact – paid for bank insolvency, and found that the government did.

Here the bets are one-way only, although, subject to three qualifications:

(1) if there are, absolutely and positively, no public resources available to pay for bank insolvency in a particular economy, the insolvent bank is resolved by the courts alone under general insolvency law, or by third parties (the 'poor home country' exception); or
(2) during a crisis, taxpayer resistance may reach the point at which the legislature, through the current state budget (a) precludes any use of public resources bailouts, which may happen in the particular circumstances of a country (for example, when there is no benefit to the taxpayers themselves, as may be the case with trans-boundary bailouts), or (b) reneges even on a statutory obligation to replenish non-self-financing deposit insurance funds (which happened, for example, in the USA where the deposit insurance funds became insolvent, and the Congress refused to replenish them forthwith); or
(3) in the immediate aftermath of a crisis, taxpayer resistance may well reach the point at which the legislature, given that experience, same mistake being repeated, exempts the resolution of banks from general insolvency law (as the USA did in 1840), sets up the necessary administrative arrangements for it, and, based on the review of any experience, updates the law and underlying institutions (the USA did so following the 1980s savings and loan fiasco).

In larger banking systems that operate under centralized supervision, bank insolvencies may be rather frequent events, depending on how the exit policy works. Indeed, if insolvent banks are invariably resolved without undue delay, as they should be resolved, that policy does not in itself restrict the size and incidence of financial accidents. Indeed, exit policies deal with symptoms rather than causes of bank insolvency. However, dealing with such incidents enhances the authorities' ability to handle whatever new situation arises and to thrive on it. This is not the case in smaller countries with large banking systems in which there is a very small number of large banks (banks that are large even relative to the largest banks in the larger countries).

Experience shows that the legislative response to locally unthinkable banking crises is to deal with financial accidents as unforeseeable contingencies, to be provided for in the State budget and bank insolvency legislation as soon as shape of the problem becomes visible through the receding fog of confidence. Generally, legislators do not want to challenge the soundness of their national banking system in the interest of emergency preparedness for remote contingencies, but there are exceptions, especially the recent reform of the FDIC in the USA which laid down the trip wires that terminate any insolvent banks forthwith, with the famous 'systemic exception'. There were no other major benefits for banking interests, but they incurred detriment in the form of prescribed restrictions on bailout ('open bank policy'). There is now in place a robust exit policy which, coupled with the depositor preference, axiomatically leads to uninsured non-depositor haircuts.

- First of all, bank insolvency presents the question of money. If there is no public money available to bail out banks, there are no bailouts that set aside the prescribed legal effects and consequences of pre-crisis bank insolvency laws. In those situations there are no voluntary contributions forthcoming from third parties other than the government (that is, from future tax receipts), or the central bank (from future central bank profits).
- Second, if not, then the bank insolvency law must decide who will pay for bank insolvency. Both bailout policies and any legal changes that 'benefit' insolvent banks at the expense of the public treasury are easy ways out because, by definition, they are 'cure alls' which can make a beneficiary retroactively solvent;
- Third, bank insolvency laws that redistribute losses and re-allocate entitlements between banks and third parties cannot be retroactive. If they are, they are subject to challenge in parliaments, courts and tribunals. The risk of constitutional and other litigation is overwhelming.

2.6 Implications of the degree of 'openness' of bank insolvency regimes?

From the international vantage point, the architecture of the European banking system is open in the sense that the depositors and other creditors of head offices and foreign branches are treated equally in terms of deposit insurance coverage and liquidation preferences, as opposed to the US banking system which is insulated from paying certain liabilities of US banks' foreign branches. The critical definitions under the US bank insolvency regime exclude (1) the deposit liabilities of foreign branches from any deposit insurance coverage; (2) the application of the depositor preference to the liquidation of the assets and liabilities of foreign branches; (3) the US branches of foreign banks as uninsured 'separate entities' from deposit insurance coverage, and the application of US bank insolvency law; and (4) the US-related assets and liabilities of foreign banks from the application of the same (foreign banks come under federal bankruptcy laws).

While the question of using public resources to bail out banks is at least debatable, the question of using public resources for the others as direct beneficiaries of subsidies and aid has to be answered in the negative. Among institutions that may receive funds from the public (for example, savings), the banks enjoy the privilege for the reason that they take deposits and make loans, and serve as channels of payment. Taking deposits and providing loans makes the institution a depositary institution. More specifically, banks stand ready to perform the first of the three functions on their own account: they offer deposits in the form of balances that are subject to withdrawal in currency, on demand and at par.

The first condition relates to the fact that bank balances are not 'legal tender', but an entitlement to receive notes and coin upon their withdrawal at the counters of the bank or from central bank balances in situations in which the account-holder is another (local) bank. Here, the historical move was from the gold standard (via the international gold-exchange standard) to a cash standard when a public law obligation was imposed on creditors to accept bank transfers in the payment of taxes and other debts (under local law). Many countries now prescribe that certain bank balances may also do as a medium of final payment, placing specialized responsibilities on banks.

The second condition pertains to demand and matured time deposits, and other similar claims on banks. The legal characteristics of demand liabilities vary according to the debtor: unlike other insolvent debtors, an insolvent bank cannot close at will, and stop making payments and transfers, but has to satisfy customers on a first-come-first-served basis at its own counters, until closed by the authorities or a moratorium takes effect. Banks have to face the run on deposits even if that, indeed, violates the *pari passu* principle that prohibits trading while insolvent.

The third condition pertains to the principle of 'equal value' that must apply to the exchange of bank balances for currency at the counters of the issuer of the deposit liabilities in question. In other words, a bank is one that discharges, or meets its obligations, and liabilities 'at par'.

For explanation, the fundamental condition of financial stability is that the value of deposits is maintained at any point of time, and over time, in money-for-money transactions: all prices can vary, except the price of bank balances in terms of the value of physical currency (at the prescribed 'numeraire' of the banking system (which is typically the currency of the country)).

Notes

1. Of course, it is debatable whether a page has been turned, and there now exists a European banking system of sorts, as opposed to an American banking system. By logical necessity, if there is a European System of Central Banks, there must be under that conceptual 'roof' a 'European System of National Banking Systems' as well, at least regarding countries in the euro zone: indeed, there is a prohibition on the issue of local currency to pay for bank insolvency (arrangements laid down by the ECB include limitations that preclude the issuance of euros (notes and coin) for the purpose). True, the other countries may issue local currency to pay for bank insolvency, but they are, nevertheless, bound to observe the same principles of bank insolvency law as the countries that are part of the euro zone, including the same principles of corporation law with respect to insolvent banks 'in reorganization' that under the provisions of the Second Capital Directive (that applies to all banks that are so called 'public limited liability companies'; all major banks are).
2. But for the legal constraints identified in the main text, it would appear that the general scheme fits with the kinds of banking systems that prevail today. The exception is banks that are in sole government or public sector ownership, which typically operate either directly under the state budget as a single entity with the public treasury, or, although financially autonomous on paper, may come under a (permanent) public sector guarantee of reserves. The public sector successor liability may apply to some banks (for example, after nationalization). The scheme is predicated on a single entity approach regarding the legal and regulatory status of a bank, and its branches abroad: a separate entity approach requires some adjustments. As it evolves, the scheme will incorporate provisions regarding cross-border operations and transactions; for example, to help adjust bank indebtedness (a) (i) that is governed by a law other than national law of the bank and (ii) gives a foreign court jurisdiction over any claims that may arise under the indebtedness; or (b) that is payable in a foreign country (which may arise when indebtedness is denominated in foreign currency). Provisions that facilitate reciprocal judicial assistance for the marshalling of assets and the collection of debts, may be necessary. These will be supplied later, as necessary, along with bank insolvency law provisions pertaining to groupings of banks and other entities that are under centralized management ('concerns' or other similar groups), including those incorporated in different countries ('trans-boundary groupings').

Part II

How Big is the Problem?

3

Disclosure as a Cure for Moral Hazard: Necessary but Insufficient*

Gary H. Stern

The title of this book is 'Who Pays for Bank Insolvency?'. If the question were 'who should pay?' then the answer would be owners, uninsured creditors, and senior managers. But since the question refers to current practice, the answer is likely to exclude some creditors and to include taxpayers. The principal point of this chapter is to explain why, in the US setting, increased disclosure is unlikely to get the taxpayer off the hook. Several suggestions that would help to reduce the taxpayer's potential liability are also offered.

Disclosure has been touted as an effective way to address the moral hazard problem and the resulting excessive risk-taking by commercial banks. Indeed, it is the basis for the third pillar of the new Basel standards, and it underlies those parts of FDICIA Federal Deposit Insurance Corporation Improvement Act of 1991 designed to increase the transparency of decision-making at the bank regulatory agencies in the USA. However, there are doubts about the effectiveness of disclosure, taken alone, to increase market discipline, especially in the case of large, complex, too-big-to-fail (TBTF) banking organizations. The concern stems from recognition that the current environment gives uninsured depositors at such institutions only modest incentive to pay attention to the additional information which increased disclosure would provide, and to incorporate it into their decisions and, therefore, into market prices. After all, if depositors believe the bank is TBTF, why should they devote significant resources to assessing whatever further information is disclosed?

Moreover, it is doubtful that requiring additional disclosure about regulatory agency decision-making will, by itself, increase reluctance to bail out large banks or convince creditors that such bailouts are unlikely. There is ample precedent to suggest that the procedures mandated by FDICIA will have little if any impact on these matters.

In light of these mostly critical observations, some constructive proposals are offered that will address moral hazard and reduce the prospect of bailouts. These proposals involve several steps, including both putting uninsured creditors of large banks at genuine risk of loss and implementing policies which limit the potential spillover effects of large bank failures.

The preceding paragraphs are a brief summary of the issues raised and points made in the body of this chapter. The chapter is organized along the following lines. In the first section, the case for increased disclosure is spelled out and then it is argued that disclosure by itself will accomplish little unless accompanied by significant 'regime change' which ensures that creditors have ample incentive to utilize the additional information. The second section explains why there is good reason to believe that the TBTF problem has, if anything, grown more severe over the past several years. The third section describes US legislation – FDICIA – designed to address the issue, and explains why it is inadequate. Finally, the fourth section offers some bare-bones suggestions for steps necessary, in the author's judgment, to effectively establish policy-maker credibility, rein in TBTF, and make disclosure a valuable adjunct in addressing moral hazard.

3.1 Disclosure: pros and cons

The general notion that increased disclosure of relevant information, by and about large complex banking organizations, would improve market discipline and reduce moral hazard is, on the surface, attractive. Many apparently think that disclosure would improve both direct and indirect market discipline of such banks. Direct discipline would improve, it is argued, because, with additional information, creditors would be able to assess the riskiness of various institutions more accurately. Hence, market prices should more truly reflect the financial condition of the bank. Indirect discipline should be enhanced because bank supervisors will find market signals more valuable in forming their view of the bank.

Despite the straightforward appeal of these assertions, there is one potential flaw. Greater availability of information will have diminished effect unless creditors have ample incentive to exploit it fully and it is far from obvious that there is such incentive in current circumstances for banks deemed TBTF. After all, it requires resources to analyse data about banks and it is not clear that rational market participants will want to devote more resources to the effort when they believe some government protection is likely in the event of trouble.

This point was made unequivocally by Federal Reserve Board Chairman Alan Greenspan (2001):

> Expanded disclosure will be critical to enhanced market discipline, but the additional information will be irrelevant unless counterparties believe that they are, in fact, at risk. That is why the second prerequisite to effective market discipline is the belief by uninsured creditors that at least they *may* be at risk of loss. Uninsured counterparties have little reason to engage in risk analysis, let alone act on such analysis, if they believe that they will always be made whole under a *de facto* TBTF policy by government's recourse to the procedure for exception to the least-cost resolution requirements of FDICIA.

Granting the Chairman's point, it seems at best premature to emphasize disclosure without assuring that market participants will make use of the information. Others might challenge our claim, pointing to a widely cited body of research showing that the prices of subordinated debt and uninsured CDs vary in the 'right' direction *vis-à-vis* the risk-taking of banks (as measured through standard financial ratios). This literature demonstrates that creditors of large banks believe they are at some risk of loss. But note that such a result is far from a claim that prices of bank liabilities today would be the same as the prices in a world without conjectural government guarantees.

Many of those who advocate increased disclosure at this stage apparently assume that we are very close to a world without implicit support for the creditors of TBTF banks. In their view, FDICIA has curtailed TBTF sufficiently so that additional information from disclosure would make a contribution. We review these claims in turn. First, we will point to evidence, admittedly qualitative in many respects, which leads us to think that implied TBTF support persists. Second, we discuss FDICIA and explain why we doubt those provisions, aimed at reducing TBTF expectations, will in fact accomplish the task.

3.2 The persistence of TBTF

We might be a lot less concerned about the effectiveness of disclosure and related proposals if we thought the TBTF problem had diminished. Unfortunately, our suspicion is that, if anything, it has grown.[1] Looking specifically at the banking industry, it appears, first, that, in almost all industrial countries, the largest banks control an ever-increasing share of banking assets. Second, we are convinced that more banks have reached the minimum size necessary to be considered TBTF by creditors.

We acknowledge that this is a qualitative judgment, but the US experience provides some data to support this view. Further, there are banks of more moderate size but distinguished by their essential role in the clearing and settlement of securities transactions, for example, that are likely to carry the perception of TBTF.

In addition to size and provision of some key payments services, we think that the growing reliance of large banks on capital market funding, significant participation by these banks in markets for a wide range of new, sophisticated financial instruments, and entrance into relatively unfamiliar lines of business all increase the likelihood of TBTF protection and that creditors realize this. Moreover, we doubt that bank supervisors, despite admirable effort, have been able to keep pace with these trends in order to rein in risk-taking.

Besides developments in banking *per se*, a second body of evidence suggesting the persistence of TBTF comes from the credit-rating agencies. While perhaps not widely appreciated, the large rating agencies (Moody's, S&P and Fitch IBCA) prepare and issue two distinct sets of ratings for banks, one which incorporates and reflects potential government support and one which does not. The gap between the two measures can be viewed, roughly, as a measure of potential TBTF protection. Not surprisingly, given our message here, comparison of the ratings reveals that the agencies anticipate considerable TBTF support for a large number of banks.

This observation leads to the final point in this section. Whether we look at banking in Japan, recent actions of the IMF or the experience with LTCM in the USA, we do not see policy-makers moving to curtail TBTF. On the contrary, it appears to us that, at least for the USA, once the Federal Deposit Insurance Corporation (FDIC) sanctioned government support for bank creditors on an exception basis (and this initially involved small banks with minority ownership), the trend has been toward irregular but discernible increases in TBTF coverage. Again, this trend is not lost on uninsured creditors.

In total, the available trends and evidence suggest to us that expectations for TBTF coverage are unlikely to have diminished and could have increased. Moreover, we find the reform that allegedly put the end to TBTF coverage unlikely to have such a salubrious effect.

3.3 Does FDICIA effectively address TBTF?

A large number of analysts view FDICIA as a model of TBTF management, arguing that it reduces the probability of providing uninsured coverage to negligible levels.[2] Not surprisingly then, outside advisers often direct countries looking to manage potential TBTF exposure better to the reforms found in FDICIA (Kaufman, 1997a, p. 41). Claims that FDICIA has largely solved the TBTF problem in the USA often appear as fact, even in articles where TBTF is mentioned tangentially. Consider a recent Federal Reserve article on the performance of small banks:

> The competitiveness of the largest banks would also be improved if depositors believe that the government will treat these banks as 'too big to fail' ... However, the Federal Deposit Insurance Corporation Act of 1991 substantially circumscribed the ability of regulators to use TBTF by requiring that the Federal Deposit Insurance Corporation (FDIC) pursue the resolution method that minimizes the cost to its insurance fund. In addition, exceptions to the 'least cost' method are allowed only with the approval of at least two-thirds of both the Federal Reserve Board and FDIC board of directors and the approval of the Secretary of the Treasury in consultation with the President. (Basset and Brady, 2001, p. 720)

While commentators who view FDICIA in a positive light compliment other aspects of the legislation, most focus on the disclosure aspect of the reform that the above quotation highlights. Simply put, the harsh spotlight of voting and disclosure will stop policy-makers from protecting uninsured creditors. Creditors realize this and thus no longer expect TBTF coverage.

In fact, compared to the regime that preceded it, FDICIA does not appear to have significantly reduced the chance that US policy-makers will provide coverage to uninsured depositors of large, complex TBTF banks. This view originated because FDICIA did not significantly alter the important incentives that govern the TBTF coverage decision. In particular, it does not make a material change to costs and benefits that the supervisory agencies and Treasury will weigh when deciding if and to what extent they should bail out uninsured creditors of large banks.

To illustrate this point, the pre- and post-FDICIA regimes have been compared in order to judge the adequacy of the FDICIA TBTF reforms. The repeated praise for the major components of FDICIA imply that prior to its passage:

(1) supervisors did not have to formally seek special dispensation from standard resolution practices and cost tests when providing

TBTF-like protection,
(2) supervisors did not consult with one another and the administration in power, and
(3) these decisions were not subject to intense public scrutiny.

In reviewing these conditions, we think that the difference between the pre- and post-FDICIA regimes are greatly exaggerated.

For example, the Garn-St. Germain Act of 1982 formalized both the notion of a cost test and an exception to it. The act stated that 'no assistance... shall be provided... in an amount in excess of that... necessary to save the cost of liquidation.' A finding of essentiality would allow exemption from the cost test. The essentiality finding was made formally by the board of the FDIC. Garn-St Germain also coupled an exception to the cost test with concerns of systemic risk. It allowed the FDIC to assist a failed bank if 'severe financial conditions exist which threaten the stability of a significant number of insured banks or of insured banks possessing significant financial resources, as long as the finding of essentiality is made' (Senate Report, 1982, p. 3099).

The main difference between the ability of policy-makers to protect uninsured creditors at large, complex banks in the pre- and post-FDICIA world, therefore, is the public involvement of the Federal Reserve and the Treasury. Establishing a cost test and allowing exceptions to it during exceptional circumstances, as noted, was not new. Moreover, considerations of systemic risk when considering exceptions to the cost test were not revert to FDICIA. The key question is whether the difference amounts to much in substance. In fact, we do not believe a more formal, more visible role for the Federal Reserve and the Treasury will lead to a significant change in the incentives that policy-makers face when confronted with the bailout decision.

Agency Involvement and Publicity. Before FDICIA, both the Federal Reserve and Treasury appear to have been intimately involved in deciding when and whether to provide bailouts to large bank creditors. Consider a description of the bailout of Continental Illinois. According to the Comptroller:

> We debated at some length how to handle the Continental situation... Participating in those debates were the directors of the FDIC, the Chairman of the Federal Reserve Board, and the Secretary of the Treasury. In our collective judgment, had Continental failed and been treated in a way in which depositors and creditors were not made whole, we could very well have seen a national, if not an international,

> financial crisis the dimensions of which were difficult to imagine. None of us wanted to find out. (Inquiry into Continental Illinois Corp. and Continental Illinois National Bank (1984, pp. 287–8)).

Comptroller Conover was later asked, 'Is it correct to say that the decisions made on what the Government would and would not do with respect to Continental Illinois and its holding company, those decisions were made by yourself, Mr. Volcker [Chairman of the Board of Governors of the Federal Reserve System], Mr. Regan [Secretary of Treasury], and Mr. Issac [Chairman of the FDIC]?' The Comptroller responded, 'Yes, that is correct' (p. 345).

According to the FDIC, significant involvement by the Treasury and the Federal Reserve was not restricted to Continental Illinois. In testifying to Congress about FDICIA-like reforms to limit TBTF, the Chairman of the FDIC noted:

> The provisions that the Treasury has proposed will make very little difference. We gave you the four cases where we actually invoked that [essentiality] doctrine. In every case we have been encouraged to invoke it by the Federal Reserve, and at least the Treasury has not been willing to say that they would advise us not to invoke it. I am concerned that we look at reality in terms of what is really going on. (Seidman, 1991, p. 13)

Chairman Seidman later repeated the same point even more strongly, claiming that he gave the Treasury power to veto the bailout of the Bank of New England (pp. 35–6). His characterization was not disputed by Treasury and Federal Reserve officials with whom he testified.

While FDICIA creates a more public process, it seems insupportable in our view to believe that the Chairman of the Federal Reserve, the Chairman of the FDIC, or the Secretary of the Treasury thought their involvement in the Continental Illinois case or in other large failures were secrets. Congressional hearings and spotlights on the role that supervisors played in bank failures have a long tradition, preceding the Great Depression, that Continental Illinois merely affirmed.

Others have argued that the increased formality of the *ex-post facto* review of large bank resolutions is a significant change. For example, a prominent academic and former Federal Reserve official has argued 'An extremely important part of FDICIA that is often overlooked is that FDICIA requires a mandatory review of any bank failure that imposes costs on the FDIC... These provisions of FDICIA are extremely important because they increase the incentives of regulators to prevent costly bank failures' (Mishkin, 1997, p. 24). The General Accounting Office (GAO) carries out these reviews (as does the Inspector General of the FDIC). But these reviews are hardly new. GAO staff were assigned to the House Committee on Banking to investigate the failure of Continental Illinois, testified during the hearings on Continental Illinois, and prepared a report evaluating the bailout of Continental Illinois (Dugger, 1984; General Accounting Office, 1984). Again, Continental Illinois was not the genesis of this practice. The Congress has a long history of using its staff to investigate bank failures. To cite one example, the Committee on Government Operations held 'Oversight Hearings into the Effectiveness of Federal Bank Regulation: Franklin National Bank Failure' in 1976. The GAO played a central role in providing information on the behaviour of thrift supervisors (General Accounting Office, 1989).

Finally, it is worth noting that an emphasis on scrutiny and publicity must recognise that supervisors and government officials may view refusal to provide TBTF coverage as posing an equal or even greater threat to their reputations than the provision of excessive coverage. Indeed, it has been typical Congressional behaviour to criticize government officials for either choice. If bank supervisors and insurers will be criticized publicly for making the 'tough calls' that policy-makers ostensibly want them to make, then requiring a more public process for TBTF coverage may not have much effect on behaviour.

3.4 If not FDICIA, then what?

If the approach in FDICIA is inadequate for dealing with TBTF and moral hazard, and, as argued earlier, increased disclosure alone is of little value, what alternatives are available? There would seem to be no single, straightforward solution; rather the answer lies in a series of coordinated steps that would serve to curtail TBTF. For example, the appointment of 'conservative' policy-makers indisposed to TBTF bailouts would be constructive, as would heightened preparation by supervisory agencies for dealing with severe financial problems at one or more large banks. Recognition of the budgetary implications of implicit TBTF guarantees would also be helpful in identifying their resource consequences.

Moreover, we think it important that uninsured creditors of large banks be at risk of loss. Such a step, if credible, will directly strengthen market discipline, since market prices will more accurately reflect risk-taking, and it will add to indirect discipline as well since bank supervisors will have the benefit of improved market signals.

However, achieving credibility with uninsured depositors may be no easy task, for this group understands the incentives and concerns of policy-makers. Somehow, uninsured creditors must become convinced that policy-makers will permit a big bank to fail. In turn, for policy-makers to be prepared to take this step, they must themselves be convinced that such a failure is unlikely to have large and devastating effects on the banking and financial system and on the economy as a whole.

While this chapter is not a forum for detailing proposals along these lines at length, probably the greatest concern policy-makers have about large bank failures is their potential spillover effects to the real economy. In order to reduce if not alleviate this concern, we need safeguards which limit but do not eliminate the exposure of uninsured creditors to losses at such institutions. In other contexts we have proposed a version of coinsurance, wherein uninsured depositors could lose up to x (say 20) per cent of the uninsured portion of their account but no more (Feldman and Rolnick, 1998). A loss of, say, 20 per cent is a significant departure from full TBTF coverage, so such depositors should have incentive to monitor and evaluate their banks. At the same time, the size of the potential spillover is capped. Similarly, we would limit inter-bank exposures in the payments system so that even the demise of a large institution would be unlikely to threaten the solvency of many other banks.

With these safeguards, policymakers would be more confident than they are today that a large failure would not have widespread consequences. Uninsured creditors, realizing this, would have more incentive than at the present to assess the quality of the banking institutions with which they do business. In short, we would expect market discipline to improve and moral hazard to be reduced, and we would expect increased disclosure to be of real value.

Notes

* Thanks are also due to the Federal Reserve Bank of Minneapolis for their permission to publish this Chapter 3; for which it holds the copyright.

1. This discussion is based on Stern and Feldman (2003).
2. For favourable views see the essays in Kaufman (1997b) and Benston and Kaufman (1997).

4

The Incentive-Compatible Design of Deposit Insurance and Bank Failure Resolution: Concepts and Country Studies*

Thorsten Beck

Deposit insurance and bank failure resolution are important parts of the financial safety net and an incentive-compatible design of both can minimize the probability and cost of financial fragility. The absence of explicit deposit insurance or the proper design of an explicit scheme can encourage large depositors and creditors to monitor banks and exert market discipline, thus reducing the risk of aggressive risk-taking by banks and thus the risk of financial fragility. Effective and timely resolution of failed banks can decrease the cost that bank failures can cause to the banking system. An incentive-compatible design of bank failure resolution can contain aggressive risk-taking by banks and thus reduce the probability of bank failures *ex-ante*.

The financial safety net has opposing public policy objectives. On the one hand, it is supposed to protect small depositors, prevent bank runs and the breakdown of financial intermediation. On the other hand, a financial safety net has to be designed so that it minimizes aggressive risk-taking by banks, which can result in financial fragility. To understand these opposing public policy objectives, one has to consider the incentives of the major participants in the financial safety net;

(i) bank management and owners,
(ii) depositors and other creditors,
(iii) the managers of the financial safety net and
(iv) the owners of the financial safety net (ultimately the tax payer). (Kane, 2000)

Given the put-option character of bank equity, bank shareholders participate only in the up-side risk of the bank business and have therefore strong incentives to take overly aggressive risks, ignoring sound and prudent risk management. Effective bank regulation and supervision, as well as market discipline exercised by large depositors and creditors can keep banks in check.

The existence and design of deposit insurance and the effectiveness of bank failure resolution can have profound impact on market discipline. Depositors care mostly about the safety of their deposits. A generous deposit insurance scheme decreases incentives to exert market discipline, even of large depositors and other creditors that are not covered, if the introduction of deposit insurance signals the authorities' willingness to bail out all creditors in the case of bank failure. The owners of the financial safety net, often and, in its ultimate consequences, always the taxpayers, want to minimize its costs, while its managers might have other interests and time horizons and might represent the interests of specific groups, such as politicians and banks.

While both deposit insurance and bank failure resolution are important in minimizing the risk of financial fragility, the proper functioning of each depends on the proper functioning of the other and the overall safety net. A deposit insurance scheme can maintain market discipline and minimize moral hazard risk only if accompanied by efficient and timely resolution of failed banks upon market signals of distress. A poorly designed deposit insurance scheme can increase financial fragility by giving banks perverse incentives and thus overload even an efficiently working bank failure resolution scheme.

While not all countries have explicit deposit insurance schemes and bank failure resolution systems, both components of the financial safety net are almost always present. Unless explicitly excluded by law, depositors often perceive the existence of implicit deposit insurance, especially for government and TBTF banks. Even in the absence of a formal institutional structure to resolve failing banks, authorities are forced to address bank fragility. Perhaps paradoxically, even the complete lack of addressing failing banks constitutes a sort of bank failure resolution, though certainly not the most incentive-compatible one.

This chapter discusses the incentive-compatible design of deposit insurance, bank failure resolution and their potential interactions and presents and compares the financial safety net arrangements in three countries: Germany, Brazil and Russia.[1] While recent empirical cross-country studies have evaluated the effect of deposit insurance on market discipline, financial fragility and financial development, country case studies can complement them by providing valuable insights into the institutional features of the safety net and the interaction of its different components.

The remainder of this chapter is organized as follows. Section 4.1 discusses the incentive-compatible design of deposit insurance schemes and empirical cross-country evidence on its effect on banking system stability. Section 4.2 discusses the incentive-compatible design of bank failure resolution schemes and its interaction with deposit insurance. Section 4.3 describes and compares the financial safety net arrangements in Germany, Brazil and Russia and Section 4.4 presents the conclusions.

4.1 Deposit insurance

This section discusses the incentive-compatible design of deposit insurance schemes and summarizes the results of the recent cross-country literature on the effects of deposit insurance on market discipline and financial fragility.[2]

4.1.1 Deposit insurance – conceptual ideas

Deposit insurance schemes are asked to fulfil conflicting public-policy objectives: on the one hand, they are supposed to protect small depositors and ensure financial stability, on the other hand, they are supposed to minimize banks' incentives to take aggressive risks. While establishing a deposit insurance scheme can promote bank stability by preventing bank runs, it is also a potential source of moral hazard. Banks can transfer some of the downside risk of their business to the owners of the deposit insurance scheme, often the taxpayer. Risk-shifting can become so substantial that rather than promoting bank stability, deposit insurance increases bank fragility.

To understand the risks of deposit insurance, one has to consider the incentive structure of bankers. Given the put-option character of bank equity, bankers face strong incentives to lend aggressively, ignoring prudent risk management. The lower their capital base, the less they have to lose and the more they can gain through aggressive lending. Market discipline exerted by creditors and regulatory and supervisory discipline from the authorities can help reduce this form of aggressive risk-taking. Bank creditors can withdraw funds or demand a risk premium if observing a decline in banks' liquidity and solvency. Large creditors and depositors, such as other banks or non-financial enterprises, have the capacity to follow closely the banks they entrust with their deposits. Since small depositors do not have the ability or incentives to monitor banks carefully, they rely on a strong regulatory and supervisory authority, which is willing to take prompt action against weak banks, or free-ride on the efforts of large creditors.

There are several risks inherent in a deposit insurance scheme. By encouraging the confidence of depositors in the safety of their deposits, they can make depositors complacent and decrease their incentives to monitor banks. In particular, the large depositors, that are the most likely and most able to monitor banks, might reduce their efforts, if they perceive the introduction of a deposit insurance scheme for small depositors as a signal that the coverage will be extended to them in times of crisis. The existence of a deposit insurance scheme and the resulting reduced market discipline can also change the incentive structure for bank owners and managers. In the presence of insured deposits, a low capital base reduces the downside of risk even more and, when hit by a negative shock, a bank is therefore more likely to take large aggressive risks. Generous deposit insurance thus has the effect of subsidizing this aggressive risk-taking.

Several features of explicit deposit insurance can make it more incentive-compatible, decreasing moral hazard and agency costs. One such feature is to assign a margin of loss to private parties to force them to monitor banks and so increase market discipline. It is desirable to identify a group that is able and likely to exert market discipline when forced to do so. Limited coverage makes the insurance incomplete, and forces large depositors to monitor banks. Similarly, co-insurance forces at least some depositors to bear a certain share of losses, since they are reimbursed for less than 100 per cent of their deposits. Excluding interbank deposits from the insurance forces banks to monitor and discipline one another. Excluding insider deposits (that is, the accounts of management and influential owners) reduces moral hazard by making owners and managers participate personally in the downside risk of the bank business.

A second feature is to structure the management and funding of the scheme in an incentive-compatible way. Industry-based funding and management can decrease agency problems between owners and managers of the deposit insurance scheme. Funding of the deposit insurance scheme through premiums levied on the member banks makes banks pay for the risks they take and thus reduces their incentives to take aggressive risks, thereby abusing the insurance scheme. Management by the banks can further reduce incentive problems; the member banks do not only have the capacity to monitor each other, they also have the strongest incentives to avoid insurance losses, especially if they have to pay for these losses. A complete privatization, however, might not be possible, as we will discuss in the next section. Finally, mandatory membership or strong incentives to belong to a deposit insurance scheme are important to avoid adverse selection, with strong banks leaving the scheme in order to avoid cross-subsidization of weak banks.

Not only the source of funding, but also its correct level is important.[3] The adequate pricing of premiums assessed on member banks not only ensures the viability of the fund, but also reduces moral hazard risks by making banks pay for the risks they are taking. Finally, it shows openly the cost of deposit insurance. One step further is the application of differential premiums depending on the risks banks are taking and are therefore posing to the scheme. While theoretically superior to a flat premium, which implies cross-subsidies from less risky to more risky banks, risk-based premiums are difficult to implement in reality, due to severe information problems. Rather than a perfect risk-premium match, banks are therefore often assigned to risk buckets.

While industry-based funding is more incentive-compatible than public funding, the accumulation of liquid resources is not only inefficient but risky in weak institutional environments, where large 'pots of money' invite abuse and looting. While insufficient resources in the deposit insurance fund might undermine depositors' confidence in the scheme and prevent authorities from closing unviable banks, sufficient funds can be ensured by giving the deposit insurer access to contingent financing, either from the market or the government. This additional financing can then be repaid by additional premiums levied on the surviving banks.

While a proper design of an explicit deposit insurance scheme along the different dimensions can minimize moral hazard risk and thus the risk of financial fragility, the interaction of these design features is as important. Industry-based funding and management are important complements. Industry-based funding and public management of the scheme can make the deposit insurance fund subject to political capture and looting by politicians. Public funding and industry-based management subjects the fund to the risk of looting by the banking system. Further, industry-based management of the deposit insurance should be complemented by some role for the deposit insurer in the regulation and supervision of the member banks. While this does not imply having a parallel supervisory structure, which would be too costly for many developing countries, certain supervisory powers of the deposit insurer can enhance significantly the market discipline. This can include:

(i) mandatory participation in the licensing process,
(ii) the right to request extraordinary audits of banks that it perceives as unsound, and

(iii) the power to exclude member banks that it perceives to be recklessly managed.

While the latter, especially, might be a 'nuclear bomb' never used, it can have sufficiently strong deterrent power.[4]

4.1.2 Deposit insurance – cross-country evidence

While the risks and benefits of deposit insurance have been discussed extensively in the literature, until recently there was no empirical cross-country evidence on the relative weights of the risks and benefits of introducing deposit insurance and specific design features. A recent data compilation has allowed to assess the effects of deposit insurance on market discipline, financial fragility and financial development (Demirgüç-Kunt and Sobaci, 2001).

Recent cross-country comparisons have shown the risks of adopting explicit deposit insurance schemes. The likelihood of a banking crisis tends to increase in the presence of a poorly designed deposit insurance scheme (Demirgüç-Kunt and Detriagache, 2003). The likelihood is even greater in countries with deregulated interest rates and an institutional environment that lacks transparency. The US savings and loan crisis of the 1980s has been widely explained by the coexistence of a generous deposit insurance scheme, financial liberalization, and the failure of regulators to intervene promptly in failing institutions.[5]

Recent empirical research has shown that specific design features, such as the coverage and the funding of a deposit insurance scheme are related with its success in terms of preventing bank runs and providing small depositor protection, while maintaining market discipline and avoiding aggressive risk-taking by banks that would result in banking crises. Demirgüç-Kunt and Huizinga (1999) find that higher explicit coverage and having a funded scheme reduce market discipline, that is, the sensitivity of the deposit interest rate the bank has to pay to changes in profits and liquidity ratios. Demirgüç-Kunt and Detragiache (2003) likewise find that the probability of having a banking crisis increases in the coverage limit and in having a funded scheme. They also find that in countries with more efficient institutions the moral hazard problems stemming from explicit deposit insurance and some of its characteristics are lower or non-existent. This raises the importance of country-specific approaches to deposit insurance schemes, taking into account other elements of the safety net and the institutional environment. Finally, Cull *et al.* (2001) find a significantly negative impact of a poorly designed deposit insurance scheme on financial development.

The pricing of deposit insurance schemes has also been found to be important for their effect on banks' risk-taking behavior. Laeven (2002b) shows that most deposit insurance schemes are not properly priced. Using different methods of calculating the actuarially fair deposit insurance premium, reflecting the risk banks take, Laeven finds that many countries do not charge their banks the actuarially fair premium, implying a subsidization of risks banks are taking. Hovakimian *et al.* (2002) show that risk-shifting to the government or subsidization of risk-taking is stronger in poor institutional environments but can be reduced with an incentive-compatible design.

Cross-country evidence on the effects of deposit insurance has been augmented by country studies. A large literature discusses success stories and failures of state-level deposit insurance schemes in the USA.[6] The successful examples functioned mostly like clubs, had strong regulatory and supervisory powers over their members and exit from the scheme was hard or even impossible. Furthermore, advantages of belonging to the 'club' included liquidity support in times of crisis. A small number of members and unlimited mutual liability prevented free-riding on the collective insurance.

4.2 Bank failure resolution and its interaction with deposit insurance

This section discusses the incentive-compatible design of bank failure resolution systems and its interaction with deposit insurance schemes. Underlying non-systemic bank failure resolution is the objective of protecting the banking system, but not the individual bank. To the contrary, the organized and effective exit of banks is as much part of an efficient banking system as the entry of new banks.

4.2.1 Bank failure resolution – conceptual ideas[7]

As deposit insurance, bank failure resolution has two conflicting public-policy objectives. On the one hand, it has the task of minimizing the disruption and cost of failing banks by providing for their efficient and timely exit. This includes minimizing the risk of contagion that might arise from individual bank failures. On the other hand, the incentive-compatible design of bank failure resolution is important to minimize aggressive risk-taking by banks. If bankers know that they face immediate exit combined with the complete loss of all equity in the case of insolvency, they are less willing to take aggressive risks. If depositors and creditors know that they will suffer losses in the case of bank failure, they will be more willing to exert market discipline. If, on the other hand, the authorities give shareholders and creditors the opportunity to shift risk to the taxpayer, by providing for generous bailouts and late intervention and closure, this increases incentives for aggressive risk-taking and increases the probability and extent of financial fragility. As in the case of deposit insurance, bank failure resolution has thus to be designed to avoid problems of moral hazard – aggressive risk-taking by banks – principal-agent problems between managers and owners of the system and adverse selection between banks.

In order to provide for the quick and timely exit of failing banks, while minimizing the risk of contagion and disruption to the financial sector, bank failure resolution has to address two major problems that correspond to the two sides of a bank's balance sheet. First, in order to maintain debtor discipline and access to credit, as well as the information value of an ongoing credit relationship, performing loans should be kept within the financial system and not be liquidated. Second, an interruption of the access that depositors have to their savings in the failed bank, can cause contagion and runs on other, fundamentally sound, banks. In the Argentine context, these two problems have been also referred to as refrigeration and hostage problems; efficient bank failure resolution wants to avoid 'perishable assets' leaving the refrigerator, that is, the banking system, and wants to take the 'hostages', that is, the depositors, out first. Minimizing the risk of contagion and asset decay demands solutions other than liquidation of the bank, since liquidation of banks implies:

(i) closure of bank, thus blocking the access of depositors to their savings, and
(ii) loss of incentives for bank management to maintain debtor discipline.

Even in the most efficient judicial systems, a liquidation is therefore often not the most efficient resolution mechanism.

Alternatives to liquidation include private sector solutions, such as merger and acquisition, and mixed private–public sector solutions such as purchase and assumption techniques. While private sector solutions do not involve any public or deposit insurance resources, moral persuasion and other active participation by supervisors or other financial safety net agents might be necessary to bring about such a solution. A purchase and assumption implies the transfer of assets and preferred liabilities to other financial institutions, before revoking a bank's licence. Only impaired assets are left in the failing banks, together with certain liabilities, and are subject to liquidation. A rapidly performed purchase and assumption transaction can minimize both the risks of contagion, since depositors will lack access to their funds only for a short time period, if at all and of asset decay, especially since most credits do not leave the financial system.[8] If done in time, before assets fall below liabilities, a completely private solution can be envisioned. If the 'good' assets are not sufficient to cover the liabilities that the authorities want to transfer, additional resources are required, either from a deposit insurance fund or public resources.

Bank failure resolution, however, also has the task of minimizing aggressive risk-taking *ex-ante* and thus reducing financial fragility. Specifically, it can be designed in a way that minimizes moral hazard risk *ex-ante* and distributes the costs of bank failure in a fair way *ex-post*. First, an incentive-compatible distribution of losses should be made clear *ex-ante* and strictly observed *ex-post*. Shareholders should be the first ones to suffer losses by seeing their equity wiped out. Incentives of shareholders can be further improved by making them liable for losses beyond the level of the paid-in capital.[9] This would make stock prices more sensitive to changes in underlying bank fundamentals and have shareholders participate more fully in the downside risk. Finally, subordinated debt can be used to create a class of debt-holders required to take the first hit. The holders of subordinated debt would therefore have a strong incentive to monitor banks and exercise market discipline.[10]

Second, intervention in a failing bank should be timely, preferably well before assets fall below liabilities. This is especially important since, as discussed in Section 4.1, incentives for aggressive risk-taking increase as the capital falls towards zero. Further, timely intervention and resolution also avoids distortionary effects on bank competition by failing banks' attempts to attract additional deposit resources through higher rates, extend aggressively their lending portfolio and their negative effects on borrower discipline. Avoiding moral hazard risk also speaks against resolution techniques that involve a bailout of banks with public resources or regulatory forbearance to enable the bank to recover a sound capital base.

The institutional structure of bank failure resolution can be designed in an incentive-compatible way, by assigning the responsibility of intervening and resolving to the agent with the highest incentives to minimize losses. Bank supervisors often have the best information for intervening early and resolving troubled banks. The ability to intervene also strengthens their power *vis-à-vis* the banks in their supervison (Quintyn and Taylor, 2002). Bank supervisors, however, do not always have good incentives to intervene in banks, but rather to avoid intervening during their tenure (Kane, 1989). Reputational concerns might prevent them from intervening early (Boot and Thakor, 1993). Political pressure and regulatory capture, together with personal liability can prevent supervisors from intervening. The deposit insurance agency might have appropriate incentives to intervene but most likely, only if managed and at least partially funded by the banking industry, and thus with strong incentives to minimize losses. Finally, even if the formal authority rests with supervisory or regulatory authorities, the private sector, especially other banks, is often involved in the resolution, since it has at least complementary, if not even better, information about troubled banks than bank supervisors, and strong incentives to intervene early.[11] Merger and acquisition and purchase and assumption techniques, described above, imply the involvement of other banks in the resolution of a troubled bank, most likely under the guidance of bank supervisory authorities. The involvement of other banks and a deposit insurance scheme financed by banks can also help reduce principal-agent problems between owners and managers of a bank failure resolution scheme and the banks themselves.

There are parallels between incentive-compatible design features of deposit insurance and incentive-compatible design features of bank failure resolution. Deposits of insiders, such as senior management and controlling shareholders should be excluded from deposit insurance coverage; the same groups should be among the last to receive compensation in bank failure resolution. Deposit insurance aims at protecting small depositors, by setting a coverage limit. Similarly, bank failure resolution can include priority ranking for small depositors in liquidation and the transfer of deposits only up to a certain limit in a purchase and assumption model.

4.2.2 The interaction of bank failure resolution and deposit insurance

Both deposit insurance and bank failure resolution are subject to the trade-off between two conflicting public-policy objectives. On the one hand, they are supposed to provide financial stability and protect small depositors. On the other hand, they have to minimize aggressive risk-taking and avoid moral hazard. In order to strike the right balance between both objectives, both components of the financial safety net have to be consistent with each other and other components of the safety net, such as supervision and lender-of-last-resort facilities. An incentive-compatible deposit insurance scheme that ensures monitoring by large depositors and creditors, has to be accompanied by a bank failure resolution system that does intervene and close banks when the markets signal fragility. While large depositors can exert market discipline, a bailout of bank owners minimizes the effect of this discipline. A bank failure system that provides implicit deposit insurance for all depositors, not just small ones, can undermine the market discipline imposed by the explicit deposit insurance scheme. The insurance losses of deposit insurance can be minimized by an efficient bank failure resolution system that does not only allow for liquidation, but alternative resolution techniques (as, for example, set out in the first two chapters of this book).

Consistency with other components of the financial safety net is as important. Unlimited access of failing banks to lender-of-last-resort facilities can give perverse incentives to supervisors to grant regulatory forbearance in order to avoid recognition of substantial losses to the authorities in charge of lender-of-last-resort facilities. Efficient bank failure resolution and incentive-compatible deposit insurance require effective supervision to

(i) enable early intervention, thus minimizing resolution costs, and
(ii) compensate for the partial loss of market discipline that deposit insurance implies.

Finally, private agents do not only need incentives, but also the instruments to monitor banks.[12]

The technique of purchase and assumption together with implicit or explicit deposit insurance exemplifies this trade-off between conflicting public-policy objectives of the financial safety net. While contagion concerns might speak in favour of transferring a large amount of deposits to other financial institutions, moral hazard considerations would favour a strict limitation. While the coverage limit should be set sufficiently low to enhance market discipline, an efficient application of the purchase and assumption technique requires a certain minimum of deposits to be transferred to the new bank. In order to avoid moral hazard in the context of a purchase and assumption mechanism, one can apply the least-cost criterion, which requires the technique to be applied that implies the lowest cost for the government or the deposit insurer. This would imply that any solution other than liquidation would have to incur costs less than the cost of paying out insured deposits minus recoveries. This would in most cases restrict the transfer of non-deposit creditors and shareholders.[13] Another element to improve market discipline is to statutorily limit the liabilities than can be transferred to the good bank.

Applying the least-cost criterion, however, faces several problems. First, only estimates are available about potential asset recoveries and the cost of a potential liquidation. Second, cost calculations typically do not take into account effects of the chosen resolution method on the behaviour of borrowers and depositors, on the one side, and the behaviour of other banks, on the other side. Failure resolution resulting in asset decay and depositor run increases overall failure resolution costs. Failure resolution that creates perverse incentives for other banks to take aggressive risk might ultimately increase resolution costs of other failing banks. Resolution methods with seemingly low short-term costs might thus result in large long-term costs if substantially increasing contagion or moral hazard risks.

The chosen balance between the stability and the moral hazard objectives of the financial safety net might vary with the size of the bank. Specifically, in the case of banks that are considered to be too big to close, public-policy considerations might override financial considerations of the least-cost criterion discussed so far. The economic cost calculation, in terms of financial stability, and other criteria, such as access to finance issues, might tip the balance in favour of resolution mechanisms that are not optimal from the viewpoint of avoiding moral hazard and from the financial standpoint of the deposit insurer. This includes open-bank assistance; injection of public resources in the form of debt, equity or purchase of non-performing assets, while the bank stays open for business. This can come with or without direct managerial involvement by the authorities.

Open-bank assistance poses considerable incentive and agency problems as well as legal and financial risk for the government. If the existing management and ownership structure is kept in place, risk-taking decisions are taken by agents that have little or no more downside risk and thus large incentives to take aggressive risks. This poses considerable challenges to bank supervisors to control such aggressive risk-taking. If management of the bank is taken over by authorities, the deficiencies of government ownership of banks are often revealed. Cross-country experience has shown the risks of such open-bank assistance: many intervened banks had to be liquidated at the end, with the financial cost being higher than if the bank had been closed earlier. Finally, special treatment for large banks creates adverse selection problems since banks are treated differently depending on their size. Nevertheless, macroeconomic and political considerations often override this negative experience. This raises issues concerning the predictability of such a situation and the involvement of an explicit deposit insurance scheme.

Overriding established rules of the financial safety net by public-policy considerations in the case of TBTF banks can be done on an *ad hoc* basis, with the event being unpredictable, or by establishing specific rules of the game, such as in the USA. As in the case of deposit insurance, the optimal choice might very much depend on the institutional development of a country. While explicit deposit insurance and specific rules for open-bank assistance might be preferable in a strong legal and institutional environment, the ambiguity of an implicit deposit insurance scheme and discretion in open-bank assistance might be optimal in a weak institutional environment.

While public-policy considerations might override microeconomic considerations, deposit insurance funds should not be used for open-bank assistance. If deposit insurance is financed by the banking industry, its use for open-bank assistance would clearly constitute a case of political abuse. Further, a political decision to keep a failing bank open, should be accompanied by funding on the political level, that is, the general budget. This would also increase the transparency of the decision and the accountability of the decision-makers.

The close interaction of deposit insurance and bank failure resolution in their effects on market discipline and financial fragility raises the question of institutional interaction. Across the countries with explicit deposit insurance schemes different set-ups can be observed, ranging from the deposit insurance agency being a pure pay-box – such as in Brazil – to deposit insurers with broad mandates in supervision and failure resolution – such as in the USA. Other schemes have narrow formal powers, but yield much larger powers in reality, such as the deposit insurer in Germany. More important, however, than the institutional setting is the incentive-compatible overall structure of the financial safety net. Purchase and assumption techniques can be applied across different institutional settings, as the examples of the USA and Argentina show.

4.3 Three country studies

This section describes the financial safety net arrangements in three countries: Germany, Brazil and Russia. These three countries do not only show very different designs in deposit insurance and bank failure resolution, but also have different levels of financial, institutional and economic development and banking sector structure. While Germany and Brazil have already deposit insurance schemes, Russia is currently discussing the introduction of such a scheme. In the following, I describe and analyse the different financial safety net arrangements, taking into account the structure of the respective banking system.

4.3.1 Germany – a private solution

The German banking market comprises three main sectors, the largest being the savings banks, owned by cities, counties and states, followed in size by the privately-owned commercial banks and the cooperative banks, owned by their members.[14] Due to the geographic limitation of individual savings and cooperative banks, competition between the different groups of banks is much greater than between members of each group. While savings and cooperative banks are not necessarily profit-maximizing institutions, due to their ownership structure, the commercial banks cannot be assumed to maximize shareholder-value either. The large commercial banks hold a large part of the votes at their respective shareholder meetings themselves and there is substantial cross-ownership of commercial banks (Gottschalk, 1988). The German financial safety net is largely industry-based. Before the introduction of a compulsory deposit insurance scheme following the adoption of a EU mandate in 1994, three deposit insurance schemes, for cooperative, savings and commercial banks, respectively, were completely industry-based, voluntary, outside government supervision and without government-back-up funds. Rather than the Bundesbank, a separate institution, the Liquidity Consortium Bank, jointly owned by the Bundesbank and large banks of all three sectors, provides lender-of-last-resort facilities. The supervision by the Federal Banking Supervisory Office (FBSO) is complemented by supervision by the deposit insurance schemes and bank failures are mostly resolved with substantial organizational and financial involvement by the industry.[15]

After the Herstatt crisis in 1974, the three banking groups introduced their respective industry-based schemes to avoid political pressure and deeper government involvement in the financial sector. Savings and cooperative banks have both regional insurance schemes and a national compensation scheme. The schemes of both savings and cooperative banks do not directly guarantee deposits, but rather the institutions themselves, thus offering unlimited depositor protection. On top of the deposit insurance scheme, depositors of savings banks are protected by an explicit institutional guarantee of the public owners.

The design of Germany's deposit insurance scheme for commercial banks seems at odds with some of the principles laid down above. It is a voluntary scheme with a very high coverage – all non-bank deposits are covered up to 30 per cent of the liable capital of a bank.[16] There is no co-insurance and only interbank accounts, bonds payable to bearer and insider accounts are excluded from coverage. Financing and management, on the other hand, are completely private. Banks pay an annual premium of 0.03 per cent per year, with higher premiums for banks that are perceived to be more risky. The risk assessment is undertaken by the Auditing Association of the German Bank Association but kept secret. The premiums can be raised or set at zero, depending on the financial situation of the deposit insurance fund. There is no public funding and the Bundesbank is prohibited by law from functioning as lender of last resort to deposit insurance schemes. The deposit insurance scheme, organized within the German Bank Association, has substantial regulatory and supervisory powers *vis-à-vis* its members. The deposit insurance scheme gives a non-binding opinion to the FBSO on new bank licence applications. The Auditing Association of German Banks can impose corrective actions on member banks if circumstances indicate an increased riskiness in the bank's business or violations of the Banking Act or other laws governing banks. Penalties may restrict the volume of deposit business or particular types of lending. Finally, members may be expelled from the scheme, especially for missing or wrong information, and for being classified in the worst risk class for more than two years in a row.

With nearly unlimited coverage and no co-insurance, the German deposit insurance scheme offers little incentives for depositors to exercise market discipline. Monitoring by peer banks replaces monitoring by depositors in the German commercial banking sector. This is accomplished by:

(i) the completely industry-based nature of funding and management of the scheme,
(ii) the exclusion of interbank deposits from the insurance, and
(iii) the almost complete coverage of deposits.

The fact that interbank deposits are excluded increases the incentives for banks to monitor one another, while the almost-complete coverage of non-bank depositors seems to increase market discipline exercised by the banks.[17] Given the completely private nature of the scheme and the lack of public back-up funding, the member banks cannot expect to externalize any costs stemming from a distressed member bank. The almost-complete coverage therefore increases pressure on the member banks to monitor one another.

The resolution of failed banks is undertaken jointly by FBSO and banks. Cooperative and savings banks enjoy the institutional support of other banks in their respective groups. The resolution of commercial banks is mostly done in informal cooperation between FBSO and bank creditors of the troubled banks. The resolution of Schröder, Münchmeyer, Hengst and Co (SMH) in 1983, a small private bank, is an example of such cooperation. Under pressure from the Bundesbank and the Federal Banking Supervisory Office, banks with outstanding claims on SMH agreed to convert their claims into subordinated debt, in exchange for managerial control. The deposit insurance scheme stepped in to compensate depositors and foreign creditors. A month later, the bank was split into a good and a bad bank, with the good bank being sold to Lloyds Bank and the bad bank being taken over by the German Bank Association and liquidated. Interestingly enough, the problems at SMH were discovered by the Bank Association, not by the Supervisory Office, and the German Bank Association stood at the centre of the rescue.[18]

The private character of the German financial safety net has its roots in the structure of the German banking system. Both deposit insurance and bank failure resolution of commercial banks are completely integrated in the German Banking Association, the first formally, the latter more informally. The commercial banking sector therefore resembles a club that enforces mutual monitoring, but also mutual support. This club character also minimizes the adverse selection problem that might arise from the voluntary character of the deposit insurance scheme by preventing the exit of member banks.[19] The high concentration reinforces the club character and allows the quick resolution of troubled banks by involving only a few large players. Having separate deposit insurance schemes for each group of banks (public, cooperative and private) reinforces the club-like nature of the deposit insurance schemes by aligning the interests of individual banks more closely.[20]

The private nature of the financial safety net reduces agency cost between owners of the safety net, its managers and banks, since these three groups coincide in the German case. Unlike in most other countries, the taxpayer is not the safety net owner, thus eliminating potential agency problems between public managers and the taxpayers as owners of the safety net.

While Germany has not suffered from any systemic banking crisis or large bank failure over the last 25 years – an indication of the success of its safety net – this has to be interpreted within the country's institutional framework, legal tradition and banking structure. The high level of institutional development and an anti-bankruptcy bias in Germany can partly explain the lack of aggressive risk-taking. The ownership patterns and the resulting lack of shareholder-value-maximizing behaviour might decrease efficiency in the banking sector, but might also help reduce aggressive risk taking.

4.3.2 Brazil – a financial safety net in development

The Brazilian financial system is dominated by two large banks that are owned by the federal government. Together with the largest three privately owned banks, they account for over 50 per cent of total banking system assets. This contrasts with a large number of privately owned small banks. A recent wave of privatization and liquidation has reduced the importance of banks owned by the Brazilian states. Failure of several large privately-owned banks in the mid-1990s was resolved with a good-bank-bad-bank model, with the Central Bank providing resources to fill the balance-sheet gap. Subsequently, bank regulation has been tightened and bank supervision significantly improved. While the Central Bank used to be responsible for all four components of the financial safety net – bank failure resolution, deposit insurance, regulation and supervision and lender-of-last-resort facilities – the 1988 Constitution prohibited the use of any public money for the protection of depositors, prompting the set-up of an industry-based scheme in the wake of the banking crisis of the mid-1990s.[21]

Many elements of the Brazilian deposit insurance scheme – Fundo de Garantidor de Creditos (FGC) – reflect the incentive-compatible standards as described above. It was established in 1995 as a mandatory insurance scheme for all deposit-taking banks, with a relatively low coverage (currently around US$6,000, or twice GDP per capita).[22] There is no co-insurance but interbank, non-resident and insider deposits were initially excluded.[23] The scheme is financed by premiums assessed on the banks (currently 0.3 per cent per year), and there is no public back-up funding due to the constitutional ban mentioned above. While there are provisions for increasing premiums in times of need, premiums do not vary according to riskiness of banks. The statutes mandate a build-up of liquid assets up to 5 per cent of covered deposits, thus making it an *ex ante* scheme. FGC is managed by the banking industry, but under public policy guidance.[24]

Unlike in Germany, the deposit insurance agency FGC is limited to a pay-box function. It does not have any involvement in the supervision of its member banks and no role in the resolution of failed banks. While the limited coverage, the compulsory membership and the industry-based financing and management are incentive-compatible, reducing problems of moral hazard, principal-agent problems and adverse selection, the scheme could be strengthened by an increased role of the deposit insurer in supervising its members and allowing it to apply disciplinary measures against member banks. Finally, while the institutional framework does not give concerns on the potential abuse of the current *ex ante* financing, *ex post* contingent financing seems more efficient, especially in the light of very high interest spreads in the Brazilian financial market.

The Brazilian deposit insurance scheme has had to deal mostly with small bank failures, with one notable exception. Most likely, it has contributed to the trust and the relative stability in the Brazilian banking system after the banking crisis in the mid-1990s, by paying out insured deposits of failed banks relatively quickly.

The resolution of troubled banks in Brazil is an extrajudicial process, led by interveners and liquidators appointed by the Central Bank. While the extrajudicial character of bank failure resolution was introduced to avoid the inefficiency and slowness of the judicial insolvency process and to benefit from the expertise of the Central Bank in the banking system, the results have been disappointing. Liquidations are protracted since liquidators do not have any incentives to terminate the process rapidly and carry subjective liability for any of their actions during liquidation. Liquidations are also hampered by court interventions by owners and other stakeholders. Given the unlimited priority ranking of tax liabilities and labour claims, other creditors do not have incentives to press for rapid liquidation. Most of the failed banks are liquidated, resulting in asset decay and destruction of credit relationships. While intervention, a six-month period that can be extended once and during which the bank is closed, has the objective of saving the bank, it has mostly resulted in subsequent liquidation. Purchase and assumption techniques, that involved the sale of good assets and deposits to another bank, were applied only to a few large banks during the banking crisis of the mid-1990s. The Central Bank took the leading role in this process, identifying purchasers for troubled banks and providing liquidity support to fill the balance-sheet gap. The resolution of these banks also allowed foreign bank entry into the Brazilian financial market.

While the deposit insurance scheme shows many elements that reduce the risk of moral hazard and financial fragility, it is not well linked to the rest of the safety net and the deficiencies in the bank failure resolution system limit its effectiveness in reducing moral hazard risks. While financing and management by the banking industry help decrease agency problems between managers and owners of the scheme and help minimize risks of regulatory and political capture, regulatory and supervisory powers *vis-à-vis* its member banks might strengthen the scheme in the long term. These might include non-binding recommendations on new bank licence applications, the ability to request extraordinary audits of banks it perceives to be unsound, and the power to exclude members it perceives as recklessly managed. These are powers similar to the ones that the German deposit insurer has and do not need the build-up of any additional supervisory capacity, as the German example shows.[25] Further, a more extensive role for the deposit insurer can be considered in the context of a reform of the bank failure resolution system. On the one side, one can envisage the introduction of a purchase and assumption model as in Argentina, with the deposit insurer continuing with its pay-box role and supplying funds to cover any balance-sheet gap that is left after the separation of good assets and preferential creditors (such as insured depositors) from the bad bank that is sent to liquidation.[26] This would imply however, the statutory application of the least-cost criterion to avoid political abuse of banks' premium payments. On the other side, one can imagine a model closer to the US case, with a more substantial role of the deposit insurer in intervening and resolving troubled banks.

The current bank failure resolution system can be significantly improved upon, by providing for a purchase and assumption technique that allows the transfer of performing assets and preferential creditors – including insured deposits – to another bank, while the remaining assets and non-preferential liabilities – including shareholders' claims – stay behind in the bank to be liquidated. This would avoid problems of asset decay and potential contagion through depositor runs. While the liquidation of small troubled banks over the last couple of years, involving payout of insured deposits by FGC, has implied only a relatively small economic cost, such a purchase and assumption model would not only be more efficient for small banks but be indispensable for the resolution of medium-sized or larger banks.

4.3.3 Does Russia need deposit insurance?[27]

Russia's banking sector suffered a major setback in the 1998 banking crisis. The unilateral restructuring of government debt resulted in a collapse of the payment system and depositor runs. Since there was no formal deposit insurance scheme in place, a large part of household deposits were protected by transfer from privately owned banks to the government-owned Sberbank, the former savings bank. These new resources and the collapse of several private banks allowed Sberbank subsequently to transform itself into a universal bank, building up a large loan portfolio. Currently, Sberbank dominates the retail deposit market with over 75 per cent market share and its assets constitute around 25 per cent of total banking system assets. Many of the private banks do not function as intermediaries, but limit their lending activity to enterprises in their business groups.

The 1998 crisis and the subsequent years have brought to light significant weaknesses in the regulation and supervision of banks. The response to the crisis was limited to regulatory forbearance and liquidity support to selected banks without disclosure of the criteria with which these banks were chosen. Regulatory forbearance, while intended to relieve pressure from the banks, allowed bank owners to strip assets and facilitated capital flight. The dual role of the Central Bank as owner and regulator of the largest two banks in the banking system – Sberbank and Vneshtorgbank – leads inevitably to conflicts of interest. A special bank restructuring agency (ARCO), created to deal with the resolution of large troubled banks, has had a very mixed record. Several of the intervened banks stayed open and in several cases, shareholders and management could stay on. The liquidation of other banks by ARCO has been very slow.

The bank failure resolution shows significant deficiencies both in its legal and institutional structure as well as in its enforcement. With the exception of the banks referred to ARCO, the Central Bank is responsible for intervention and the resolution of troubled banks. However, it was not until 1998 that a Bank Bankruptcy Law was enacted and not until 2002 that the revocation of a bank licence by the Central Bank led automatically to its liquidation. Before the 2002 amendment, a court had to find a de-licensed bank to be bankrupt before liquidation could begin, resulting in a large number of phantom banks. Further, the Central Bank does not use its powers to intervene sufficiently early in a troubled bank. The liquidation process is administered by a court-appointed liquidator and has been reported to be extremely slow and non-transparent. Further, the legal priority for household deposits has often been ignored in favour of large creditors and shareholders.

Overall, the existing financial safety net does not seem incentive-compatible, posing significant moral hazard, principal-agent and adverse selection problems. Banks are not thoroughly supervised and shareholders not punished in the case of failures, thus giving them opportunities and incentives for aggressive risk-taking. There does not seem to be a level playing field between banks, given the dual role of the Central Bank as regulator and owner of the largest two banks and the preferential treatment of politically well-connected private banks.

Late intervention, slow liquidation and partial bailouts of shareholders and large creditors create perverse incentives.

While there is currently no industry-wide deposit insurance scheme, the Russian government is preparing for the introduction of such a scheme in the near future. Thus, Russia hopes to increase trust in the financial system, develop financial intermediation, and hence foster economic development. It is also believed that the extension of deposit insurance to all banks would reduce the competitive advantage that the state-owned banks, especially the former savings bank Sberbank, hold over private banks in attracting retail deposits. The scheme would be compulsory for all banks, including Sberbank. The proposal provides for a coverage limit of 95,000 Rubles (around US$3,000), which approximately equals GDP per capita, with a co-insurance of 25 per cent on deposits over 20,000 Rubles. Coverage would be limited to household deposits, but include both Ruble and foreign-exchange accounts. The scheme would be jointly financed by premiums assessed on the banks – 0.6 per cent on covered deposits – and budget support from the government. Management would be public and under guidance from the Central Bank that is also responsible for regulating and supervising the banking system. The scheme would be reduced to a pay-box function, without any role in the supervision of its member banks.

While the limited coverage of the proposed scheme is incentive-compatible, the proposed public management and joint private and public financing increases the risks of political and regulatory capture and poses significant moral hazard risks. The envisaged *ex-ante* accumulation of liquid resources invites political abuse and looting. The lack of any regulatory and supervisory powers *vis-à-vis* its member banks deprives the deposit insurer of any means of minimizing insurance losses by imposing market discipline on banks, while the availability of backup funding by the government decreases the incentives to do so.

Given the extremely weak supervisory and regulatory framework and deficiencies in the bank failure resolution system, the introduction of a deposit insurance scheme at this stage seems premature. The lack of serious supervision and prompt supervisory action means that such a scheme would pose a high risk of moral hazard to the system. In the absence of the necessary market and regulatory discipline, the increased ability that an insurance scheme would give to private banks to attract additional resources would be likely to encourage those banks to lend aggressively and imprudently.

While a deposit insurance scheme has been proposed to level the playing field between government-owned and privately owned banks, the effect of the deposit insurance scheme on the relative competitive position of government-owned *vis-à-vis* private banks depends on a hard-budget constraint being imposed on the government-owned banks, so that they price risk correctly and function according to fully commercial terms.

4.4 Conclusions

This chapter discussed the incentive-compatible design of deposit insurance and bank failure resolution in the context of the overall financial safety net. An incentive-compatible design has to address problems of moral hazard – inherent incentives for banks to take aggressive risks, principal-agent problems between owners and managers of the financial safety as well as the banks and problems of adverse selection of banks. Limited coverage, industry-based funding and management and compulsory membership can reduce moral hazard, principal-agent and adverse selection problems in deposit insurance schemes. Prompt intervention and wiping out equity and, potentially, claims of large creditors, significant financial and organizational involvement of banking sector in the resolution of troubled banks and equal treatment of all banks can minimize these risks in bank failure resolution systems. The effectiveness of deposit insurance and bank failure resolution in reducing the risk of financial fragility does not only depend on the incentive-compatible structure of each, but also on the effective interaction of both. Purchase and assumption techniques exemplify the close interdependence of both, but also the tensions.

The analysis of the financial safety nets in Germany, Brazil and Russia underlines the importance of analysing the whole financial safety net, taking into account the structure of the banking system and the level of institutional development, when assessing deposit insurance schemes and bank failure resolution systems. The structure of the German banking system facilitates a financial safety net with a completely private deposit insurance scheme and a bank failure resolution scheme that relies heavily on financial and organizational support from other banks. While the Brazilian deposit insurance scheme is incentive-compatible in many dimensions, it is not well integrated into the overall financial safety net, and the current system of bank failure resolution that consists mainly of liquidation is inefficient and inadequate for the failure of medium and large banks. The Russian bank failure resolution system, finally, gives perverse incentives to bank owners and managers, by intervening too late and often in favour of shareholders and managers who took the decisions that led to the fragility in the first place. Given these deficiencies and a weak supervisory and institutional framework, the proposed introduction of a deposit insurance scheme seems a risky undertaking that will most probably increase the probability of financial fragility rather than reducing it.

Since a country's financial safety net has to be adapted to a country's level of institutional development and banking structure, one can certainly not simply export Germany's private solution to other, especially developing, countries. However, one can learn certain lessons. First, embedding the financial safety net and its different components in the banking community can reduce principal-agent problems by making banks the managers and owners of the safety net. Second, assessing risk-based premiums based on auditing by the deposit insurer itself helps to align the incentives to banks and deposit insurers and thus minimize moral hazard risk. Finally, while a completely private solution might not be possible, especially in the case of a systemic crisis, a private-public partnership that relies on a completely industry-based solution for non-systemic crises can reduce risks to the financial safety net. A legal prohibition of public depositor protection, as in the cases of Germany and Brazil, not only forces banks to bear the cost of deposit protection, but can also force them to actively participate in bank failure resolution, as the German case shows.

Notes

* The author would like to thank Robert Cull, Augusto de la Torre and participants at the Bank Insolvency Conference of the Bank of Finland for useful comments and discussions. This chapter's findings, interpretations, and conclusions are entirely those of the author and do not necessarily represent the views of the World Bank, its Executive Directors, or the countries they represent.

1. This chapter does not discuss the resolution of systemic banking crises, but rather focuses on the resolution of individual banks.
2. For an overview of the theoretical and empirical literature on deposit insurance, see Demirgüç-Kunt and Kane (2002).
3. For an overview of the literature on deposit insurance pricing, see Laeven (2002b).
4. The deposit insurance scheme of the German commercial banks has the power to exclude members but this has not been applied in the 27 years of its existence (Beck, 2002). Spain's deposit insurance scheme also has the right to expel members in order to coerce failing banks into failure resolution by the deposit insurance scheme (De Juan, undated).
5. See, among others, Kane (1989).
6. For a description of successful and failed deposit insurance schemes in the USA, see Calomiris (1989, 1990) and English (1993).
7. See also Glaessner and Mas (1995) for a discussion of the incentive-compatible design of bank failure resolution schemes.
8. A variant of the purchase and assumption technique is the model of a bridge bank applied to very large banks, where the deposit insurer or another safety

net agent takes over a failing bank for limited time before selling it to another institution.

9. A caveat has to be made here. In countries with weak liquidation systems, unlimited shareholder liability might give them perverse incentives to prolong the liquidation process, without the benefits of recovering additional resources, as the example of Brazil shows.
10. Calomiris and Powell (2000) discuss the effects of introducing a subordinated debt requirement in Argentina.
11. Insolvent banks betting on resurrection often try to attract additional liquidity from depositors by raising interest rates, thus distorting competition in the banking system. The improper resolution of a troubled bank can result in widespread depositor run and decrease in debtor discipline.
12. Barth *et al.* (2003) show the importance of private monitoring for reducing the risk of financial fragility and financial development.
13. This is more stringent than the less-cost criterion, which only requires a resolution that is less than the cost of a liquidation and reimbursement of all depositors and creditors, including uninsured ones.
14. The respective share in total banking assets in 1999 were 36 per cent for the savings banks, 25 per cent for the commercial banks and 13 per cent for the cooperative banks. See Beck (2002).
15. For more details on the German deposit insurance schemes, see Beck (2002).
16. Given that the average equity size of a commercial bank was 295.5 million in 2000, the average limit is around 90 million or 300 times GDP per capita.
17. Laeven (2002a) finds that, out of a sample of 12 countries, German banks take the lowest risk. The chapter by Granlund in this volume also shows that German banks face the smallest spreads in raising market finance among the major markets.
18. The failure of Schmidtbank, another small private bank, is a more recent example. In 2001, the supervisory authorities forced the shareholders to sell the bank for one euro to the four major private banks and the regional Landesbank.
19. Only a few small banks do not participate in the private deposit insurance scheme. However, they are still subject to mandatory limited deposit insurance according to the EU mandate.
20. There is a trade-off in the optimal number of participating banks in a deposit insurance scheme, between diversification, requiring a large number of banks, and monitoring and disciplining, working better with a small number of banks.
21. See Lundberg (1999) for a historic and technical overview over the Brazilian financial safety net.
22. While the coverage has been constant in local currency, the devaluation has continuously reduced the coverage in US dollar terms.
23. A change in statutes approved in late 2002 includes interbank and insider deposits in the coverage.
24. The statutes have to be approved by the National Monetary Council, a body including the Central Bank governor and the Minister of Finance among others.
25. The German Banking Association and the Auditing Association contract auditors for any audit.
26. See de la Torre (2000) for a detailed analysis of the Argentine model.
27. See Chapters 5, 10, 11 and 12 in World Bank (2002).

5

Small Countries, Large Multi-Country Banks: A Challenge to Supervisors – the Example of the Nordic-Baltic Area

*Jón Sigurðsson**

The experience of the Nordic-Baltic region in recent years provides an excellent illustration of the way that the developments of the banking system and financial markets have outgrown the traditional country-based system of regulation and concern. The size, complexity, inter-relational and multinational character of the banking system means that not only is the problem of TBTF writ large but it is not clear whether the authorities are in a position to handle a major failure should it occur. Indeed the problem is in many respects the reverse of what is traditionally understood. Traditional thinking was that society could not afford the costs of failure and hence the authorities would choose to bail out a bank in difficulty. Now the concern is that the banks are so large and complex compared with the individual countries that society could not afford to bail them out. They are thus in a real sense 'too big to save' (TBTS).

Sections 5.1 to 5.3 document the structure of the banking system in the Nordic-Baltic region and how it has become increasingly concentrated and multinational. Sections 5.4 to 5.6 go on to show the challenge this poses for supervisors and suggest how the challenge might be met in order to reduce the systemic risk to acceptable levels.

5.1 The structure of banking in the Nordic-Baltic region

The past two decades have brought home to us in no uncertain manner the impact of financial market liberalization and technological change on banking world-wide. Increased competitive pressures, declining barriers to entry and the emergence of new suppliers of financial services, free flow of capital across borders, changes in regulation and prudential supervision and financial innovation – all of these combined with technological change have greatly affected the structure of the banking sector. Developments in the banking systems of the five Nordic countries offer striking examples of the consolidation – both domestic and cross-border – that has been the response to these drivers of change. The Nordic countries – Denmark, Finland, Iceland, Norway and Sweden – have seen a dramatic reduction in the number of banks and branch offices and in banking employment since the pre-deregulation peak of Nordic banking in the 1980s (Figures 5.1–5.3 and Tables 5.1–5.4).[1]

More recently, banking in the three Baltic countries – Estonia, Latvia and Lithuania – has followed suit. In the early 1990s, after these countries had regained their independence following the dissolution of the Soviet Union, there was a flurry of bank establishments. By 1993 they all had a large number of banks – especially considering the small size of their economies – succeeding the mono-banks of the communist era. But during the last ten years the number of banks in the Baltic region has been reduced drastically, while the number of foreign-owned banks has increased strongly, as have their market shares (Figures 5.4–5.5 and Tables 5.5–5.6); see Bonin and Wachtel (2002, pp. 53–4).

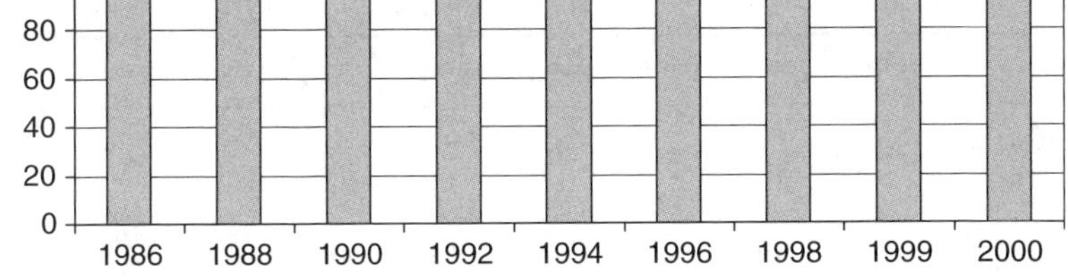

Figure 5.1 Number of commercial banks in the Nordic countries
Source: National banking statistics.

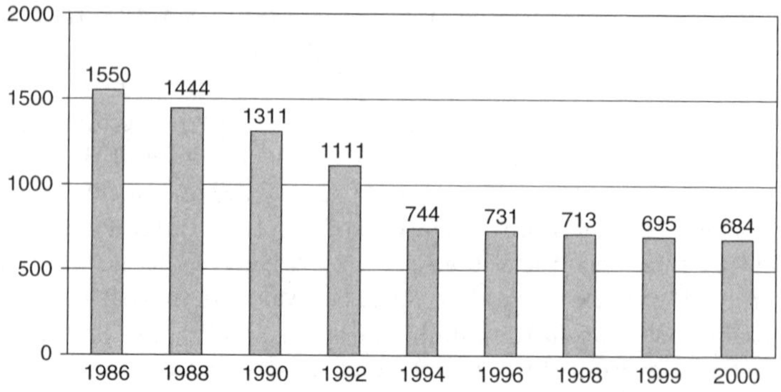

Figure 5.2 Number of savings banks and cooperative banks in the Nordic countries
Source: National banking statistics.

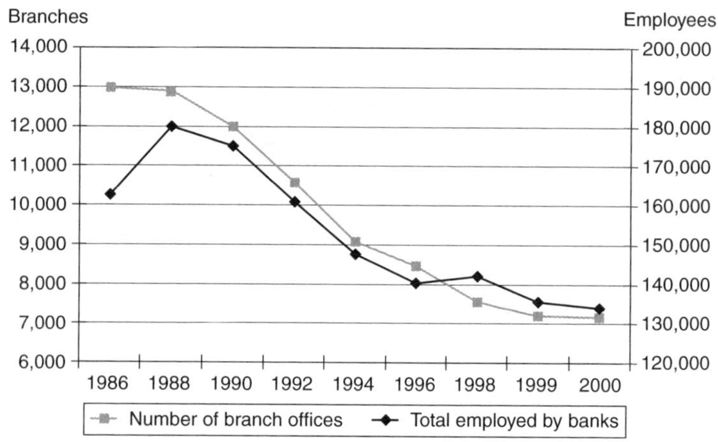

Figure 5.3 Bank branches and employment in the banking sector of the Nordic countries
Source: National banking statistics.

Table 5.1 Number of commercial banks in the Nordic countries

	1986	1988	1990	1992	1994	1996	1998	1999	2000
Denmark	70	74	71	67	61	61	57	64	64
Finland	10	10	14	15	14	11	9	9	8
Iceland	7	7	3	3	4	4	4	4	4
Norway	23	19	14	13	13	16	14	13	13
Sweden	20	21	21	26	16	16	16	20	24
Total	130	131	123	124	108	108	100	110	113

Source: National banking statistics.

Table 5.2 Number of savings banks and cooperative banks in the Nordic countries

	1986	1988	1990	1992	1994	1996	1998	1999	2000
Denmark	201	176	162	152	150	138	138	124	121
Finland	611	578	488	370	342	341	329	329	326
Iceland	38	34	32	33	30	30	26	25	25
Norway	192	158	142	134	132	133	133	131	130
Sweden	508	498	487	422	90	89	87	86	82
Total	1,550	1,444	1,311	1,111	744	731	713	695	684

Source: National banking statistics.

Table 5.3 Number of branches (all deposit banks) in the Nordic countries

	1986	1988	1990	1992	1994	1996	1998	1999	2000
Denmark	3,642	3,571	3,333	2,798	2,452	2,413	2,369	2,188	2,197
Finland	3,537	3,517	3,302	2,817	2,151	1,720	1,591	1,524	1,550
Iceland	174	180	175	178	178	177	187	184	180
Norway	2,138	2,166	1,885	1,661	1,378	1,537	1,568	1,483	1,472
Sweden	3,490	3,468	3,290	3,125	2,911	2,612	1,850	1,819	1,756
Total	12,981	12,902	11,985	10,579	9,070	8,459	7,565	7,198	7,155

Source: National banking statistics.

5.2 Concentration in the Nordic-Baltic banking sector

The rapid pace of consolidation in recent years has led to increasing concentration in the banking sector of the Nordic-Baltic area. Measured as a percentage of total bank lending to the private sector, the share of the three largest banks in each of the Nordic countries rose markedly (as shown in Figure 5.6 and Tables 5.7–5.8).

While this statistical yardstick may have its limitations as a true indicator of concentration, due to changes in the structure of the financial sector, it is abundantly clear that by any criterion the degree of concentration in the financial sector on a national basis is very high in the five Nordic countries. This is true in a double sense, as not only is the banking sector in each country dominated by a very limited number of banks, but its lending is historically concentrated on domestic industry, and furthermore, in some of the countries at least, on lending to relatively few companies. This implies that the stability of the banking

Table 5.4 Number of employees (all deposit banks) in the Nordic countries

	1986	1988	1990	1992	1994	1996	1998	1999	2000
Denmark	49,744	50,793	49,466	47,560	45,465	42,850	43,081	40,018	40,907
Finland	42,690	51,749	50,088	42,225	36,175	28,100	29,260	28,245	29,496
Iceland	2,894	3,080	2,831	2,725	2,572	2,552	2,810	3,016	3,158
Norway	29,267	33,400	31,200	23,935	23,168	24,441	22,965	22,300	21,513
Sweden	38,056	40,882	41,337	44,323	40,230	42,368	43,970	42,077	38,832
Total	162,651	179,904	174,922	160,768	147,610	140,311	142,086	135,656	133,906

Source: National banking statistics.

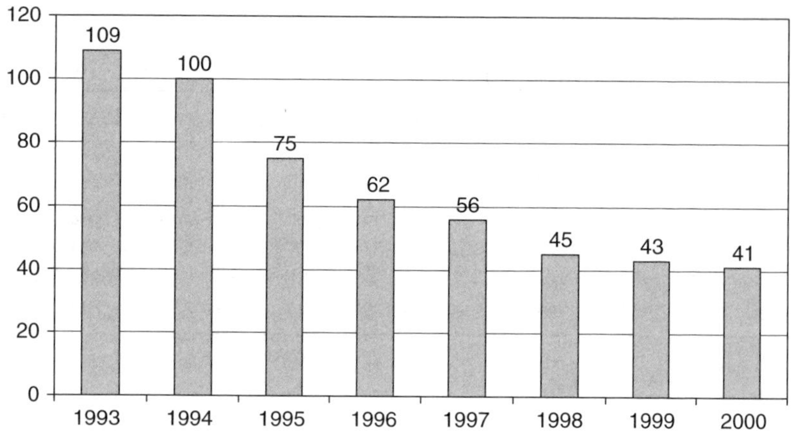

Figure 5.4 Number of banks in the Baltic countries
Source: Bonin and Wachtel, 2002.

system rests on very few banks and is at the same time vulnerable to fluctuations in each country's economy. The latter source of potential instability may have been mitigated somewhat by the creation of multi-country banks within the region. This effect, however, is undoubtedly weakened by the fact that there has also been a strong trend towards cross-border mergers and acquisitions in the industrial sector of the region – that is, among the banks' borrowers – during the last decade. It is also worth noting that the cyclical behaviour of the countries of the region is similar, due to similarities in resource base, international trade patterns, capital and investment linkages, as well as economic and social systems. Consequently, the diversification effect of multi-country banking within the region may not be very strong.

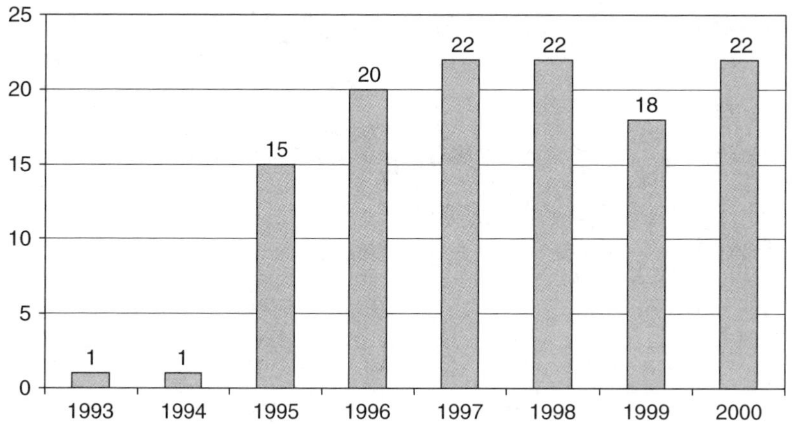

Figure 5.5 Number of foreign-owned banks in the Baltic countries
Source: Bonin and Wachtel, 2002.

Table 5.5 Number of banks in the Baltic countries (all deposit banks)

	1992	1993	1994	1995	1996	1997	1998	1999	2000
Estonia	–	21	22	18	15	12	6	7	7
Latvia	–	62	56	42	35	32	27	23	21
Lithuania	–	26	22	15	12	12	12	13	13
Total	–	109	100	75	62	56	45	43	41

Source: Bonin and Wachtel, 2002.

Table 5.6 Number of foreign-owned banks in the Baltic countries (all deposit banks)

	1992	1993	1994	1995	1996	1997	1998	1999	2000
Estonia	–	1	1	4	3	3	2	2	4
Latvia	–	–	–	11	14	15	15	12	12
Lithuania	–	0	0	0	3	4	5	4	6
Total	–	1	1	15	20	22	22	18	22

Source: Bonin and Wachtel 2002.

The share of the three biggest banks in each of the three Baltic countries in total commercial bank lending to the private sector has risen strongly over the last five years (Figure 5.7). In Estonia this figure was 65 per cent in 1996, rising to 91 per cent in 2001. For Latvia and

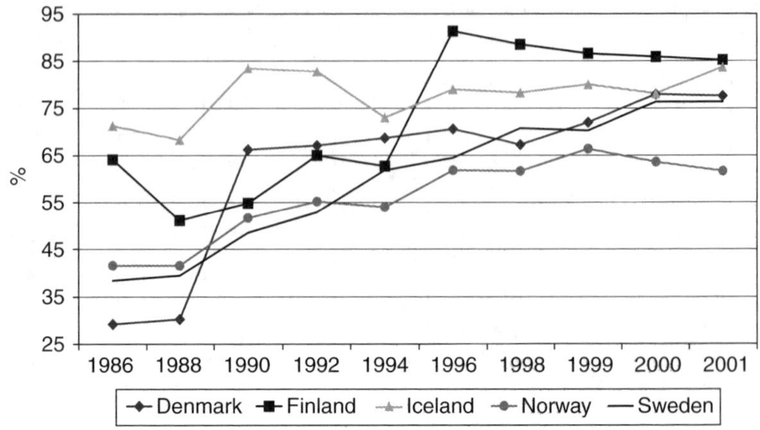

Figure 5.6 Concentration in the banking sector of the Nordic countries: market share of the three largest banks in each country (% of total lending to the private sector)

Source: BankScope and national banking statistics.

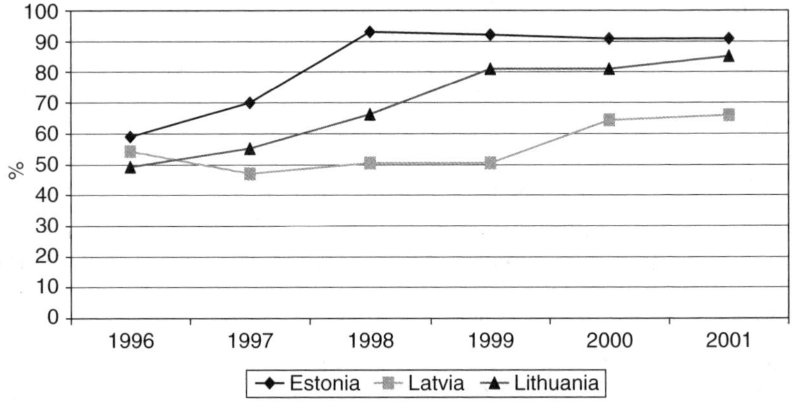

Figure 5.7 Concentration in the banking sector of the Baltic countries: market share of the three largest banks in each country (% of total lending to the private sector)

Source: BankScope.

Table 5.7 Market share of the three largest banks in each Nordic country (% of total lending to private sector)

	1986	1988	1990	1992	1994	1996	1998	1999	2000	2001
Denmark	29.1	30.2	66.1	67.1	68.6	70.5	67.3	72.0	77.8	77.5
Finland	64.1	51.2	54.9	65.0	62.7	91.4	88.6	86.6	85.9	85.2
Iceland	71.3	68.3	83.4	82.7	73.0	79.0	78.3	80.0	78.1	83.7
Norway	41.6	41.6	51.6	55.2	54.0	61.8	61.6	66.4	63.6	61.6
Sweden	38.5	39.4	48.6	53.0	61.8	64.5	70.8	70.2	76.3	76.3

Source: BankScope and national banking statistics.

Table 5.8 Market share of the three largest banks in each Baltic country (% of total lending to private sector)

	1996	1997	1998	1999	2000	2001
Estonia	59.0	70.0	93.0	92.0	91.0	91.0
Latvia	54.1	47.1	50.5	50.4	64.4	65.9
Lithuania	49.2	55.1	66.3	81.2	80.9	85.2

Source: BankScope.

Lithuania the corresponding statistics were 54 and 50 per cent, respectively, in 1996, but 66 and 86 per cent, respectively, in 2001. So the degree of concentration is even higher in some of the Baltic countries than in the Nordic area.

Another way of looking at concentration is to compare the total assets of the largest banks with the GDP of the country of operations or the legal domicile of the banking group's headquarters. For the five Nordic countries these numbers show a very significant increase in the concentration of exposure to risk of bank failures for the national financial safety nets of the region (Tables 5.9 and 5.10).

The total assets of the single largest bank in Sweden had increased from 32 per cent of GDP in 1994 to 105 per cent in 2001, if the comparison is based on the balance sheet and domicile of the group's holding company, but to 54 per cent in 2001, if based on Sweden's share in the single largest bank's operations. In Denmark the comparable increase was even greater for the largest bank, namely from 37 per cent in 1994 to 116 per cent of GDP in 2001 (Figures 5.8 and 5.9). These figures are, of course, only intended to indicate orders of magnitude in relation to economic activity in each country and should not be regarded as a measure of risk in particular cases.

In the Baltic region, the size of the largest bank relative to GDP of the country of operation has also increased dramatically since the

Table 5.9 Largest bank in each Nordic country: total assets relative to GDP of home country of parent company (%)

	1994	1995	1996	1997	1998	1999	2000	2001
Denmark	36.9	43.5	45.7	47.0	51.3	57.7	106.0	115.7
Finland	28.6	46.9	44.7	46.6	43.8	43.8	46.5	44.3
Iceland	24.8	25.5	24.5	22.5	27.7	36.7	44.5	46.8
Norway	17.9	18.8	19.9	19.2	20.9	27.2	24.1	24.6
Sweden	31.7	33.9	35.0	44.8	49.6	46.6	50.3	54.3

Source: BankScope and *International Financial Statistics Yearbook 2002.*

Table 5.10 Largest bank in each Nordic country: total assets relative to GDP on the basis of country of operations (%)

	1994	1995	1996	1997	1998	1999	2000	2001
Denmark	36.9	43.5	45.7	47.0	51.3	57.7	106.0	115.7
Finland	28.6	46.9	44.7	46.6	20.1	23.4	20.6	22.2
Iceland	24.8	25.5	24.5	22.5	27.7	36.7	44.5	46.8
Norway	17.9	18.8	19.9	19.2	20.9	27.2	24.1	24.6
Sweden	31.7	33.9	35.0	44.8	49.6	44.4	94.3	105.0

Source: BankScope and *International Financial Statistics Yearbook 2002.*

mid-1990s (Figure 5.10, Table 5.11). In the case of Estonia, for instance, the largest bank's balance sheet shows a total increase from 9 per cent of GDP in 1995 to 76 per cent in 2001.

It is obvious that exposure to big bank failures and consequently to systemic risk has increased dramatically throughout the Nordic-Baltic area.

5.3 Corporate structure of the largest banks

The process of consolidation has not only led to concentration. It has also led to the creation of large and complex financial institutions, with both cross-sector and cross-border characteristics.

Looking at the corporate structure of the three largest banks in each country of the Nordic-Baltic region, we find that in all eight countries, except Iceland, at least one or two of the three biggest banks – and indeed in six of the countries, the biggest bank – belong to a multi-country banking group with the parent of the group having its legal domicile in one of the Nordic countries.

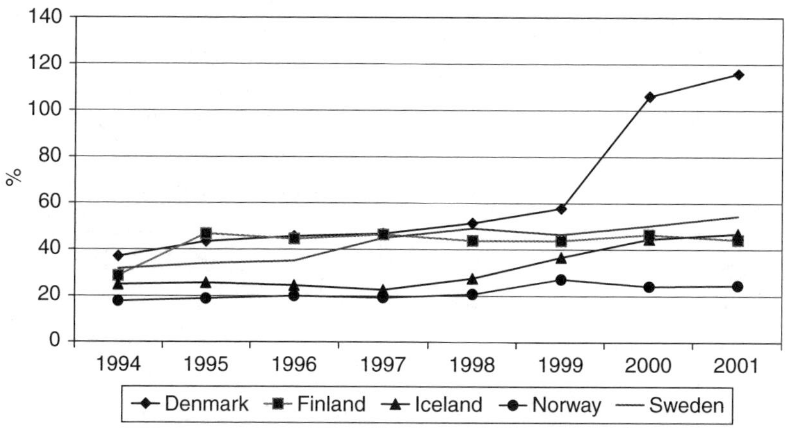

Figure 5.8 Concentration in the banking sector of the Nordic countries: largest bank by country of operation (total assets relative to GDP (%))

Source: BankScope and *International Financial Statistics Yearbook 2002.*

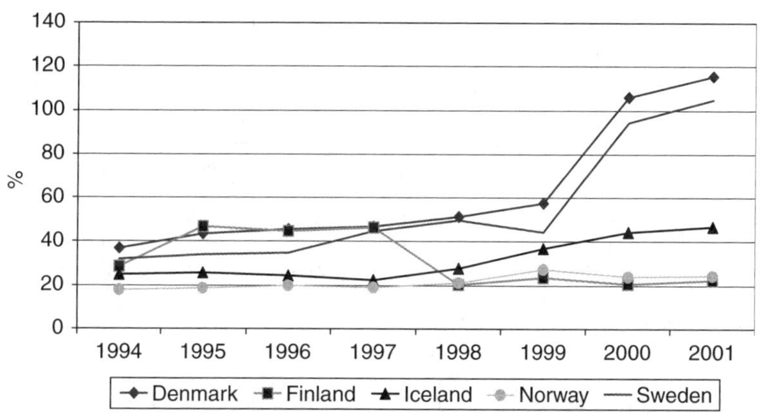

Figure 5.9 Concentration in the banking sector of the Nordic countries: largest bank by parent company (total assets relative to GDP of home country (%))

Source: BankScope and *International Financial Statistics Yearbook 2002.*

Using the terminology of Liuksila in Chapter 2, we have clear examples of both kinds of complex groupings in our Nordic-Baltic sample of the largest banks in these countries:

(a) a bank that consists of a head office and domestic as well as cross-border branches subject to the concurrent jurisdiction of two or

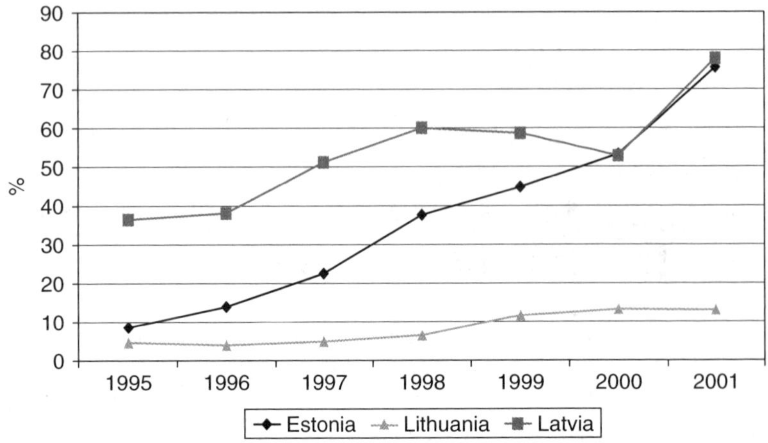

Figure 5.10 Concentration in the banking sector of the Baltic countries: largest bank (total assets relative to GDP (%))

Source: BankScope and *International Financial Statistics Year Book 2002.*

Table 5.12 Largest bank in each Baltic country: total assets relative to GDP of home country (%)

	1995	1996	1997	1998	1999	2000	2001
Estonia	8.5	14.0	22.5	37.7	44.9	53.4	75.6
Latvia	4.8	4.0	4.8	6.5	11.6	13.1	12.9
Lithuania	36.5	38.1	51.2	60.0	58.8	52.8	78.0

Source: BankScope and *International Financial Statistics Yearbook 2002.*

several countries, even if it forms, from the point of view of the home country, a single corporate structure under centralized management. This could be instanced with Svenska Handelsbanken, even though its structure also includes a holding company element.

(b) a grouping consisting of a dominant legal entity and one or more dependent but separate legal entities (for example, banks that are run as limited companies) in more than one country's jurisdiction, consolidated by means of a centralized management. This kind of grouping may form a banking concern consisting of a holding company, subsidiaries and affiliates, which in turn may have branches domestically and cross-border. The Nordea Group illustrates this kind of grouping.

As Liuksila has pointed out, the distinction between these two kinds of structure may, indeed, be a distinction without a difference in economic terms, but when it comes to dealing with insolvency or near-insolvency of banks under current national and, where applicable, EEA regimes, there are differences that may create difficulties for depositors, other creditors, shareholders and the relevant authorities. Due to the high degree of concentration in the financial sector of the Nordic-Baltic area, the authorities of these countries are faced with the prospect of having to deal with insolvencies or near-insolvencies of a number of bank-assurance groups that would be systemic on their own, either nationally or even for the Nordic-Baltic region as a whole. We have in effect moved from national to regional financial markets, without creating a corresponding regional version of national regulation or national safety nets. This is in fact true of the whole of the EU/EEA area, with significant consequences in extreme situations, such as in the event of reorganization or winding-up of financial institutions, even if the countries in question all belong to the EU or the EEA, as the case may be. All five Nordic countries belong to the EU/EEA area and the three Baltic countries will soon join the EU.

The national supervisory authorities have developed and enhanced their cooperation to ensure effective execution of supervision and corrective action in the increasingly integrated financial system of the region, but it is important to come to grips with the inadequacies of the present EU/EEA system of supervision based on the concept of home country supervisory responsibility and reciprocal recognition of national legislation. It may not be enough for the national supervisors to enter into *ad hoc* memoranda of understanding to deal with cross-border banks' supervision if the final responsibility for dealing with ailing or insolvent banks is unclear.

The existence of a number of cross-border banks may have increased the gap between the costs and benefits of intervention for national supervisors and central banks. This is worrisome for the smallest countries of the region if branches or affiliates of foreign banks account for a large share of their domestic banking system. Here the home country supervisor and central bank might be willing to accept liquidation without fully considering the systemic consequences for the host country. For some of the Baltic banking systems this might be a cause for concern.

The widespread market perception is that all liabilities of EU/EEA banks – possibly with the exception of their equity – will *de facto* be guaranteed by the government or even by two or more governments in the case of multi-country banks. This market perception needs to be corrected, and there is also a need for clarity in defining which authorities should deal with reorganization, exit and liquidation of ailing or insolvent banks, and in what manner. While there may be a role for constructive ambiguity regarding the role of the lender of last resort, and in answering the question who will pay for bank insolvencies, there is a pressing need to clear up a number of questions in this connection.

5.4 Improving supervision

The blanks in the map of the current EU/EEA regime identified by Mayes, Halme and Liuksila, and the proposals they make for addressing these problems, constitute a valuable input into the ongoing debate on the development of the regulatory environment for banking within the EU/EEA; see Mayes *et al.* (2001).

There is undoubtedly increasing taxpayer resistance in EU/EEA countries to bailouts from the public treasury to rescue ailing banks. The ongoing process of privatization in the financial sector has strengthened this trend. It is worth noting that before the Nordic banking crisis in the early 1990s governments held a relatively low share of the banking sector's equity. As a consequence of government rescue efforts, the public share in the bank sector's equity was temporarily increased. This has since been reversed through privatization. If there is extensive public ownership, the line between shareholders and governments is blurred when it comes to decisions on government intervention and support for the banking sector (Sigurðsson, 1995, pp. 4–6).

Another important element in this connection is that the scope for governments to provide risk capital support for banks is now limited by the watch kept by the EU/EEA on state aid in the EU/EEA area. The introduction of the euro also means that, within the Eurozone, measures for supporting single national banking systems to protect their national currency reserves are ruled out. While not directly applicable to non-EMU EU countries, this may also affect the scope for such actions by their governments. This means that blanket state support for whole national banking systems, such as was provided in Norway, Sweden and Finland in the early 1990s, may be a thing of the past (Andrews *et al.*,

2002, p. 29). This makes it all the more important to clarify the relevant codes of law, regulations and directives. In some parts, the present policy-based regime needs to be replaced with binding rules. It seems clear that harmonization and reciprocal recognition of national legislation leaves too many unanswered questions. Proper conditionality for official support for reorganization, exit and winding up of banks, burden-sharing and ranking of claims among stakeholders, the access to all the assets of a banking concern whether domestic or cross-border in a reorganization, and the 'reorganization hair-cut' of various claims are of particular importance.

The legal difficulties in drafting and implementing a special insolvency procedure for banks separate from the general bankruptcy legislation for companies should not, however, be underestimated, not least because of the fluid state of the corporate structures of the financial services sector.

It is important that public funds should not be used to bail out shareholders of failed or failing banks. The problem of cross-country subsidization also needs to be addressed explicitly. In all of this, cross-border cooperation is needed but may not be enough. A carefully considered balance between deposit guarantee schemes and the provisions on bank failure resolution is an important ingredient in the financial safety net. A balance needs to be struck between proper consumer protection for depositors to avoid runs on banks on the one hand, and the prevention of aggressive risk-taking by banks on the other. The safety net must avoid fostering moral hazard. In the final analysis this may require more than harmonization of national legislation.[2] It may call for common rules and institutionalization for the whole of the EU/EEA area. This is important not only in the interest of sound macroeconomic management but also for the protection of the legal rights of individual depositors and other creditors of European banks.

5.5 Importance of capital markets

The European financial system is evolving from a system dominated by banks to one relying more on direct access to capital markets for credit and other forms of capital provision. This may lead to greater volatility in interest rates and asset prices and financial flows, which is not necessarily a source of instability as it opens up possibilities of market adjustment instead of collapse of banks. But this volatility may also occasionally give rise to serious banking problems. The other significant trend is the internationalization of banking activities with an increasing share of cross-border transactions in the interbank payments system. Both of these trends are important in the process of consolidation. Both indicate channels of transmission of potential financial instabilities. The focus of supervision needs to be on these areas deriving from cross-border consolidation. This means paying particular attention to short-term interbank loan exposures and cross-border transfers and derivatives exposures.

The concerns raised by the authors of *Improving Banking Supervision* (Mayes *et al.*, 2001), concerning the lack of clarity regarding final, legal responsibility for bank liabilities are relevant for the everyday activities of banks, in their lending as well as their operations in the bond and derivatives markets, and not only in extreme situations such as the resolution of bank failures. A particular, fairly recent, characteristic of European banking is that the banks are themselves the largest borrowers from the bond markets and they themselves or their subsidiaries are the most important distributors of bonds and derivative products. To take currency and interest rate swaps as an example – instruments used in risk management by all modern banks – the same problems arise when it comes to assigning ultimate responsibility for the counterparty in swap agreements. This is of great significance for the possibilities for 'netting' of such exposures among different parts of banking groups. Greater clarity in EU/EEA directives and legislation on the role and responsibilities of banking groups with cross-border characteristics would facilitate secure derivatives trading and ease 'netting' as well as the use of collateral agreements on a Europe-wide standard. Such a standard needs to be based on a reliable and clear mechanism for the resolution of bank insolvencies that is capable of dealing with the realities of corporate structures in today's financial markets.

There is a need to step back and look at the corporate structures in the financial sector and the laws and directives that shape them within the EU/EEA area. There might be a case for an EU/EEA directive on the company structures that are allowed for holders of banking licences within the EU/EEA area, before accommodating legislation is drafted for the structures that have emerged. Is there perhaps a case for European rather than national financial services companies? A directive on the creation of European companies has been under discussion for a long time within the EU without any conclusion so far (Werlauff, 1998, pp. 19–28).

5.6 Systemic risk

Complex corporate structures can be a source of systemic risk. Because of capital adequacy and other regulatory requirements that are costly, banks have securitized and sold part of their loan books. Banks are also trying to shield themselves from bad debt by selling credit exposure to other financial institutions, insurance companies, hedge funds etc. But they may not be able to discard these risks in the end. There are limits to the extent the banking system can change from being the originator and holder of credit risk to becoming the originator and distributor of credit risk in concentrated and consolidated banking systems. Banks may in the end have to provide liquidity to the investing institutions that have taken on credit risks from the banks. A bank belonging to the same financial services group as an insurance company or an asset management firm that has taken on credit derivatives from banks may be hit in the end. What goes around comes around. Shortcircuiting of this kind can turn out to be a source of systemic risk. A system-wide supervisory focus on banking risk needs to take this into account to be macro-prudential. The micro-prudential approach to supervision is best organized by a sharp focus on depositor protection. The focus for supervision in today's cross-border financial markets needs to be more on systemic risk and on reactions of international bank creditors and derivatives markets to bank ailments. Current accounting, auditing and regulatory regimes may, unfortunately, not be well equipped to deal with the explosion of financial engineering that has taken place in recent years. The ideas put forward by Mayes *et al.* (2001) are a welcome contribution to the discussion on how to improve banking supervision to meet the needs of today's open financial markets in a fiscally responsible manner.

Appendix: deposit guarantee schemes in the Nordic and Baltic countries

Table A1 Deposit guarantee schemes in the Nordic countries

	Denmark	Finland	Iceland	Norway	Sweden
Institutions	**THE GUARANTEE FUND FOR DEPOSITORS AND INVESTORS** (GARANTIFONDEN FOR INDSKYDERE OG INVESTORER) (established in 1987)	**DEPOSIT GUARANTEE FUND** (TALLETUSSUOJARAHASTO, INSÄTTNINGSGARANTIFONDEN) (established in 1998)	**DEPOSITORS' AND INVESTORS' GUARANTEE FUND** (TRYGGINGARSJOÐUR INNSTÆÐUEIGENDA OG FJÁRFESTA) (established in 2000)	**COMMERCIAL BANKS' GUARANTEE FUND**, CGBF (FORETNINGSBANKENES SIKRINGSFOND) (established in 1961) **SAVINGS BANKS' GUARANTEE FUND**, SBGF (SPAREBANKENES SIKRINGSFOND) (established in 1961)	**DEPOSIT GUARANTEE BOARD** (INSÄTTNINGSGARANTI-NÄMNDEN) (The Bank Support Authority, 'Bankstödsnämnden', was converted into the Deposit Guarantee Board as of 1.7.1996)
Coverage	All deposit banks, mortgage banks and investment companies operating in Denmark. The scheme also covers banks on the Faeroe Islands and Greenland and branches of credit institutions from other (non-EU) countries. Branches of a credit institution authorized in another EU or EEA country are covered by the support scheme if the branches have joined the Fund. The scheme covers a customer's registered cash deposits with banks, cash amounts in mortgage institutions and investment companies relating to investment services.	All deposit banks operating in Finland must be members of the Deposit Guarantee Fund. A credit institution authorized in an EEA country may apply for membership for its branch in Finland in order to supplement the cover provided by the institution's home country. In respect of branches of non-EEA institutions, the Ministry of Finance decides on the membership. The scheme covers deposits held by private persons, companies, foundations and public bodies in member banks and their foreign branches as well as in branches of foreign banks, provided these have joined the guarantee scheme.	The scheme covers deposits in all deposit banks and companies offering investment services in Iceland as well as their foreign branches. Furthermore the scheme covers subsidiaries of foreign banks operating in Iceland.	All deposit banks operating in Norway must be members of a Deposit Guarantee Fund. A credit institution authorized in an EEA country may apply for membership for its branch in Norway in order to supplement the cover provided by the institution's home country.	The scheme covers deposits (nominal balances available to the depositor at short notice) with Swedish banks or securities companies licensed to take deposits as well as with their branches in other EEA countries. Upon application the Board may decide that the scheme shall cover deposits with a branch of a Swedish institution outside the EEA or with a branch of a foreign institution operating in Sweden.
Limits on deposits covered	Max. DKK300,000 (net) for each customer.	Max. €25,000 for each customer and institution. Banks wholly or partly responsible for each other's commitments or liabilities are treated as one bank (the group of cooperative banks).	Minimum ISK1.7 million (€20,000) for each customer. No upper limit for the compensation as long as the Fund's assets are sufficient.	At least NOK2,000,000 for each customer and institution.	Max. SEK250,000 for each customer and institution.

Funding	The capital of the Fund comprises cash contributions and guarantees from the members of the Fund as well as accumulated profits. The Fund is divided into three departments. The total capital must be at least DKK 3.2 billion.	The Fund is financed through annual fees payable by the member banks. The annual fee comprises a fixed fee of 0.5% of the institution's covered deposits and a fee that varies depending on the institution's capital adequacy. The latter fee amounts to a maximum of 0.25% of the institution's covered deposits. When the net assets of the Fund amount to 2% of the aggregate deposits covered by the scheme the fees may be lowered to 1/3 and when net assets amount to 10% the collection of fees may be suspended.	Fees from the institutions. The assets of the Fund shall amount to a minimum of 1% of the average deposits for the previous year. The annual fees depend on whether the fund shows a surplus or deficit. However, the fee may amount to a maximum of 0.15% of the aggregate guaranteed deposits of the institutions.	Fees from the members. The total annual fee is (a) a fixed fee of 0.1% of the institution's deposits covered by the scheme and (b) a fee of at least 0.5% of the risk-weighted balance of the institution. The fees are determined taking into consideration *inter alia* the capital adequacy ratio (Tier 1) of the institutions. The capital of the Funds must amount to at least 1.5% of the aggregate deposits covered by the scheme and 0.5% of the risk-weighted assets.	Fees from the institutions. The annual fee is 0.1% of the institution's deposits covered by the scheme if the fees in total amount to a sum that is the equivalent of at least 2.5% of the aggregate deposits covered by the scheme. If this level is not reached, the annual fees will be charged at a percentage that is necessary in order to reach this level, however in the range of a minimum of 0.1% and a maximum of 0.3%. The fees are determined taking into consideration *inter alia* the capital adequacy ratio of the institutions.
Financial position	By the end of 2001 the assets of the fund amounted to DKK3.37 billion, which was approximately 0.94% of the aggregate net deposits under the scheme (DKK360 billion).	By the end of 2001 the assets of the fund amounted to €189.7 million, which was approximately 0.6% of the aggregate deposits under the scheme (€32.3 billion). By the end of 2002 the assets of the fund amounted to €236.2 million.	By the end of 2002 the assets of the Fund amounted to ISK3.233 million, which was 0.8975% of the average guaranteed deposits for the previous year.	By the end of 2001 the capital of CBGF amounted to NOK3.02 billion, which was approximately 1.2% of the deposits covered by the scheme (31.12.2000). By the end of 2001 the capital of SBGF amounted to NOK5.9 billion, which was approximately 2.8% of the deposits covered by the scheme (31.12.2000).	By the end of 2001 the assets of the Board amounted to SEK11.1 billion, which was the equivalent of approximately 2.6% of the aggregate deposits under the scheme (SEK428.2 billion). By the end of 2002 the aggregate assets stood at SEK12.3 billion.
Covering of funding shortfalls	If the Fund's financial resources for compensation, in any of the three departments, are not sufficient, the departments may borrow from one another up to certain limits. If that is not sufficient the Fund may finance itself through external loans. Such loans may be guaranteed by the Minister of Economic Affairs.	If the Fund's financial resources for compensation are not sufficient the Fund may borrow from the member banks. Member banks are obliged to grant loans to the Fund.	If the Fund's financial resources for compensation are not sufficient the member institutions are obliged to issue a 'declaration of liability'. The declaration may amount to a maximum of 1/10 of the Fund's assets. The Fund is also allowed to borrow money.	Shortfalls in the Funds are guaranteed by the members.	If the Board's financial resources for compensation are not sufficient, the Board may borrow from the National Debt Office (Riksgäldskontoret).

Sources: The deposit guarantee institutions and the national financial supervision agencies.

Table A2 Deposit guarantee schemes in the Baltic countries

	Estonia	Latvia	Lithuania
Institution	**DEPOSIT GUARANTEE FUND** (TAGATISFOND) (established 1998)	**DEPOSIT GUARANTEE FUND** (NOGULDĪJUMU GARANTIJU FONDA) (established 1998)	**DEPOSIT AND INVESTMENT INSURANCE STATE COMPANY** (INDÉLU IR INVESTICIJŲ DRAUDIMAS) (established 1996)
Coverage	The Fund shall guarantee and compensate the deposits taken by credit institutions and Estonian branches of foreign credit institutions registered in Estonia. Deposits of a branch shall not be guaranteed if the deposits of the branch are guaranteed by a guarantee scheme of the home country of the branch to the same or higher level than prescribed by the Guarantee Fund Act. The Fund shall compensate for the guaranteed deposits together with the interest to the extent of 90% in every credit institution.	All commercial banks, foreign bank branches and credit unions operating in Latvia. (Credit unions as from 1.1.2003.) The scheme covers private and legal persons' (legal persons as from 1.1.2003) deposits in Latvian banks, credit unions and foreign bank branches in Latvia unless they have a similar or better guarantee scheme in their country of origin. Branches of Latvian credit institutions abroad if there is no similar or better guarantee scheme in the host country.	Deposits are insured by commercial banks, branches of foreign banks and credit unions. The scheme covers private and legal persons' deposits in Lithuanian credit institutions and foreign credit institutions with branches in Lithuania unless they have a similar or better guarantee scheme in their country of origin.

Limits on deposits covered	Max: EEK20,000 before 1.1.2000 EEK40,000 from 1.1.2000 EEK100,000 from 31.12.2003 EEK200,000 from 31.12.2005 EUR20,000 from 31.12.2007	Max: LVL500 before 31.12.1999 LVL1,000 1.1.2000–31.12.2001 LVL3,000 1.1.2002–31.12.2003 LVL6,000 1.1.2004–31.12.2005 LVL9,000 1.1.2006–31.12.2007 LVL13,000 from 1.1.2008	Max: LTL45,000 before 31.12.2003 LTL50,000 from 1.1.2004 LTL60,000 from 1.1.2007 EUR20,000 from 1.1.2008
Funding	Credit institutions make a single payment of EEK50,000 as the banking licence is granted. Quarterly paid fee 0.125% of the guaranteed deposits (fees in 1998–2001 0.124%; in 2002 0.1% and from 2003 0.07%). The Fund may suspend the collection of quarterly fees if the assets of the Fund are at least 3% of the total amount of deposits guaranteed.	A licensed bank pays a single initial payment of LVL50,000 and 0.5% of average balance of the guaranteed deposit quarterly (till 1.1.2003 payment was 0.075% of average private person deposits). A credit union single initial payment is LVL100 (and 0.05% quarterly payment).	Fees from the member institutions. Annual fees: (1) Commercial banks 0.45% of the average deposit amount. (2) Other credit institutions, credit unions 0.2% of the average deposit amount.
Financial position	By the end of 2001 the total assets of the Fund amounted to EEK417 millions, ca. 1% of total deposits and 1.2% of guaranteed deposits.	By the end of 2001 total assets of the Deposit Guarantee Fund was LVL5.1 million, ca. 0.2% of total deposits.	By the end of 2001 the total assets of the Fund were LTL272 millions, ca. 2.8% of total deposits.

Table A2 (Contd.)

	Estonia	Latvia	Lithuania
Covering of funding shortfall	If the Fund's financial resources are not sufficient for compensation the Fund may (1) borrow from credit institutions, or (2) borrow from the Estonian government or ask for a government guarantee for loans.	Where the Fund's money resources are insufficient the shortfall shall be paid from the government budget.	Where the Fund's resources are insufficient the Fund can borrow on the capital market.

Sources: Central banks and deposit guarantee institutions in Estonia, Latvia, Lithuania.

Notes

* The views expressed are those of the author and do not necessarily reflect the views of the Nordic Investment Bank.

1. Llewellyn (1994), pp. 22–32; Sigurðsson (1995), pp. 2–5; and (2002) pp. 1–2.
2. It is noteworthy that, even among the five Nordic countries with broadly similar financial sector legislation and regulation, there are differences in the deposit guarantee provisions that complicate cross-border mergers of banks and leave unanswered questions on responsibility for multi-country operations. In the appendix to this chapter there is a schematic overview of the deposit guarantee systems in the Nordic and Baltic countries that brings these differences out very clearly.

6

The Economic Impact of Insolvency Law

*Bethany Blowers and Garry Young**

Dissatisfaction with the current system for handling bank insolvencies has led Mayes, Halme and Liuksila (2001) (henceforth MHL) to propose a range of reforms. These are put forward within the context of the situation as it currently applies in much of Europe, although MHL are also concerned about the handling of bank insolvencies internationally. These reforms are intended to eliminate the costs and risks that the taxpayer might otherwise incur in the event of bank insolvency, the moral hazard that 'always attaches to extending state aid to insolvent banks' and the 'undue delay' that causes losses of bank assets in reorganizations. The essence of the MHL proposals is to empower a government agency to seize control of an insolvent bank and effectively allow it to reduce the claims on the bank until the point at which it may be sold as a going concern or liquidated in an orderly manner.[1] In this way the judicial insolvency process is avoided, although the reduction of claims of insolvent banks will lead to losses for pre-existing shareholders and uninsured creditors in the same way as formal insolvency.

One of the key reasons for the proposed reform is to reduce and possibly eliminate the cost to the taxpayer of any bank failure by transferring the burden to the private sector claimants on the failing bank. It is likely that any change in the size and allocation of costs when banks fail will affect *ex-ante* incentives and business arrangements, possibly making failure less likely. Indeed, the proposed reform is intended to eliminate the moral hazard arising when state aid is extended to insolvent banks.

This chapter does *not* attempt to analyse in detail the MHL proposals for reform of insolvency arrangements applying specifically to banks. Instead it tries to draw attention to the lessons that have been learned from recent analysis of the general insolvency arrangements that apply to non-financial companies, non-incorporated businesses and individuals (referred to here as 'general insolvency law').[2] This includes discussion on the design of appropriate insolvency law where important contributions have been made in setting out what the law should seek to achieve. The paper goes on to summarize empirical evidence, looking at the *ex-ante* effect of insolvency arrangements on loan rates, the availability of credit and the rate of insolvency. The conclusion from this review is that insolvency arrangements can have a significant effect on incentives and the operation and efficiency of the financial system.

We also look at recent evidence on the *ex-post* effect of insolvency arrangements by describing the management of corporate workouts by UK banks and discuss proposed changes to UK insolvency law designed to overcome some difficulties with it that have been identified. We also outline the role played by the Bank of England in corporate debt workouts under the 'London Approach' where a collective approach that promotes effective coordination among creditors and debtors is used to preserve value at the pre-insolvency stage.

The chapter then outlines arrangements for dealing with bank failures in the UK where banks and non-financial companies are subject to the same insolvency law. We discuss how other differences in the institutional arrangements facing financial and non-financial companies at the pre-insolvency stage are intended to prevent financial instability without encouraging moral hazard. We also discuss some differences between workouts of financial and non-financial companies in the UK.

The chapter is organized as follows. Section 6.1 outlines the principles of general insolvency law, focusing particularly on what the law should seek to achieve from an economic perspective. Section 6.2 considers the evidence on the economic effects of general insolvency law. Section 6.3 describes some features of corporate workouts in the UK. Section 6.4 discusses the extent to which bank insolvency differs from that of non-bank companies and whether the previous analysis needs to be modified to cover banks. Section 6.5 summarizes the conclusions.

6.1 The principles of general insolvency law

A widely quoted rationale for the provision of insolvency law,[3] over and above that provided by standard contract law, is that the market on its own may fail to achieve a Pareto optimal distribution amongst creditors of the debtor's assets. When insolvent, a firm's assets do not cover its liabilities; so creditors have an incentive to try and collect their debts ahead of other creditors, as there is not enough to go around all of them. Such a race might lead to the firm's assets being dismantled at fire-sale prices, with a consequent loss of value for all creditors. Pareto efficiency might be improved then through the firm's assets being disposed of in an orderly manner: this is the remit of the insolvency process.[4]

Aghion, Hart and Moore (1992) and Hart (1999) suggest three goals of a good insolvency law, each of which is aimed at making this process efficient. According to their Goal 1, a good insolvency law should maximize the total value (in money terms) available to be divided amongst the insolvent firm's appropriate stakeholders. It should also (Goal 2) adequately penalize incumbent management and shareholders so as to preserve the bonding role of debt, and (Goal 3) observe in insolvency the absolute priority of contracts negotiated *ex ante*.[5]

These criteria are quite weak in terms of giving guidance on the relative strengths of different insolvency regimes, or prescribing how a regime should be designed. Instead, they are more like a set of minimum standards which any regime should meet and, subject to that, countries can choose from a range of systems. Hart (1999) and Aghion *et al.* (1992) suggest a possible two-step procedure for meeting these goals.[6]

First, the firm's debts are cancelled, and an automatic debt-equity swap is made for all existing creditors of the insolvent firm. This replaces multi-layered creditor classes, each bargaining with different objectives, with a homogeneous group of shareholders. Rights to the shares of the 'new' all-equity firm are allocated according to the absolute priority of creditors' *ex-ante* claims. For the (common) case where the true value of the firm is not known, this might be done by allocation of options to creditors to 'buy' units of the reorganized company that they will exercise depending on their assessment of the company's future value (Bebchuk, 1988). What is most important is that Goal 3 is achieved.

Second, these new shareholders must decide on the firm's future, specifically whether the firm should continue as a going concern, or be closed down. Bids are invited for the firm's assets and its operations; these can be either cash bids, or proposals (non-cash bids) for how the company can be restructured, this latter to avoid cash-constrained bidders (incumbent management, for example) being unable to compete. Shareholders choose between them, either by vote, or through standard corporate governance procedures (that is, a new board of directors is first elected by the new equity holders). Goals 1 and 2 are achieved: each new shareholder has the incentive to vote for the option which he believes maximizes the value of the firm, since this is in his interests of getting his money back. Existing managers are penalized if the new shareholders vote not to accept their proposal for the future of the firm and dismiss them.[7] Thus by achieving all three goals, this two-step procedure should promote an efficient resolution of a firm in distress.

The MHL proposals for orderly bank exit can be evaluated in terms of these three goals. The main thrust of the proposals is that when the government determines that a bank is economically insolvent it has the authority to take over the bank, replacing the incumbent management. The bank would then be restructured at the date of takeover, with the claims of pre-existing shareholders being wiped out; in reverse order of priority the claims of subordinated debt-holders and other junior creditors would be eliminated up to the point that the bank is again viable. The newly solvent bank would then be sold as a going concern or liquidated by the government depending on how much can be realized by each alternative.

It would appear that the MHL proposals could satisfy the Aghion *et al.* goals in that the government attempts to maximize the value of the insolvent firm (Goal 1), the incumbent management and shareholders are punished (Goal 2) and priority of contracts is observed since the relative priority of different classes of creditors would be reflected in the way they were treated in the insolvency (Goal 3). In practice, the optimality of this approach as a means of restructuring an insolvent bank would depend on the government being competent to make these decisions without any judicial process to challenge it. There is no guarantee that this is the case and more private sector involvement in the procedure might be warranted.[8]

6.2 Evidence on the economic effect of general insolvency law

Whether these, or any, insolvency procedures achieve economic efficiency will depend in part also on the incentives the regime creates *ex-ante* for both debtors and creditors. For example, if the general insolvency law is too strict, potential entrepreneurs might be deterred from setting up in business, because they believe the consequences of failure are too high. In this case, productivity, and so growth, might be lower as a result. But if lenders do not believe they will get their money back – that is, the law is too soft – they will be reluctant to lend, at least at prevailing prices: businesses will be credit rationed, and again productivity may be lower. Also, whilst there should be an incentive for honest bankrupts to try again, it is not the case that all decisions to become entrepreneurs are efficient. A tougher bankruptcy law may discourage those whose comparative advantage lies elsewhere from becoming entrepreneurs. This trade-off between a hard and a soft law has been considered from a historical perspective. Di Martino (2002) finds from a comparison of English and Italian personal bankruptcy law between 1880 and 1930, that the relatively more strict continental personal bankruptcy law in Italy was less efficient than the English one in reducing the general costs of insolvency. There was also a lower incidence of corruption in England, even though Italian law was relatively more strict; insolvency law should as well be able to select between 'good' and 'fraudulent' debtors in order to avoid the costs of fraud.

6.2.1 Evidence from Scotland

Scotland saw a marked increase in the number of personal bankrupts after a change in law there in 1985 altered the way that bankruptcy proceedings were financed. Bankruptcy law impacts on an entrepreneur's incentives to exit from business, or an individual's incentives to become bankrupt, as well as on creditors' incentives to petition for their exit. Other things being equal, a debtor might be more inclined to enter bankruptcy, and so gain protection from his creditors, if the cost to him of the process were lower now and in the future. Creditors will be reluctant to petition for the debtor to be made bankrupt if the costs of doing so outweigh the amount they are likely to recoup.

On being declared bankrupt in Scotland, a debtor's assets are transferred to a trustee, whose duty is to sell the assets and distribute proceeds to creditors, after first meeting his professional fees from these proceeds (this process is known as 'sequestration' in Scotland). Until 1985, these costs were met indirectly by creditors: they received proceeds from the debtor's estate only after the trustee had been paid.

In 1982, a report from the Scottish Law Commission identified two key problems with this process. First, few trustees were prepared to act in sequestration cases unless they could be reasonably assured that enough money would be realized from the estate to cover their professional fees and the cost of the process. In some cases this meant that although the court awarded a creditor petition for sequestration of a debtor, no action was taken as no trustee was appointed. In others, it meant that debtors were unable to obtain sequestration by their own petition. Second, some cases were then not completed: without a discharge from their debts, debtors were unable to make a 'fresh start'.

This led to a change in law embodied in the Bankruptcy (Scotland) Act 1985, to ensure a trustee was appointed for every bankruptcy case. Where there were insufficient funds available from the debtor's estate to

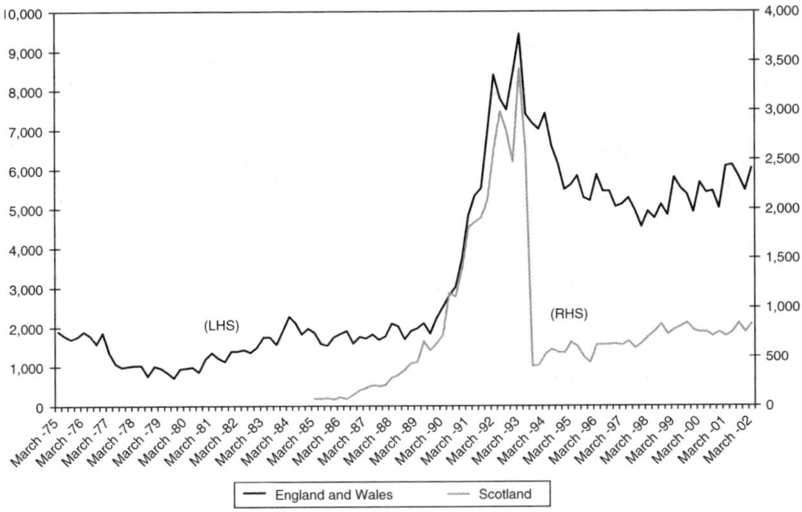

Figure 6.1 Bankruptcies in Scotland compared with England and Wales

Sources: Individual bankruptcy orders. England and Wales, *Financial Statistics*, Table 6.1A (ONS code: AIHW).
Individual sequestrations, Scotland, supplied by Department of Trade and Industry.

cover the costs of the process, the state would meet the shortfall, and underwrite the trustee's costs. Figure 6.1 shows the number of bankruptcies each year in Scotland, after this change was made. Between 1980 and 1985 there were between 150 and 300 sequestrations in Scotland each year. In 1992, there were over 10,000 partly reflecting the economic downturn at that time, evidenced by the rise in bankruptcies in England and Wales, but also reflecting the change in Scottish law. The cost of providing public funds was estimated at the time of the change of the law to be £10,000 a year. By 1993, the cost was £26 million. In 1993 the Bankruptcy Act was amended, with two key changes. First an attempt was made to prevent inappropriate bankruptcies by restricting petition rights. Second, instead of the public purse underwriting private sector trustees' costs in bankruptcy, a public official (the Accountant in Bankruptcy) would act as trustee for any cases where the debtor's estate did not cover costs. The effect of this reform was to reduce bankruptcies in Scotland from around 3,500 to 500 per quarter.

6.2.2 Evidence from the USA

Recent evidence from the USA also throws light on the impact of insolvency law.

Entrepreneurship

Fan and White (2002) find that the level of entrepreneurial activity in different states of the USA depends on the personal bankruptcy law in those states.[9] Each state sets the value of a bankrupt's home that is exempt from surrender to creditors in bankruptcy: the homestead exemption level. This level varies amongst states, from zero to unlimited (that is, from no exemption, to debtors in bankruptcy being able to keep the entire value of their home). The median exemption in 1993 was $15,000. Fan and White show that families who are homeowners are around one-third more likely to own businesses if they live in states with a high or unlimited, rather than low, homestead exemption – that is when they face a less strict law. These families are also approximately one-quarter more likely to start a business. Thus entrepreneurship is encouraged.

Bankruptcy rates

The variation in bankruptcy laws across the states of the USA also makes it possible to examine their effect on the bankruptcy rate itself. Lehnert and Maki (2002) find that generous bankruptcy laws lead to increased state-level bankruptcy rates. They estimate logistic equations for the bankruptcy rate for 51 US states from 1984 to 1999 and find a significant effect from the size of the homestead exemption. They use their estimates to quantify the size of this effect by considering the effect of a policy experiment where all homestead exemptions in the top three quartiles of the distribution are forced into the bottom quartile. They estimate that such a policy would have reduced bankruptcy filings by 18 per cent had it been enacted in 1999.

Interest rates and credit availability

The potential for higher bankruptcy rates in states with more generous homestead exemptions is likely to affect lending decisions. Berkowitz and White (2002) find evidence for this. In states with high rather than low homestead exemptions, they show that small businesses are more likely to be denied credit or discouraged from applying for it. For non-corporate firms they find that if the homestead exemption rises from the 25th percentile to unlimited, then the probability of credit rationing rises from 0.127 to 0.171; for corporate firms, the probability of credit rationing rises from 0.198 to 0.236. They also find that for firms accepted for credit, these businesses receive smaller loans at a higher rate of interest. For non-corporate firms they find that if the homestead exemption rises from the 25th percentile to unlimited, then the interest rate rises by 4.4 percentage points and the average loan size falls by $265. For corporate firms the effects are smaller; the interest rate rise is 1.4 percentage points and the loan size reduction is $194.

In the USA the size of the homestead exemption offers a form of insurance to homeowning borrowers, limiting the size of their downside risk. Perhaps not surprisingly, the evidence suggests that the more insurance there is the more risks are likely to be undertaken.

6.3 Corporate workouts

6.3.1 The London Approach

This evidence from the USA shows the *ex ante* impact on managers' and individuals' incentives of a hard or soft bankruptcy law. One of the risks of making a bankruptcy regime harder by removing a government lifeline of liquidity for a distressed firm is that it could lead to more failures, especially of firms that are solvent but facing short-term liquidity problems. One way of avoiding that is through pre-insolvency workouts. In this case, insolvency law becomes the procedure to which creditors and debtors turn if the workout cannot be agreed, and so impacts on players' incentives to take part in the restructuring process.

In the UK, there is a recognized tradition of large corporate workouts. The Bank of England in the early 1990s coordinated the development of a set of non-statutory principles for how banks should respond to news of serious financial difficulty in one of their corporate customers, where there is more than one bank involved in the lending. The Bank's role in this 'London Approach' is to facilitate discussions between banks if there is disagreement between them on the right course of action, to ensure that decisions are made on the basis of a full sharing and understanding of relevant information. These principles are reflected in the global approach to multi-creditor workouts agreed by insolvency professionals (INSOL, 2000).

Armour and Deakin (2000) find that the non-statutory social norms that are the basis of the London Approach can provide a substitute for legal procedures in ensuring collective creditor action, because non-statutory enforcement mechanisms exist such that creditors behave according to these norms. One example is the fear that failure to act in accordance with the norms may mean creditors are excluded by fellow creditors from future collective lending. They note also the important role state institutions, in this case the Bank of England, play in creating the environment in which the norms become established in the first place.

Workouts may allow for efficiency gains if the cost of the coordinated debt renegotiation is lower than the cost incurred when a firm moves into the formal insolvency process. The indirect cost of a loss of goodwill associated with a distressed firm might be much lower: legal insolvency procedures are public, whereas debt renegotiations under the London Approach, for example, are private. Further, empirical evidence suggests that the rate of recoveries is higher under pre-insolvency workouts than under statutory insolvency procedures (Franks *et al.*, 1996).[10]

6.3.2 Evidence from UK lenders and the Enterprise Act

Franks and Sussman (2002) examine the extent to which banks restructure the small to medium-sized firms to which they lend. In the sample of distressed firms they examined, the equity structure was such that liquidation and control rights in the event of insolvency were concentrated with the firm's main bank, as senior lender, typically with a fixed or floating charge (or both). Probably as a result of this, Franks and Sussman found that the insolvency process was not characterized by creditor races. But there was mixed evidence for the efficiency of the restructuring process.

There was some evidence of sophisticated monitoring by banks: over 85 per cent of the firms came out of distress as going concerns, after a rescue process lasting on average 7.5 months. The data also suggested that banks had used their control rights to increase their recovery rates at the expense of other creditors. In particular, where firms were put into insolvency, banks had timed it to the point where the value of unsecured creditors' claims was largely eroded, and so the value of the firm in insolvency was not maximized. There is a practical problem for lenders in ensuring an efficient outcome in a period of economic downturn. With an increasing number of defaulting debtors, banks may have insufficient resources to consider restructuring every company in distress; some viable but liquidity-constrained firms may be liquidated as a result. Nonetheless, on average, trade creditors in Franks and Sussman's dataset had recovery rates of close to zero, whilst for the banks it was close to 100 per cent.

Thus, the effect of control rights being concentrated within the main lending bank is that decisions regarding insolvency are not taken in the interests of all creditors, but only that one with the control rights. Restricting the control rights of single creditors in insolvency is one of the aims of the insolvency reforms contained in the UK Government's Enterprise Act, which received Royal Assent on 7 November 2002 and came into force on 15 September 2003. The Act seeks to achieve this by restricting the use of administrative receivership for insolvent firms – where a single secured creditor has effective control – and shifting the balance in favour of administration – which takes account of the interests of all creditors. At the same time, reforms to personal bankruptcy law are designed to give a second chance to entrepreneurs who fail through no fault of their own, but also make reckless or culpable bankrupts subject to a more stringent regime. That is, the proposals seek to make more efficient both crisis resolution and entrepreneurs' incentives.

6.4 The economic effect of bank insolvency arrangements

The previous sections have considered some of the economic consequences of general insolvency law as it applies to non-financial companies and individuals. In this section we discuss how bank insolvency differs from that of other companies and how this may modify the previous analysis.

Applying the previous logic would suggest that a change in the insolvency regime which raised the costs to pre-existing shareholders and uninsured creditors of a failing bank would raise the *ex-ante* costs of finance to the bank unless it acted to make failure less likely. This would provide an incentive to reduce the probability of failure and so provide market discipline that would be generally helpful to improving financial stability. Honohan and Klingebiel (2000) provide some evidence which suggests that a 'strict' regime helps to contain the fiscal costs of banking crises. In particular, they find that 'unlimited deposit guarantees, open-ended liquidity support, repeated recapitalisations, debtor bail-outs and regulatory forbearance add significantly and sizably to costs'.

Thus, it is likely that banks are similar to other companies in the way in which they respond to the incentives provided by the insolvency regime. But it is also likely that the welfare costs of bank insolvencies are larger than those for other, non-financial, companies, suggesting that an 'optimal' insolvency regime would make insolvencies less common among banks. In the next section the arrangements for handling bank insolvency in the UK are outlined, describing the differences that are intended to reduce the risks of systemic banking crises.

6.4.1 The UK arrangements

Unlike many other countries, the UK does not have any special insolvency regime for banks.[11] When there is a need for an insolvency procedure, banks are subject to the same legal provisions as any other company. However, there are important differences between banks and other companies that may prevent banks from getting to this stage.

First, the banks alongside building societies, investment firms, insurance companies and friendly societies are authorized, supervised and regulated by the Financial Services Authority (FSA). Second, some bank liabilities are insured through a scheme funded by the banks themselves. Third, the Bank of England, being responsible for the overall stability of the financial system, is able in exceptional circumstances to undertake official financial operations to limit the risk of problems in particular institutions spreading to other parts of the financial system.[12]

This lender-of-last-resort function and the principles underlying its use are described fully by the former Governor in George (1994). It is important to stress that lender-of-last-resort support is directed to safeguarding the financial system as a whole and not any particular institution.[13] It does not mean that banks are prevented from failing:[14]

> We do not see it as our job to prevent each and every bank from failing. The possibility of failure is necessary to the health of the financial system, as it is to the efficiency of all other economic activity. (George, 1994, p. 63)

The principles of last-resort assistance are such that the cost of providing it does not generally fall on the Bank of England or on the UK taxpayer via lower dividend payments to HM Treasury. In particular, the Bank explores every option for a commercial solution before committing its own funds. When it does provide support, the Bank takes collateral and its support is structured so that any losses fall first on the shareholders and benefits come first to the Bank. Moreover, the aim of support is to help illiquid banks, not those known to be insolvent.

It is clear then that in the UK the path to insolvency is different for failing financial and non-financial companies despite both types of companies being subject to the same insolvency law. Before reaching the insolvency courts, the failing financial institution must be judged not to represent a threat to the financial system as a whole. There may be circumstances when this leads to some injection of capital, although the principles of last-resort assistance are designed to prevent this, especially in any predictable way. While the Bank of England is clear about its willingness to consider lending in systemic situations, it does not say what those precise circumstances would be and no single institution could take such support for granted. An important question is whether this additional test affects the incentives of financial and non-financial companies in relation to possible insolvency. For example, it has been argued that some large, complex, banking organizations are perceived to be 'too-big-to-fail' (TBTF) and that this weakens market discipline (see Stern in Chapter 3). While market discipline may be weakened to the extent that creditors perceive some institutions to be TBTF, the managers of banks and their shareholders will not expect protection and as such the response of companies to insolvency laws should be the same for financial and non-financial companies alike. This arises because there is no guarantee in the UK that an individual failing bank will be supported; even if it is, the support will not be necessarily beneficial to its shareholders so the treatment of financial companies cannot be expected to be any different from that of non-financial companies.

Of course, this similarity of effect would not apply in countries where an injection of capital into a failing bank could reasonably be expected; in that case, the impact of bank insolvency arrangements would be different from that applying to other types of companies.

6.4.2 Bank workouts

Despite similarities in the incentives of financial and non-financial companies in relation to insolvency law, financial sector restructurings are likely to be much more complicated than those of non-financial companies. This arises from the greater diversity of claims and the need to act quickly and finally in the case of financial sector restructurings.[15] Brierley and Vlieghe (1999) and Clementi (2001) both compare some dimensions of financial sector restructurings with those of non-financial corporate workouts. Here we summarize some of the main points of these articles. The common themes are:

- The first step in any restructuring would be an assessment of the long-run viability of the company. This will determine whether liquidity support is justified or whether it should be closed. With financial institutions, the time available to make an assessment and reach a decision is likely to be limited.
- There would be a need for cooperation between all relevant parties based on full exchanges of information and the need for equitable treatment of similar classes of creditors, investors and depositors. It would be hard not to envisage the authorities playing a facilitating role in a private sector solution, raising parallels with the Bank's role in the London Approach.

The complications are:

- Depositors or policyholders are in a different position from ordinary creditors, having less information, being greater in number and less well organized to recover their assets than professional creditors.

- Consolidation of financial groups has given rise to a range of large complex financial institutions or LCFIs. Restructuring one of these groups would be far from straightforward and has been the subject of recent discussion among central banks.
- This is further complicated by the degree to which financial groups operate in a number of different jurisdictions. While this applies also to some non-financial companies, these difficulties are more likely to be present for banks. It has been argued that further difficulties are likely to arise within the euro area where the ECB has no fiscal counterpart, possibly making burden-sharing between national authorities more complicated. Moreover, countries differ in the extent to which their insolvency laws embody a universal or territorial approach to cross-border insolvencies.
- The role of supervisors would need to be recognized explicitly and workout principles would need to be consistent with internationally recognized principles of banking and insurance regulation.

Many of these same points are made in Bank for International Settlements (2002) which draws particular attention to the problems of dealing with large, internationally active financial institutions who trade in a range of jurisdictions. It is argued that this weakens the power of creditors since no one creditor has sufficient influence to encourage workouts. Also, it is claimed that banks are able to 'shop' between jurisdictions with the result that legal certainty, one of the criteria by which the BIS assesses different regimes, is reduced.

Further complications arise when banks face major problems arising from their corporate loan books since this may make them reluctant to participate in corporate workouts. In such circumstances bank restructuring programmes have often transferred distressed corporate debt to separate government agencies, or asset management companies (AMCs). This could lead to tensions between maximizing short-term debt recoveries to limit the public costs of bank recapitalization and preserving longer-term corporate value. Effectively, the public authorities might liquidate companies prematurely, although evidence suggests that asset sales have been slow (Klingebiel, 2000). Further, recent financial innovations, such as credit derivatives, weaken the incentive of the covered creditors to monitor and take part in workouts.

Despite these difficulties, Campbell and Cartwright (2002) provide some recent case studies where administration has been used in connection with distressed banks in the UK. Clementi (2001) is clear about the need for a cooperative approach in organizing workouts of this type.

6.5 Conclusion

The MHL proposals for reform of bank insolvency procedures represent a radical change in insolvency arrangements designed to reduce moral hazard and the potential costs to the taxpayer of bank rescue. We have not looked at these proposals in detail, but they may be viewed in the light of the wider literature on insolvency that we have discussed. These proposals would appear to respect the Aghion *et al.* principles that insolvency law should attempt to maximize the value of assets in the insolvent firm, punish incumbent management and respect the priority of claims. However, MHL recommend that decision-making authority in the restructured bank be passed to a government agency rather than to those with remaining claims on the restructured bank. It is unlikely that this will result in decisions that are in the best interests of these claimants. We have also summarized some of the recent literature looking at the wider economic effect of different insolvency arrangements. This suggests that there is a clear effect of incentives provided by insolvency arrangements on behaviour. This evidence suggests that a stricter insolvency regime tends to be associated with less insolvency, lower interest rates, less credit rationing and lower fiscal costs. This suggests that a less debtor-oriented insolvency regime of the type recommended by MHL would improve market discipline so as to make insolvency less likely, although this should be weighed against the potential deterrent to new banks starting up and making capitalism less dynamic. We have also explored the use of debt-workouts at the pre-insolvency stage which prevent the failure of solvent companies with liquidity problems. These have been useful in restructuring non-financial companies and some banks in the UK, but the potential problems involved in restructuring LCFIs require continued discussion of the type proposed by MHL.

Notes

* This chapter is published with the kind permission of the Bank of England, but the views expressed are those of the authors, not necessarily those of the Bank of England. We are grateful to conference participants, Bill Allen, Peter Brierley, Alastair Clark, Glenn Hoggarth, Geoffrey Wood and John Young for comments. They are not responsible for any remaining errors.

1. The effects of government ownership during banking crises is discussed with reference to the Nordic countries in Sandal (2002).
2. We draw heavily on papers presented at a recent Bank of England conference, 'The Economics of Insolvency Law: effects on debtors, creditors and enterprise'. This is summarized in Blowers (2002).

3. In England and Wales, bankruptcy is the term used for personal as opposed to corporate insolvency proceedings.
4. Jackson (1982) illustrates this via a two-creditor 'prisoner's dilemma' example. Take a debtor, D, whose business at the point of insolvency is worth £60,000. The firm has two creditors, C1 and C2, each of whom has loaned D £50,000. On hearing of D's financial distress, each has a 50 per cent chance of being paid in full (£50,000) if they act individually and are first to (win the race to) claim. Hence, each has a 50 per cent chance of receiving only £10,000 if they are last. But if C1 and C2 share in D's distress, they are each guaranteed £30,000. In this example, the expected pay-off for each creditor under each scenario (racing or sharing) is £30,000. But assuming that creditors are essentially risk-averse, more value might be placed on the certain outcome available through sharing (that is, coordinated and collective action) than the uncertain outcome possible through racing (that is, individual action). If he shares, each creditor knows with certainty that he will receive an equal share of aggregate assets (in his asset class), and does not face the uncertainty of receiving an amount dependent on who wins the race to claim. Assuming a value is attached to certainty, each creditor may be better off through sharing without either being made worse off. This holds particularly since the race itself also bears administrative costs.
5. The Bank for International Settlements (2002) identifies three similar goals: efficiency (in terms of more to be shared out), equity (people getting what they should, relative to each other) and the reduction of legal and financial uncertainty.
6. Note that Hart finds it is difficult for economists to derive an optimal insolvency procedure from first principles because they do not at this point have a satisfactory theory of why parties cannot design their own bankruptcy procedures; that is, why contracts are incomplete.
7. Problems might occur here if creditors have horizons that are shorter term than the time necessary to turn the firm around. Equally, creditors might be reluctant to take on equity exposure in certain situations: where the stock is illiquid, for example, or where the company is not listed, both making it difficult to on-sell the equity. These problems are not necessarily peculiar to these procedures, however; Hart notes that the procedures might do better – and certainly not worse – than existing regimes in handling them.
8. The benefits of market-based insolvency mechanisms have been noted by a number of authors. For example, see Bank for International Settlements (2002).
9. Owners of small firms may come under the jurisdiction of personal bankruptcy law if the firm is unincorporated, or in the common case where the owner has personally guaranteed a loan made to the firm.
10. As a set of guiding principles, Armour and Deakin note the London Approach may have a flexibility that provides an efficiency advantage over the public or private legal procedures to which, over time, parties are bound. But equally, given the fluid character of the financial markets (both in terms of new participants, who may be unaware of the principles, and new financial products such as the trading of distressed debt), the stability of the norms may be put at risk.

11. In the European Union, Germany and Ireland are the only other jurisdictions dealing with insolvent banks under the general insolvency laws (Campbell and Cartwright, 2002).
12. The arrangements for cooperation between the FSA, the Bank of England and HM Treasury in the field of financial stability are set out in a memorandum of understanding (MOU) between the three parties concerned.
13. This is also the case in other countries. Marino and Shibut (2002) note a similar policy in the USA: 'While twenty years ago it was generally understood that the likelihood of losses to uninsured depositors and general creditors (of a bank) was fairly small, this is no longer the case today.' The key, they argue, is for the deposit insurer to 'develop ways to conduct an orderly failure'.
14. Individual bank failures do occur in the UK. See Campbell and Cartwright (2002), Hoggarth and Soussa (2001) and Jackson (1996).
15. The need for a fast resolution is also highlighted in Bank for International Settlements (2002), 'perhaps the most important source of uncertainty and inefficiency lies in the slowness of traditional insolvency processes'.

7
Do Bank Exit Regimes Affect Banking Conditions?

Peik Granlund

This chapter explores the extent to which bank exit regimes affect banking conditions by undertaking an empirical study of the effects of exit regimes on bank refinancing costs.

Bank exit regimes do not only direct how bank losses are distributed between bank creditors, depositors, bank shareholders, the banking industry and taxpayers in the case of bank failure. They also affect the current distribution of income and wealth by influencing the conditions under which banking is carried out. To show the implications of bank exit regimes on commercial banks' refinancing costs, the exit regimes of New York, London, Frankfurt and Tokyo during the years 1999–2002 are investigated. The specific question addressed in the analysis is: 'Do differences in bank exit regimes of significance to bank creditors generate differences in bank refinancing costs?'

To answer the question, the various exit regimes are compared and evaluated quantitatively. A search for correlation between the various exit regimes and individual bank refinancing costs characterizes the evaluation. Evidence supporting assumptions of causal relations between exit regimes and bank refinancing costs is gathered using regression techniques. The analysis has three separate stages. First, all bank exit regimes are indexed according to bank creditor interests. Then, exit regimes are compared with bank refinancing costs using regression techniques. Finally, the results of the analysis are discussed in a broader theoretical context.[1]

Section 7.1 concentrates on how the bank exit regimes can be indexed, specified and quantified in terms of legislation and practice. Attention is focused on those aspects of the bank exit regimes that matter to bank creditors from an economic point of view. The provisions and practices dealt with concern the level of security (financial assistance to banks) and the extent of powers (right to commence bankruptcy, risk for capital loss in bank reorganization and so on) that the legislation provides bank creditors. Bank refinancing costs are specified, principles for the collection of data presented and calculations made in Section 7.2. Bank refinancing costs are specified as the refinancing spread on publicly traded bank bonds. The spread is the difference between the bank bond yield and a risk-free rate of return (government bond) of equal maturity. In Sections 7.3 and 7.4 results are interpreted and conclusions drawn. Interpretation is made in the light of existing theories and empirical findings on spreads.[2]

7.1 Specification and quantification of bank exit regimes according to bank creditor interests

7.1.1 The Financial Assistance Index (FAI) as an attribute for assistance probability

The aim of this section is to specify and quantify the bank exit regimes to the extent these concern bank creditors in a manner that makes them amenable to econometric analysis. The focus is on those aspects of the regimes that matter to bank creditors in an economic sense. Aspects of this kind relate to

- *the degree of security that the regimes provide the creditors' investments,* and
- *the powers that the bank exit provisions transfer to bank creditors* in the reorganization and liquidation of banks.

These aspects of bank exit regimes mainly deal with features related to eventual creditor capital loss. Other aspects of bank exit regimes may also affect creditor security and rights, and may have implications for market conditions similar to the aspects analysed. The sections that follow explore correlations between the specified aspects of the bank exit regimes and market conditions.

Two types of *indexes* are introduced to specify and quantify bank exit regimes to the extent these concern bank creditors. The characteristics of the bank exit regimes to be included in the indexes are specified below. The indexes are *graded* for each financial centre in each time period, with values from 15 to 0. 15 indicates a high degree of security for creditor investments or large transfers of powers to creditors and 0 indicates no security or power-transfer. As the regimes change so do the grades. The first index is labelled the *Financial Assistance Index* (*FAI*).

FAI deals with the overall probability of banks receiving financial assistance in various financial centres. The second index is the *Bank-Creditor Rights Index (BCRI)*. BCRI focuses on certain basic creditor rights in the reorganization and liquidation of banks.[3]

FAI concentrates on the *probability* of banks receiving financial assistance. It is apparent that substantial differences exist between the regimes in several respects.

First, one can differentiate the *legal bases* for financial assistance from the *practice* of how assistance is applied. The legal bases vary from the highly specified to the imprecise. Practice in directing financial assistance to problem banks pursuant to the varying principles set out by the bank exit legislation also varies considerably.

Second, *conditions* for assistance need to be identified. Practice can be more restricted than the discretionary principles set out by the law. In other cases, one may be of the opinion that practice is more liberal than the law originally intended.[4]

Third, we can distinguish the *form of assistance* from the perspective of the different stakeholders in the bank. In theory, the form of the assistance determines which bank stakeholders will benefit from the assistance. The priority accorded to financial assistance will affect the position of existing creditors. Financial assistance in the form of ordinary (or prior) debt may be needed to create the conditions for the redevelopment of the bank, but it also establishes a claim against the debtor's assets of the same (or better) priority as any creditor claim, deteriorating the position of former creditors. Still, practice has shown that this aspect of assistance is not the most important when estimating the effects of eventual financial assistance on market behaviour. Consequently, the format of FAI mainly focuses on the overall probability of any major financial assistance, irrelevant of its form.

Fourth, in some financial centres some *uncertainty* regarding the conditions, timing and content of eventual assistance is promoted. As a result, the exact assistance practice is difficult to estimate in advance. The uncertainty relates to the notion of 'constructive ambiguity' and is a means of inhibiting the development of moral hazard problems.[5]

Actual grading of bank exit regimes according to FAI

We take the bank exit regimes of New York, London, Frankfurt and Tokyo in turn.

US banks Legal provisions concerning assistance state that Federal Deposit Insurance Corporation (FDIC) funds constitute US financial assistance to (deposit) insured banks faced with financial problems.

Conditions for assistance are mainly dependent on FDIC discretion. The main alternatives for the FDIC to handle bank failures comprise the pay-off of depositors or direct financial assistance to banks. In practice, assistance is in the form of ordinary or subordinated debt. The FDIC has to choose those alternatives that would minimize the loss for the FDIC. Only in the case of systemic implications, may the FDIC deviate from this restriction. From the mid-1990s, depositors' claims have priority in relation to ordinary creditors in the realization of bank assets. Moreover, paid-off depositors' claims are subrogated to the FDIC. Since the FDIC must minimize loss, the probability of such financial assistance to banks under circumstances that would benefit bank creditors is very low. As for US bank exit *practice*, small bank failures without systemic implications have been handled in a legalistic and prompt manner, implying losses for bank creditors. For larger bank failures, with eventual systemic implications, the approach has been more liberal. Large banks have been more likely to receive financial assistance, with such assistance also clearly benefiting bank creditors. Still, the probability of financial assistance to large US banks is seen as lower than in other bank exit regimes. This derives from the fact that the US bank exit regime is characterized by the concept of 'constructive ambiguity' and general reservations about governmental intervention. As a result, US banks, other than the largest, receive a grade of 3/15 while the FAI of large US banks is 12/15.[6]

UK banks The situation is quite different from that in the USA. There is no *legal base* for financial assistance to UK banks. Eventual financial assistance to UK banks will most probably be lender of last resort (LLR) or other support from the Bank of England (BoE) due to the Memorandum of Understanding (MoU) instigated by HM Treasury, the BoE and the Financial Services Authority (FSA) in 1997 (see also Chapter 6). According to the MoU, assistance may be given *normally*, only in the case of a genuine threat to the financial system. The form of the assistance is not specified in the MoU. This means that the assistance may take the form of loans, subordinated loans or subsidies. The Financial Services Compensation Scheme (FSCS, deposit insurance) may not assist banks directly. Before the establishment of the FSA the UK assistance *practice* had been for the Bank of England to be fairly active in the handling of banking crises. There have been examples of support to smaller insolvent banks and denial of support to larger failed banks without systemic implications (for example, Barings). Consequently, the grade given to all but the largest UK banks in the FAI is 8–9/15. For large UK banks it is 13/15. The relatively high scores also reflect the establishment of the FSA, the recent introduction of the new Financial Services Market Act

(FSMA) and the Bank of England's ambitions in the area of financial stability.[7]

German banks The role of the German Central Bank (Bundesbank) as a source of assistance differs strongly from the UK model. In principle, in *legal terms*, there are two channels for a German bank to receive financial assistance. The Liquidity Consortium Bank (LCB) handles the Central Bank's lender-of-last-resort (LLR) function but may grant loans only to banks of unquestioned soundness. The Voluntary Deposit Protection Scheme administered by the Association of German Banks may directly assist member-banks. The assistance to member-banks may be in any form. The scheme is entitled to support the member-banks but it has no obligation to assist them. Furthermore, the funds of the scheme are limited. Although no other formal assistance procedures exist, the actual role of the Bundesbank in a major crisis is not clear. Partly, this depends on the capacity of the LCB. In exit *practice*, no larger German banks have faced serious problems during the last decade. Bank problems have always been dealt with beforehand, in a manner accepted by the industry and the authorities. The extent to which German insolvency laws apply to bank failures is unspecified. Accordingly, the probability of assistance in the case of a failure may be considered high. The FAI for German banks is given a grade of 13/15 while the FAI for the largest German banks is assumed to be 15/15.[8]

Japanese banks The *rules* applicable to Japanese banks state that banks may receive financial aid from the Japanese Deposit Insurance Corporation (DIC). The financial aid may be in any form. Until 1996 financial aid to banks was only possible in order to facilitate mergers between a failing and a healthy bank. From 1997 onwards, DIC was also able to finance mergers between ailing banks. Initially, the amount of financial aid was limited to the potential pay-off cost to depositors. In 1996, the Japanese Government committed to protect all deposits to their full amount. Accordingly, the limits for financial assistance to banks were extended. These principles still apply. In addition, the Bank of Japan (BoJ) is in some cases entitled to provide assistance to insolvent banks, even without sufficient security. In exit *practice*, the role of the BoJ has been more central than the laws indicate. Historically the BoJ has organized rescue operations involving public capital (DIC funds), BoJ funds and funds from the private sector. The decision over the use of public funds is taken by the Prime Minister's Office. Since there is solid evidence of financial assistance to Japanese banks, the FAI grades for the Japanese banks are fairly high. Still, one should not forget that Japan faces a large public deficit, eventually restricting future supportive operations. Consequently,

Table 7.1 Financial centre grades according to the Financial Assistance Index (FAI)

	1999	2000	2001	2002	Mean
Probability of assistance to any bank (FAI)					
New York regime	3	3	3	3	3.0/15
London regime	8	9	9	9	8.7/15
Frankfurt regime	13	13	13	13	13.0/15
Tokyo regime	12	12	11	11	11.5/15
Probability of assistance to largest banks (FAI_L)					
New York regime	12	12	12	12	12.0/15
London regime	13	13	13	13	13.0/15
Frankfurt regime	15	15	15	15	15.0/15
Tokyo regime	15	15	14	14	14.5/15

for the largest Japanese banks the FAI grade is 14–15/15. For other than the largest banks the grade is somewhat lower, 11–12/15. This is a result of the lack of systemic implications of failures in smaller banks and the fact that the refinancing of rescue operations may become a problem.[9]

Table 7.1 summarizes the FAI gradings of the US, UK, German and Japanese banking systems.

7.1.2 The Bank Creditor-Rights Index (BCRI) reflecting legal creditor rights

The second index is the Bank Creditor-Rights Index (BCRI), concentrating on certain basic creditor rights listed in the various bank exit rules. In contrast to the FAI, which focused on the probability of financial assistance (that is, the combination of rules and practice), the BCRI only deals with *legislative issues*. Since the rules are fairly stable over time, the probability of diachronic changes in BCRI is small. On the other hand, major differences exist in the BCRI grades for the various financial centre bank exit regimes. Three facets are taken into account in forming the BCRI:

- First, BCRI concentrates on the *existence of certain reorganization provisions* in the regimes significant to bank creditors. The focus is on the formal reorganization means whereby *creditor claims are cut* to secure the continuance of bank activities. Creditor voting or/and court approval constitute conditions for cutting creditor claims. The procedures have no effect on the position of shareholders.
- Second, BCRI also deals with the *judicial possibility for creditors to start bankruptcy proceedings* against banks. In other words, it looks into the

Table 7.2 Financial centre grades according to the Bank-Creditor Rights Index (BCRI)

	1999	2000	2001	2002	Mean
New York regime, total	5	5	5	5	5.0/15
Elimination of claims	5	5	5	5	
Initiation of bankruptcy	0	0	0	0	
Subordination of claims	0	0	0	0	
London regime, total	10	10	10	10	10.0/15
Elimination of claims	0	0	0	0	
Initiation of bankruptcy	5	5	5	5	
Subordination of claims	5	5	5	5	
Frankfurt regime, total	7.5	7.5	7.5	7.5	7.5/15
Elimination of claims	2.5	2.5	2.5	2.5	
Initiation of bankruptcy	0	0	0	0	
Subordination of claims	5	5	5	5	
Tokyo regime, total	10	10	10	10	10.0/15
Elimination of claims	0	0	0	0	
Initiation of bankruptcy	5	5	5	5	
Subordination of claims	5	5	5	5	

powers of the *creditors*, not the security that authorities may provide by initiating compulsory liquidation. In practice, authorities in all financial centres have the right to initiate compulsory liquidation on financial grounds. Whether they do it or not is a question of:

(a) receiving adequate information about the condition of banks,
(b) the type and precision of existing insolvency criteria, and
(c) the will or obligation to act.

Although one might assume that any creditor has the right to initiate a bankruptcy, this is not a feature of all the regimes.

- Third, BCRI also takes into account *whether creditors are subordinated depositors* in the realization of bank assets. Depositor priority (US preference) significantly impairs the position of ordinary creditors in the realization.[10]

In grading for the various financial centres, each of the three aspects just listed are given equal weight. Each aspect is graded in the range 0 to 5 and the BCRI grade is the sum of those three grades, as shown in Table 7.2.

The existence of certain reorganization provisions

US banks The US procedure for bank reorganization is given the value 5. This is because the US bank exit regime does not recognize any reorganization procedures that would cut creditor claims without affecting shareholders. Reorganization of US banks is carried out through conservatorship (or receivership) and the powers given to the conservator are considerable. Still, shareholder responsibility for the bank failure is emphasized in all situations.

UK banks The procedures for the reorganization of UK banks assessed from the banks' creditors' perspective is graded 0. This implies that the UK jurisdiction contains measures whereby creditor claims are cut. Various bank stakeholders may initiate a court-directed reorganization procedure. Measures taken are subject to creditor/shareholder-voting and/or court approval. In the UK, there is no specific reorganization procedure for banks. Procedures apply to all companies.

German banks Reorganization in accordance with German laws is graded 2.5. The grade reflects uncertainty whether reorganization provisions apply. The German Banking Act does not include actual reorganization measures. In principle, reorganization is possible in accordance with the Insolvency Act, which provides for a procedure through which creditor claims are cut. Still, the extent to which this act applies to failed banks is not specified. The preceding insolvency acts (before 1998) recognized two composition procedures based on creditor voting whereby creditor claims were cut.

Japanese banks Here, reorganization relative to bank creditors is graded 0. The Japanese legislation provides for both a reorganization scheme and a composition scheme that may be used to cut creditors' claims. Creditors vote on both schemes. Although the Japanese banking sector has been characterized by several ailing banks, the banks have been dealt with differently. Assisted mergers have been the most frequently used measure.[11]

The judicial possibility for bank creditors to start bankruptcy proceedings

US banks Bank exit rules are graded 0. The US bank exit regime does not give creditors any rights to initiate the liquidation (receivership) of a bank. Authorities make all the decisions. However, the 'Prompt Corrective Action' (PCA) scheme introduces a detailed procedure focusing on capital adequacy that entitles/obliges authorities to initiate compulsory liquidation.

UK banks The UK jurisdiction is graded 5. The fact that general laws apply to UK bank liquidation, opens up the possibility for creditors to initiate bankruptcy proceedings against banks as one type of compulsory winding up. A bank's inability to pay its debts is the judicial criterion for the commencement of bankruptcy in the UK. In addition, courts may wind up any bank if this is considered just and equitable.

German banks In Germany, bank creditors are not able to initiate bankruptcy proceedings against banks. As a result, the German jurisdiction is graded 0. The Banking Act states that the only party entitled to initiate liquidation proceedings on insolvency grounds against German banks is the Financial Supervisory Authority (FSA). There are two types of insolvency criteria that may be used as financial grounds for compulsory liquidation under the Act, insolvency and over-indebtedness. The terms are not further specified.

Japanese banks The powers of Japanese bank creditors to initiate bank bankruptcy in accordance with the Japanese bank exit regime are graded 5. Theoretically, bank creditors may initiate bankruptcy in accordance with the general Japanese bankruptcy laws. Authorities received the right to initiate compulsory liquidation proceedings in 1996. Criteria for the commencement of bankruptcy comprise the debtor's inability to pay his debts, suspension of debt payments and debtor liabilities exceeding assets. In 1998, a 'Prompt Corrective Action' scheme was established for Japanese banks. This scheme provided for capital adequacy-orientated, objective criteria for action against banks. Although formal bankruptcy and liquidation procedures exist, they are seldom used. Failing banks (especially larger ones) have been dealt with through assisted mergers.

The subordination of ordinary creditor claims in relation to depositor claims

US banks Exit rules are graded 0. The position of ordinary US bank creditors is weak on this point. In the liquidation of US banks, ordinary creditor claims are subordinated to depositor claims. Similarly, depositor claims transferred to the FDIC as a result of paying off depositors are in priority in the realization of bank assets. Before the amendments of the legislation in the mid-1990s, ordinary creditor claims were not subordinated relative to depositor claims.

UK, German and Japanese banks The bank exit regimes of all the other financial centres are graded 5. The position of ordinary bank creditors is strong. Their claims are not subordinated to depositor claims.

7.2 Collection of data on bank refinancing costs and presentation of calculations and results

7.2.1 Collecting data on bank bond spreads

We focus on bank refinancing costs in evaluating the impact of bank exit regimes from a bank-creditor perspective. The data collected on refinancing costs have both cross-sectional and diachronic dimensions. In the remainder of this section we consider

(a) *the choice and definition of refinancing costs* as a market attribute,
(b) *the structure of the data search,*
(c) *the collection of bank bond yield data,* and
(d) *the collection of government bond yield data.*

Choice of market attribute There are several alternative choices of market attributes for creditor interests. These include credit agreement terms, ratings carried out by third parties and even authority measures. In the analysis, the market attribute chosen is the *cost for capital provided by the bank creditor*. There are two main motives for this choice. First is the fact that the attribute is a *primary* source of information. Creditors and debtors agree on the cost of capital. Consequently, it is likely to be highly (empirically) valid. Second, the cost of capital, in a causal theory sense, should be relatively dependent on the features of the bank exit regimes directing creditor security and powers. Since features of the bank exit regimes direct creditor security and powers relative to credit agreements, they also should affect the cost of creditor capital. The cost of creditor capital may be specified in three dimensions:

- it comprises traditional external capital in the form of senior debt.
- it is reduced to a question about the spread of creditor capital, defined as the difference between creditor capital yields and the risk-free rate of return. The risk-free rate of return is considered to correspond with the yield of government bonds in each financial centre.
- it only includes debt in the form of publicly issued and notified securities (that is bonds). Moreover, collateral or pledges should not secure the creditor capital in question.[12]

The structure of the data The data cover market conditions in New York, London, Frankfurt and Tokyo, *quarterly* over the period 1999–2002. The aim was to create a sample of banks from each of the markets to form a panel (observations start on 27 July 1999 and end on 27 April 2002, giving 12 measurement points). The banks are divided into two separate groups: those representing 'too large too fail', or at least a group of banks that may be treated preferentially under the threat of insolvency, and the remainder.[13] The original aim was to observe bank bond yields for three large and three other banks (a total of six banks) on each date. In practice, there are fewer observations as not all banks have bond quotations on each occasion. Thus out of a potential 288 observations there are only 161 recorded, 75 relating to large banks and 86 to the others. The 'Large banks' group is the three largest (*Bankers' Magazine* ranking) in each financial centre. The 'Other banks' group comprises banks picked on a random basis from the remaining banks in that financial centre. The component banks in the two groups varied over time – in the case of the large group because the largest three may not always be the same and in the other group because randomization is repeated each quarter. The total number of banks (with bond yield observations) in the sample is 48. Bond yields were obtained from the Bloomberg database, while other indicators of the condition of individual banks used were taken from the Bankscope database and *Bankers' Magazine*.

The are some problems in selecting the appropriate banks in each financial centre. Clearly the overriding criterion for inclusion in the sample is the applicability of the bank exit regimes of those specific financial centres on the particular banks. In this sense, the domicile of the banks is central. The banks analysed are commercially-oriented, deposit-taking, retail banks in the form of limited-liability companies. The *judicial structure* of the banks analysed raises some questions. Banks may form independent entities or constitute subsidiaries to bank holding companies. In the first case, capital is directly injected into the bank as a separate judicial entity. If the bank is confronted with problems, an eventual bank exit will have direct implications on bank creditors. In the second case, capital in the bank may be invested through the bank holding company. Such an approach is frequent and may be motivated by fiscal and other grounds. The capital received by the bank holding company may be transferred to the subsidiary bank in any form. In this study, both judicial forms are accepted. This derives from the fact that an eventual exit of a bank subsidiary will reflect in the value of the bank holding company. An eventual bank exit will have indirect implications on bank holding company creditors of the same type as it would have on bank creditors.[14]

Characteristics of the bonds Creditor capital must be in the form of senior, non-secured debt issued and notified publicly. Some restrictions on the currency of bonds apply. Bonds analysed are issued in the local currency of the financial centre. The maturity of all bonds analysed is approximately three years. It is assumed that such a maturity is sufficiently long and such bank bond yields will comprise information concerning the possibility of a bank exit. Yields of bonds with a very short maturity will be less affected by the possibility of bank exit unless there are serious questions about solvency.

Yields on government bonds These are also required for the estimation of the 'risk-free' rate, against which the bank bond spreads are to be computed. The bonds were issued by the governments in each financial centre and in the respective currencies. The aim was to include government bonds of exactly the same maturity (approximately three years) and date of observation as the bank bonds. As the probability of finding government bonds of exactly the same maturity as bank bonds is small, *hypothetical government bond yields* for bonds of exactly the same maturity as the bank bonds are constructed, using the yields from the bonds with the nearest shorter and longer maturities. The hypothetical government bond yield is computed as a weighted average of these two nearest values, based on the assumption that the yield curve is linear between the observations.[15]

The data are presented in Table 7.3.

7.2.2 The calculations and the results

The components of the two indexes used (FAI and BCRI) are normally combined in the analysis that follows. This is partly because they are inter-related and hence treated in combination by markets rather than as independent facets – in any case one can only choose between the available markets and not pick and choose among their components. From a more practical point of view, since many of the individual components remain unchanged over the observation period in a particular market, it is only through combination that we can observe variation in the time-series dimension.[16]

In the calculations the indexes are combined in three ways:

- first using the FAI on its own without the BCRI, labelled *FAI100*,
- second applying equal weights to the two indexes, labelled *FAI50*
- lastly, the FAI is given a weight of 25 per cent and the BCRI a weight of 75 per cent, labelling the result *FAI25*.[17]

This enables an exploration of the relative importance of the components.

As can be seen from Table 7.4, simple ordinary least squares regression is employed (using E-Views), with bank spreads as the dependent variable. The sample is analysed in four ways, first looking at all banks and second just at the large (TBTF) banks (panels (a) and (b) of the Table 7.4, respectively). Large banks are distinguished because the probability of financial assistance is different (FAI is different) for large banks. Each panel includes three regressions, one for each of the weights applied to FAI and BCRI as described in the previous paragraph. Second, low-solvency banks are identified separately both for the whole sample and

Table 7.3 Bank bond spreads 1999–2002

		1999	2000	2001	2002	1999–2002
All banks						
New York	Observations	7	15	18	10	50
	Number of banks	7	11	10	6	18
	Mean	92.61	113.27	113.57	91.27	105.22
	SD	(18.96)	(24.67)	(26.88)	(11.01)	(24.02)
London	Observations	1	9	9	2	21
	Number of banks	1	6	6	2	9
	Mean	85.20	94.31	64.43	77.73	79.54
	SD	(NA)	(20.18)	(25.72)	(0.09)	(23.99)
Frankfurt	Observations	5	15	19	9	48
	Number of banks	4	8	12	8	13
	Mean	26.53	33.01	35.84	34.53	33.64
	SD	(5.32)	(7.86)	(8.88)	(10.69)	(8.90)
Tokyo	Observations	3	13	15	11	42
	Number of banks	2	5	6	6	8
	Mean	70.58	57.70	42.58	57.56	54.24
	SD	(54.72)	(54.89)	(31.76)	(37.59)	(39.88)
Large banks						
New York	Observations	1	5	11	6	23
	Number of banks	1	2	3	3	3
	Mean	70.85	103.66	95.52	89.52	92.59
	SD	(NA)	(14.71)	(10.51)	(5.18)	(12.56)
London	Observations	0	3	3	0	6
	Number of banks	0	1	2	0	2
	Mean	NA	77.11	47.07	NA	57.08
	SD	(NA)	(NA)	(5.19)	(NA)	(17.73)
Frankfurt	Observations	3	7	7	3	20
	Number of banks	2	3	3	2	3
	Mean	30.30	39.98	44.30	33.22	37.99
	SD	(5.29)	(3.84)	(8.68)	(3.03)	(7.55)
Tokyo	Observations	2	9	9	6	26
	Number of banks	1	3	3	3	3
	Mean	31.89	17.63	22.43	40.42	27.33
	SD	(NA)	(2.16)	(7.67)	(26.03)	(16.23)
Other banks						
New York	Observations	6	10	7	4	27
	Number of banks	6	9	7	3	15
	Mean	96.24	115.41	121.31	93.02	109.77
	SD	(17.91)	(26.56)	(28.54)	(16.35)	(25.68)
London	Observations	1	6	6	2	15
	Number of banks	1	5	4	2	7
	Mean	85.20	97.75	73.10	77.73	85.15
	SD	(NA)	(20.50)	(28.14)	(0.09)	(22.44)
Frankfurt	Observations	2	8	12	6	28
	Number of banks	2	5	9	6	10
	Mean	22.76	28.83	33.02	34.97	31.67
	SD	(0.47)	(6.51)	(7.35)	(12.54)	(8.91)
Tokyo	Observations	1	4	6	5	16
	Number of banks	1	2	3	3	5
	Mean	109.27	117.80	62.72	74.70	84.13
	SD	(NA)	(1.25)	(35.29)	(44.43)	(37.05)

Table 7.4 Regression results

(a) All banks									(b) Large banks								
	FAI100			***FAI50***			***FAI25***			***FAI_L100***			***FAI_L50***			***FAI_L25***	
Exv	**Corr**	**Stder**	**Exv**	**Corr**	**Stder**	**Exv**	**Corr**	**Stder**	**Exv**	**Corr**	**Stder**	**Exv**	**Corr**	**Stder**	**Exv**	**Corr**	**Stder**
FAI100	−8.23	0.99	*FAI50*	−8.90	1.40	*FAI25*	−7.20	1.60	*FAI_L100*	−23.77	5.39	*FAI_L50*	−16.80	2.68	*FAI_L25*	−10.47	2.03
E/TA	−3.28	1.45	*E/TA*	−0.80	1.48	*E/TA*	1.95	1.42	*E/TA*	−3.57	4.08	*E/TA*	1.87	2.27	*E/TA*	6.23	2.01
SIZE	−0.04	0.01	*SIZE*	−0.05	0.01	*SIZE*	−0.05	0.01	*SIZE*	−0.01	0.01	*SIZE*	−0.02	0.01	*SIZE*	−0.02	0.01
	$R^2 = 0.57$			$R^2 = 0.49$			$R^2 = 0.42$			$R^2 = 0.67$			$R^2 = 0.74$			$R^2 = 0.70$	

(c) All low-solvency banks									(d) Large low-solvency banks								
	FAI100			***FAI50***			***FAI25***			***FAI_L100***			***FAI_L50***			***FAI_L25***	
Exv	**Corr**	**Stder**	**Exv**	**Corr**	**Stder**	**Exv**	**Corr**	**Stder**	**Exv**	**Corr**	**Stder**	**Exv**	**Corr**	**Stder**	**Exv**	**Corr**	**Stder**
FAI100	−11.03	1.51	*FAI50*	−9.69	1.96	*FAI25*	−7.31	2.07	*FAI_L100*	−24.43	9.97	*FAI_L50*	−15.13	3.63	*FAI_L25*	−9.17	2.54
E/TA	−7.95	2.60	*E/TA*	−1.41	2.48	*E/TA*	2.73	2.27	*E/TA*	−5.13	8.94	*E/TA*	4.31	3.61	*E/TA*	9.28	3.03
SIZE	−0.03	0.01	*SIZE*	−0.04	0.01	*SIZE*	−0.04	0.01	*SIZE*	0.00	0.02	*SIZE*	−0.02	0.01	*SIZE*	−0.02	0.01
	$R^2 = 0.57$			$R^2 = 0.45$			$R^2 = 0.37$			$R^2 = 0.56$			$R^2 = 0.66$			$R^2 = 0.63$	

FAI100–25 – indexes and combinations of indexes applicable to all banks. *$FAI_L100–25$* – indexes and combinations of indexes applicable to large banks. Exv – exogenous variable. E/TA – equity to total assets (balance sheet end sum). SIZE – balance sheet end sum in billion USD.

for large banks, shown in panels (c) and (d) of Table 7.4. This enables an investigation of the hypothesis that in cases of low solvency, bank creditors will be more sensitive to whether they will experience a capital loss or not. Consequently, issues like bank creditor security and rights should become more central. Low solvency is described as being below mean solvency in a particular market in a particular time period. Thus the sample of low-solvency banks change from one time period to the next.

The regression equations also control for the level of solvency and the size of banks as these are widely expected to affect spreads. The level of solvency is defined as equity to total assets. Size is measured as the balance sheet end sum in billion US dollars.

The regression results in Table 7.4 seem *prima facie* reasonable. They support the initial assumption that bank exit regimes affect bank refinancing costs. Not only are the estimates clearly significant but over 50 per cent of the variance in bank bond spreads can be explained by the variables in the model in most cases. The values of the estimates appear reasonable in quantitative terms and their signs fit with the theoretical priors. A one unit difference in the level of FAI (that is, 1/15) corresponds with a 7.20–24.43 basis point difference in spreads. Five features stand out:

- The probability of financial assistance (FAI) is more important than the legal features (BCRI) of the bank exit regimes in explaining the level of spreads for all banks and all low solvency banks. This is not clearly the case for large banks and large low-solvency banks.
- Bank exit regimes seem to be more important when explaining spreads of large banks than spreads of small banks.
- The probability of assistance (FAI) and bank creditor rights (BCRI) are negatively correlated with the spreads, as expected.
- Solvency does not seem in general to work well as a control variable.
- Bank size on the other hand is negatively correlated with the level of spreads in all regressions, although only marginally.[18]

7.3 Regression results in the light of theory and previous empirical findings on credit spread determinants

The *existing theoretical framework* on credit spreads currently covers a wide variety of determinants, for example, structural models of default, the existence of embedded bond options in relation to interest-rate volatility and the implications of the interest-rate term structure. The discussion here distinguishes between determinants relating to market dynamics, bank-specific determinants and market-structure-oriented determinants. *Determinants relating to market dynamics* include the business cycle, the interest-rate level, interest-rate volatility and the term structure of the yield curve. *Bank-specific credit spread determinants* can in turn be separated into determinants relating to the leverage of the debtor company and others relating to the value of the debtor company.[19] However, previous research in the area is limited, particularly with regard to the market structure determinants that are the focus of this study.[20]

The *general business cycle* is the most widely addressed element of the effect of *market dynamics* on credit spreads.[21] One way of considering this is through quality spread theory, which focuses on the relation between company and government bonds as features of separate sectors of the bond market during varied economic times. Earnings and cash flows of debt providers are reduced during *difficult economic times*. This is also true for debtor companies. Asset values that form eventual collateral for debt issued are likely to deteriorate. In this situation, rational investors demand an increasing risk premium to accept high-risk non-government (that is, company) bonds. Conversely, in a *strong economic situation*, earnings and cash flows of debt providers and debtor companies increase and asset values continue to grow. Rational investors then also accept risky non-government bonds. As the demand for bonds increases, the risk premiums provided by the debtor companies to debt providers decrease.

The *level of interest rates* may also affect the nature of spreads directly according to yield ratio theory. It is not the *difference* between company and government bond yields (that is, spreads) that is most informative but the *ratio of non-government to government bond yields* that will be more stable and informative than their absolute spread. The underlying idea of the yield-ratio approach is quite contrary to that of the quality spread. The yield-ratio theory builds on the assumption that times of high interest-rate levels are characterized by wide spreads and times of low levels by narrow spreads, that is, it emphasizes proportionality.[22]

Interest-rate volatility is linked to the level of bond spreads in three ways.

- First, it can have a *direct effect* through embedded options in the debt contracts, as many corporate bonds have cash call, refunding or put provisions. In combination with such terms, interest-rate volatility creates uncertainty about returns on existing bonds. Consequently, investors require higher yields to compensate for the increased bond risks, leading to a decrease in bond price. The effects of bond terms on bond yields and bond prices vary depending on the specific character of the terms. These terms include various conditions for debtor action. In some cases a *documented change in market conditions* is needed, for example, to legitimate optional measures by the debtor. In others, the legal terms may give the debtor *independent options* without regard to market conditions. In these latter situations, increasing volatility implies an even higher degree of uncertainty, since optional measures may be taken on whatever grounds.

- Second, interest-rate volatility may relate to – that is, cause changes in or derive from – the general business cycle, implying *indirect effects* on or correlation with spread movements. Changes in interest rates impair the ability of companies to make investment decisions and the consumers to consume. High interest-rate volatility often precedes periods of economic stagnation or contraction. During such times rational investors demand an increasing risk premium in order to accept corporate bonds as an alternative to government bonds.[23]
- Third, the relative liquidity of bond markets affects the impact of interest rate volatility on corporate bond spreads. Corporate bonds are usually less liquid than government bonds. In such markets, the bid-ask spread is wider than in well-functioning markets. Consequently, the variation in yields (and spreads) agreed upon is higher than in well-functioning markets.[24]

The second group of theoretical spread determinants is *company* (that is, *bank*) *specific*. As so-called 'structural' models of default for identifying determinants of credit spread changes concentrate on the level of debt outstanding, they are analysed first, before moving on to other determinants linked to the character of the debtor company.

Company-specific *determinants focusing on leverage*, may be viewed from two angles. In the first case, the view on debt in relation to own funds follows a *balance-sheet logic*. Determinants deal directly with the amount or proportion of debt in relation to own funds. Large amounts of debt are considered problematic, since own funds may not be sufficient to cover debts in the event of default, leading investors to demand a wider spread. The second angle, from which determinants focusing on leverage may be viewed, follows a *profit/loss account logic*. In this situation, it is not the amount of debt in itself that affects the spreads – it is the cost generated by the debt as a function of the amount of debt and the level of interest rates. According to this perspective, the interest-rate level in combination with the amount of debt is a crucial determinant of the observed spreads. For a profitable company the spreads may narrow, since cash flow is sufficient to cover the interest paid and decrease the amount of outstanding debt. Still, worth remembering is that a simplified view of the amount of debt and the level of interest rates may be misleading. The construction of spread determinants focusing on leverage also incorporates the maturity structure of company debt and future liquidity needs. In other words, the spot (interest) rate is not necessarily a determinant of the costs generated by the debt. For many companies the major part of existing debt is fixed rate and long term. Such costs of debt are not affected by the spot (interest) rate. Companies with unexpected capital outflows (that is, liquidity needs) are the ones most influenced by changes in the spot (interest) rate.[25]

There is a wide range of *other determinants* linked to the character of the debtor company. In the theoretical debate, these determinants mainly relate to the value of the debtor company and changes in the company's business climate. Transparency plays a key role in affecting the potential effects of these determinants on credit spreads. In practice the environment is not characterized by free, instant information flow in the disclosure of company data. For determinants focusing on the *value of the debtor company*, the underlying theoretical assumptions are that an increase in debtor-company value should generate lower spreads. This derives from the fact that the higher company value constitutes a guarantee for the capital invested by company creditors. Still, the exact procedures for how changes in company value generate changes in credit spreads have not been established. *Changes in the company's business climate* are also often reflected in the value of the company. Improvements of the business climate are expected to generate narrower spreads.[26]

Apart from these theoretical considerations, empirical research on bank bond spreads has found *aspects of the market structure*, that is, country-specific features, contribute to explaining the level of spreads. Signs of underlying systematic factors affecting the levels of spreads have been identified in comparative studies but there has been uncertainty about what these factors represent.[27] Two characteristics stand out in studies of bank performance: determinants associated with the *role of banks* in various financial systems and also directly with *features of the regulatory system*. Traditionally, a distinction between relationship and transactional banks has been made, signalling country-specific differences in functions between German-related and Anglo-Saxon banks. Furthermore, when focusing on regulatory systems, the emphasis has mostly been on the general investor protection provided by the legislation. In this sense, this study clearly contributes to an area not yet investigated. This study clearly implies that certain detailed features of the regulatory system affect the level of bank bond spreads.[28]

7.4 Summary

The regression results imply that bank exit regimes affect *bank refinancing costs*. Banks receive a competitive advantage in the form of lower spreads if situated in financial centres with regimes providing bank creditors with higher grades of security and better rights in the case of bank failure. Traditional determinants of spread levels usually considered in theoretical discussions, in this case solvency and size, were not found to affect spread levels significantly. A separate question concerns the implications of the fact that spread levels vary under different bank exit regimes. One could assume that banks strive to compensate for the higher refinancing costs through various arrangements. This is an area for future research.

Notes

1. See Granlund (2003) for a discussion of methodological approaches to legislation evaluation.
2. See Granlund (2002) for a presentation of the bank exit legislation of the various financial centres.
3. This analysis develops approaches for the specification and quantification of legal regimes similar to those used elsewhere; La Porta *et al.* (1997), for example. Initially, in such quantification, traditional (0–1) scales were used on the grounds that the law either does or does not regulate certain features. Second, simple cardinal scales relating to a certain legal feature were used (assuming grade differences between countries exist). Finally, cardinal scales, based on aggregating the individual series were employed and contrasted with the individual indexes used jointly.
4. See Granlund (2002) for a presentation of the legal basis for financial assistance to banks and of the assistance practice followed in the various financial centres.
5. For literature on the subject of constructive ambiguity see Freixas *et al.* (2000, p. 74).,
6. The most recent rescue of a major US bank was of the Continental Illinois National Bank and Trust Co. (CINB) in 1984. As a result of a run of uninsured depositors and implications of systemic effects the government provided the CINB with a US$2 billion assistance package. Only bank shareholders suffered losses due to FDIC arrangements. On the other hand, smaller US banks are seldom bailed out or dealt with in a way that would benefit bank creditors directly or indirectly.

7. The most recent UK bank failures and government actions taken include Barings Bank and Re Chancery plc. In the case of Barings Bank, the Bank of England (BoE) tried to arrange for a rescue of the bank. The rescue failed but the administrator was allowed to negotiate an immediate contract with the Internationale Nederlanden Groep (ING) without consulting bank creditors. No public capital was required. In 1991, the Re Chancery plc. was reorganized on a voluntary basis. Similarly, no public capital was involved.
8. Surprisingly, in 1974 Bankhaus Herstatt was allowed to fail without governmental intervention. Still, it is clear that the German assistance practice is supportive. The problems of the banking industry are dealt with in close cooperation with the supervisory institutions. Recently failed banks, like Schmidt Bank and Bankgesellschaft Berlin in 2002, have received capital injections.
9. In Japan, there is a long history of bank bailouts and the Bank of Japan has led arrangements to secure the continuance of banks' activities as separate independent or merged entities. One example of a larger bank recently receiving financial aid is the Long Term Credit Bank. Smaller banks have also usually received support, although there are a few examples of it being denied.
10. For viewpoints on all these legal features of the financial centre bank exit regimes see Granlund (2002).
11. The current trend in the formulation of bank exit regulation seems to be the replacement of composition with broader authority-administered reorganization. In Frankfurt, for example, such amendments have been made to the national legislation.
12. The reason for focusing on senior rather than subordinated debt is that senior debt should be more sensitive to changes in the banks' environment. In the realization of the banks' assets, senior debt-holders may regain all their capital or lose some or all of it. For subordinated debt-holders this question is not as topical. It is rare for subordinated debt-holders to receive anything in the realization of debtor-assets. The reason for concentrating on spreads instead of yields eliminates a substantial amount of variation in the cost of capital and improves conditions for the drawing of conclusions based on regressions results. By considering debt only in the form of publicly traded bonds, another type of sensitivity relating to market efficiency is introduced. According to economic theory, publicly traded bond prices should signal the full extent of the knowledge (information) about the debtor and its environment.
13. The criterion for inclusion in the top three category is the amount of total assets according to the bank's balance sheet. Balance sheet data are analysed on a yearly basis.
14. Another area requiring some additional explanation is the treatment of international banking groups in the study. Such groups should not constitute a problem for the study as all banks considered in the analysis are separate judicial entities to which the local bank exit regime applies. In addition, in order to eliminate any bias in bank refinancing costs generating from parent company jurisdictions, all banks with an apparent foreign bank subsidiary status have been excluded from the analysis.

15. Sometimes, bank failures may be very costly to deal with. According to Milhaupt (1999) costs may rise to 20–50 per cent of the affected country's GDP when bailing out troubled banks. In these cases, government bond yields may also be affected by bank failures. Then, spreads as attributes for individual bank conditions are biased.
16. There are some balances to be made in considering combination of indexes. Some of the distinctions among the components, such as that between the legal features and the practice of the authorities in implementing them, may represent very different dimensions that affect behaviour. Where possible the separate application of these influences needs to be attempted before resorting to combination if this is not compelled for statistical reasons.
17. Since the grades of the FAI applied to large banks are different from the grades of the FAI applied to all banks (the grades of the BCRI are the same), the indexes are separately indentified with the label *L*: FAI_L100, FAI_L50 and FAI_L25.
18. There is a small problem of serial correlation in the residuals since the Durbin-Watson statistic is between 0.33 and 0.77. This may depend on the fairly low number of spread observations for each quarter. It may also be a result of the fact that the underlying model is fairly static, although spread movements themselves are dynamic.
19. There is also some debate about how bank spreads across markets should be related to other company spreads across the same markets.
20. For related examples concerning the implications of the market structure on bank performance see Allen and Rai (1996), Chakravarty and Molyneux (1996) and Dewenter and Hess (1998).
21. Fama and French (1989), for example, discuss the relation between business conditions and expected returns on bonds and find that credit spreads widen when economic conditions weaken.
22. For more detailed viewpoints on the yield ratio as an alternative market attribute see Dialynas and Edington (1992).
23. Closely related to this question are considerations concerning local supply and demand shocks as major determinants of the level of spreads. In some studies, this concept has been introduced as a complementary explanation for existing spread levels, since other significant determinants have not been identified.
24. Credit spreads of corporate bonds may also be affected by *the term structure of the yield curve*. Bond spreads are influenced by the shape of the yield curve, independent of the general level of interest rates. Spreads are assumed to decrease when the yield curve has a sharply positive slope and increase when the yield curve is flat or inverted. Here the term structure of the yield curve in relation to the level of credit spreads is seen as an expression of the quality spread theory discussed earlier.
25. Merton (1974) introduced structural models of default. Since then, the empirical validity of the models has been debated. Brown (2000) has found evidence supporting the opposite view that credit spread changes are due to non-credit-risk factors.
26. Bryis and de Varenne (1997) speak in favour of models focusing on firm value in the estimation and explanation of credit-spread levels. The regression results of *this study* indicate that other factors than firm value direct the

level of spreads. Similarly, based on this analysis, company size does not seem to affect the level of spreads very much.

27. Collin-Dufresne *et al.* (2001).
28. See Allen and Rai (1996) and Dewenter and Hess (1998). See also La Porta *et al.* (1997, 1998, 1999).

Part III

Approaches to Solving the Problem

8
A European Approach to Banking Crises

Henk Brouwer, Gerbert Hebbink and Sandra Wesseling

Financial crises happen. More specifically, banking crises happen. Most of the times, these crises have a number of common features, like a combination of adverse market or other external conditions and poor risk management practices. However, we can also observe that banking crises are never identical. For every banking crisis there are different immediate causes. Every setting or situation is different and also the characteristics of the problematic institutions differ. Causes of financial problems can differ widely. The problems can become manifest at the financial institutions themselves, whether these are banks, insurance companies, securities firms or financial conglomerates, as was shown with BCCI and Barings. Shocks can also originate in and be transmitted through financial markets, as was shown by the Asia crisis and the LTCM affair. Moreover, payment and settlement systems can be channels of financial instability, as was feared after the terrorist attacks in September 2001. Finally, the implications of a crisis can be very different, depending on the type of crisis and the type of institution. The type of institution, its relation with other financial institutions, its cross-border linkages and its position on certain financial markets determine, *inter alia,* whether there is a potential danger for contagion to other markets and institutions.

For these reasons, national authorities deal with banking crises on a case-by-case basis and take all the relevant aspects connected with each crisis into consideration. For these reasons also, it is clear that there is no – and should be no – blueprint for crisis management, either at the national level or at the European level. Another argument for this is to limit moral hazard, that is, the phenomenon that market participants are less risk averse than they would be, because they discount the authorities' readiness to rescue.

In this chapter we focus on financial crisis management, in particular the European approach to banking crises. On the one hand, it is clear that national authorities remain responsible for handling banking crises, mainly because their authority is embedded in an environment of national regulations. On the other hand, some broad and general principles which need to be addressed during a crisis have emerged, and it may be useful to sum up here what has been achieved so far in the EU. In the course of the chapter we illustrate how diverse the European banking environment is, and, consequently, how dissimilar any future banking crisis will be from previous crises. In the first section, we discuss the key principle of private sector involvement. This principle guides many initiatives around the issues of crisis prevention and crisis management in the EU. In Section 8.2 we focus on the kind of information that financial sector authorities should try to have available to address any future crisis. Crisis management is the subject of Section 8.3, where we start with some general issues that need to be prepared in advance. Some of these may be considered obvious, like liquidity assistance and a deposit insurance system. Besides, authorities need to be prepared by having arrangements for the exchange of information in crisis situations. We elaborate on the specific European rules and directives in this regard. In the second part of Section 8.3, we focus on actual crisis management, where we have arranged possible responses to a crisis according to the degree of systemic risk that the authorities perceive at the time. We sum up the main findings in Section 8.4, and conclude by drawing up a list of steps that have to be taken in addressing a bank crisis.

8.1 Private sector involvement

In principle, the private sector should be involved as much as possible in both crisis prevention and, if this fails, in crisis management. Each financial institution is responsible for its own safety and soundness. If financial losses occur, the firm's shareholders should bear their share of the costs and its management should suffer the consequences. Alternative options for private sector solutions among other things are takeovers, lifeboats or purchase-and-assumption transaction. This includes splitting-up the institution followed by takeovers of the parts, in line with the dictum that institutions that might be too-big-to-fail are not necessarily too-big-to-shrink. Finally, the winding down of the institution may be a sensible strategy when the systemic consequences are considered to be small.[1]

There are several considerations for promoting private sector involvement. First, bank failures are inherent to risk-taking in a competitive environment. Banks enjoy the benefits of profits during favourable economic conditions and should also bear the losses in times of adverse economic developments. Supervision cannot and should not provide an absolute assurance that banks will not fail. Therefore, the objectives of protecting the financial system and the interests of depositors are not incompatible with individual bank failures.

Second, a least-cost criterion should guide the authorities when making choices between alternative actions. All costs and benefits, including those of a stable financial system, should be taken into consideration by the supervisor in deciding on a course of action.[2] A private sector solution, that does not impose a cost on taxpayers and introduces the least distortions in the banking sector, is in line with the least-cost criterion. This usually entails finding a healthy institution that is interested in ownership of (parts of) the bank. From an economic point of view, private sector solutions are the least distortionary, in the sense that allocation of resources is left to market forces.

Finally, moral hazard should be avoided as far as possible. Supervisory action should not create incentives for banks to engage in risk-taking behaviour that entails costs which those banks do not have to bear entirely. Shareholders should not be compensated for losses when an institution gets into difficulty; otherwise it will encourage comparable institutions to behave less prudently in the expectation that they will receive a similar kind of bailout if problems occur. Equally, supervisory action should not protect the interests of the bank's corporate officers. In general, private sector solutions will be such that this is avoided.

These considerations imply that the authorities should only step in when private sector solutions are exhausted. The importance of this increases with the risk of financial instability, as the latter will fuel market perceptions of a public safety net. In the current international financial system there are strong indications that financial instability risks are greater than in the past. For example, international capital markets are increasingly correlated and financial institutions are increasingly linked to each other; within countries and across borders. These linkages may lead to increased instability, for example, through contagion or other systemic events. It could be argued, however, that other developments have led to reduced risks of financial instability, like financial market innovations, use of derivatives, enhanced risk management, improved economic policies, and wider adherence to codes and standards. A particular development is risk diversification, through the emergence of larger financial institutions. Although these developments may contribute to a reduced probability of individual bank crises, it is clear that authorities have to be aware that systemic events, once they occur, will have more severe consequences than in the past. Consequently, regarding crisis *prevention*, it is increasingly important to have a supervisory focus on risk management, stress tests and so on.

8.2 Information on the specific nature of a financial crisis

As we have argued, financial crises come in all shapes and sizes. How the private sector or public authorities respond to a specific crisis will depend on the character of the financial problems and the characteristics of the financial institution. Consequently, there is a strong need to identify the problems the financial institution has run into and their possible effects. Adequate information is crucial; in the first phase of the crisis in particular. In this phase many questions have to be answered, mainly concerning recognition and identification of the problem.[3]

A first set of questions that have to be answered relates to the type of institution and the nature of the particular crisis. The focus of many of these questions will be whether there is a liquidity or solvency crisis. However, these two are not easy to disentangle. An up-to-date organization chart is required to verify the legal structure of the financial institution (or the group). Recent balance sheet and income statements, as well as off-balance-sheet information, are needed, in order to gain insight into the potential impact of current risk exposures on the institution's financial condition. Information on the liquidity and funding profile, including the maturity of major funding arrangements, is of vital importance, because this indicates how long the financial institution can withstand a situation of financial stress. The financial institution should have performed stress tests and have contingency procedures, which address the liquidity and capital needs, funding options, downsizing options and spillover effects in specific scenarios. These are helpful in gauging the potential size of the ultimate loss.

A second question to be addressed by the authorities in the early stage of a crisis relates to the response of the financial institution itself to its critical situation. It also entails mapping out the likely reaction of its direct counterparties (wholesale and retail clients, exchanges and clearing houses), in particular whether they are willing to enter into new funding or trading transactions. Moreover, it concerns information on upcoming settlements, actual and expected margin and collateral calls. Also relevant is the extent to which close affiliates of the financial institution are affected, necessitating information on the size and the nature of intercompany balances, exposures, and current flows of funds.

A third question concerns information that enables authorities to weigh up the indirect impact of the crisis situation on financial institutions and markets. Linkages between the strained financial institution and other financial institutions and markets may threaten financial stability, particularly when the institution has large cross-sector or cross-border positions. However, in an integrated financial area it may be difficult to identify *a priori* the systemic implications of a crisis at a major financial institution. For example, the strained institution may affect other institutions through common creditors. Another possible channel through which the effects are difficult to measure runs through off-balance-sheet items.

8.3 Management of banking crises in the EU

There are some general measures that will be taken in any case, mainly in the early stages of a crisis, when liquidity problems need to be addressed. These are discussed in Section 8.3.1. Next, instead of trying to formulate a uniform methodology of crisis management, in Section 8.3.2 we describe policy responses to problems taking place in various types of financial institutions.[4] We structure this description using a broad – though not comprehensive – set of characteristics of the banking institutions involved. In the process, we use some comparative evidence on the EU banking sector.

8.3.1 General considerations

Deposit insurance

Once it becomes clear that a crisis requires public policy measures, because a bank is possibly insolvent, the authorities have to consider the distribution of costs between taxpayers on the one hand and creditors and shareholders on the other hand. In line with the principle of private sector involvement, public authorities will try to limit the taxpayers' bill as much as possible. Irrespective of additional public sector involvement in the crisis, a deposit insurance system may be available, in order to cover part of depositors' losses. (The interaction of the structure of the deposit insurance system and bank insolvency is the explicit subject of Chapter 4. It is also a critical feature of the proposals discussed in Chapters 1 and 2.) In European countries, deposit insurance is generally funded by the banking sector.[5] A deposit insurance system may have the added value of limiting or restoring the depositors' and the public's confidence in the banking system. Still, the effect may be limited, since the coverage of most deposit insurance schemes is subject to a ceiling. In past banking-crisis episodes, however, this has led some governments to announce a blanket guarantee, which may raise the immediate public costs to a sizable level.[6]

Within the EU, national deposit insurance schemes are controlled by the home country. In case of a crisis at a foreign branch, this means that the home country's deposit insurance system covers losses to foreign depositors at the branch office.[7]

Liquidity assistance

In order to prevent a liquidity crisis from developing into a solvency crisis, it is essential for public authorities to shore up confidence. This may be done by providing information to financial market participants, for instance on the readiness of the authorities, in practice the central bank, to provide liquidity assistance if needed. However, in order to prevent any bailout expectations from taking root, most central banks in the EU adhere to a policy of so-called constructive ambiguity and do not disclose their emergency liquidity assistance (ELA) policy options beforehand.

Nonetheless, in case of an imminent bank crisis, there is a general understanding that, once it is decided to provide liquidity support, this has to take place in an early stage. An important advantage of ELA, inherent to its purpose, is that it provides valuable time during the onset of a crisis. Authorities can benefit by using this time to analyse the situation, collect information, and contact relevant parties.

From the start of EMU it has been made clear that any existing arrangements for ELA within the countries of the Eurosystem remain the responsibility of national central banks, and not of the European Central Bank. National central banks also bear the costs of any ELA provision.[8] Obviously, the ECB must be kept informed, since liquidity injections may interfere with the single monetary policy and may need to be sterilized. Specific arrangements for a proper exchange of information have been made. As a rule, official liquidity support is provided to solvent banks, against collateral, and only for the short term. Hence, initially, there are no direct fiscal costs involved in this stage of crisis management.

Responsibilities with regard to crisis management

It is important to recall that EU countries differ in their organization of the regulatory and supervisory framework for the financial sector. Banks, in particular, are either supervised by national central banks, by a separate supervisory institution or by a combination of the two.

Moreover, countries differ in their relationship between supervisors and national governments.[9] In general, banking supervision in the EU is organized according to the principle of home country responsibility, which means that the country of residence is responsible for solvency supervision. The principle of home country control however is not applicable to foreign subsidiaries. Host country authorities are obliged to treat these as domestic institutions with their own legal identity. In the event of a crisis at a foreign subsidiary, the host country supervisor can take any preventive measure envisaged in this context.

Moreover, key common principles regarding the supervision of the financial sector have been agreed in the EU, as defined in a core set of harmonized concepts and rules.[10] However, there are no specific references to crisis management in EU directives. Of particular relevance is the question of the distribution of responsibilities in crises that may have cross-border implications. In such cases, there is a need for coordination on a cross-border and cross-sector basis between the various authorities. For banks the identification of the coordinating supervisor is relatively straightforward, for instance the supervisor who exercises consolidated supervision is generally considered to be the coordinator. Even if a coordinator has been identified, the responsibilities of the authorities involved have not changed. This means that, although there are no specific references to crisis management in EU directives, the presumption exists that the home country supervisor is responsible for decisions on crisis management, at least regarding individual institutions and their branches.

Information sharing

In the previous section, we argued that gathering information is vital in the early stage of a crisis. This is also a prominent issue in two recent reports on financial stability prepared for the ministers and governors of the EU.[11] Of course, in this stage there should be intense cooperation and discussion between supervisors and other relevant authorities. In this context, some general principles for cooperation and information exchange apply in the EU. These principles have been incorporated into EU directives. Crucially, the relevant EU directives do not impose an obligation for information sharing in *crisis situations*, nor do they provide for the content and timing of the information to be exchanged in such circumstances. In practice, information exchange in crisis situations relies on cooperative arrangements between the competent authorities belonging to different geographical jurisdictions. The infrastructure for information sharing in the EU consists of three components: day-to-day contacts between supervisors and central banks; the existence of committees, like the Banking Supervision Committee (BSC) of the ESCB and the Groupe de Contact; and bilateral Memoranda of Understanding (MoUs). Currently, a multilateral MoU is in preparation on high-level principles of cooperation between banking supervisors and central banks of the European Union in crisis management situations. The BSC fulfils an important role in enhancing cross-border cooperation and information exchange between central banks and supervisors.[12] In addition, the BSC has a responsibility in crisis prevention, by performing macroprudential analyses and analyses of banking developments for the purpose of assessing the soundness of the EU banking sector.

Enforcing a private sector solution

In order to enforce a private sector solution the authorities may take on a role as independent, 'honest broker'. As a neutral intermediary, they may encourage the involved parties to share information and to find a private sector solution, such as some type of reorganization, a merger, an acquisition by another bank, or a purchase-and-assumption transaction.[13]

If the private sector cannot resolve the crisis, the option to close and liquidate the bank, including (possibly partial) repayment of the depositors, will have to be considered. In the case of smaller banks, without significant systemic risks, the usual liquidation procedures may imply that the bank's shareholders and creditors bear a loss.[14] Moreover, supervisory authorities will hold the bank's management accountable for any possible misbehaviour. For banks within the EU, a liquidation decision is within the competence of national, home country authorities.[15] They are committed to inform authorities in other countries that might be affected by the liquidation.

8.3.2 Public sector involvement and systemic risk

When a private sector solution does not appear to be feasible and intermediating action by the authorities does not work, it may be necessary to consider the use of public funds to speed up an orderly resolution of the crisis. A large set of options exists, predominantly under the heading of recapitalization. The options range from complete nationalization of the institution, to temporary use of public funds in a bridge bank.

The decision to intervene in a crisis by providing 'taxpayer's money', however, should only be taken after a solid cost-benefit analysis. This is a complex issue, which has to be settled in a situation that is characterized by lack of time and information. As indicated, it requires an assessment of the costs of (future) moral hazard and the alternative costs of financial instability. Thus, the authorities' decision process will need to gauge the extent of systemic risk.

Although it should be acknowledged that any solvency crisis is a unique event, the authorities can attempt to infer the potential for systemic risk by analysing the general characteristics of the institution, its counterparts and the markets in which it operates, as well as the source of the incurred losses. In this section, we try to structure the possible cases that may emerge from this analysis and discuss the possible policy responses. This overview also illustrates the point that a one-size-fits-all solution does not exist, because these cases differ widely across the EU.

Relative size

A significant characteristic of any insolvent institution that will be taken into account by public authorities is the *size* of the bank, as, for example, measured by its balance sheet. First, this is a factor that is related to the feasibility of private sector solutions, because it affects the maximum loss that may be incurred by the institution(s) that takes over the insolvent bank. Hence, if the insolvent bank is relatively small, private institutions may be more interested in taking part in the solution.

The relative size of an insolvent bank is also relevant, because it functions as an indicator of possible systemic risk, in particular through stress in financial markets. Liquidation of assets of insolvent banks could significantly affect financial markets, acting as a channel of systemic risk. For this reason, in the case of insolvency at a relatively small bank, public authorities would be less inclined to become further involved in the solution of the crisis.

In recent years, the average size of banks in the EU has increased.[16] During the 1990s, the number of banks has mainly declined due to mergers between smaller institutions at regional and national levels (Table 8.1). Similarly, as a result of mergers, the relative size of universal banks has increased further. Over the past decade, the concentration of banks has increased in almost all EU countries. *Ceteris paribus*, this indicates that the systemic implications of a defaulting institution have increased.[17] On the other hand, the presence of large institutions also increases the capacity of the private sector to take over a problematic institution (possibly in another country). Figure 8.1 illustrates how the concentration ratios differ significantly among EU countries. Therefore, the extent to which crisis management is able to rely on private sector solutions, as well as the kind of solutions that are feasible, differs across EU countries.

Table 8.1 Number of MFIs in the EU, end of year

	1998	2000
Credit institutions	8,320	7,464
Money market	1,516	1,604
Other institutions	8	8
Total	9,844	9,076

Note: The 1998 data refer to the euro area-wide numbers of MFIs as at 1 January 1999.

Source: Data from ECB, *Report on Financial Structures*, 2002.

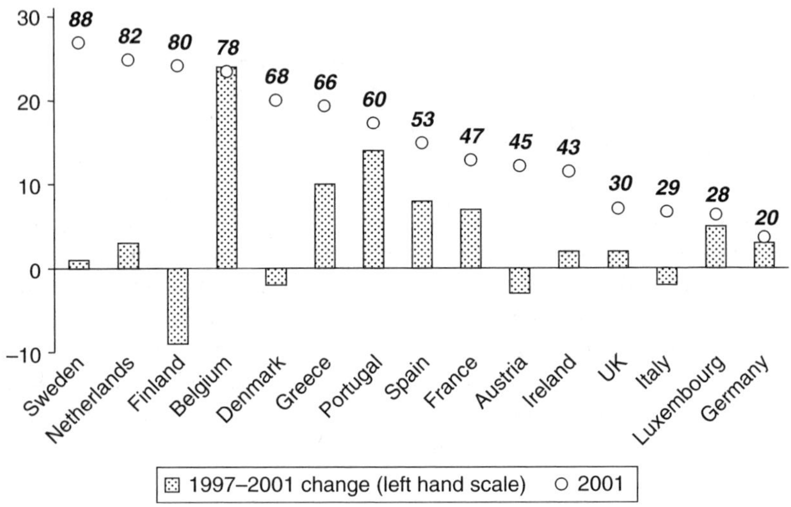

Figure 8.1 Share of five largest credit institutions in total assets

Note: Non-consolidated basis; Sweden 2001 is value for 2000.

Source: Data from ECB, *Structural Analysis of the EU Banking Sector*, 2002.

Related to the size of a bank's balance sheet is its *exposure to other banks*. This may be considered as an additional indicator of systemic risk, through the channel of balance sheet contagion. First, banks exposed to the distressed bank are directly affected, because of losses on their exposures. In addition, they may be forced to liquidate other assets, because their solvency ratios have decreased. Authorities, interested in maintaining financial stability, will have to take this effect on the solvency of other banks into account in the decision whether to support an insolvent bank. Moreover, indirect exposures, for example

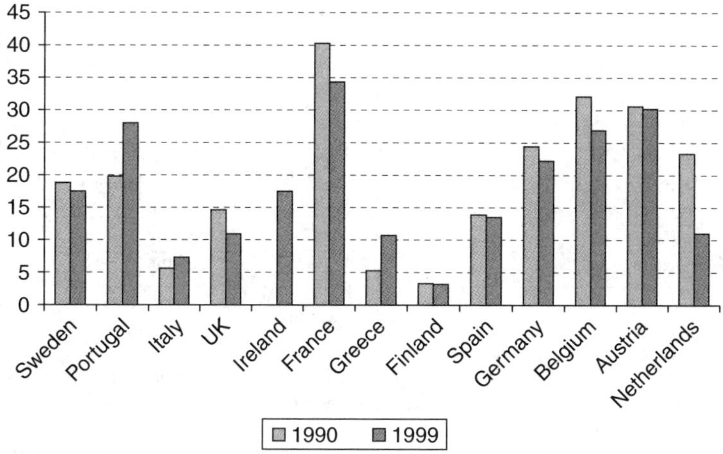

Figure 8.2 Interbank claims as a percentage of total assets
Source: Data from *Bank Profitability*, OECD, 2000.

credit derivatives, have to be taken into consideration. These credit-risk transfer instruments are used more and more, and large financial groups have been able to transfer part of their risks to other players. However, these risks have not disappeared from the financial system but supervisory authorities do not have a very clear idea where they are located. Figure 8.2 shows the level of interbank exposure during the 1990s.

Besides interbanking exposures, banks hold exposures in other financial institutions, like investment funds, pension funds and insurance companies. These *cross-sector exposures* may be an additional source of systemic risk, because weaknesses in these other sectors may lead to losses in banks. Moreover, other financial sectors are taking over credit risk from banks. This might be efficient, since it may contribute to optimal risk allocation. However, it is not always clear whether credit risk has been transferred entirely, or whether non-bank institutions are sufficiently aware of the kind of risks they are taking on.

There is evidence that non-financial sectors increasingly hold financial assets in financial intermediaries other than banks. In particular, this trend can be observed in the euro area within the 1998–2000 period. However, Figure 8.3 illustrates that the relative size of non-bank intermediaries differs significantly across the euro area. Hence, the potential for cross-sectoral systemic risk will vary across the EU. As a separate indicator of potential systemic effects, *cross-border linkages* should be considered. The most important type of cross-border linkage

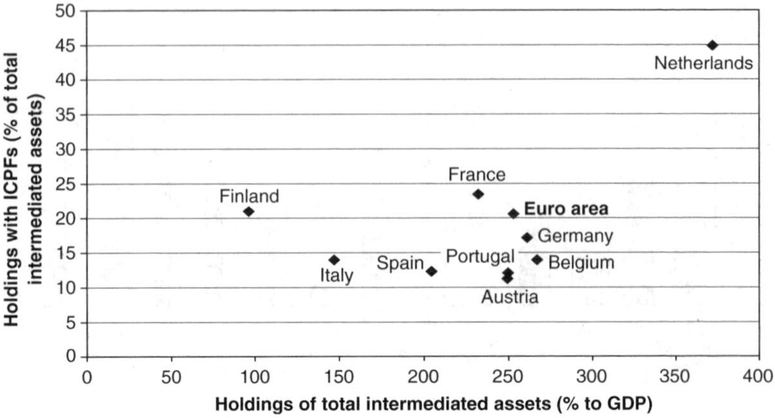

Figure 8.3 Percentage of holdings with insurance corporations and pension funds of intermediated assets (end-2000)

Source: ECB, *Report on Financial Structures*, 2002, p. 25.

is foreign banking exposures. Although cross-border exposures in themselves do not have to lead to additional systemic risks, these require specific attention of authorities in periods of distress. Insolvency at a bank with sizable cross-border holdings in other banks or foreign subsidiaries has implications for supervisory authorities in the host countries. According to Figure 8.4, euro area banks hold significant claims on banks in other euro area countries, though the relative size differs across countries.

Moreover, according to Figure 8.5, banks in most euro area countries have increased the share of euro area banks in their total foreign bank claims. However, Figure 8.5 also conveys the opposite message that European banks still have significant links to banks outside the euro area. This is supported by data on revenues of large financial groups, which show that European financial institutions in 2000 received 25 per cent of their revenues from other European countries, against 30 per cent from non-European countries.[18] Hence, European cooperation with regard to crisis management should not be too inward-looking, neglecting cross-border linkages to non-euro area countries.

Additional types of cross-border linkages are cross-shareholding interests. Often, this type of linkage is combined with cross-sector exposures or exists in the form of *financial conglomerates*. In general, conglomerates may warrant specific attention regarding systemic risk, in particular

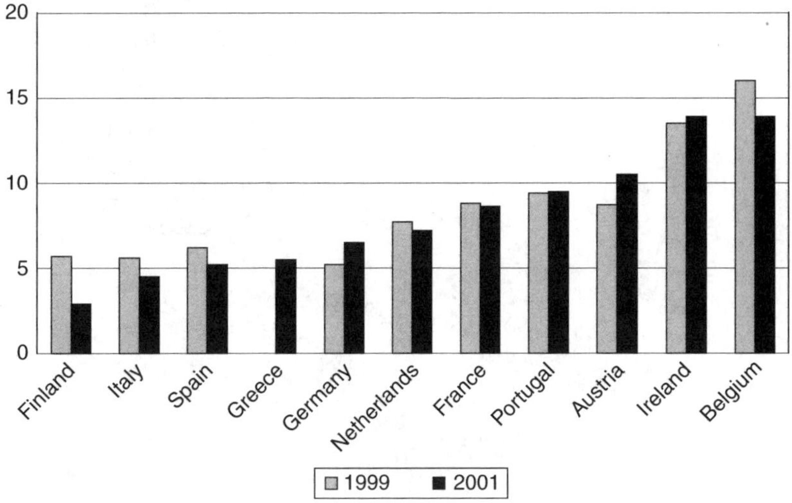

Figure 8.4 Claims on banks in other euro area countries (percentage of total claims)

Source: Data from IMF, *International Financial Statistics*.

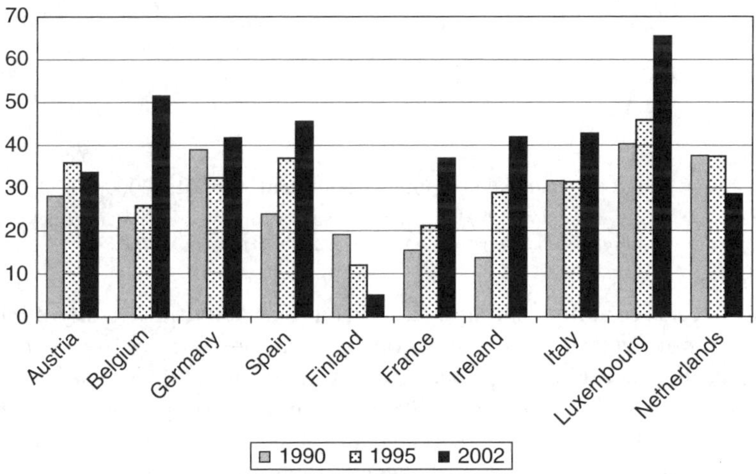

Figure 8.5 Cross-border claims on euro area banks (percentage of total claims on banks)

Source: Data from BIS locational statistics.

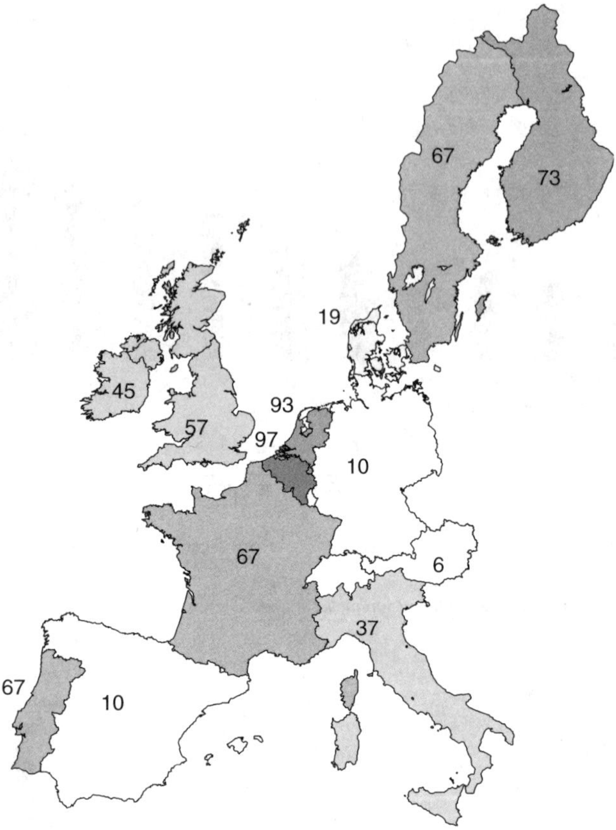

Figure 8.6 Share of financial conglomerates in bank deposits (2000, %)

Source: I. van Lelyveld and A. Schilder, 'Risk in Financial Conglomerates: Management and Supervision', *Research Series Supervision*, No. 49, The Netherlands Bank, 2002.

those that combine banking and insurance activities. It should be noted, however, that the risk of contagion among entities in the group should not be higher than among other institutions, since separate solvency requirements apply to banks and insurance companies within the group. Besides, conglomerates have an increased potential to diversify their credit and market risks. However, problems in one part of the conglomerate can spillover to other parts through the reputation of the group as a whole. Another channel of contagion runs through the holding of the conglomerate, which may be less well supervised than the separate entities. If the solvency of a bank within a conglomerate is at risk, it is even more vital to obtain information, in particular from other parts of the group. Currently, an EU directive is being prepared, which aims to improve supervisory practices for conglomerates. One of the proposals is to appoint a coordinating supervisor.

Figure 8.6 illustrates the variation within European countries with respect to the relevance of financial conglomerates to the banking sector. The significance of conglomerates is particularly high in Belgium and the Netherlands.

A final specific source of systemic risk may arise due to a bank's relation to national or international *payment systems*, especially concerning large-value interbank fund transfer systems. Oversight of payment systems in the EU is exercised by national overseers and the ECB. Credit institutions in the EU are free to access the payment system in any member state, hence a crisis at an individual bank could have systemic effects on banks in other EU countries, through its settlement obligations in payment systems. It is important, therefore, that relevant information is transferred between overseers and supervisors. In order to provide for exchange of such information, overseers and supervisors have agreed on a Memorandum of Understanding on specific arrangements for cooperation and information sharing.[19]

8.4 Conclusion

Although financial crises, and bank insolvencies in particular, will happen, they are never identical. Moreover, national financial systems differ widely, even across the EU countries. For practical reasons, therefore, there can be no blueprint for management of bank crises. However, there is general agreement on some principles to which the public authorities should adhere in a bank crisis. First, private sector solutions are to be preferred. They prevent moral hazard, are cost effective, and limit the costs to the taxpayer. Second, due to increased cross-sectoral and international linkages, flows of information between supervisors and central banks should be optimal. Third, emergency lending arrangements should be in place and could be used in the early stage of a crisis. This creates precious time that may be required to collect information and prepare a solution to a crisis.

In their decision on how much public funds might be devoted to the resolution of a crisis, authorities should be prepared to perform a proper cost-benefit analysis. Indispensable in this analysis is an assessment of the potential costs of financial instability that might evolve from the crisis. On the one hand, systemic risks are more contained than before, because of enhanced risk management procedures and increased potential for diversification. On the other hand, it might well be clear that the potential costs of a crisis, once it occurs, have risen dramatically.

Finally, although bank crises are never the same, and many practical caveats exist, the most important steps in the decision process that public authorities should go through might be summed up in the following list.

- buy time:
  - ✓ ELA
- provide confidence:
  - ✓ depositor guarantee
  - ✓ liquidity in interbank markets
- acquire information:
  - ✓ existing information
  - ✓ additional information from crisis institution
  - ✓ additional information from cross-sector and cross-border authorities
- encourage private sector solution:
  - ✓ honest broker/curator
  - ✓ assess maximum loss
- assess risk of financial instability and quantify costs:
  - ✓ channels of contagion
- make a decision: winding down or intervene with public funds
  - ✓ process available information
  - ✓ cost-benefit analysis
- formulate a type of intervention:
  - ✓ recapitalization
  - ✓ limited funding combined with private sector solution

Notes

1. *Supervisory Guidance on Dealing with Weak Banks*, Basel Committee Publications, No. 88, March 2002 (www.bis.org/publ/bcbs88.htm).
2. A formal model of cost-benefit analysis is proposed in E.J. Frydl and M. Quintyn (2000) 'The Benefits and Costs of Intervening in Banking Crises', *Working Paper*, WP/00/147, IMF.
3. Danièle Nouy (1999) 'Cooperation of Supervisory Authorities and Possible Harmonization of Applicable Rules', in Giovanoli and Heinrich (1999).
4. See, for example, *Supervisory Guidance on Dealing with Weak Banks*, Basel Committee Publications, No. 88, March 2002 (www.bis.org/publ/ bcbs88.htm).
5. World Bank, database on bank regulation and supervision (www.worldbank.org/research/projects/bank_regulation.htm). For an overview focusing on practical issues, see *Guidance for Developing Effective Deposit Insurance Systems*,

Financial Stability Forum, September 2001 (www.fsforum.org/reports/depositinsurancefinal.html).

6. See Ingves and Lind (1996).
7. EU directive on deposit guarantee schemes.
8. ECB, *Annual Report*, 1999.
9. For an overview see, for example, *Monthly Bulletin*, ECB, April 2000.
10. EU directives on the winding-up and liquidation of banks and of insurance companies.
11. 'Report on Financial Stability', *Economic Paper*, No. 143, European Commission, Economic and Financial Committee, May 2000; 'Report on Financial Crisis Management', *Economic Paper*, No. 156, European Commission, Economic and Financial Committee, July 2001.
12. In addition, the Groupe de Contact, consisting of EEA banking supervisors, is concerned with implementation of regulations and supervisory practices.
13. See also *Supervisory Guidance on Dealing with Weak Banks* (footnote 1).
14. Currently, a project group of the Group of Ten is collecting and analysing comparative information on bank resolution procedures, contract enforceability and insolvency arrangements in the principal international financial jurisdictions. A report will be released as a consultation document. See 'Ongoing and Recent Work Relevant to Sound Financial Systems', 26 September 2002, www.fsforum.org.
15. 'European Directive on the Reorganisation and Winding Down of Credit Institutions' (2001/24/EG).
16. See also *Consolidation in the Financial Sector*, Group of Ten, Bank for International Settlements, January 2001 (www.bis.org/publ/gten05.htm).
17. *Consolidation in the Financial Sector*, footnote 16.
18. See van der Zwet (2003).
19. 'Memorandum of Understanding on co-operation between payment system overseers and banking supervisors in stage three of Economic and Monetary Union', Press release, ECB, 2 April 2001 (www.ecb.int).

9

Avoiding a Crisis: Lessons from the Danish Experience

Eigil Mølgaard

During the years 1720 to 1987 there were 36 financial crises in the Western World (Lybeck, 1992). That makes a crisis every 7–8 years on average. However, such events appear to have become more common wherever one looks. Over the 15 years from 1987 until 2002 it looks as if the intervals have been shorter: at the beginning of the 1990s there were crises in three Nordic countries, France, UK, Japan and the United States. In the last years of the century we experienced events in Asia, Russia and Latin America. Japan and some countries in Latin America are still suffering from heavy losses in their banking systems.

Is it possible to avoid crises in financial systems? Most probably the answer is 'no', as they are events in open markets and these markets cannot be managed or controlled by governments, central banks or supervisory authorities, whatever purpose they might have. However, during the last decade attention has increased on a number of new risks in financial markets and – in parallel – towards ways and means of strengthening the 'International Financial Architecture'.

Governments and international organisations do have an obligation to try to improve financial stability and prepare some contingency planning in case crises occur. This is most likely the background for numerous initiatives taken by international organisations, such as the IMF, the World Bank, EU, the European Central Bank and also the G8 countries. The level of activity appears to have been higher over the last few years than maybe during the preceding 25 years.

In Denmark during 1987–93 we had crises in several credit institutions, in a few conglomerates and in some insurance companies. How did we avert a systemic crisis and how could we weather the restructuring of so many ailing institutions in such a long period of time? I give my personal view in the last section of this chapter.

However, let me focus briefly on the term 'crisis'. In my view, a crisis only exists when a financial institution, such as a bank or a banking *system*, cannot carry on without *financial or other support from outside.* I mention this because, during the recession of the period mentioned above, the news media were often quick to claim that there was a crisis in the banking system or in a particular undertaking, just because it was in difficulty, for instance due to heavy losses, large provisions, a deficit in a few years or the exit of the general manager. As long as the bank and/or the system is pulling through, there is no crisis. The media have a great impact upon public opinion and that in itself may contribute to a real crisis. The Danish banking system could continue its operations based on its own vigour and there was no systemic crisis, though the banks suffered from big losses and low profitability and many of them did not survive.

9.1 The home economy in the 1980s

There must be some macroeconomic conditions which create the *background* for a 'countrywide' crisis: for example, a recession and deflation, high real interest rates, quick deregulation and financial innovations. Then all the well-known *risks become hard facts*: credit risks, volatility in the capital market, and so on. Finally, the banks that do not have the necessary resources because they are financially weak and maybe badly managed, will have to 'surrender': *go bankrupt, merge, be reorganized and so on.*

That was the pattern we experienced from 1987 until 1995. However, from 1982 to the end of 1986 there was very high economic growth. This sharp output growth was primarily driven by a significant expansion of private consumption and private investment. The growth was greatly based upon borrowing from banks, mortgage credit institutions and other sources. This was encouraged by a low nominal rate of interest. This situation had negative consequences of course. The high level of domestic activity led to major growth in imports and a widening current external deficit. In 1986 the deficit peaked at 5.5 per cent of GDP. Foreign debt had risen to 40 per cent of GDP.

Against this background, economic policy was tightened in several ways at the end of 1985 and in 1986. A tax reform reduced the deductible value of interest payments from just over 70 per cent to about 50 per cent. In addition, a tight fiscal policy was implemented, which, for a period of time, resulted in a 20 per cent tax on interest on consumer loans, tightened up the repayment terms for all new loans on mortgage and increased various stamp duties on legal documents drawn up when transferring real estate and taking loans. All this pulled about DKK15 billion out of the economy (US$2 billion),[1] compared to the state annual budget of around DKK250 billion (US$34 billion).

This was the beginning of the longest period of stagnation in the post-war era. The consequence of the higher costs for financing both private consumption and commercial investment was a fall in 1987 and 1988. The slow growth should also be seen in the light of the subdued economic activity in world markets.

All parts of economic life were affected, with reduced profitability and a strong decline in business. Fixed investments and all major components of private demand showed either stagnation or decline. Some of the results were:

- Decline in prices of commercial buildings and family houses
- Strong increase in forced sales of such buildings
- Increase in the rate of unemployment
- The number of bankruptcies became extremely high
- The building industry was in difficulty
- Unstable securities markets.

9.2 How did the banks and mortgage banks react to this development?

Let me answer by quoting a Norwegian phrase – first presented by the former Governor of Norges Bank, Hermod Skånland, when he described the three main causes of the banking crisis: *'bad luck, bad policies and bad banking'*. However, that is only relevant to credit institutions which failed or at least were in serious difficulties.

'Bad luck' refers to the international recession, the length of which had been unprecedented. It had some effect in Denmark, as mentioned above. Apart from that I am not in fact able to quote any circumstance that may be called 'bad luck' as an excuse for the bad credit institutions.

'Bad policies' could refer to the very sudden and tough intervention by the parliament and government in 1985–86. It is still known as 'The Potato Diet' and it is my opinion that the politicians still have the emergency situation which they created on their minds and no government will dare use that 'prescription' again.

'Bad banking' refers to the banks' own mistakes, such as lack of caution and excessive risk-taking in lending and investment. During the 1980s banks built up relatively cost-intensive organizations, partly by taking on more staff. The sector became one of the most

labour-intensive in the world with considerable excess capacity for the domestic market.

As a result of the cyclical upturn and the bright economic outlook in the first half of the 1980s, lending rose rapidly, exceeding the growth in nominal GDP. Experience from many countries shows that such periods of strong growth almost invariably result in an increase in losses and provisions, with some time lag. In 1992 and 1993, losses and provisions amounted to 2.5 per cent of outstanding loans and guarantees. Historically, this was a relatively high level. Thus heavy losses and provisions were the main source of profitability problems.

While low inflation is the basis for stable and sustainable growth, the recession created problems for many businesses. Projects that were appropriate and profitable in a higher inflation environment ran into problems instead. The sharp fall in property prices further eroded the value of the underlying security for some bank loans and resulted in losses in the property portfolio.

The strong balance sheet growth in the first half of the 1980s was increasingly financed by money market loans from foreign credit institutions and through the issue of bonds. In 1991, the balance sheet growth led to a deposit deficit. This made the banks that exposed themselves in that way very vulnerable in case of loss of confidence in the Danish banking system and, in fact, a number of banks had their access to loans from foreign credit institutions cut in 1992.

Danish mortgage banks play a very important role in financing all sorts of real estate. Their total balance sheet exceeded that of all universal banks and savings banks. Three banks dominated the market and two of them suffered such big losses that they had to be reorganized and to have their capital restored. In that sense the Danish real estate-market saw the same problems as other countries, mainly in the big cities.

9.3 The institutions involved in the rescue operations

Figure 9.1 shows 'who is responsible for what' in some order of priority. It also indicates who were the most important stakeholders. I will refer to Figure 9.1 again in Section 9.7 and explain its merits a little bit more. At this juncture I only offer some remarks about the Financial Supervisory Authority (FSA), which had a major role to play in the situation.

Components	*Responsible*
Acts and rules of law (on supervision, company law, accounting, auditing, and so on)	Parliament Government Banking Supervisory Authority
Management. Corporate Governance	Board of Directors, managers
Control system – in the local environment	External and internal audit Internal control Audit committee
Control system – state	Banking Supervisory Authority
Sanctions (compensation, punishment, dismissal)	Prosecuting authority, courts of law
'Social contract' in 'political cases', too important to fail, and so on	Minister responsible for: the Central Bank the banking sector Deposit Insurance Scheme Banking Supervisory Authority
'Supranational' agreements	EU, Basel Committee and others

Figure 9.1 The Prudential System for the banking sector

The Danish FSA is an institution under the umbrella of the Minister for Economic and Commercial Affairs. Its activities take place within three core areas:

- Supervision
- Regulation
- Information

The FSA is an integrated authority, which is responsible for the supervision of the entire financial sector. It was established in its present form on 1 January 1988. At that time the institution supervised almost 800 enterprises in the financial sector, which employed a total of 70,000 employees and had combined assets of approximately DKK 2.400 billion (US$330 billion). The authority had a staff of 120 to carry out its many different tasks. (In 2001 there were about 900 enterprises – including 230 insurance brokers – and the staff numbered 170.)

The institution will have to add new responsibilities to the role of supervision, in a narrow sense, in a period of difficulties in the banking sector. Under normal conditions, they do not include remedial actions, such as searching for new capital and shareholders, arranging takeovers, assisting in selling off good or bad loans, making calculations, solving legal problems or intermediating between interested parties.

It is hard enough to identify the problems and causes in the individual bank and to decide what legal actions must be taken, if no rehabilitation is possible. There was, however, an unwritten 'law': 'There must be no failures in the financial sector.' From the time of the first collapse during the recession, it soon became obvious that this was the position of the government, partly to avoid any expectations of government support and thus to avoid risks of moral hazard. This meant a strong professional obligation on the FSA to do its utmost to obtain solutions for banks that seemed doomed to fail.

On the other hand it is the responsibility of the supervision to close the bank if it is a consequence of the law and not to show undue 'forbearance'. Other stakeholders did not normally want to be involved in this business, which could mean merely hard work, wasted money and heavy criticism as the reward. One exception was the Central Bank which acted in its own interest as a possible 'lender of last resort' and as a guardian of stability in the financial system, but also in practical and useful cooperation with the FSA in some very difficult cases.

As one case after another passed the FSA, staff gradually gained experience and established a collection of bank rehabilitation techniques and models. In this way they were able to support all the interests that were dependent on the banking system, even if experience shows that hardly any crisis in a particular bank is similar to the previous ones. Some things are certain:

- the crisis should be handled and managed quickly;
- the elements in the final solution are not known in advance;
- the task is complicated practically;
- the task is financially and economically complicated;
- this area is not regulated by law;

 but

- some 'modules' are known; and
- experience and preparedness should be in place.

The last bullet point touches upon the so-called 'human resources' – all the skilled, hard-working and patient colleagues who were prepared to invest all their capacity – day and night – to tackle failures for which they had no responsibility at all.

9.4 How wrong did things go? The financial institutions that did not survive

Between the beginning of 1987 and the end of 1995, 102 credit institutions (banks, savings banks and cooperative banks) ceased to exist.

In many cases they were not in difficulties, but – maybe advised by the FSA – concluded that it was better to merge or to be taken over while they could decide the point of time, partner and conditions for themselves.

Of these institutions, 51 were in crisis, normally because they had lost their capital. The FSA intervened in 47 of these banks and ordered them to find a solution if they wanted to avoid withdrawal of their licence, suspension of payments or other measures.

Apart from the credit institutions, there were two other groups of financial institution which had to close down. The first group comprised some specialized undertakings (11), stockbrokers (22 – our 'big bang') and 4 insurance companies, all of them relatively small ones. Fourteen were closed by the FSA. Second, there were a number of very big financial undertakings – 34 in total including some banks – which were in a dangerous economic situation but still functioning. Their situation was known to be an emergency by the financial sector but not by the general public, which meant that there was no reaction from the depositors or the shareholders.

Two 'members' of this group were very big conglomerates (Hafnia and Baltica), originally established as insurance groups. They expanded, however, into banking and other financial and non-financial activities in the mid-1980s. Both companies suffered huge losses and were dissolved in the early 1990s. Two other big enterprises in this group were two of the three biggest mortgage banks. This gave rise to concern about the 'reputation' of mortgage bonds, since they are used as long-term investment by foreign life insurance companies and pension funds.

The total 'population' of ailing financial institutions was thus 122. They needed considerable attention from the FSA to enable them to survive or were closed in the period from 1987 until 1995. That makes an average of 13 cases per year or approximately one per month year in and year out during those 9 years!

9.5 Why did things go wrong in the individual institutions?

Obviously there are several reasons why some financial enterprises fail in difficult times while others maintain business as usual – more or less – even though they are working in the same market under the same macroeconomic conditions. What made the difference? This issue may be discussed in a broader sense and may be illustrated in detail based upon concrete examples.

In a broader perspective, the answer is quite simple in its form but complicated in substance: difference in corporate governance and management quality. High-quality management is the most valuable 'asset' and bad management the most dangerous 'liability' in a bank. But what is good corporate governance and management?

Turning to the background in detail, shortly after the bank crisis had come to an end, an expert group examined its context, causes, and so on. The main conclusion in their report (Ministry of Economic Affairs, 1994, pp. 72, 78) was that deficiencies in general management and weak board supervision were characteristic of most of the credit institutions that were closed down.

The working group applied two methods to identify some common features in the banks which failed:

- The FSA had developed an Early Warning System (EWS) (certain key figures), and it was applied (retroactively) to 38 closed banks together with a parallel group of 38 banks, which had had no serious problems.
- An inquiry among the FSA inspectors and examiners who had been responsible for the failed banks.

The EWS test Many banks in the parallel group had the same key figures as the closed banks. Therefore it was not possible to select a set of characteristics which could identify banks that had started on a downward path. Nevertheless, there were some facts which were found frequently in the closed banks: those closed in the mid-1980s were strongly fixed on increasing market share, growth and earnings. The period between the expansion of the loan portfolio and the crisis was rather short. This indicates a low level of internal risk management systems, particularly with respect to credit risks. The banks that remained after 1990 had adapted to the recession, while the smaller banks had still run an excessive growth and risk-taking policy.

The banks which were liquidated during the last part of the crisis period had low profitability in their core business. Profitability decreased continuously until the close-down and was low compared to other credit institutions. These banks had a very low core capital compared to their loan portfolio. Thus they were particularly at risk from fluctuations in the internal economy. The solvency ratio was lower than the average of the banking system.

The inquiry The main causes of the failures were in day-to-day management: unrealistic valuation of credit risks or no interest in controlling these risks, lack of current control of large exposures and no overview of the bank in its entirety. Also the panel of inspectors considered volume at the cost of profitability as an essential factor on the part of the managers. Likewise, they found unrealistic assessment or lack of control of market risks.

A weak board of directors had been decisive in two-thirds of the cases examined. The concept 'weak' is ambiguous: it may mean weakness of professional skills or education *or* little ability to keep control over the management. However, the last phenomenon is often a consequence of the first. The importance of strong external and internal auditors was very often underestimated – and bad auditors were even appointed in order to save costs.

Finally, the following are some general observations on the loan portfolio. One of the major causes of failure was the concentration of large exposures. Also mentioned is the concentration of credits to certain branches of industry (agriculture, property developers, retail trading, hotels, transportation and so on) and misjudgement of the economic development. It is not surprising that there is a correlation between these two categories of concentration and the lack of ability on the part of the managers to supervise and control major clients.

9.6 Policy response: crisis strategy and implementation of measures

It must be said immediately that the Danish authorities who became involved in crisis administration *had no ready-made master plan* to consult when the initial bank failures developed into a current process. There had been some cases now and then, but they were normally settled by the banking industry itself and gave no reason to anticipate crises in a large number of credit institutions. This meant that each case had to be handled on its own merits. Two qualities were decisive in these circumstances:

- Improvising talent and smooth and effective cooperation between all parties: the bank staff and the banks' auditors and lawyers, the government administration, Central Bank, FSA, the bankers' association and many others.
- Highly qualified staff ready to do the job whenever needed. As the FSA had to make the diagnosis, this institution would normally be the meeting place and initiator of negotiations in order to avert a bankruptcy.

Intervention in a bank is a totally different activity from the day-to-day activities of off-site surveillance and on-site inspections. In contrast to these activities, which primarily involve evaluation of banks' financial condition and observance of prudential regulations, intervention requires resolute action. Because such action will affect bank owners, managers, employees and customers, it may sometimes be controversial and provoke resistance. Consequently, supervisory intervention must be based on a solid legal and regulatory foundation and be carried out decisively. Although intervention should be free of political constraints, an awareness of the political context and skills for handling the political implications are also indispensable assets.

In a typical case, the bank in question will have an operating loss, either accumulated over several years or of more recent origin, resulting in the reduction or complete loss of the liable capital of the bank. In most cases the problems of a bank have been detected during the review of the exposures by the supervisors in an inspection. Only in a few cases have the auditors of the bank or management contacted the FSA. In certain cases the situation in a bank came to the attention of the FSA as a consequence of information from the banking market.

As a rule, no matter how serious the problems are, a clarification will be required within a very short period. Otherwise, rumours about the situation might lead to a run on the bank. Moreover, it would be negligent on the part of the supervisors, with respect to depositors in particular, to let a bank stay open, for even a week, in the full knowledge that the bank does not meet the conditions for keeping its 'banking licence'. There is a parallel problem if the shares or commercial bonds are listed in the stock exchange. The solution must therefore usually be implemented within a very tight deadline.

It may be extremely difficult to strike a balance between the interests of depositors and shareholders, the supervisory obligations according to the banking law and other relevant laws and the strong political wish to avoid bankruptcies. This was particularly relevant as the 'intermediaries' (the FSA and the Central Bank) had no funds to invest as a contributory element in a reconstruction. The Deposit Insurance Fund now has a legal authority to pay a contribution in case of, for example, a takeover if the amount will be less than the compensation that must be paid in case of bankruptcy.

The legal instrument of 'suspension of payment' has proved not to be applicable as a 'break' in the negotiations. It was applied in six cases which all ended in bankruptcy. Possible investors lose interest in a takeover and clients will have lost confidence in the bank, even if it opens again. Apart from that, there are numerous problems related to trade in the money market and securities, settlement and payment systems, liquidity supply, and so on. Eight small banks were declared bankrupt.

Experience of solving crises in Danish banks can be divided into solutions *without* public funds and solutions *with* public funds. The public support provided to banks through the Central Bank was however rather modest and directed to only a few small and medium-sized banks from 1984 until 1993. The total amount was DKK5 billion (approximately US$685 million), granted to 5 banks. The risks attached to DKK3 billion were removed gradually up to 1995.

As a rule, solutions *without public funds* were based on an evaluation of which parties had a direct or indirect interest in preventing the compulsory liquidation of the bank. The models used or considered range from simple or more indirect capital injection, to mergers or separation into a 'good bank and a bad bank' to bankruptcy. Merger was the most widely used model, although it became increasingly difficult to comply with some of the conditions of this model towards the end of the crisis period. For example, most larger banks had neither the opportunity nor the desire to expand by means of takeovers. In some cases, their own capital was written down to zero, and the assets and liabilities were transferred to another bank. The now 'empty company', the former bank, was then declared bankrupt. An asset management company was only established in one case.

One problem present in many cases was that shareholders and subordinate capital investors or other creditors were not willing to write off a loss and at the same time surrender influence over the continuing enterprise. This also applies to some quite special creditors, including data-processing centres and the Deposit Insurance Fund. All parties are strongly motivated to preserve their ownership interests and leave the costs of avoiding liquidation to others.

In other cases, the authorities also sought to involve other parties who might incur indirect costs in case of liquidation, for example other banks that ought to be concerned for the reputation of the sector. However, the government and/or the Central Bank had to exercise some pressure upon the banks or their associations to gain their support. A fundamental policy was to avoid public co-ownership of a bank. Shareholders, other investors and as many other parties as possible, were thus required to make their contribution in the first instance. If public funds were available, it was only at a certain cost. In most cases the board and the management were also replaced.

Finally, a few remarks are in order public support organizations or rescue facilities which were *not applied*. No special bank support organizations were established, such as a specialized authority or asset management companies. No government guarantee fund or investment fund or funds were established by the banking industry. No explicit guarantee for the liabilities (deposits) of all the banks or capital adequacy or guarantee for the asset quality was given and there was no forbearance generally or in individual cases, such as lowering of solvency or liquidity requirements.

9.7 Some reflections on bankruptcy vs. rehabilitation

Most politicians will agree with the general statement that banks should be allowed to go bankrupt. However, when it comes to a specific case, the political decision is much more difficult, and chances are that politicians will override central bank and supervisory objections.

In Denmark a bank as small as US$150 million was 'saved'. On the other hand, saving banks with balance sheets of less than US$50 million were allowed to go into bankruptcy. If the same had happened to larger banks, it would certainly have caused political fury. This would be even more likely if the government had a minority in the parliament, because the opposition would be enthusiastic about bank failures as ammunition in the political infight. Thus, we were operating in a very different environment from the one suggested by the traditional TBTF arguments. The argument for saving small banks cannot be avoidance of systemic problems, for example, domino effects on other banks. With the trend in many countries towards collateralized intrabank lending and limits on credit risks, the validity of these arguments also appears to have decreased.

Politically, the determinants seem to be losses to depositors – depositors are voters – and a general political responsibility for the well-being of banks. Even the existence of fairly generous deposit insurance schemes does not seem to eliminate the political concerns. A more sophisticated line of argument for saving even small banks can be made by looking at the role of a bank in a modern society. A bank is a key link in the payment and settlement systems moving deposits or granting credits. Thus, payments cannot be made for some time. If a small bank has a high market share in a special region, the regional impact of a bankruptcy can also be quite severe.

In one case the costs of a bankruptcy compared to the actual solution (transfer of assets and liabilities to a major bank) were estimated as follows:

	million DKK
Balance sheet	864
Guarantees	372
Off balance items	153
Extra costs in case of bankruptcy	*227*

Børsens Nyhedsmagasin (no. 7, 7 April 1995, pp. 18–22) made a comparable calculation for three banks:

	Rescue (million DKK)	Bankruptcy (million DKK)
Major bank	457	744
Medium-sized bank	79	187
Small credit union	9	24

Table 9.1 summarizes the problems inherent in forcing bankruptcy or providing government support.

Table 9.1 Summary of the problems that arise in bankruptcy or government support

Bankruptcy for credit institutions

- Loss for large deposits
- It may take years before dividends are paid
- Credits and accounts are closed
- Refinancing may be difficult or even impossible
- Severe consequences for local business clients and public or semi-public depositors
- Value of assets is reduced
- Large costs in the bankruptcy proceedings

Systemic crisis – additionally

- Reaction from foreign markets: credit lines are cut off and low confidence in the banking system in the country in question
- Limited access to foreign exchange, securities and derivatives markets
- Payment and settlement systems become disintegrated
- Domino effect
- Confidence is generally reduced

Government support for credit institutions

- Expensive for the state budget
- Means transfer of losses from creditors to taxpayers
- Moral hazard
- Market discipline with respect to risk-taking is reduced
- Distortion of competition
- Violation of EU rules on state aid
- Everybody having an economic interest (depositors, borrowers) in the banks which are supported will expect to be treated with flexibility as to their claims because the state has taken responsibility for the future of those banks
- In the end the authorities may be the permanent owners of the banks

Systemic crisis – additionally

- Formidable expenditure for the state budget
- Creates claims on the state and puts its credibility on the line
- Several banks in public ownership
- Difficulties in the re-privatization process

9.8 A new scheme for the resolution of bank insolvencies?

It must be recognized that bank failures are inevitable unless much that is of value to users of a banking system is to be lost. In earlier periods of crisis, governments and authorities mainly applied the following 'scenarios' in the case of bank failures:

- Bankruptcy
- Takeovers, mergers, and so on, arranged only between private parties, and
- Government support, if possible together with the deposit insurance institution.

As pointed out by Mayes and Liuksila in Chapters 1 and 2, however, there are several reasons for trying to eliminate the last-mentioned possibility, in order to correct for the assumption that the public treasury is in many cases ready to assist in bank rescues.

While the 'New Scheme' will of course be a political 'hot potato' and will present a lot of difficult issues it might be a way out of the dilemma, if the general public is properly informed that in future there is a risk of a 'semi-bankruptcy' and not automatically a rescue in case of a failure. It is easy to put forward objections and hesitations by politicians, depositors, bankers and so on but as some experts have presented a new idea, it should be 'tested' by some EEA government in open discussion to examine if it is realistic from all points of view (including the extremely important background), with the intention of implementing the scheme, if it is considered acceptable. After all, such fundamentally new ideas can only be tested in their 'natural environment'.

9.9 How did Denmark escape a systemic crisis?

In my opinion the answer is in the 15 items listed in Table 9.2. As will be shown, the capability to cope with a crisis in a few banks, many banks or a systemic crisis depends on several skills, policies and processes.

Looking back and assessing why Denmark was able to weather the crisis in the banking system, it is possible to identify a good deal of these elements. Hopefully, they may serve as 'core principles' for the preparedness also in other countries – but with a reservation for new risks or causes in the financial markets that were not known 10 to 15 years ago. This list is unlikely to be exhaustive and there may be differences of opinion over some issues. It is not an academic study but the experience gained by a practitioner. It is, however, in accordance with the main conclusions in reports from official expert groups.

It may be useful to keep in mind Figure 9.1 (p. 226). It represents the supervisor's ideal view of the significant elements for the protection of a financial system. This summary is useful for pinpointing who is actually responsible for the quality of the financial institutions and for the system itself. Far too often, public opinion, as well as the politicians, will blame the supervisory authority (and the auditors) for negligence in a case of failure and not the board or the management of the bank. That is a fallacy of course: the supervision contributes perhaps as little as 15 per cent of the safety net and the other parties 85 per cent. Therefore, the model also shows where the legislator and the supervisor should concentrate their efforts. It is clear that it does not necessarily mean a strengthening of the supervision but of the three 'upper floors' of the 'building'. Some further comments on Figure 9.1 will appear in the following sections.

When we consider the measures taken in Denmark to avert the banking crisis we have to distinguish between the 'security net', which had been created before the failures (for example, laws and regulations), and the 'inventions', which we made while the operations took place (for example, legal and technical models, political involvement and attitudes). There had not been many failures since the 1930s and they had been managed case by case. Thus, not having much experience in managing a number of failures at the same time, an important conclusion is that the major factor is the human resource provision – the staff – who need to be sufficient in number, well qualified and in attendance from the beginning of the crisis events. It requires a very high degree of attention on the part of management to ensure that the supervisor is able to draw upon such 'human resources', not from time to time, but all the time. They are *the supervision!*

Table 9.2 'Core Principles for a Sustainable Banking System' – Danish version

The criteria are drawn up in order of priority.

Section I

The most important provisions are:

1. Good up-to-date *legislation*. The relevant legislation was currently updated. A new banking law was adopted in 1974 and then continuously updated, in response to internal needs and additionally based upon the implementation of EU banking directives. *Legislation* is included in this survey as the most important principle, because it lays down the requirements that are intended to keep discipline in the individual bank and in the banking system and

Table 9.2 (Contd.)

determines the actions that the supervisory authority may take in case of failures. It is a matter of fact in democratic societies that the administration cannot go further than permitted by the decisions of parliament, that is, by law. This is sometimes not properly understood by the parliamentarians themselves or the news media when they blame the supervisory authority for taking action too late.

However, a special banking law cannot regulate the banking system alone. Company law or similar legislation must regulate the banks as legal persons, particularly when important decisions must be taken because of economic difficulties, mergers, liquidation and so on. Other examples are accounting legislation, securities law, bankruptcy law and criminal law. This whole bundle of legislation was updated and satisfactory to the authorities that had to act during Denmark's banking crisis.

2. Financial supervision, like the Danish Financial Supervision, that is adapted to the requirements of the sector, which means that its qualifications are 5 per cent better than those of the banks and has:

- clear, transparent and updated objectives,
- adequate resources and powers,
- efficient administration,
- the ability to adapt quickly to new conditions, and
- continuously planned activities.

The fact that the supervision 'works efficiently' means, among other things, having thorough, practical knowledge of the functions and current state of banks, obtained by such means as extensive use of on-the-spot inspections. Supervisors need to focus on the valuation of loans and guarantees. They cannot rely on analysis of accounting statements from the banks and their auditors. If loans and guarantees are not properly valued, the contents of these statements are meaningless. Valuation of loans is a mixture of art and craft. Valuing loans requires on-site inspections to review the relevant material. It was recognized among other Nordic countries that Denmark's better performance may partly be explained by its tradition of on-site inspections (Ministry of Economic Affairs, 1994, 1995a,b, 1997). It was also Denmark's experience that certified accountants are generally not sufficiently specialized to value loans. All of the approximately 50–60 problem banks were identified by the supervisory authority, none by the accountants.

As to the Danish Financial Supervision's performance before and during the banking crisis, I think that we may maintain that it:

- was well equipped, being a relatively big and integrated institution,
- was alert to the danger of an approaching crisis in the economy,
- had in-depth knowledge of the functions of the banking system and its current state,
- was able to react in time with a range of influences and interventions, either by known methods or specially developed for the particular situation, and
- had reasonable political relations and good connections with other public institutions that were involved, for example the Central Bank and the

Table 9.2 (Contd.)

Deposit Insurance Scheme. In some cases that network was essential for a successful outcome.

3. *Liable capital* (own funds and supplementary capital) in abundance and consisting of high-quality elements. The Danish rules on solvency calculation underwent fundamental changes from 1990 when the new EC banking directives took effect, including the Solvency Directive. The adaptation to the EC system was achieved through a reduction from an average of just below 14 per cent to 8 per cent according to the new method of calculation. The Supervisory Authority feared that the surplus capital would be used for a risky expansion. However, the demand for capital had dropped drastically. Instead the surplus capital had, to a great extent, been used to absorb heavy losses and provisions and thus large deficits in the banking sector. Thus, the Danish banking system could benefit from a perfect but accidental timing. This is an essential part of the reasons why Denmark escaped a systemic crisis.
4. *Rules governing provisions,* which are adapted to current needs and therefore result in comparatively large reserves to cover losses.

   During the crisis the Supervisory Authority tightened the requirements for the banks and their auditors with regard to provisioning. In the mid-1980s it introduced annual circulars to the banks, dealing with special matters of which they ought be aware when presenting annual accounts. Later it introduced a circular that was issued prior to publication of interim accounts. These circulars were known as the Christmas Letter and Midsummer Letter, respectively. Monthly balance sheets were delivered and banks reported quarterly profit and loss accounts to the supervision.

   Looking at the losses and provisions for the 19 years 1975–93, one can observe that the last 7 years of this period represent 36 per cent of the time period, whereas the provisions constitute 75 per cent of the total provisions for loans and guarantees. The aggregate amounts are DKK101 billion and DKK75.3 billion, respectively. By comparison, own funds averaged approximately DKK70 billion in 1990 and DKK53 billion in 1993. These two figures also show that own funds had to pay a price for the recession. Annual provisions in 1993 amounted to approximately 2.5 per cent of loans and guarantees – the same as in 1982 and the highest ever. Reserves based on the annual provisions amounted to approximately 6.3 per cent of loans and guarantees in 1993 – the highest in Denmark's financial history.

   The conclusion is that the banking system was able to cover very high losses – and nevertheless to survive.
5. *Stable and adequate earnings* from the actual banking operations. These do not include gains on the securities portfolio. Profits due to market fluctuations are unstable. The profitability forecasts should be based on the ordinary banking and cost control. Many of the Danish credit institutions that failed had used the windfall profits between 1983 and 1985 as a capital basis for a huge increase in their credit portfolio and to expand their administration. *The majority of the banking system did not adopt a policy like this and avoided difficulties.*

Table 9.2 (Contd.)

6. *External auditors.* Denmark had (and have) a reliable and qualified profession of State Authorised Public Accountants, who served well during the banking crisis. The auditors are elected by the general meeting. None is appointed by public authorities. The FSA may:

- order the auditors to provide information on the credit institution,
- arrange for an extraordinary audit,
- dismiss an auditor who has been found to be manifestly unqualified.

The auditor must be completely independent of the credit institution, and must report to the FSA on all events that may have an impact on the future of the credit institution. The regulations on audit and accounting were made more rigorous during the crisis, and the responsibilities of the auditors were extended.

The auditors are in a somehow difficult position: engaged by and serving the credit institution but on the other hand confirming to the general public and shareholders that the annual statement and report express a true and fair view. Besides they have strong obligations to the FSA. The auditors function properly in the normal state of affairs but during the crisis there were some problems. The audit profession was, however, an indispensable and useful participant in all the efforts to identify ailing credit institutions and in the negotiations on actions to be taken.

Section II

There are other matters which are actually just as important, but more difficult to define:

1. *The vigour of the political system,* that is, the ability and willingness of the government to see and understand signals about a dangerous trend in the banking system, for example, as reported by the supervisor, and its willingness to take the necessary initiatives, such as the introduction of legislation in the parliament. The wish for vigour obviously applies equally to the latter. If no effective action is taken against emerging crises, the consequences could be disastrous. In this respect the FSA had no ground for complaint: laws were amended, resources were allocated to the supervision, economic support granted in the few cases, (unfounded) complaints from the closed banks were normally rejected.
2. It is to the credit of the politicians that, since the Second World War, it has been generally acceptable to *let enterprises fail* that could not support themselves. It applied to all industries, including the financial institutions. There had never been political interventions in the business of the banks, such as 'policy loans' on favourable conditions to selected industries. Restrictions upon these institutions were kept at a minimum as far as possible and effective competition was an important goal. The financial market was opened at an early stage for direct investments and acquisitions. The restrictions in the capital market were lifted gradually and this process had come to an end before the financial crisis. Thus, there was no *liberalization which gave a shock to the banking industry.*

Table 9.2 (Contd.)

The generally accepted policy towards insolvent banks was an *'early merger'*. More than 40 out of the 50 to 60 problem banks were merged in due time. 'Due time' meaning, while there was still sufficient equity to pay for a merger. This practice substituted an explicit government programme for support to rehabilitation of banks.

3. The government's *demonstration* of its willingness in a few cases to *grant loans, issue guarantees* and – through the Central Bank – to *grant liquidity* support to ailing banks contributed to the stability. Two big banks which were quite clearly TBTF benefited from this policy, which was endorsed by all parties in parliament. A *deposit insurance fund* was established immediately after the first bankruptcy.
4. *The banking sector* showed both ability and willingness to collaborate in mergers and takeovers and provide capital for restructuring. If not, the 40 cases mentioned above could not have been managed. The negotiations were often difficult, as the bank that was taking over had to take care of its own interests above all. The motivation for this assistance was, generally, the possibility of making a good deal, saving own investments or protecting the reputation of the whole sector.

Section III

Finally, there are certain conditions of a good banking system which are more difficult to describe in concrete terms. Nevertheless, they did – to a greater or lesser extent – play a role in protecting the banks against a systemic crisis.

1. The majority of the banks was characterized by a *good quality of management.* By this I mean not only the functioning of the boards and the managers but also such matters as strategic planning, geographic and administrative organization, reporting system, internal control and audit, and so on.
2. Although *business ethics* were not as developed as nowadays, in the author's experience, well-developed business ethics led to a reduced risk of loss – that is, actually gain. This to be understood in the way that those banks avoid some dirty businesses and transactions and some shady clients.
3. Most banks did not pursue an *expansionary strategy.*
4. The structure of the banking system was dominated by *universal banks* (risk diversification) and not specialist banks. There were only a few big banks.
5. The banks were used to *competition in their home market.* They were internationally experienced and generally able to control subsidiary banks and branches abroad.

9.10 Final comments

While it was generally felt that the FSA did a good job, there was occasional criticism of the FSA regarding some cases and solutions. On this, the author makes only one comment: nobody else was willing to take the overall responsibility for decisions on insolvency together with efforts to find solutions that would save large sums for the banking industry and its customers. If so, they would have been welcome to take over the rescue operations. While it must be admitted that sometimes the FSA could have done a better job, it is only those who are doing nothing, who do not fail!

9.10.1 Lessons to be learnt? What was done after the crisis?

A few expert groups analysed the experience and made proposals for improvements of the security net. Numerous amendments of the financial legislation have been adopted. New supervisory methods have been implemented. In the year 2000 an 'all interested parties committee' (25 members) delivered a report called 'The Financial Sector after Year 2000', which was the basis for even more new legislation, adopted in a single act in 2002/03 – and it has not yet exhausted its power! (Ministry of Economic Affairs, 1999).

Note

1. 1989 exchange rates.

10

Learning Lessons and Implementing a New Approach to Bank Insolvency Resolution in Switzerland*

Eva H.G. Hüpkes

On 3 October 2003 the Swiss Parliament adopted a new legal framework for resolving bank insolvencies which will enter into force in early 2004. This chapter discusses this proposed new framework in the light of the approach proposed in Mayes, Halme and Liuksila (2001) ('MHL proposal'). Under the new Swiss framework, Switzerland's bank supervisor, the Swiss Federal Banking Commission (SFBC) will assume functions traditionally exercised by the bankruptcy courts. The proposed reorganization regime will offer an alternative to the outright compulsory liquidation of banks that are no longer able to comply with solvency requirements. In keeping with the general principle that private sector problems require private sector solutions the regime excludes any form of public assistance. In the case of the cantonal banks it is however generally the canton as main shareholder that provides the necessary funds for a recapitalization or the guaranteeing creditors' claims. The characteristics of the Swiss financial sector with its large number of small banks and two major 'global players', UBS and Credit Suisse, illustrate the impossibility of drawing up a bank insolvency framework that is 'one size fits all'.

10.1 Banking problems in Switzerland

During the last century significant banking crises occurred in the 1930s and 1990s. The result of both these crises was to alert the law-makers and the public to the need for an improvement to the existing laws which would enable the bank supervisor to deal with insolvent banks more effectively. The new framework was developed in response to the crisis in the 1990s.[1]

10.1.1 The banking crisis in the 1930s – a first awakening

As in many other parts of the world, Switzerland suffered a severe financial crisis in the 1930s. It was started by the effects of the stock market crash in New York on 24 October 1929, which spread quickly to Europe and affected Switzerland's economy and banking sector severely. Several banks became insolvent or were on the verge of insolvency. Over 10 per cent of the 520 active banking institutions became subject to reorganization or liquidation proceedings. Although the 1934 Banking Act provided some important preventive measures, it did not confer any powers on the SFBC to deal with the crisis effectively. Interestingly, very little has changed since then; the legal framework for dealing with insolvent banks is essentially the same today as it was in 1934. Under the 1934 Banking Act, in practice only the bankruptcy judge and the Federal Council had powers to act. In reality, neither the bankruptcy judge nor the Federal Council were in a position to make an informed decision without seeking the opinion of the SFBC. Given the severity of the crisis and the lack of adequate procedures, the Federal Council adopted an emergency ordinance giving the SFBC the authority to conduct a bank reorganization. Depending upon the specific condition of the bank in question, a range of different measures was applied, which included a stay on the enforcement of all claims, comprising, if necessary, secured or privileged claims, combined with the write-off of debts and the issuance of new shares, and the creation of temporary entities to take over bad debt. Several failing banks were successfully reorganized under this regime.

One lesson from the experience of the 1930s is that a regulator-centred procedure allows banking problems to be dealt with more effectively than a court-centred procedure. This is also the presumption at the basis of the MHL proposal which seeks to avoid the judicial process used in the insolvency of non-financial companies. As the ordinance had been created through an extraordinary legislative act, it was only of temporary nature and, therefore, needed to be regularized and implemented through the ordinary legislative process. Several attempts were undertaken to this end, however without much success. As is often the case, it took another crisis to remind the authorities of the urgency of this matter.

10.1.2 The failure of the Spar & Leihkasse Thun – the wake up call

In the 1980s, the Swiss real estate market boomed. The total amount of mortgages more than doubled in the 1980s, with mortgage growth even higher than that of real estate prices. Real estate prices doubled, peaking in 1989 and remaining high until 1991 when they started to fall sharply. As a result, many banks encountered problems. On the asset side, the recession adversely affected the ability of bank customers to service their debts, and large sums had to be written off. On the liability side, banks lost deposits as customers shifted to bond, equity and mutual fund investments. Problems due to adverse market conditions were compounded with weak day-to-day management and control mechanisms, inadequate management of credit risks and a lack of control of large exposures. The total losses incurred between 1991 and 1996 are estimated at CHF 42 billion, or nearly 8 per cent of the total loan volume. At a first glance, the large banks seemed to have been hit the hardest, as they incurred about three-quarters of total loan losses. However, due to their well-diversified portfolios, their profits were sufficient to cover these losses. Thus, it was the regional and the cantonal banks that suffered most from the crisis.

In 1991, the SFBC took action against Spar & Leihkasse Thun (SLT), a medium-sized regional bank with assets of CHF 1.1 billion. SLT had suffered significant loan losses and attempts to arrange a merger or acquisition by other financial institutions had failed. In October 1991, the SFBC withdrew the banking licence and ordered the compulsory liquidation. As the institution turned out to be over-indebted, judicial insolvency proceedings had to be initiated shortly thereafter.

The situation came as quite a shock for a country used to a stable financial system. Thus, there was a strong interest in avoiding a repetition of this set of circumstances. Since other banks were also in a bad condition, the SFBC cooperated with the Swiss Bankers Association (SBA) and the Swiss National Bank (SNB) to arrange takeovers of banks threatened by insolvency. Banks that were thought likely to run into problems in the long run were 'forced' to look for a stronger partner. With offers to buy from existing shareholders or by taking over all the assets and liabilities, larger banks, and also to some extent the cantonal banks, took over banks affected by the structural changes thus saving them from closure and liquidation by the SFBC. As a result, only very few banks were liquidated and, with the single exception of the SLT, no creditors suffered any losses. No public funds were used. Mergers and acquisitions served as the main instruments for the resolution of the problems.

In a more and more competitive business environment it is unlikely, however, that mergers and acquisitions can be relied upon exclusively to resolve failing banks in a future crisis. Since bank failures typically occur in a weak economic environment, it will be difficult to find investors that are willing to agree to an immediate takeover. Interested investors may need time to conduct due diligence on the assets and to assess whether they would be able to absorb the impact of taking over an insolvent bank. Hence, there is a need for some form of regulatory support or statutory framework that assists in that process. MHL propose a temporary assumption of the ownership of the insolvent institution by the government. The Swiss framework, as will be seen in the following pages, provides – under the legal umbrella of a bank reorganization procedure – for the appointment of an administrator to take stock and assess options for reorganization while acting to minimize or avoid further losses to creditors and preventing contagion of the financial system.

10.1.3 Restructuring with public funds

Several cantonal banks – heavily engaged in the commercial real estate mortgage business and therefore dependent on the economic growth of a limited geographic region – encountered serious economic difficulties during the 1990s crisis. All cantonal institutions, with the exception of those in the cantons of Vaud and Geneva, benefit from a full guarantee from the canton for all their liabilities.[2] In case of undercapitalization, the canton would be required to provide additional funds to the cantonal bank.[3] Furthermore, should a cantonal bank be liquidated, the canton would have to ensure that all creditors and depositors are fully repaid and, if necessary, put up additional funds to this end.[4]

Several cantons had to inject money in order to restore the financial situation of their banks, which had been hit hard in the crisis of the 1990s.[5] A financial restructuring became necessary to solve their financial problems in the cantons of Bern (1991), Geneva (1999) and Vaud (2001). In 1991, serious financial losses on loan operations of the cantonal Bank of Berne (Berner Kantonalbank (BEKB)) led to a rescue operation consisting of a recapitalization and the establishment of an asset management company.[6] The asset management company was established as a 100 per cent subsidiary of BEKB and acquired all non-performing assets of BEKB. It was financed by a loan from BEKB equal to the value of the assets transferred to it. The canton recapitalized BEKB and extended the state guarantee to all liabilities transferred to the asset management company. A similar solution was adopted to resolve the problems of the cantonal Bank of Geneva (Banque Cantonale de Genève (BCG)), in 1999. All impaired loans were transferred to a foundation, which became BCG's new debtor. The foundation was given a guarantee from the Canton of Geneva for the totality of the loans.

The foundation's sole function was to sell the real estate of the impaired debtors gradually. Whenever a sale was achieved the proceeds would be transferred to the bank to reduce the debt of the foundation. The canton agreed to pay the difference between the proceeds from the sale and the nominal value of the loan. Finally, the problems of the cantonal bank of Vaud, which surfaced only in 2001 but also had their roots in the real estate crisis of the 1990s, required a significant infusion of new capital by the canton.

The problems Switzerland experienced with its cantonal banks raise the question of whether the government should be directly involved in the banking business. While one would expect that unlimited liability creates an added incentive for prudent bank management there is always a high risk that the bank management is susceptible to political influence. In the above-mentioned cases, corporate governance and political involvement in management decisions were, at least partly, to blame for the problems.

Interim government ownership and public administration with creditors' claims being guaranteed by the public treasury are critical components of the MHL proposal. There is obviously a difference between the case of the cantonal banks and the state of play at the basis of the MHL approach. Contrary to MHL, in the case of the cantonal banks, state ownership coupled with an explicit guarantee of all liabilities renders the banks' creditors immune from loss. The canton and possibly other shareholders absorb all losses. In contrast, the MHL proposal provides for a debt and equity restructuring whereby in reverse order of priority the interests of pre-existing shareholders, subordinated debt-holders and other junior creditors are eliminated up to the point that claims equal the value of the bank's assets. Following this debt and equity restructuring the remaining depositor and other creditor claims will be fixed and guaranteed by the government. The case of the cantonal banks demonstrates that state ownership and the availability of public funds for the purpose of guaranteeing creditors' claims significantly facilitate financial restructuring, but at a political price. In implementing the MHL proposal it is important to avoid entangling the government authority in charge of the restructuring in the political process. To this end it seems advisable that the authority be independent from the government and protected from political influence. Ideally, the government authority should be overseeing the restructuring at arm's length with the direct administration of temporarily nationalized banks being placed in the hand of competent and experienced bankers.

10.2 Weaknesses of the current *lex generalis* approach

The experience with bank failures in Switzerland, sketched out in the preceding section, revealed several shortcomings in the existing legal framework. Most of them relate to the fact that the current law does not take into account the particularities of bank insolvency. In the terminology of MHL, the current legal framework follows a *lex generalis* approach, in that failing banks are subject to general bankruptcy law, which is administered by cantonal judicial authorities. The key weaknesses of this approach are the following:

- The complex interplay between *lex specialis*, that is, the banking statutes[7] on the one hand and *lex generalis*, that is, the Bankruptcy Act,[8] on the other causes legal uncertainty.
- Along with the application of two different types of statutes, two authorities – the bank supervisor and the bankruptcy courts – are involved in the process. The most striking example of the complex interplay between regulatory and bankruptcy law is the case of a bank placed into compulsory liquidation by the SFBC that subsequently turns out to be insolvent and therefore becomes subject to bankruptcy proceedings.[9] When the SFBC withdraws a licence, it simultaneously orders the compulsory liquidation and appoints liquidators. If the bank turns out to be insolvent, the bankruptcy court will appoint a commissioner and impose a moratorium,[10] which may be followed by an out-of-court settlement, formal court proceedings for an arrangement with creditors or bank bankruptcy proceedings.[11] Past experience with this regime has shown that the resulting joint administration by the court-appointed commissioner and the liquidator appointed by the SFBC can give rise to conflicts of competencies between the appointed officials which in turn cause unnecessary delays and additional costs.[12]
- Under current law a bank that is no longer complying with the licensing requirements and is experiencing financial difficulties will have its licence withdrawn. Licence withdrawal is followed by liquidation. There is no alternative or intermediate solution, such as provisional administration, as found in other jurisdictions.[13] Neither is there a statutory framework for reorganization that would include a stay of debt enforcement action against the bank, which could provide some 'breathing space' to support an attempt to reorganize the bank, thus saving it from liquidation. A stay of enforcement action can be obtained only upon the initiation of judicial bankruptcy

proceedings which most of the time render any prospect for reorganization illusive. In the aftermath of the failure of SLT, the SFBC was criticized for closing the bank too quickly. It was held that an alternative and less damaging solution would have been possible and that there would have been ways of maximizing the value of the bank's assets. A lot of value was lost through piecemeal liquidation. However, the applicable legal framework did not offer an alternative.

- Finally, the failure of SLT in 1991 also revealed the shortcomings of the deposit protection system. Compensation was paid on the basis of a voluntary arrangement among Swiss banks.[14] Approximately CHF 73 million had been employed to compensate for the deposits protected under the scheme. However, the protected deposits included only certain types of savings accounts, holders of checking accounts did not receive any compensation. The loss suffered by non-protected depositors, amounted to about CHF 107 million. The principal weakness affecting this system, besides its selective coverage, appears to be its voluntary nature. Banks have no legal obligation to participate in the system and, as opposed to what is required under the European Directive on Deposit Protection Schemes,[15] depositors have no legal claim to receiving payment.

10.3 Guiding principles of the new framework

Although there was much debate about the details, the architects of the new framework quickly reached an agreement on its basic underlying principles, which are the following:

- the need for special rules,
- the pivotal role of the bank supervisor, and
- the strict application of market discipline.

10.3.1 Special rules for dealing with distressed banks

The drafters of the new framework reached the same conclusion as MHL regarding the inadequacy of general bankruptcy for dealing with bank insolvencies in an expedient manner. The Swiss framework therefore introduces special provisions for reorganization and bankruptcy liquidation into the banking act and transfers the powers to conduct those proceedings from the bankruptcy courts to the bank supervisor. However, all issues of material law, for instance regarding the schedule of claims, the verification of claims, the avoidance of pre-insolvency transactions and so on continue to be governed by the Bankruptcy Act.[16]

Whether a special legal framework for banks is necessary is dealt with extensively in the academic literature.[17] It is generally recognized that banks, as financial intermediaries and providers of financial services, play a special role in the economy. They perform financial services, such as credit extension, deposit-taking and payment processing, both within and across national borders. Furthermore, they are essential instruments in the execution of monetary policy. Even in economies where a significant number of firms can turn to the capital market for financing, banks retain important roles as providers of payment facilities and short-term credit. The specific nature of the banking business characterized by a liquidity mismatch, that is the funding of illiquid loans by short-term deposits, creates a potential for market failure. For those reasons, both because of their important function and to counterbalance the tendency towards increased risk-taking, banks are subject to prudential supervision, notably minimum capital requirements and risk management systems. It is generally argued that special rules are also necessary to deal with stress situations because the insolvency of a bank poses different problems to those of other types of corporations. Whereas general insolvency law is a collective procedure aimed at maximizing the insolvency estate for the benefit of the creditors, the main objective of a banking regulation is to ensure the stability of the financial system as a whole and to prevent systemic problems.[18] Hence, besides ensuring the orderly and fair treatment of all creditors, a bank insolvency procedure has to take into account the systemic impact on the financial system.

10.3.2 Sole competence of the bank supervisor

When bank insolvency regimes in major legal systems are compared, two models are generally found. They all lie between the two polar regimes described in MHL, the *lex specialis* and the *lex generalis* approach. The first involves a special bank insolvency procedure administered by the bank supervisor or the deposit protection agency, as for instance in Canada,[19] Italy[20] and the United States.[21] The second, which is prevalent in European countries, uses court-administered regimes.[22] In Europe, the conduct of bankruptcy proceedings is traditionally a judicial function, which may be one explanation for the reluctance of legislators to transfer certain 'judicial' functions to the bank supervisory authority.

Some maintain that bank supervisors should deal only with 'living' banks, while 'fatally ill' or 'dead' banks should be turned over to the 'mortician', the bankruptcy court: since an insolvent bank can no longer conduct the business of banking, it is no longer a bank and thus should be treated just like any other bankrupt corporation.[23] This argument holds only in part. Banks are already subject to special regulation which determines the conditions of their operation. It is, therefore, only the bank supervisor – and not a bankruptcy judge or a meeting of creditors – who is in a position to determine whether a bank is viable. Thus, the bank supervisor must have a voice in the insolvency procedure. Moreover, the banking law defines the general mandate of banking supervision in terms of its objectives, that is, the stability of the financial system and the protection of the depositors as a whole. Since the presence of insolvent banks or banks on the verge of insolvency presents a threat to the financial system, it is important that the bank supervisor has the requisite powers to deal with such situations.

The transfer to the bank supervisor of some of those 'judicial' functions, such as the power to order a stay on enforcement action and freeze assets, and to conduct reorganization or liquidation proceedings, can in fact result in increased efficiency. Decisions regarding protective measures, a moratorium or the closure of an institution, and the need for restructuring or reducing a specific market exposure generally need to be taken in a very narrow time frame. Due to its continual supervisory function, the bank supervisor, as opposed to the courts, is already in the possession of the necessary information about the institution, its business structure and its operations. It also has the necessary technical expertise which enables it to act more expeditiously. Given its expertise and proximity to the financial sector, the bank supervisor is better placed to assess whether or not specific measures are appropriate under the circumstances.

For those reasons, and in the light of past experience in Switzerland with judicial bank insolvency proceedings paralleling regulatory action taken by the SFBC, it was found that the SFBC alone, excluding the courts, should be given the power to initiate and oversee reorganization and insolvency liquidation proceedings. The experience of the 1930s described earlier confirmed that the objectives of speed, cost-efficiency and minimal disruption to the banking operations can be better achieved through a regulator-centred process.

10.3.3 Market discipline – no state assistance

As discussed in MHL, ensuring a strong measure of market discipline is key to an efficient and equitable resolution of troubled banks. A framework for reorganization must not undermine market discipline. Therefore, public funds must not be used for restructuring or resolving financial institutions.[24] Any losses derived from a bank failure must be allocated among shareholders and creditors of the bank. There was agreement among the drafters of the new framework that a key aspect of market discipline is the understanding that bank failures are possible and that the bank supervisor will allow those banks that become insolvent to fail. In order for market incentives to work, the regulatory process must be credible to the regulated entities and the public.[25] Having acknowledged the special role of banks earlier, it should be stressed that it is the function performed by banks, not the existence of any particular bank or group of banks, that is essential to an economy. Bank failures are part of risk-taking in a competitive environment. Supervision cannot and should not provide an absolute assurance that banks will not fail.[26] When a bank is no longer competitive, resources must not be wasted to keep that bank alive and a reorganization procedure must not be abused to postpone the decision on licence withdrawal or liquidation. In other words, bank closure and compulsory liquidation also serve the 'healthy' purpose of weeding out non-viable financial institutions.

10.4 The main features of the new bank insolvency framework

10.4.1 Intervention

MHL recommend the definition of precise intervention triggers in terms of capital levels. This system of mandatory graduated corrective measures, sometimes referred to as '*Structured Early Intervention and Resolution*' (SEIR),[27] serves to reduce regulatory discretion. As such, in the United States the Federal Deposit Insurance Corporation Improvement Act [FDICIA], which was passed in 1991 to correct what was perceived as regulatory forbearance towards undercapitalized banks during the 1980s,[28] provides for mandatory remedial action of increasing severity as the level of a bank's capital decreases ('*prompt corrective action*') [PCA].[29] It was intended to oblige examiners to act more promptly.[30]

Triggers for intervention

The proposed Swiss framework codifies a number of intervention measures, which include the power to replace management, alter, reduce or terminate any activity that poses excessive risk and restrict an institution's business activities. The drafters of the new framework refrained, however, from defining precise trigger points in terms of capital levels. Under the proposal the SFBC can order protective measures where it identifies a threat to depositors' interests. Such a situation is deemed to exist where a bank fails to comply with capital adequacy requirements on a continuing basis. A threat to depositors' interests is further presumed where a bank encounters liquidity problems and has difficulty in obtaining liquidity under market conditions, or where there are any other indications suggesting that a bank may no longer be able to satisfy its obligations towards its creditors in the near future.

Instead of defining *ex-ante* mandatory intervention criteria, which may be too crude to ensure that intervention occurs early enough (but not too early!), the Swiss framework provides the supervisor with some flexibility in pursuing the optimal solution in terms of timing and type of action in each individual case. It is understood that for a discretion-based system to function well the banking supervisory authority must have the necessary resolve to implement a firm policy. A consistent and transparent regulatory practice has to send clear signals to the banks and to the public and make the banking supervisory authority's choice of remedial and intervention measures predictable.

The intervenor

The new law introduces the new instrument of an investigator or intervenor who can be appointed for different purposes to establish the extent of financial difficulties and take corrective actions and also to examine other problems, such as compliance with anti-money laundering provisions or to verify the implementation of measures ordered by the SFBC. In its appointment order the SFBC defines the mandate as well as the powers and competencies of the investigator, which may include the authority to enter the premises of all offices and other facilities of the institution, to obtain access to the bank's computer systems and all other information relating to the operations and affairs of the undertaking, and to examine accounts, books, documents and other records. It is considered key to successful intervention that the investigator or intervenor has the necessary powers to achieve the objectives of intervention, namely the avoidance of the dissipation of assets and further losses to creditors. The SFBC may therefore delegate certain administration powers to the investigator and allow the investigator to act in lieu of the bank's managers and directors. The appointment of an investigator need not be publicly announced. It can be a secret measure, which may be desirable in the circumstances, to avoid alerting the public and triggering a crisis of confidence.

Regulatory moratorium

The most powerful new instrument at the disposal of the SFBC is the power to order a stay of all execution proceedings (moratorium) against the bank, keeping creditors from continuing or engaging in forced execution and seizure of assets. If under current law the SFBC orders a bank to suspend its payments – a measure that may be necessary to prevent a further outflow of liquidity – the order does not have the effect of halting civil debt enforcement action. Thus, paradoxically, the bank supervisor can bar a bank from fulfilling its contractual payment obligations, but does not have the power to give any relief from enforcement action. Creditors, upon not receiving their due payments, therefore immediately commence a debt enforcement action in court. In order to stop such debt enforcement actions, the bank has no other option but to petition the competent bankruptcy court for the initiation of insolvency proceedings.[31] Once formal court proceedings have been initiated any realistic prospects for reorganization will have vanished.

The regulatory moratorium provided for under the new framework fixes this incongruity. It gives adequate protection to the bank creditors by prohibiting any uncontrolled disposition of the bank's assets while at the same time allowing some additional time ('breathing space') to arrange a financial restructuring or a sale or merger with another financial institution. The width of this window of opportunity ultimately depends on the bank's ability to maintain a degree of confidence in its future and the practicability of a reorganization.

The moratorium has far-reaching effects on creditors in that they cannot enforce their claims for its duration. A general moratorium, as typically provided for under ordinary bankruptcy law that blocks all payment streams, will be inappropriate in most cases given the needs of bank customers and households. Even in a situation of severe financial difficulty it is not possible to halt all bank activities. In order to reduce the potential for systemic risk, the bank will have to continue to operate, even as it scales down the size of its books. The new regulatory moratorium therefore allows for some deviations from general insolvency law.

10.4.2 Reorganization

If a bank experiences financial distress the SFBC will, in the first instance, encourage a silent reorganization. Such a solution could entail finding strategic investors, selling off parts of the institution or arranging a merger or an acquisition by a stronger financial institution. For the authorities, a private sector solution is the least costly, and for investors and creditors it preserves more value in their investments. Should such efforts fail the present Banking Act requires the SFBC to revoke the banking licence immediately and order the liquidation.[32]

The new framework offers the alternative option of a reorganization procedure. The proposed procedure emulates the procedure applied under the emergency ordinance in the 1930s described earlier.[33] A reorganization should only be an option where there are reasonable prospects for its success. While it may be possible to overcome organizational shortcomings or significant loan losses that are due to adverse market conditions, it would not be reasonable to attempt to rehabilitate a bank that, due to structural changes in the financial sector in which it operates, is unable to survive in the long run. The objective of reorganization is not the rescue of the bank as such, rather it is the realization of the optimal economic solution for the bank's creditors and the financial sector as a whole.

A central role for the bank supervisor

MHL recommend that decision-making authority regarding the restructuring be passed to a government agency, which acquires temporary ownership of the institution. In Switzerland it is believed that the bank supervisor should not be involved in the day-to-day business of running banks and that bank reorganization should, as a matter of principle, be left to the private sector. The statutory framework for reorganization should merely facilitate and create appropriate incentives for private initiatives. The bank supervisor (or a person appointed by the supervisor) may act as an honest broker and draw up reorganization plans using its moral persuasion to reinforce commitment amongst all parties affected by the plan, but should not be directly involved in the reorganization process. There is concern that direct government involvement in the reorganization process, as proposed by MHL, would expose the state to significant liability risk. Direct governmental involvement could give rise to the expectation that, in cases of unsuccessful management and failure to return the bank back to solvency, the government would guarantee all additional losses suffered by creditors. To avoid such an outcome it is necessary to communicate clearly to the banks and the public that regulatory measures that support reorganization cannot be interpreted as a guarantee for a successful reorganization or a commitment to subsequent official support if the reorganization fails.

Prospects for reorganization

How is reorganization carried out under the new framework? As a first step, the SFBC has to determine whether or not the distressed institution would be economically viable and could be reorganized. At this stage, private attempts to solve the financial problem, for example, arrange a merger or takeover, may have already failed. The current law in force requires the SFBC to withdraw a bank's licence and order its compulsory liquidation.[34] The draft proposal would provide the SFBC henceforth with the option of abstaining from immediate licence withdrawal and instead taking protective measures and initiating a reorganization procedure.[35]

If the SFBC decides that there are reasonable prospects for reorganization, it will mandate an administrator with the elaboration of a reorganization plan. In the meantime, the bank's business may be continued on a reduced scale according to guidance from the administrator and the SFBC.

The reorganization plan

The reorganization administrator has the task of working out a reorganization plan, which indicates how and in what time frame the identified financial problems and possible organizational shortcomings are to be corrected. The core of the reorganization plan is the financial restructuring, which may consist of the sale of the whole or parts of the entity to another institution, a restructuring or reorientation of the business activities, recapitalization by existing or new shareholders or a debt-equity swap. The debt-equity swap is a simple and effective reorganization tool whereby creditor's claims are transformed into ownership rights. Existing overindebtedness is eliminated, the balance sheet shows the equity capital intact again.[36] In most European jurisdictions, corporate law requires that every capital contribution be equivalent to the issue price of the subscribed shares[37] and the 'intact' value of the claims be taken into account in the settlement. If the company is insolvent or overindebted the claims of the creditors against it are, however, no longer of intact value. The claim thus may not be offset at the nominal value but at a reduced value. Under the new law the terms of the debt-equity swap, which may provide for reduction of the value of the claims which are set-off against the newly subscribed shares, would be defined irrevocably in the reorganization plan.

The 'reorganization haircut'

Experience with the regime of the 1930s in Switzerland and bank reorganizations in other countries has demonstrated that successful reorganizations have a price and cannot be achieved without sacrifice on the part of the owners and possibly the creditors. A 'haircut' imposed upon owners and creditors – that is, a writing down of shareholder equity and a reduction of creditors' claims – is almost always a necessary component of a financial restructuring.

According to MHL a 'reorganization haircut' must distribute the cost of the loss to pre-existing shareholders and uninsured creditors according to the ranking of claims under ordinary insolvency law. Those who are primarily to blame for the failure, that is the bank management and the shareholders, should not get a free ride by not sharing in the losses while reaping all the benefits and future gains from the reorganization. The Swiss framework adopts the same approach. The law explicitly stipulates that the reorganization plan should respect the ranking of the stakeholders, placing secured creditors first, then preferred claims, unsecured claims, subordinated debt and finally equity.

What is the legal mechanism for forcing some or all owners, investors or creditors to share in the losses? MHL renounce any form of negotiation or bargaining among stakeholders. The 'reorganization haircut' is decided by official act of the government. At first glance, this proposal seems appealing. Publicity requirements and other procedural requirements in formal judicial insolvency proceedings, such as creditors' meetings, invariably tend to lengthen the bankruptcy procedure and can have adverse effects on the value of assets and destroy liquidity. In the United States, it has been observed that, because it typically causes significant delays in returning the assets of failed companies to the private sector, the bankruptcy system could not have acted as quickly as did the Federal Deposit Insurance Corporation (FDIC) in the Savings & Loans crisis.[38] The analysis by Peik Granlund in Chapter 7 also seems to indicate that there is a clear correlation between the powers of stakeholders in the insolvency process and the efficiency and likely speed of resolution. A unitary decision-making process under regulatory law proves faster than the negotiated process under ordinary insolvency law. Yet, the authoritative approach proposed by MHL raises some due process and creditors' rights issues, which are addressed in more detail by Christos Hadjiemmanuil in Chapter 11. The Swiss approach attempts to take into account those concerns and may be seen as a compromise between the authoritative action of a government agency and a negotiated process among all stakeholders.

The drafters of the new Swiss law found that the stakeholder should have a say in the decision-making process if the reorganization plan directly affects its legal rights, for instance, by way of a reduction or rescheduling of claims, the write-down of shareholder equity. The new law does not provide for an assembly of all creditors as provided for under ordinary insolvency law. Instead, the concerned creditors and shareholders have (merely) the right to submit objections to the proposed plan. The reorganization administrator is required to take into account those objections when drawing up the final plan for submission to the SFBC, however, only to the extent that they do not conflict with the general objectives and criteria for the reorganization plan as defined in the law.

As opposed to the typical bankruptcy procedures a formal vote on the plan is not required. However, it cannot be imposed against a majority of creditors either. As such, the only remedy against the plan is a majority vote of the creditors in favour of an immediate bankruptcy liquidation. A majority of the creditors representing the majority of claims, not counting secured creditors and those who have priority in bankruptcy, can reject the reorganization plan and request the initiation of liquidation proceedings. Priority creditors and secured creditors are excluded from voting to prevent them forcing liquidation in order to obtain rapid repayment of their claims.

Approval of the reorganization plan

The reorganization plan is subject to approval by the SFBC. The need for approval serves to ensure that reorganization is only carried out when there are realistic prospects for success and will not be used to put off an inevitable liquidation and thereby cause additional losses to the creditors. The new law provides for a number of criteria that the SFBC has to take into account in the approval process. As such, a necessary precondition for a successful implementation of the reorganization plan is a truthful assessment of the financial situation and a conservative evaluation of the bank's assets. The current economic situation as well as the expected economic developments will also have to be taken into consideration. The reorganization plan must ensure that full compliance with all reorganization criteria is achieved within a reasonable period of time. Another approval criterion is that no creditor is placed in a worse position than in a liquidation. In other words, the reorganization should be Pareto-superior to a hypothetical liquidation.

The approval by the SFBC is subject to legal review and may be appealed to the Federal Supreme Court. While defining criteria for the approval of a plan, the proposal confers some discretion to the bank supervisor in the appreciation and application of the criteria. It should therefore be expected that, unless it is established that the plan is wholly unreasonable, the court will not lightly interfere with the reorganization process.

No vote by the shareholders

Even though under Swiss corporate law an increase or a reduction of the capital as well as a merger with another bank requires the approval by the general assembly of shareholders a reorganization plan that would include similar measures is not subject to approval by the general assembly.[39] The objective of the new law is clearly to allow for a rapid reorganization and to avoid the possibility of a few large shareholders boycotting the reorganization plan. The requirement of full shareholder participation would create additional obstacles (more cost, more time) to the swift restructuring of a bank on the verge of failure, and can even make that failure more likely.

A critical question, also raised by Christos Hadjiemmanuil in Chapter 11, is whether a reorganization procedure that allows for the imposition of changes to the capital structure of a company without shareholder approval would be admissible from an EU company law perspective.[40] The case commonly cited in this context is *Panagis Pafitis and other* v. *Trapeza Kentrikis Ellados AE and others* ('Pafitis case').[41] In the Pafitis case, the ECJ was asked to address the prejudicial question of whether the rules of the Second Company Law Directive 77/91[42] were applicable to a bank that had been placed under provisional administration by the bank supervisor, the Central Bank of Greece. The provisional administrator had decided a capital increase without having previously obtained the formal approval by the general assembly of shareholders. The ECJ stated that member states must not adopt bank reorganization measures that violate the minimum level of protection for shareholders, which includes, in particular, the shareholders' right to decide upon changes in the capital structure of a banking corporation. According to the ECJ, an administrative act to this end without a resolution of the general meeting is contrary to Article 25(1) of the Directive.

Would the ECJ have decided otherwise had the ousting of existing shareholders occurred in the context of formal insolvency proceedings furnished with all procedural guarantees? It would seem that the rights of shareholders to make changes to the capital structure of their company, referred to by the ECJ as their 'most intimate and unrelinquishable rights', are not absolute. There is no higher legal norm that prohibits any derogations. In a bank reorganization scenario, there is a conflict between the objectives of the *lex generalis*, that is, the company law, and the objectives of the *lex specialis*, that is, the banking and bank insolvency law. Whereas the first pursues the protection of shareholder rights as its goal, the second pursues the protection of depositors' and more generally creditors' rights. In weighing the values at stake it would appear that a limitation on the rights of shareholders is justifiable if it is shown that it allows the interests of the bank's creditors to be better safeguarded. In a reorganization scenario, the protection of depositor rights carries greater weight than the protection of shareholder rights.[43]

10.4.3 Bank bankruptcy

Where there are no prospects for reorganization, or where the reorganization has failed, the SFBC must order the immediate liquidation of the insolvent bank. The new law provides for an insolvency liquidation ('bank bankruptcy') procedure under the sole responsibility of the SFBC. Powers currently exercised by the courts are assumed by the SFBC. As such, the SFBC appoints the liquidators and oversees the liquidation process thus becoming a quasi-bankruptcy authority.

Exclusive right to initiate proceedings

The SFBC alone has the right to initiate bankruptcy proceedings against a bank. Thus, if a creditor lodges a bankruptcy petition against a bank, the bankruptcy court must forward the petition to the SFBC. It is believed that limiting the ability to commence liquidation proceedings to the bank supervisor gives the supervisor a better opportunity to consider the wider impact of the bank failure and to control the issues that affect public confidence, such as the timing of the measures, the notice to the public and the overall impact on the financial system.

Applicability of ordinary bankruptcy rules

As a rule, the Bankruptcy Act applies unless derogated by special rules in the Banking Act. The liquidators have the right in accordance with the rules laid down in the Bankruptcy Act, to avoid or otherwise render ineffective acts prejudicial to creditors, such as transfers of property or rights, encumbrances of property and obligations incurred. They may take action to nullify transactions that were intended to deceive creditors by removing assets otherwise available to them on insolvency. They have to take all steps necessary for preserving and keeping assets comprised in the estate, selling the assets at the best price reasonably obtainable in the market, examining and admitting claims, preparing a statement as to admitted and contested claims and responding to reasonable requests for information concerning the insolvency estate or its administration. They must ensure that the liquidation proceeds are ultimately distributed to the bank's creditors in the order provided for by the law[44] and that the estate is closed promptly and in accordance with the best interests of the creditors.[45]

Immediate pay-out of small deposits

As a measure to simplify the proceedings, the SFBC is given the discretion to decide that small depositors with account holdings up to

CHF 5,000 be paid out immediately, notwithstanding any counterclaims of the bank. A survey showed that such immediate payment for small depositors would, in the case of a medium-sized bank, make it possible to satisfy claims of about 60 per cent of the depositors fully with approximately 6 per cent of the assets. It is expected to simplify the liquidation procedure significantly by eliminating the requirement to inventory those small accounts. The SFBC may further reduce (but not increase) the amount of CHF 5,000.

Oversight by the bank supervisor

The liquidators are accountable to the SFBC and must report to the creditors on the progress of the liquidation at least annually. A creditor committee may be appointed to monitor the liquidation proceedings and to consult with the liquidator regarding the disposition of significant assets, the conduct of significant liquidation operations and the continuation of certain business transactions. Complaints against individual acts of the liquidator may be submitted to the SFBC. The SFBC can remove a liquidator if it determines that the liquidator has acted with gross incompetence and failed to perform the duties assigned by the SFBC.

10.5 Deposit protection

Another component of the new framework is a reform of the deposit protection system. It has generally been recognized that there is a need for a system whereby less-financially-sophisticated depositors are protected from the loss of their deposits when banks fail.[46] The new law introduces a deposit protection system which largely follows the precepts set out in the European Directive on Deposit Guarantee Schemes.[47] In keeping with the Swiss tradition of self-regulation in the financial sector, the future deposit-protection system will be an industry-run system.

Mandatory membership

In the majority of industrialized countries, and contrary to the current situation in Switzerland, banks are by law required to join a deposit insurance system.[48] Within the EU, mandatory deposit protection was introduced with the Deposit Insurance Directive.[49] The rationale of mandatory membership is to reduce adverse selection, which occurs when the weakest institutions choose to join a voluntary system while the strongest remain outside. Although compulsory membership involves a degree of cross-subsidization of weak institutions by strong ones, all members, even the strongest ones, benefit from having a more stable financial sector.[50] The new law therefore declares membership in a deposit protection system mandatory for all financial institutions in Switzerland that take deposits from the public, including branches and subsidiaries of foreign banks and securities firms with client accounts.

Limited coverage

The new law extends mandatory deposit insurance of CHF 30,000 to all types of accounts. As seen earlier, the voluntary scheme currently limits deposit protection to certain types of accounts excluding, for instance, cheque accounts. Since foreign currency deposits, in particular deposits in euro and US$, are widely used in Switzerland, the coverage also extends to deposits denominated in currencies other than the Swiss franc. In contrast, however, to the system adopted by the European Directive,[51] coverage only applies to local deposits excluding deposits of foreign branches of Swiss banks.[52] Compensation of the sum of deposits held by one individual depositor in a bank will be paid up to a limit of CHF 30,000. If a depositor's holdings exceed the amount covered under the system, the depositor will take a place in line with other creditors to receive the proceeds recovered over time from the liquidated assets of the failed bank.

Depositor preference

In addition to the deposit protection scheme, a bankruptcy priority applies to bank deposits. In contrast to the United States where the depositor preference extends to the full amount of the deposits, the Swiss statute limits the priority to the maximum amount of CHF 30,000, that is the amount also protected under the deposit insurance system.[53] The deposit protection agency will become subrogated in the rights of the depositors and thus be able to recover the funds from the liquidation proceeds as preferred creditor. A survey in a representative selection of small, medium-sized and large banks has shown that, on average, the volume of privileged deposits amounts to 20 per cent to 30 per cent of the balance sheet total booked in Switzerland. A bank would have to suffer a loss of more than 70 per cent of its value for privileged deposits to be no longer covered. Hence, there is a considerable likelihood that privileged deposits can be fully recovered from the liquidation proceeds.

Transparency

In order to ensure the transparency necessary for market discipline to work, the banks will have to disclose the amount of privileged deposits in their annual financial statements to enable non-privileged creditors to evaluate their risk position in a hypothetical insolvency.

An industry-run system

The deposit protection system is to be set up by the industry through self-regulation. The new law lays down certain minimum requirements that must be fulfilled and verified by the SFBC. As such, the system must be adequately organized and be in a position to ensure the payout of compensation within no more than three months of the suspension of the bank's payments.[54] The new law provides, however, that the Federal Council will take the necessary measures to establish a government-run system should the banks fail to set up a functioning deposit protection system or should their system prove inadequate.

The details of the financing of the deposit protection system are not set out in the new law. They are to be defined by the banks subject to authorization by the SFBC.[55] There is a preference for an *ex-post* system similar to the existing deposit insurance system devised by the Agreement of the Swiss Bankers Association, which relies on the ability of surviving banks to fund losses after they have been incurred.

Additional liquidity

In many cases, the need to pay assessments or levies to deal with failures occurs at an inopportune time, when the obligation to provide funding may impose a significant financial burden on the industry. To ensure the ability of the banks to contribute their part to the compensation paid to depositors of failed banks, the new law introduces the obligation on all banks to provide for permanent liquidity coverage of half of the maximum contribution that could be imposed upon them. This liquidity requirement is complementary to the general regulatory liquidity requirements.

Systemic limit

In response to the banks' concern that they would become subject to an open-ended obligation to contribute to compensation payments for depositors of failed banks, the new law explicitly spells out the maximum coverage of CHF 4 billion. Recognising an explicit limit will however raise additional questions. Should this limit be crossed, will the government automatically step in to provide the lacking funding or will it bail out the failing bank given that systemic implications are likely?

In the case of a large bank failure it may in fact be hazardous to ask all 'surviving' banks to cover the losses. Given the structure of the Swiss banking sector with essentially two large banks, it can reasonably be questioned whether the proposed self-regulatory scheme would be able to cope with the difficulties of one of the two. While it is necessary that the two large banks participate in the scheme as they provide additional stability to the system, it is likely that, should a large bank face financial distress, the smaller banks would simply be unable to provide enough liquidity for paying off the preferred depositors immediately.

One possibility that was discussed during the elaboration of the new law was to require larger banks to procure additional protection for the amount of deposits that exceeded a defined 'systemic limit', understood as a hypothetical maximum amount that all banks together could afford to guarantee without risking their own financial health. Such additional protection could be provided by private insurance, the issuance of bonds or express guarantees of the parent companies. Given the extremely low probability on the one side but the unlimited loss potential on the other, only large insurance companies would be able to provide such insurance coverage.[56] In the absence of any practical experience with such private market solutions and considering the costs that these solutions would entail for the industry, this proposal was rejected during the formal consultation process. Instead, it was decided to write an explicit limit of the deposit protection system into the law, subject to adjustment by the Federal Council. This explicit limit is intended to make clear that the objective of the deposit protection system is to protect small depositors' funds in normal times and to help avoid unjustified runs and that it cannot be expected to maintain systemic stability in the face of any severe shocks to the entire financial system.[57] In such a case, the government may have to decide to take emergency action to preserve the system.[58]

10.6 Challenges ahead

For the new legal framework it can be said that one size does not fit all. The discussion on deposit insurance already hinted at the particular features of the Swiss system which create unique challenges to the architects of Switzerland's bank insolvency law. Switzerland is the home of two global players, UBS and Credit Suisse Group (CSG). Both UBS and CSG have their main activities and the associated risks outside the jurisdiction of incorporation of the parent company, which is in Switzerland. They are managed from a multitude of financial centres and their operations span multiple legal jurisdictions and time zones. The international diversification of these two large banking groups may constitute a shock absorber for the Swiss system since their globally diversified international activities could provide a cushion against domestic shocks. On the other hand, the large banks can more easily spread global turbulence to Switzerland. They are closely linked with other global financial institutions through inter-bank exposures, OTC market counter party exposures and through trading, clearing, and settlement relationships. A shock that threatens one of the large Swiss banks could have severe repercussions on the Swiss financial system and on the Swiss economy as a whole. However, effective crisis management could not be handled by the SFBC alone but would require a close cooperation between various regulators at the international level.

The G10 Study of Financial Sector Consolidation,[59] which was released to the public in January 2001, pointed out the potential issues arising from financial consolidation and the recent creation of a significant number of large, and in some cases increasingly complex, financial groups. The study observes that the damaging effects of a failure of such an institution could be reduced by stepped-up efforts in contingency planning and improved communication and cooperation among central banks, finance ministries and other supervisory authorities, both domestically and internationally. The study gives no further detail on how such communication and cooperation should take place and what action would need to be taken to effectively deal with problems imperilling the viability of a large financial group. On the European level the *Report on Financial Stability* of May 2000 ('Brouwer Report') examined the impact of the major financial trends on the stability of the financial system in Europe as well as the arrangements in the European Union (EU) aimed at safeguarding financial stability.[60] (See also Chapter 11 by Brouwer, Hebbink and Wesseling.) This report likewise recommends enhanced cooperation and information sharing among supervisors and the conclusion of memoranda of understanding among all concerned regulators and recommends the designation of a lead coordinator, a concept introduced in the draft European Directive on Financial Conglomerates.[61] As observed by Sigurðsson in Chapter 5, it may, however, not be enough for national supervisors to enter into MOUs for the purpose of cross-border cooperation and information exchange if the final responsibility for dealing with ailing financial groups is not clear. The problem is that in the case of a large and complex financial group that is 'too complex to fail' and of systemic relevance the question of which country's treasury and eventually taxpayers would bear the cost for the rescue is unresolved.[62]

An approach that has been discussed occasionally is to set up a 'supranational regulator' for the 'super-league' of globally active financial groups.[63] The supranational regulator would exercise the same functions as a home supervisor under the present framework of consolidated supervision and would thus be solely responsible for crisis management and coordination of a global winding-up of the group. A single clear responsibility for ongoing supervision and crisis management at the group level and a supervisory system tailor-made for large and complex financial groups would be established by international agreement. The implementation of such an idea would, however, require national regulators to surrender considerable supervisory powers and competencies to a supranational regulator.

While the creation of a supranational regulator on a global level may still appear a chimerical vision, it may be less so at the European level. Significant regulatory developments over the past thirty years have led to an almost full integration of the banking and capital markets in the European Union. It would seem that the necessary groundwork has been done.

10.7 Concluding remarks

The prominent innovators in bankruptcy theory, Aghion, Hart and Moore (1992), described three characteristics of good bankruptcy procedures.[64]

- First, a good bankruptcy procedure should deliver an *ex-post* efficient outcome, that is, it should maximize the total value available to be divided between the debtor, creditors and shareholders.
- Second, a good bankruptcy procedure should preserve the bonding role of debt by penalizing managers and shareholders adequately in bankruptcy states.
- Third, a good bankruptcy procedure should preserve the absolute priority of claims.

With respect to the first goal, both the MHL proposal as well as the new Swiss framework seek to preserve the value of the bank's assets with minimal disruption to bank operations and counterparties. In Switzerland, this objective is to be achieved through the replacement of management (if necessary) and the temporary appointment of an official with powers to temporarily oversee the bank's operation until a reorganization or an orderly winding-down has been achieved. The MHL proposal achieves the objective of continuity through an immediate take-over of the failing institution by a government agency.

With respect to the second goal, both proposals stress the importance of penalizing those in charge of running the bank (and responsible for its problems). Both provide for the possibility of removing management and nullifying shareholder rights by writing down the share value.

With respect to the third goal, both proposals stress the importance of adhering to the absolute priority of claims and thereby avoiding adverse incentives in favour of either reorganization or bankruptcy. As such, a prerequisite for approval of the reorganization plan under the new Swiss framework is that it respects the ranking of all stakeholders. Even depositors are not insulated from market discipline since they may not receive more than the limits of the deposit protection system. Under the MHL proposal the debt restructuring that is an essential component of the reorganization procedure must respect the ranking of the claims on the bank.

Both proposals seem to achieve the overall objectives of good bankruptcy procedures and both procedures accord a dominant role to the regulatory authority. The MHL proposal goes one step further in that it provides for the temporary takeover by the government of failing banks for the purpose of reorganization. Which procedure is better? The answer probably depends on the circumstances, for instance, the resources available to the government agency to carry out reorganizations. In some instances, it may be cheaper to hive off the important parts of the bank rather than maintaining loss-making operations by trying to save the entire institution. For banks without a strong banking franchise, a lower cost resolution may be achieved through an instant piecemeal liquidation. In the case of a large bank failure, however, which could put at risk the entire financial system, a temporary bank nationalization may in fact be the preferred resolution method. Ideally, a legal framework would provide for a choice of appropriate tools and procedures to allow for the necessary flexibility to cope with each specific case. While the MHL proposal puts forward a practical answer to the question of who pays for bank insolvency in a national setting, the answer to the question is more difficult in a cross-border setting. With the increasing number of cross-border and cross-sector mergers and alliances, the number of institutions with systemic relevance and considered TBTF, in other words, 'too complex to be closed and liquidated', is increasing. The issue of how to deal with an insolvency of such an entity is becoming more important and it is obvious that the national regulator alone is not the answer. 'Who pays for the insolvency of an internationally active financial group?' is therefore likely to be the next question.

Notes

* The views expressed are those of the author alone.

1. The proposal, which takes the form of an amendment to the Banking Act, and the explanatory report were published for submission to parliament in November 2002 and can be downloaded in German, French and Italian at http://www.bk.admin.ch/ch/d/ff/2002/8117.pdf (legislative proposal) http://www.bk.admin.ch/ch/d/ff/2002/8060.pdf (report). For a synopsis of the proposed new framework, see Hüpkes (2002, p. 153).
2. Between the beginning of the nineteenth century and the two first decades of the twentieth century, the various Swiss cantons separately decided to create cantonal banks. (Switzerland is composed of 26 entities, 20 cantons and 6 half-cantons.) The general objective was to provide a safe place for the savings of the general public and to give an impetus to regional economic development by making loans at low interest to the local economy.
3. Following the amendment to the Banking Act in 1999, the cantonal guarantee is no longer a condition for the recognition of a bank as 'cantonal bank'. The 'cantonal bank' label now presupposes that the canton holds a participation of more than one-third of the capital and of the shareholder voting rights.
4. The cantons of Vaud and Geneva set up banking institutions with a limited guarantee in favour of all depositors. In Vaud, the guarantee is limited to CHF 40,000 per depositor for saving accounts. In Geneva, the guarantee amounts to CHF 500,000 for saving deposits and CHF 3 million for the deposits of pension funds.
5. The most important cases were those of the cantons of Jura and Valais. In the cantons of Solothurn and Appenzell-Ausserrhoden, the local legislative power decided to sell the cantonal bank to large private banks.
6. See Swiss Federal Banking Commission, *Annual Report 1991*, pp. 22 *et seq*.
7. See Federal Act on Banks and Savings Act of November 8, 1934 ('Banking Act') Arts. 23ter ss. The official German, French and Italian versions can be found at http://www.bk.admin.ch/ch/d/sr/c952_0.html and through the website of the SFBC http://www.ebk.admin.ch. An unofficial English translation of the Act as well as the implementing ordinances is available at http://www. kpmg.ch/library/ebk/. The provisions of the Banking Act are further elaborated in the Implementing Ordinance of 30 August 1961, the Ordinance on Banking and Savings Banks of 17 May 1972 and the Ordinance of the Federal Supreme Court regarding the Composition Procedure for Banks and Savings Banks of 11 April 1935.
8. Law on Debt and Enforcement and Bankruptcy of 1889 and 1994. The official German, French and Italian versions can be found at http://www. bk.admin. ch/ch/d/sr/c281_1.html.
9. A similar regime exists under French law, see Hüpkes (2000, p. 79).
10. A moratorium is a stay of enforcement action. As a typical bankruptcy measure a moratorium serves the interests of the creditors in preserving the

bank's financial situation, at the same time it may give the bank a respite for it to overcome the temporary financial difficulties.

11. Banking Act Art. 29.
12. Hüpkes (2000, p. 72).
13. For examples, see Hüpkes (2000, pp. 57 *et seq.*).
14. This agreement was replaced in 1993 by the Agreement on Depositor Protection in Case of Compulsory Bank Liquidation of 1 July 1993 of the Swiss Bankers Association (available on the internet at http://www.swissbanking.org/en/vereinbarung_930701_einlegerschutz_eng.pdf) in order to take into account changes introduced into the Bankruptcy Act.
15. Directive 94/19/EC of the European Parliament and of the Council of 30 May 1994 on deposit-guarantee schemes Official Journal L 135, 31/05/1994 p. 0005–0014, available via the internet at http://www.europa.eu.int/eur-lex/en/lif/dat/1994/en_394L0019.html.
16. As a consequence, all related disputes also remain within the jurisdiction of the competent cantonal courts under the Bankruptcy Act.
17. See further references in Eva Hüpkes, 'Insolvency – why a special regime for banks?', in International Monetary Fund (2003) (ed.) *Current Developments in Monetary and Financial Law*, Vol. III, Washington, available via the Internet at http://www.imf.org/external/np/leg/sem/2002/cdmfl/eng/hupkes.pdf.
18. In some countries, such as the United States, banks are therefore precluded from the scope of application of general corporate insolvency law.
19. Hüpkes (2000, pp. 66–7); D. M. Duffy, 'Canada National Report', in Giovanoli and Heinrich (1999), pp. 35, 42.
20. Hüpkes (2000, p. 64); L. Cerenza and E. Galanti, 'Italy National Report', in Giovanoli and Heinrich (1999), pp. 105, 111.
21. See Bovenzi and Spaid (1998).
22. For instance, in England, the Netherlands, Luxembourg, Germany, and Austria, see Hüpkes (2000, pp. 68–80).
23. See Ashmead (1994) (comparing the relevant rules under the Bankruptcy Code to the procedure under the Federal Deposit Insurance Act governing bank insolvencies).
24. The new framework does not deal with bank failures that have systemic implications or systemic banking crises in which cases the use of public funds may be justified. The MHL framework permits 'least-cost' resolution procedures after the authorities take over the problem bank, as would be considered in 'systemic cases'. This is a matter of choice for the government, not the administrator of the problem bank. The framework enables the reorganization of any bank without the use of public funds.
25. So far, the Swiss regulator has shown the necessary resolve with respect to banks that no longer satisfy licensing requirements. The SFBC ordered licence withdrawal and compulsory liquidation in four instances over the past ten years. In October 1991, the SFBC withdrew the banking licence of Spar & Leihkasse Thun and appointed a liquidator. In 1997, the SFBC withdrew the banking licence of Bank Rinderknecht AG, Zürich, and ordered its compulsory liquidation because of severe violations of the law, management and organizational deficiencies. In December 1998, the SFBC withdrew the licence of Bank Globo AG and ordered its liquidation. Besides severe management and organizational deficiencies, the bank had been unable to

comply with the mandatory capital requirements. In August 2002 the SFBC revoked the licence of A&A Actienbank, Zurich, which failed to comply with capital adequacy requirements. In October 2002, the SFBC revoked the licence of Bank Thorbecke on the grounds of serious organizational shortcomings and violations of securities laws.

26. Basel Committee (2002) p. 30.
27. See Benston (1995) and Kaufman (1996).
28. See T. Curry, with contributions by G. Hanc, J. O'Keefe, L. Davison and J. Reidhill (1997), 'Bank Examination and Enforcement', in Federal Deposit Insurance Corporation, *History of the Eighties – Lessons for the Future*, p. 452.
29. USA Pub. L 102–242, 105 Stat. 2236 (1991) (12 USC § 1831o).
30. See Peek and Rosengren (1997).
31. A moratorium may be imposed pursuant to Article 29 of the Banking Act if the bank is not over-indebted. Where a bank that is over-indebted or, subsequent to the imposition of a moratorium, it becomes apparent that the bank is over-indebted, it must either apply for a composition with creditors under Article 36 of the Swiss Banking Act, or petition for bank bankruptcy proceedings pursuant to Arts. 35(2) and 37 of the Banking Act. See also Decision of the Federal Supreme in re Spar & Leihkasse Thun, of 18 December 1991, BGE 117 III 83, 89, available via the website of the Federal Supreme Court at http://www.bger.ch.
32. See also Decision of the SFBC of 29 March 1983 in the matter of Banque Commercial SA, reprinted in SFBC Bulletin, 12, at 19 (1983) available via the Internet at http://www.ebk.admin.ch/e/publik/bulletin/index.htm.
33. See Section 10.1.1.
34. Banking Act Art. 23^{quinquies} (1).
35. In case of a severe violation of other rules, such as conduct of business rules, due diligence or anti-money laundering rules, licence withdrawal and compulsory liquidation remain the ultimate regulatory sanctions.
36. A framework for an efficient bankruptcy procedure based on an automatic debt-equity-swap is proposed by O. Hart (2000), 'Different Approaches to Bankruptcy', Harvard Institute of Economic Research Discussion Paper Number 1903, September, available via the Internet at http://papers.ssrn.com/paper.taf?abstract_id = 241066.
37. Art. 8 of the Capital Directive, note 42.
38. See Remarks by Ricki Helfer, Chairperson of the Federal Deposit Insurance Corporation before the Group of Thirty Conference on International Insolvency in the Financial Sector, London, 14 May 1997. (Helfer cites US bankruptcy statistics showing that from 1982 to 1995 only 491 companies in the United States successfully emerged from bankruptcy proceedings under Chapter 11, which gives companies protection from creditors while they reorganize. The average length of time for a company to emerge from this process was 17.2 months.)
39. Law of Obligations (the official German, French and Italian versions can be found at http://www.bk.admin.ch/ch/d/sr/c220.html), Art. 698 (2).
40. Note that Switzerland is not bound by the European Directives. Switzerland is not a member of the EU and, while being a member of EFTA, it is not a party to the EEA.
41. *Panagis Pafitis and other* v. *Trapeza Kentrikis Ellados AE and others* (Case C-441/93), CMLR, 9 July 1996.

42. Second Council Directive of 13 December 1976 on coordination of safeguards which, for the protection of the interests of members and others, are required by member states of companies within the meaning of the second paragraph of Article 58 of the Treaty, in respect of the formation of public limited liability companies and the maintenance and alteration of their capital, with a view to making such safeguards equivalent ('Capital Directive') (77/91/EEC) (OJ No L 26, 31. 1. 1977, p. 1) available via the Internet at http://europa.eu.int/eur-lex/en/consleg/main/1977/en_1977 L0091_index.html.
43. The fact that a bank experienced financial problems and became subject to reorganization proceedings is an indication that the existing shareholders may not have exercised their control rights and that they were either unwilling or unable to invest additional funds in the bank.
44. Under the new law, providers of 'new money', that is, funds provided during a reorganization procedure, are given a priority over other debts ('super-priority').
45. As is already the case under the current law, some special rules apply. There is no creditors' assembly as such. Given the usually very large number of depositors and other creditors, it would not be practical to hold a creditors' meeting.
46. See Financial Stability Forum (2001).
47. See note 15.
48. See overview in Garcia (2000, p. 61 *et seq.*).
49. See note 15.
50. Garcia (2000, p. 17).
51. See note 15.
52. The European Directive (see note 15) requires that all branches of a credit institution be covered by the deposit protection system of the institution's home country.
53. The priority not only applies to deposits in Swiss francs but also deposits in other currencies, for example, US dollars or euros up to the respective value of CHF 30,000. It can be expected that in the future more and more accounts will be held in euros or in US dollars so it would be unjustifiable to limit the preference to deposits in Swiss francs.
54. This is the time limit set out in Article 10 of the Directive on deposit guarantee schemes (see note 15).
55. The European Directive also merely states that the banks themselves must provide funding and that the level of financing be proportionate to the liabilities of the system. See Directive on Deposit Guarantee Schemes (note 15) Recital 23.
56. It is, however, questionable whether insurance companies would be able to provide the liquidity necessary to pay out the depositors immediately.
57. See Financial Stability Forum (2001) p. 8, which states that '[A] deposit insurance system can deal with a limited number of simultaneous bank failures, but cannot be expected to deal with a systemic banking crisis by itself'.
58. See Garcia (2000, p. 44).
59. In September 1999 finance ministers and central bank governors of the Group of Ten asked their deputies to conduct a study of financial consolidation and its potential effects. To conduct the study, a working party was

established under the auspices of finance ministry and central bank deputies of the Group of Ten. The publication can be obtained through the websites of the BIS, the IMF and the OECD: www.bis.org, www.imf.org, www.oecd.org.

60. 'Report on Financial Stability prepared by the ad hoc working group of the Economic and Financial Committee chaired by the Dutch Deputy Governor Henk Brouwer', *Economic Papers*, Nr. 143, May 2000, available via the Internet at http://europa.eu.int/comm/economy_finance/publications/economic_papers/economicpapers143_en.htm.
61. Directive on the supplementary supervision of credit institutions, insurance undertakings and investment firms in a financial conglomerate (hereinafter 'Directive on financial conglomerates'), available via the Internet at http://europa.eu.int/comm/internal_market/en/finances/cross-sector/com213en.pdf.
62. See also J. Dermine (2002), 'European Banking Past, Present and Future', Paper presented at the Second Central Banking Conference on the transformation of the European Financial System, Frankfurt, October, available via the Internet at http://faculty.insead.fr/dermine/research.htm.
63. See 'The Financial Industry in the 21st Century', introductory remarks by Daniel Zuberbühler, Director of the Secretariat, Swiss Federal Banking Commission at the 11th International Conference of Banking Supervisors, Basel, September 2000, available via the Internet at http://www.bis.org/review/rr000921c.pdf.
64. See also O. Hart (1999), 'Different Approaches to Bankruptcy', Paper presented at the Annual World Bank Conference on Development Economics, Paris.

11

Bank Resolution Policy and the Organization of Bank Insolvency Proceedings: Critical Dilemmas

*Christos Hadjiemmanuil**

How should a country deal with the financial failure of banking institutions? What policy objectives should it pursue, and by what means? The answers to these questions do not merely determine the *ex-post* resolution[1] of particular failed banks; they also affect the *ex-ante* incentive structure of market participants generally (bank owners and managers, depositors, other creditors and so on). In this manner, a country's bank resolution policies exercise a subtle but critical influence on the incidence of bank insolvency and, in consequence, on the overall stability of the financial system. The costs of inappropriate and confused bank resolution policies are extremely high for a national economy. It is, accordingly, evident that the various resolution-related decisions should be guided by clear and consistent principles. Yet, the theoretical understanding of the issues is still limited and common international approaches have not so far emerged.

Since the early 1970s, the debates concerning banking policy have focused on the prevention of failure through prudential regulation and ongoing supervision. Many academics have contributed to the elucidation of the underlying issues. At the same time, the pronouncements of the Basel Committee on Banking Supervision have set the stage for international regulatory convergence on a single dominant regulatory paradigm, primarily focused on a risk-weighted system of capital adequacy requirements.[2] For all its flaws, the Basel approach has provided a common vocabulary and a structured set of problems for further discussion, with a view to refining the applicable norms.[3] In comparison, the *ex-post* official reactions to cases of actual or impending bank insolvency – cases that, for all intents and purposes, have fallen through the supervisory net – have not received the attention that they deserve.

The main exception are certain types of public 'safety nets', involving the bailing-out of troubled banks or, as an alternative, the provision of a very high degree of protection to their depositors. This has been the subject matter of a small academic industry. In particular, two types of safety net have been studied in great detail: American-style comprehensive-coverage systems of deposit insurance;[4] and the provision of emergency support by the central bank under the rubric of lending of last resort.[5] Without doubt, the preoccupation with these issues was justified. Until recently, safety nets were the rule, rather than the exception, in cases of bank failure. In contrast, the outright closure of banking institutions, especially by way of normal liquidation proceedings, used to be exceedingly rare. This was – and continues to be, albeit to a more limited extent – a fundamental source of moral hazard, with profound implications for the incentive structure of bank managers and depositors, as many commentators have rightly emphasized.[6]

In recent years, however, one can observe an international trend towards the curtailment – though not the total elimination – of public safety nets. More aggressive resolution practices, often involving the closure of insolvent banks (whether through the withdrawal of their authorization or through their winding up and legal dissolution), have returned to centre stage. According to World Bank data, in the last five years one or more banks were formally terminated in more than 50 countries.[7] In particular, the increase in the incidence of formal insolvency proceedings affecting banking institutions is noticeable. As a result, bank insolvency law is finally attracting a measure of scholarly interest.[8] Concurrently, national and international are policy-makers are engaging in extensive discussions of the broader gamut of bank resolution policies.

All the same, national practices relating to regulatory enforcement and/or bank resolution remain haphazard. A principled approach to crisis-handling is often lacking, and the relevant legal arrangements tend to be patchy and incoherent. In many countries, the resolution-related actions of the public authorities do not even respect the elemental principle of consistency of objectives across different fields of action and over time. A lot depends on the vagaries of the prevailing public attitudes with regard to financial failures, the nature of relationships between the government and the ownership and management of banks, and the specific macroeconomic conjuncture.

Even worse, we still lack a clear conceptual framework for debating the policy issues with reference to distinct types of potential solutions and their respective legal forms. The multiplicity and heterogeneity of the legal and regulatory tools by means of which countries attempt to deal with bank failure contributes to the analytical confusion, which, in its turn, renders more difficult the streamlining and rationalization of the bank resolution regimes.

This chapter clarifies the principal issues. The discussion commences with an identification of three generic categories of resolution-related official actions: regulatory corrective and enforcement actions, financial assistance operations involving the expenditure of public funds, and formal insolvency (or collective) proceedings. These are set apart by their different legal forms, decision-makers, triggers and objectives (Section 11.1). Due to the multiplicity of actors and procedures, bank resolution policy cannot be analysed merely in terms of the stance of the banking authorities. The broader policy regime, comprising separate actors and institutions, with potentially conflicting interests, entrenched attitudes and legal constraints, must be considered.[9] To attain overall coherence, a country must strive to ensure that the scope and objectives of the various resolution-related actions are clearly delineated and carefully coordinated in the law. Most importantly, a fundamental choice must be made with regard to the general objectives and priorities. In particular, it must be decided whether bank resolution should aim at the strict enforcement of obligations or at the reorganization and survival of failed banking businesses. The relationship between the economic and disciplinary objectives of official actions must also be clarified. The ordering of objectives must be consistent both within and across fields of action, and entrenched in the law. This, however, is more easily said than done (Section 11.2).

Based on this analysis, it is shown that the recent attempt of the Basel Committee to produce guidelines for bank resolution policy is not particularly helpful. Whatever its substantive merits, the proposed approach fails to acknowledge that bank resolution policy cannot be decided by banking supervisors acting alone on the basis of their administrative discretion. Given the legally diverse but practically interconnected nature of the various components of the bank resolution regime, the implementation of a country's chosen policy on their coordination in a legally robust and transparent form. Only in this manner can the matrix composed of the various legal powers and procedures and their respective objectives operate consistently (Section 11.3).

In so far as the integration and successful implementation of bank resolution policy depends on the procedural suitability and decision-making structure of the available types of insolvency (or collective) proceedings, two closely linked questions must be answered by a country's legislators: whether banks should be subject to the collective proceedings of general corporate insolvency law, or to special proceedings of bank insolvency law; and what role should the banking regulatory agencies (supervisors or deposit insurers) play in these proceedings. Although many commentators advocate the exemption of banks from general corporate insolvency law and their subjection to administrative insolvency proceedings under the control of the regulators, there are important counterarguments, both substantive and technical (Sections 11.4 and 11.5).

The chapter concludes with a brief overview of the resolution-related norms of European law, which constrain the discretion of EU Member States with regard to certain aspects of their bank resolution policy (Section 11.6).

The resolution of systemic crises, involving the simultaneous collapse of many financial institutions, is not discussed in the following pages, which are concerned with the treatment of single bank failures. It is sufficient to note here that systemic (contagion) risk is a much-abused concept, which is often used to dramatize the potential implications of a single bank's closure and liquidation. Even so, in recent years many countries have experienced fully-fledged financial crises, bringing their whole banking system to its knees. Whatever the causes of such crises – faulty macroeconomic policy, widespread mismanagement and accumulation of losses at the level of individual banks or, less likely, contagious depositors' runs on otherwise healthy institutions – the simultaneous occurrence of numerous bank failures may force a country to intervene on a large scale for the purpose of recapitalizing and restructuring its banking sector. Insisting on a policy of strict enforcement, involving the immediate closure and liquidation of insolvent bank, which could appear justified in normal times, might be foolish in the midst of a crisis. Extreme situations require extreme measures, and even the permanent institutional framework for bank resolution might need to give way to special structures for system-wide bank restructuring with public resources, introduced by way of emergency legislation or governmental fiat. On the other hand, a country's normal resolution policies should not be modelled on the wholly exceptional – and, therefore, idiosyncratic and unpredictable – scenario of a generalized crisis. The standing resolution-related legislation should focus on the handling of isolated failures, in the expectation that a good regime for normal times would also prove effective in days of moderate crisis. As for the possibility of large-scale crises, the main task of public policy is to prevent them by seeking to minimize macroeconomic and financial fragility, not to establish in advance mechanisms for picking up the pieces once the festering underlying problems will have already destroyed the national financial infrastructure.

11.1 The fragmented landscape of bank resolution procedures

A wide range of resolution tools may be available to the state authorities under a country's legal system to deal with an insolvent, or almost insolvent, bank. At first sight, the multiplicity of potential official actions could create the impression of a carefully crafted panoply of legal powers, whose reasoned deployment by the authorities could guarantee the effective handling of almost every bank failure. The reality, however, is more complicated and less satisfactory. Few countries have achieved full coordination of their matrix of resolution powers. Thus, conflicts between different procedures and/or objectives are often possible in individual cases. More generally, most national bank resolution regimes fail to produce consistent and predictable outcomes over time.

The reasons are easy to comprehend by examining the various categories of possible resolution-related actions more closely. These can be classified in broad categories with reference to the legal nature of the relevant procedures and the identity of the decision-makers. In simplified terms, once a bank's financial difficulties have been verified, three generic categories of official intervention will be possible:

(i) corrective and enforcement actions of the supervisory authority;
(ii) public financial assistance and rescue operations of various descriptions; and
(iii) formal insolvency (or collective) proceedings.

It might be observed, from a systematic viewpoint, that this elementary classification is wanting, because the boundaries between the categories are not clear-cut and airtight.[10] Nevertheless, the classification serves a useful heuristic purpose, precisely to the extent that it brings to the forefront and makes more visible the multiple cleavages of the landscape of bank resolution procedures – in other words, the profound differences between alternative forms of action in terms of their respective legal field, party in control, scope or trigger, procedural requirements and, last but not least, objectives.

The *corrective and enforcement actions of the supervisory authority* might, at a minimum, encompass measures of a disciplinary nature, aimed at penalizing detected past misconduct (including breaches of prudential norms). Measures of this type, however, are not specifically directed to insolvent or, more generally, financially weak banks; nor do they contribute directly to their resolution. Further, and most importantly, the supervisory actions could include forcible interventions in the bank's organization and/or operations (in the form of mandated restructuring actions,[11] conditions for the bank's management, objections to the continuing presence of certain directors, restrictions on activities and so on) with a view to correcting the underlying problems. In principle, although not always in practice, such corrective measures make sense only as long as the prospect of default is not immediate; in cases where the institution has already reached a point of irreversible financial decline, there is little room for reform. As a final resort, the supervisory authority could ensure the orderly exit of the bank by withdrawing its licence and overseeing the winding up of its regulated business.

In legal and administrative terms, the corrective and enforcement actions take the form of administrative decisions, adopted in public law by the agency responsible for ongoing banking supervision. They may be triggered by a variety of regulatory infractions and, especially, by non-compliance with the basic prudential requirements relating to banks' financial situation (solvency, liquidity, large exposures).

The subcategories of actions falling under this general heading can serve a number of distinct objectives, including: disciplining of wrong-doers (in the case of punitive or enforcement actions), rectification of financial and operational weaknesses and restoration of the bank to soundness (in the case of purely corrective measures) and forced exit without actual default (in the case of timely revocation of licence). These objectives are largely inconsistent, either because the ultimate economic and legal outcomes are logically irreconcilable (for example, corrective measures will have as their final objective the survival of the bank as a legal person and the continuation of its business as a going concern, while the withdrawal of its licence will lead to a direct termination of its activities) or because the effect of an action belonging to one subcategory may hinder the achievement of the main objective of another (for example, the public announcement of penalties for wrong-doing may hamper the restoration of the bank to financial soundness).

Beyond the field of supervisory actions, the state could decide to provide *financial assistance out of public funds* for the purpose of rescuing a critically troubled or insolvent bank or, at least, of ensuring that its failure does not cause losses to depositors. To achieve this purpose, the state could extend to the bank liquidity assistance, recapitalize it, guarantee its liabilities, assume its bad assets or deposits liabilities, finance the transfer of its operations to a solvent bank, or even proceed to the bank's outright nationalization.

Rescue operations and fiscal subsidies of various descriptions are frequently perceived either as a distinct subcategory of regulatory actions or as an extension and variation of supervisory corrective measures.

This notion, however, fails to grasp the essential legal and administrative character of these operations, which involve the expenditure of public funds and which are separated from supervisory actions by a number of distinguishing traits. To start with, the relevant decisions are rarely left in the hands of the supervisory agency. Instead, the decision to bail out an insolvent bank, to nationalize it or to subsidize its restructuring by the private sector is taken by a high political authority (such as the cabinet, the prime minister or the minister of finance) and/or the central bank, depending on the exact form and fiscal implications of the operation in question.[12]

Unlike supervisory actions, financial assistance operations are typically conducted, not as ordinary administrative measures authorized by explicit provisions of standing statutory law, but as *ad hoc* or exceptional measures.[13] As such, they do not depend on predetermined legal triggers and their launching and timing is a matter of discretionary judgement. Their implementation takes the form either of contractual operations of the state, possibly backed up by fiscal spending decisions or budgetary appropriations in public law, or of contractual operations of the central bank (often conducted under the guise of lender of last resort), or of special decisions, incorporated in an emergency statute or ministerial decree, ordering the outright nationalization of the insolvent bank. Accordingly, the power to engage in such operations is derived either from the general contractual capacity of the state and/or the central bank, or from case-specific legislative authorizations (special laws, measures or decrees, including any necessary budgetary appropriations).

The evident objective of interventions of this kind is to assist the insolvent banks thereby affected to remain open for business or, at least, to facilitate the continuation of their deposit-taking operations by an acquirer. In the former case, their implementation will often require some degree of relaxation of the supervisory authority's enforcement function, or what is known as 'regulatory forbearance'; that is, the supervisory authority will need to refrain from enforcing strictly the applicable prudential and accounting norms against the troubled institution, especially where these norms would require the full recognition of its insolvency and, in consequence, the withdrawal of its banking licence and/or its immediate closure and placement in liquidation.

Like all other business entities, insolvent banks may be resolved by way of *formal insolvency* (or *collective*) *proceedings*. All countries have legal mechanisms for the commencement of liquidation or reorganization proceedings, or some functionally equivalent procedure, against banks that have already crossed the applicable benchmark of insolvency.

The common denominator of such proceedings is the replacement of the bank's management by official persons acting as administrators or liquidators, who are authorized to pursue the restructuring or winding up of the bank's business in ways that could affect the pre-existing rights of third parties without their consent.

On this matter, however, the variation of national approaches is remarkable. In some countries, the relevant proceedings are conducted under the general rules of corporate insolvency law (which is a branch of private law) under the supervision of the normal insolvency courts. In most countries, however, to deal with bank insolvency the general corporate insolvency framework is either complemented or completely replaced by special rules. In many cases, even the basic legal character of the relevant proceedings is different for banks than for non-financial enterprises: bank insolvency proceedings are organized as special administrative (public-law) measures, taken by, or under the control of, the supervisory authority or the deposit insurance agency. In similar vein, the criteria for determining whether a bank should be transferred to the applicable insolvency regime are sometimes the same as for other corporations; but special triggers of bank insolvency are used in many countries.

In some countries the available insolvency proceedings have as their only objective the orderly liquidation of insolvent banks. Elsewhere, their reorganization can also be pursued in this context – thus requiring the persons responsible in each and every case to choose between two mutually exclusive outcomes, namely, the winding up of the banking business or its continuation as a going concern. In procedural terms, while many jurisdictions recognize only one form of insolvency proceedings (that is, liquidation proceedings, or unitary insolvency proceedings leading either to reorganization or, where this is not possible, liquidation), other legal systems contain multiple sets of proceedings, with distinct triggers and objectives. In the latter case, sometimes the supervisory authority is responsible for the reorganization of banks in serious difficulties and can exercise for this purpose administrative powers in public law, but bank liquidation takes place under the norms and procedures of general corporate insolvency (that is, private) law.

In systems where bank insolvency proceedings are conducted under the control of the supervisory authority, they appear to form the extreme end of the broader spectrum of supervisory corrective and enforcement actions.[14] In contrast, where control is placed in the hands of the courts or the deposit insurance agency, a clear distinction can be drawn between the two categories of information – not only formally, but also, and more importantly, in terms of the party which takes the relevant decisions.

In any event, it is evident that decisions to take, or refrain from taking, action in any of the three directions discussed above (supervisory enforcement, public financial assistance, formal insolvency proceedings) will have immediate and profound implications in terms of the exit or survival (invariably following financial and operational restructuring) of banking institutions in a condition of insolvency or near-insolvency. To put it in another way, a troubled bank's survival, restructuring or termination is determined jointly by a number of discrete, but overlapping decisions. These are taken on the basis of a mixture of legal powers and under diverse legal forms by separate official decision-makers (regulators, governments and central banks, courts) with different – and often incompatible – objectives.

In these circumstances, the proliferation of bank resolution tools does not necessarily ensure greater effectiveness of the overall bank resolution regime, but may be a harbinger of incoherence and conflicts. To ensure that the national bank resolution policy is characterized by consistency and effectiveness, therefore, it is indispensable that the partial policies animating the three fields of action converge, that the scope and objectives of each resolution-related procedure are precisely delineated in the law and that the relative priority of procedures and objectives is clearly understood. Only in this manner can the whole matrix of legal powers operate in a harmonious manner and for the declared purposes.

11.2 The objectives of bank resolution

Evidently, the primary dilemma concerns the determination of the objectives of bank resolution. As we have seen, currently conflicting values or purposes inform the various pillars of the national resolution regimes, and even within the partial decision-making fields actions are influenced by competing legal and extralegal factors. Thus, overall consistency may be difficult to achieve in practice. Nonetheless, the issue cannot be avoided.

What is the preferred fate of failed banks? Is it desirable for the state to facilitate by legal and/or financial means the reorganization and continuation of financially unsound institutions? Or should the resolution regime give priority to the strict enforcement of regulatory norms and private claims, even by means of outright closure?

The dilemma is not confined to the banking sector. Even in the non-financial field, the proponents of reorganization[15] and a 'second chance' for insolvent enterprises are at loggerheads with the advocates of strict collective enforcement of creditors' rights, including through rapid and decisive liquidation. The positions adopted by national insolvency laws on this matter diverge widely. Even so, in the case of general corporate insolvency, the interests that must be reconciled are confined (except, perhaps, in cases of very large or economically or politically critical enterprises) to those of the relevant enterprise's ownership, on the one hand, and the various classes of direct liability holders, on the other. Formal insolvency proceedings seek to balance these interests by means of legal provisions determining the way in which creditors can exercise their rights following the declaration of the insolvency (that is, the scope and effect of the moratorium) and the procedural protections and decision-making rights of each class of claimants. Of course, the relevant rules of insolvency law generate stable expectations about the treatment of insolvent enterprises in the future, thus creating an incentive structure which is bound to influence the behaviour of economic actors prior to, and outside, the insolvency process as such. In particular, an insistence on strict enforcement will foster market discipline and reduce the *ex-ante* costs of commercial borrowing. For this reason, the norms of insolvency law are a matter of broader social interest. This interest, however, is exhausted in the general structure and operation of the normative framework; the actual treatment of specific cases concerns it indirectly, to the extent that it reveals biases in the application of the nominal rules and corroborates or undermines the related expectations. Only rarely does the insolvency of a large industrial or commercial enterprise cause significant economic disturbance or seriously affect large numbers of persons outside the circle of the immediate claimants, who have a voice in the insolvency proceedings.

Bank insolvency is thought to be different, due to the widespread external effects and potential systemic implications of the failure of individual institutions but also because of the special role played by the state both in the run-up to insolvency (when the supervisory agency is involved) and in its aftermath (at which point the law of many countries provides for deposit insurance payments). These factors may create a bias in favour of the continuation of banking enterprises, even where the market is unwilling or unable to finance their reorganization. In other words, certain special arguments are offered in justification of the active participation of the state in the restructuring of insolvent banks (potentially, even by means of direct financial assistance or even full nationalization) in situations where their financial and operational condition might point, in accordance with the criteria of general corporate insolvency law, to their closure and liquidation. The proponents of reorganization are particularly vociferous in relation to the treatment of large banks, which they consider TBTF.

In principle, everybody agrees that the resolution regime should produce incentives compatible with the long-term soundness of the banking industry. And it is trite to observe that strict enforcement serves market discipline by driving home the message of hard financial constraints, while forbearance breeds moral hazard. From this standpoint, except in the case of truly systemic crises, the choice between the early closure and liquidation of an insolvent bank, on the one hand, and its restructuring on an open-bank basis, on the other, should depend on which course of action appears, given the circumstances, to maximize the recovery value of its estate for the benefit of its depositors and other creditors.[16]

However, almost everywhere in the world, the arguments in favour of continuation even of deeply insolvent and non-viable banks converge with entrenched expectations of the general public. The latter tends to place a high value in the uninterrupted operation of financial institutions and the full protection and accessibility of depositors' savings.[17] Explicit banking failures – and especially those leading to closure and loss of deposits – are perceived by the public as 'scandalous'. Moreover, they reveal failures in the ongoing prudential supervisory process, which is thereby proven incapable of detecting pathogenic situations and preventing crises. In other words, failures do not undermine public confidence in the stability of the banking sector alone, but also in the quality of the public system of economic governance. As a result, the political dynamics usually favour a lenient treatment of insolvent banks and open-bank resolution, possibly with the support of capital injections by the state, rather than an uncompromising enforcement of the rules. The costs of closure are often exaggerated and clothed in the language of 'systemic risk', while the incentive implications of the *ex-post* validation of bad managerial and supervisory decisions are downplayed. In other words, the policy-makers' expressions of commitment to market discipline are undermined by 'time-inconsistency', and in the short run the active preference is for interventions that keep the market environment stable, even if this stability is artificial and depends on bending the general rules of the economic game.

This has significant implications both for the design of laws relating to bank resolution and for their practical implementation, including and the actual choice of resolution technique, whenever discretion can be exercised in this respect. Thus, the reorganization of insolvent institutions, regardless of cost to taxpayers, incidental hardship to certain creditors, or any perverse competitive and incentive effects, is viewed in many jurisdictions as the primary objective of bank insolvency proceedings, because it is supposed to preserve economic activity and employment and to offer better protection to normal depositors.[18] But even in countries where the law applicable to formal insolvency proceedings does not favour reorganization, regulatory forbearance and the lax use of public funds in rescue operations (sometimes disguised as 'lending of last resort') may be used to prop up unsound institutions and avert the official declaration of their insolvency and placement in liquidation. The incompatibility between the declared objectives of bank insolvency law, on the one hand, and the discretionary actions of the regulatory authorities, the central bank and the ministry of finance, on the other, is the most common source of incoherence and artificiality in bank resolution policy.

The problem of conflicting objectives is aggravated where the tools of bank resolution policy seek both to cure financial unsoundness through restructuring and to enhance market discipline by penalizing misconduct. Generally, the termination of a bank's business by revoking its licence can be used as the ultimate sanction against delinquent institutions, regardless of their financial situation. In countries where the mandatory placement of banks in liquidation is possible not only in situations of actual insolvency, but also on public-interest grounds, liquidity proceedings can serve a similar disciplinary purpose.[19] This may lead, however, to an overloading of the resolution process, which is incapable of servicing incompatible objectives simultaneously.

It is unrealistic, for instance, to expect that the disciplinary purpose will be pursued retrospectively, where a bank's position has already changed for the better and the interests of the public are no longer threatened by its continuing operation. A supervisory authority or an insolvency court would be very reluctant to terminate on grounds of past misconduct an institution which is currently managed in a sound manner, even if the law gave them this power.[20] This can be especially important where a change of ownership or management has occurred in the meantime. In such cases, fraudulent behaviour and other forms of managerial misconduct would probably be dealt with by means of less intrusive enforcement actions against the institution and/or those personally responsible,[21] but the institution would be allowed to survive.[22] Forced exit, however, is unlikely to serve the disciplinary objectives effectively or consistently even on a contemporaneous basis. Other considerations may override the need to make an example out of delinquent institutions by terminating them. The mandatory termination of large solvent institutions will rarely be politically tenable, except in the most dramatic cases of criminality. At the same time, the interplay between the financial and disciplinary objectives of bank resolution policy may paradoxically – and perversely – result in a delinquent institution being less likely to face dissolution on public-interest grounds if it is also financially weak, so that its immediate closure (and related loss of franchise value) would entail losses for depositors and other creditors.

The potential conflicts between the financial and disciplinary objectives of bank resolution cannot be avoided by simply substituting supervisory enforcement actions for formal insolvency proceedings. Thus, the disciplinary objective of the public-interest liquidation can be pursued outside the insolvency framework by way of administrative withdrawal or restriction of the banking licence. In this manner, however, the conflict may merely change form. Assuming, for instance, that the bank in question is subject to administration or reorganization proceedings under judicial control, the cancellation of its banking licence by the supervisory authority may frustrate the purposes of these proceedings, since it excludes the survival of the banking business as a going concern following recapitalization or an arrangement with creditors.[23] In this way, a problem that was hitherto internalized in the insolvency proceedings now becomes a conflict of procedures, and even of institutions (supervisors versus insolvency courts).[24]

The internal coherence of the various resolution-related procedures can, accordingly this manner, coincide with external dissonance. The objectives of one type of action may be set out in the law with precision, but still be overridden, not because the relevant decision-makers go beyond their mandate, but because another procedure has been activated. Overlapping and mutually contradictory actions, with different official actors pursuing divergent objectives, can have very negative implications for the overall policy mix. Establishing a clear order of priorities in relation to procedures and/or objectives is, thus, an essential element of a principled approach. The legal entrenchment of these priorities will occasionally require that the relationship between different procedures be transparently delineated even where these span the divide between public and private law. For instance, in countries where bank insolvency proceedings are conducted within the general corporate insolvency framework (that is, in private law), the law should not only specify the respective powers of the supervisory authority and the insolvency court, but also who should prevail in cases of conflict.

Finally, assuming that a country's resolution regime favours bank reorganization and seeks to prevent exit, for the long-term robustness of the financial economy it will be necessary to take all feasible concrete steps towards the penalization of insolvency and the containment of moral hazard. A number of measures can be adopted in this direction. It is particularly important that protracted restructuring plans, with doubtful results, be avoided. The reorganization process should not be used as an excuse for the accumulation of losses and the dissipation of assets. It is equally important that the managers of failed banks be penalized and the shareholders prevented from appropriating any benefits, at the expense of the creditors or the taxpayers. Conversely, one could envisage incentives, in the form of an attractive administration regime, to induce bank managers to declare existing problems and take corrective actions at an early stage.

11.3 The search for coherent bank resolution policies in the Basel Committee's Weak Banks report

The international banking regulatory fora have now recognized the need for coherent bank resolution policies. This is attested by a spate of ongoing international initiatives relating to various aspects of bank financial unsoundness and/or resolution and involving the Financial Stability Forum (FSF), the IMF, the World Bank, the Basel Committee, the OECD, as well as regional organizations, such as the European Union and APEC.[25]

In particular, in April 2001 the Financial Stability Forum considered the possibility of international guidelines for dealing with 'weak' banks and systemic banking crises. In response to this initiative, in July 2001 the Basel Committee, in cooperation with its Core Principles Liaison Group, set up a Task Force on Dealing with Weak Banks. Sixteen countries, as well as the World Bank, the IMF, the European Commission and the BIS Financial Stability Institute, were represented in the Task Force, whose work was concluded in March 2002 with the publication of the 'Weak Banks report' (the section that relates to insolvency is reproduced as Appendix 2 in this book).[26]

The report outlines a structured approach to issues relating to the 'identification of weak banks', the taking of 'corrective actions', and 'resolution and exit'. It defines a weak bank as 'one whose liquidity or solvency is or will be impaired unless there is a major improvement in its financial resources, risk profile, strategic business direction, risk management capabilities and/or quality of management' (para. 10) and sets out principles for the identification of weak banks by the regulator through detailed supervisory assessment (paras 25–65).

The Weak Banks report draws a relatively sharp distinction between situations where problems have been identified, but the bank's 'failure' (para. 66)[27] or 'insolvency' (para. 136 and Annex 4) does not appear imminent, and those where an institution is fast approaching this point or has already passed it. In the former case, the report encourages early regulatory intervention and the taking of proportionate but decisive corrective action, based on a broad range of tools. It suggests that the best strategy might involve a combination of 'automatic' rules for supervisory actions with room for flexibility in particular circumstances. It further prioritizes informal methods when the identified problems are not very serious and the bank's management is cooperative, but more formal intervention of a prescriptive nature and backed by the threat of penalties in the event of deeper problems or management recalcitrance. Closure of the bank through the revocation of its licence is identified as the ultimate sanction (paras 66–132).

This part of the Basel Committee's guidance essentially corresponds to the corrective and enforcement facet of bank resolution policy described in this chapter and provides a bridge to the subsequent discussion of 'resolution and exit' of banks that are not only weak but have already 'failed' or are close to this point. The implication is that corrective actions are conceptually distinct from bank resolution (which, accordingly, should be understood to include only insolvency proceedings and rescue operations), because they address problems at an earlier stage. Nonetheless, this is not always true. Undoubtedly, enforcement and corrective actions may be taken even against a bank which is financially sound (that is, not 'weak' in the report's sense). In the context of financial unsoundness, however, they form part of the same continuum as other bank resolution tools, and overlap with the latter even in terms of their timing or preconditions. For example, the revocation of a bank's licence is both an enforcement action and a form of exit or resolution. Moreover, in many jurisdictions it can be combined with administrative directions for the orderly winding up of the banking business; in this manner, it can serve as a functional equivalent to liquidation proceedings in situations of actual insolvency. Likewise, intrusive corrective actions can sometimes be used as a close substitute for reorganization-directed insolvency proceedings. In addition, as explained earlier, in many countries there can be no easy way for drawing an exact line between corrective actions and insolvency proceedings, because both take the form of administrative actions under the control of the supervisory authority.

In any event, to deal effectively with financially unsound banks by means of corrective actions, the supervisory authority will need to be vested with substantial legal powers of intervention. In many countries, these may not be available – or, at least, may not be available on a discretionary basis, but may be exercizable only when a specific threshold set out in the law has been crossed or certain procedural requirements have been complied with.[28]

With regard to situations of imminent or actual failure and/or insolvency, the Weak Banks report encourages a coherent approach, based on a template of 'resolution and exit' techniques, which are apparently set out in increasing order of severity. These include:

- restructuring schemes;
- mergers with or acquisitions by healthy banks;
- purchase-and-assumption transactions, whereby some or all of the assets together with some or all of the liabilities of a failed bank are taken over by a healthy financial institution or private investor, while the legal person of the bank and any residue of its estate are left for liquidation;
- where a private solution is possible but cannot be organized immediately, the closure of the failed bank and the creation of a 'bridge bank', licensed and controlled by the regulator, to take over the good assets and a corresponding amount of liabilities, thus maintaining the banking business as a going concern and providing time for the eventual acquisition of its surviving part by appropriate purchases;
- where no private investor can be found to take over the banking business final closure of the business and liquidation of the bank's estate; likewise, for countries with a deposit insurance scheme, where the making of direct payments to depositors out of the scheme appears less costly (presumably for the deposit insurance agency, although this is not clearly stated) than the other options, final closure and liquidation, combined with depositors' pay-off.

Before discussing the last option (closure and liquidation), the report examines the conditions under which public financial resources may be employed for the purpose of ensuring the continuation of a weak bank's operations ('open bank assistance'). The public assistance can take the form of the bank's outright rescue through direct solvency support (capital injections, emergency loans, guarantees or purchases of bad assets); this can easily lead to the bank's effective nationalization. Alternatively, public funds may be used as an incentive to the private sector for the implementation of one of the first four options, all of which preserve at least part of the bank's business in operation. The report emphasizes that

> [p]ublic funds are only for exceptional circumstances, in potentially systemic situations. An intervention of this nature should be preceded by a cost assessment of the alternatives, including the indirect cost to the economy...

> The provision of solvency support is not a resolution measure in the sense of providing a lasting solution to the underlying weaknesses of the bank. The disbursement of public monies should be made dependent on the implementation of an action plan, approved by the supervisor, including measures to restore profitability and sound and prudent management. The government should always retain the option of getting its money repaid if the resolution of the bank so allows.
>
> If public monies are used, shareholders of the weak bank should be made to bear the cost of the resolution via a dilution or even elimination of their shareholding interests. (paras 157, 161–2)

Finally, the report recognizes that the resolution of weak public-sector banks will generally require a different approach, which should take the financial and political issues into account simultaneously, leading to a longer timescale. Nonetheless, it insists that such banks should not be treated less stringently than banks with private ownership.

Overall, the suggestions in the Weak Banks report lead to the conclusion that the guiding principle that should animate national regulators' choice of resolution technique is the preservation of the value of a weak bank's assets with minimal disruption to its operations and to counterparties, subject to constraints of expediency and minimization of resolution costs. More specifically, the Committee has this to say about the choice of resolution technique:

> In a legal closure, the licence of the bank is withdrawn and the legal entity ceases to exist. In an economic closure, there is interruption or cessation of the operations of the bank which may often lead to severe disruption and possibly losses for the bank's customers. The art of resolving bank problems often entails achieving a 'legal closure' while avoiding an 'economic closure'. (para. 135)

In this manner, the report dissociates an insolvent bank's reorganization (that is, the financial and operational interventions intended to ensure that the banking enterprise will survive as a sound going concern) from its legal rehabilitation.[29]

With regard to the objectives of bank resolution policy, therefore, it is apparent that the report leans towards the continuation of insolvent banks' operations, whenever this is feasible, even where their fate as legal persons under the control of the original ownership is sealed. Economic closure, followed by collection and distribution of assets, as in a normal commercial liquidation, should only be considered when the prospect of restructuring does not appear realistic.

Whatever its theoretical advantages, the structured approach suggested in the Weak Banks report remains highly improbable, to the extent that it fails to consider properly the implications of the basic fact that a country's supervisory agency is not the only public decision-maker involved in bank resolution. As explained above, the latter spans a variety of legal procedures, with separate triggers and objectives. Multiple public-sector actors, with different functions, particular incentives and limited legal mandates, co-determine the design and implementation of bank resolution policy. Nonetheless, the report discusses the issues as if a single mind, unencumbered by legal fetters, is empowered to consider each case on its merits, in order to determine the appropriate response on a discretionary basis, by picking up that point in the continuum of potential corrective and insolvency actions which matches the stage and intensity of the underlying problem.

In particular, this assumption underpins the discussion of what the report calls 'resolution and exit' – that is, the array of reorganization and/or liquidation-related actions, or insolvency proceedings, available in relation to insolvent banks. How realistic is it, however, to imagine that the supervisory agency or, more generally, the governmental and regulatory authorities are always free to choose the most appropriate resolution technique, based on their administrative discretion? In discussing open-bank assistance, the report itself acknowledges that the supervisory authority will not be the primary actor. The relevant decisions will be taken, instead, either by the government (possibly subject to the approval of the legislature) or by the central bank (although the report refers to the latter possibility disapprovingly). As for the wider range of insolvency decisions, the report fails to notice that national legal systems assign critical roles in the relevant proceedings to a combination of different actors, which often include the supervisory agency, the deposit insurance agency, insolvency and/or administrative courts, private parties and stakeholders, and/or insolvency practitioners.

Given this variety of actors and procedures, the coherence of bank resolution policy cannot be achieved by establishing guiding principles for supervisors alone, as the Basel Committee's paper would seem to suggest. Instead, there is need for overall legislative and policy consistency, both within and outside the terrain of regulatory law. The partial arrangements of regulatory, bank insolvency and deposit insurance law should contribute to the architectonic unity of the entire bank resolution regime. The scope, procedural requirements and objectives of the available legal and regulatory instruments must be streamlined, with a view to ensuring that they are employed in a mutually reinforcing, rather than contradictory, manner. For this purpose, a country must tackle complex legislative problems, always keeping in sight the interrelationships between different areas of the law.

Assume, for instance, that the existing rules of bank insolvency law require that the persons responsible for the conduct of insolvency proceedings act for the purpose of ensuring the satisfaction of pending financial claims, in their relative order of priority, to the maximum extent possible. This would be consistent with the strict enforcement approach, in accordance with which the purpose of collective proceedings is to maximize the recovery value of the estate for the benefit of direct claimants (that is, creditors of various descriptions and, following them, the shareholders as residual claimants). But it would not appear to serve the policy outlined in the Weak Banks report. It is implausible to suggest that the discussion of resolution techniques there is merely an extremely elaborated way of restating the trivial recovery-maximization principle animating the strict enforcement approach, possibly combined with a plea for changes in the law to facilitate any forms of reorganization that may not be currently practicable for purely technical reasons. Instead, on a proper reading, the report promotes the restructuring and continuation of banking operations as a regulatory objective animated by broader systemic and depositor-protection concerns. The logical implication is that reorganization should in certain situations be pursued in the public interest even if this is inconsistent with the financial interests of the direct claimants and would not be chosen freely by the latter. In this case, however, it will be necessary either to impose additional losses on claimants or to make good the difference by use of public funds, that is, by transferring the resolution costs to the taxpayer. If this interpretation is correct, how should the rules be changed to reflect the policy?

A new, explicit operational criterion could be adopted to govern the choice of resolution technique – although it is difficult to imagine in exactly what terms this might be formulated. Alternatively, the matter could be left to the unconstrained judgement of the front-line decision-makers, in the expectation (but without any legal certainty) that these would tend to follow the proposed policy. In either case, the change might involve a weakening of the protection that the old rules afforded to the bank's direct claimants. Their concrete interests could be compromised for the benefit of another, supposedly superior, but probably ill-defined purpose. At the same time, the expenditure of public funds in support of reorganization plans would remain a question for other, high-level decision-makers. How should their decisions be integrated in the overall resolution framework? Should they remain discretionary, or be subjected to mandatory conditions? Could decision-making coherence be achieved by retaining the autonomous and discretionary nature of the decisions relating to public financial assistance, but trying to coordinate them with the main insolvency or regulatory proceedings by means of information exchanges and consultation requirements? In short, it may be exceptionally difficult to translate the proposed approach into a meaningful and effective legal framework.

Last but not least, since the policy should not be a mere fig leaf for undue forbearance, how could laxity be avoided in the course of the policy's practical implementation? The policy comprises a ladder of calibrated responses to bank insolvency, whose implementation is supposed to depend on the severity of the underlying problems and the environmental contingencies. Enabling provisions, conferring discretionary powers on decision-makers, may not be enough to tie the latter to its mast. In the absence of a strong institutional environment and an appropriate incentive structure, nominal adherence to the proposed approach is more likely to be accompanied by extensive forbearance and waste of resources, thus further aggravating moral hazard. Appropriate safeguards must be devised, but how? At the end of the day, in this policy field too, a system based on simple but robust general rules can prove in practice to be more incentive-compatible and, for that reason, more efficient than an elaborate discretionary system, seeking to discover a fine balance between competing considerations in each individual case.

11.4 Bank insolvency proceedings: is a special regime necessary?

In so far as bank resolution is pursued by way of formal insolvency proceedings, a country's law must provide answers to a number of critical questions:

- What precisely should be the statutory goals of proceedings of this category? Should the open-bank restructuring of failed institutions (that is, their reorganization and/or the continuation of their operations on a going-concern basis) be enshrined in the law? Should restructuring be incorporated as a public-interest objective, justifying continuation even at the cost of a less advantageous treatment of certain categories of creditors and/or the expenditure of public funds (for instance, by way of financial incentives provided by the deposit insurance agency or nationalization)? Or should the law treat bank insolvency as a private matter and simply focus on overcoming creditors' collective action problems, seeking to achieve the optimal realization of assets as a means towards the effective, speedy and equal satisfaction of creditors at the maximum extent possible out of the estate? Should insolvency proceedings be available as a penalty where a bank's major shareholders and/or management have acted in ways inconsistent with commercial morality? Should these or other objectives be clearly defined in the law, or should room be left, instead, for discretionary trade-offs between potentially conflicting objectives?

- Should bank insolvency proceedings be organized in the same way and under the same rules – possibly, subject to appropriate modifications – as collective proceedings for non-financial enterprises? Or should special types of reorganization and/or liquidation proceedings be available for banks? Assuming that a special regime is found to be preferable, should proceedings be conducted under the supervision of the insolvency courts? Or should these take the form of administrative proceedings, under the supervision or direct control of banking regulators?
- Should the usual definitions of insolvency in corporate insolvency law apply to the determination of bank insolvency? Or should a special trigger be adopted for this purpose? Should the trigger for bank insolvency proceedings be the same as for deposit insurance payments?
- Who should have capacity to initiate insolvency proceedings? In particular, should the supervisory authority have exclusive competence in this regard? Should creditors and other private parties be allowed to participate and be heard at this and subsequent stages in the proceedings?

Leaving aside the first group of questions, which evidently forms part of the earlier discussion concerning the objectives of bank resolution policy as a whole, the principal dilemma that a country must face is whether to include banks in the general framework of corporate insolvency law, subject to any appropriate modification, or to establish a special bank insolvency regime. In the latter case, proceedings could, in theory, remain under the supervision of the insolvency courts. In practice, jurisdictions adopting a special regime often follow the administrative model, whereby the banking authorities, not the insolvency courts, carry the responsibility for proclaiming a bank's state of insolvency, appointing the insolvency officials (administrators and/or liquidators) and supervising the reorganization and/or liquidation measures – or even for directly taking over and administering insolvent institutions themselves. Indeed, the integration of the insolvency process in the supervisory framework is a major motivation behind the creation of special regimes. As explained in Section 11.1, however, in many countries the administrative responsibility of banking authorities is limited to the reorganization (or official administration) of insolvent banks, while their liquidation is conducted according to the rules of general corporate insolvency law under judicial supervision.[30]

The world's mature financial jurisdictions follow very different paths, ranging from the most extreme versions of the administrative model to an almost unadulterated application of the court-based general insolvency framework.[31] Schematically, an Atlantic divide separates the administrative approaches of the USA and Canada from the general stance of European countries, where court-based proceedings predominate.

Thus, in the USA, depository institutions are fully exempt from general corporate insolvency law. Under special banking legislation, supervisors are authorized to close down a depository institution within 90 days after it has crossed the threshold of 'critical undercapitalization',[32] at which point the Federal Deposit Insurance Corporation (FDIC) typically steps in as receiver (that is, liquidator) or conservator (that is, administrator), with full discretionary powers for the institution's resolution.[33]

In contrast, in the UK, the Financial Services Authority (FSA) can seek the reorganization or termination of ailing banks by petitioning the insolvency courts for their placement in administration or for their winding-up.[34] The FSA is further entitled to participate and be heard in bank insolvency proceedings, whether the original petition was brought by itself or by other parties.[35] But otherwise, the general corporate insolvency law applies to banks on the same basis as to other companies.[36]

Elsewhere in Europe, the liquidation of banks is usually conducted in accordance with general corporate insolvency law. The situation is more complex in relation to reorganization (or administration) proceedings. In some countries (such as Luxembourg, the Netherlands, or Austria), bank reorganization can be pursued by way of special court-based reorganization proceedings of banking law. In many more cases, administrative procedures of various descriptions are available in relation to the reorganization of troubled banks, whereby either the approval of the supervisory authority is required for certain managerial decisions, or the management is completely expelled and full and direct managerial control is transferred to that authority or to administrators appointed by it.

It is not always easy to determine the respective scope of the administrative and court-based reorganization measures. Occasionally, the two overlap. Thus, in France, the procedure of *administration provisoire*, involving the appointment by the supervisory authority of a provisional administrator with extensive managerial powers, can coincide with the opening of court-based insolvency proceedings of the general type (*redressement judiciaire*).[37]

It must be noted that the multitude of administrative reorganization measures provided for under national banking laws in situations of underlying financial unsoundness can create an exaggerated sense of the true incidence of administrative insolvency proceedings in European countries. Returning for a moment to the distinction between bank resolution (the wider category, or genus) and insolvency proceedings (the subcategory, or kind), even if all types of reorganization belong in the former class, not all can be subsumed in the latter. Sometimes, however, the similarities in terms of name, triggers and objectives among the various reorganization measures can lead to confusion and mischaracterizations. Thus, from an objective-orientated viewpoint, it is meaningless to differentiate between reorganization measures belonging to the class of corrective and enforcement actions and those adopted by way of insolvency proceedings. Neither can the legal triggers be used as a criterion for classifying the various administrative actions, because in many systems the adoption of reorganization measures does not depend directly on the 'insolvency' or, more generally, the non-viable financial state of the bank. Finally, the intensity of the interference with the normal running of the institution can provide a reasonable but not conclusive criterion. The effect of the official actions on the governance of the institution concerned and, in particular, the termination of the role played by its insiders (shareholders and directors) in its management is, thus, often used as a basis for distinguishing between corrective and insolvency actions. Nonetheless, a line must be drawn between actions directed exclusively to the institution's internal governance structure – no matter how intrusive these may be – and actions producing mandatory legal results against third parties (depositors and other creditors, employees and so on). The normal proceedings of general corporate insolvency law typically involve, beyond the expulsion of managers and shareholders from the governance of an insolvent enterprise, significant legal alterations of the substantive and procedural rights of third parties (for instance, in relation to creditors, moratoria precluding individual enforcement of their rights, mandatory adjustments in contractual claims and/or majority-based procedures for compositions and the arrangement of claims). This automatic effect on third-party legal rights is a unique characteristic of insolvency proceedings, which provides the best possible basis for distinguishing them from simple corrective actions – even though hybrid or mixed cases (so to speak, quasi-insolvency proceedings) evidently exist and classification will often be difficult on the borderline, especially in fully administrative systems.

If an internationally dominant model does not exist, on what basis could a country decide between general and special, court-based and administrative bank insolvency proceedings? Sometimes, the proponents of an administrative approach suggest vaguely that the usual arguments about the peculiar asset-and-liability structure of depository institutions and the related threat of bank runs, which are used to justify the prudential regulation of solvent banks, somehow continue to apply in the insolvency context. It is not clear, however, why the fact that banks are regulated institutions justifies *per se* their exceptional treatment once they have become insolvent. Special proceedings can, accordingly, only be justified on either or both of two more specific grounds: that the objectives of bank insolvency law are different from those of the general corporate insolvency framework; or that the latter lacks the technical capacity to deal effectively with insolvent banks, either because it is inefficient or because it does not take into account certain unique features of banking operations.

We have already seen that, even in jurisdictions where the law does not favour the reorganization of insolvent non-financial enterprises, bank resolution practice may be characterized by a bias in favour of forbearance and continuation on a going-concern basis. In many cases, however, this is the result of *ad hoc* departures from the declared resolution policy, which promotes market discipline and strict enforcement. To this perspective, leaving banks within the general, court-based framework can be part of a strategy for narrowing down the legal possibilities for reorganization, thus partially counteracting the potentially strong propensity of discretionary decision-makers in the government and the supervisory authority towards forbearance. The issue will be further explored in the following section. To the extent, however, that the predilection for open-bank resolution is reflected in a country's official resolution policy, creating a separate framework for banks may appear preferable, and even necessary, precisely because it can institutionalize the more lenient treatment of banks as compared to other enterprises. More generally, the proponents of proceedings of the administrative type argue that these can transform the insolvency process from a mechanism for the reconciliation of conflicting private interests into an instrument for the servicing of the broader public interest, as represented by disinterested banking supervisors.

In so far as the technical structure of insolvency proceedings is concerned, it has to be recognized that the corporate insolvency framework of many nations is not flexible enough to enable the resolution of banking institutions in the manner that might appear economically most advantageous in view of the concrete circumstances. The main difficulties relate to the indissoluble link between financial assets and liabilities in a banking operation, and the resulting problem concerning the proceedings' timing and duration.

With regard to reorganization proceedings, for insolvent industrial enterprises, the effect of the moratorium is to ensure a relatively long timeframe for going-concern reorganization. The production assets and existing inventory can be employed for the continuation of the business, while the restructuring of frozen debts is attempted in parallel on a collective basis (through the submission of plans to the court, the calling of creditors' meetings and so on). In comparison, in the case of a bank, the suspension of payments will almost inexorably lead to the institution's death: the non-payment of existing liabilities will destroy any remaining goodwill, thus making it impossible for the bank to attract new deposits; in turn, this will result, not only in an inability to extend new loans, but probably also in a rapid depreciation of existing assets, that the bank may find it impossible to service. In other words, a bank's restructuring may be infeasible under a moratorium. But, without a moratorium, the publicity that the formal opening of insolvency proceedings will attract to the bank's financial difficulties could precipitate a run, making its continuing survival impossible. For this reason, restructuring must take place, whenever possible, either prior to the commencement of formal insolvency proceedings or immediately thereafter, over the proverbial long weekend, without publicity or disruption to depositors' and other creditors' rights. This, however, may be difficult to achieve where the procedural framework for reorganization proceedings is burdensome or inflexible, as is often the case. Thus, the expeditious, irreversible and secretive restructuring of insolvent banks is offered as a key justification for a special reorganization (administration) regime, with the banking authorities in direct control of the process.

In relation to liquidation proceedings, differences between banks and other companies are less easy to pinpoint. Even here, however, some problems may arise if the general law does not permit the realization of a bank's estate by means of a partial transfer of its operations to a solvent acquirer (partial going-concern restructuring, possibly in the form of US-style purchase-and-assumption transactions, combined with liquidation of the residual estate). The outright closure and liquidation of insolvent banks will generally be a suboptimal solution, possibly appropriate only in the case of deeply insolvent and highly delinquent institutions. Because of the economic structure of banking intermediation, closure followed by piecemeal collection of assets can significantly impair the value of the estate, which comprises, in large part, non-tradable financial claims in need of continuous servicing and rolling over. Closure will also eliminate a bank's franchise value. This will harm the interests of creditors. In short, the continuation of operations under new ownership is likely to protect the value of the estate and to increase creditors' dividends. Now, for a non-financial enterprise, it may be possible to sell as a group the assets which constitute the infrastructure of its ongoing business, thus allowing, in appropriate cases, a more profitable realization. In contrast, the assumption of part of an insolvent bank's operations (branches or lines of business) generally requires the lawful transfer to the acquirer, not only of a pool of assets, but also of a related amount of liabilities. However, the mandatory wholesale transfer of liabilities is not always permissible or practicable under existing general insolvency law.

Even the general triggers of corporate insolvency law may be considered inappropriate for banks. Usually, the definitions of insolvency vacillate uncomfortably between cashflow (or liquidity) and balance-sheet (or net-worth) criteria – even though the international trend is to give greater credence to the former.[38] In relation to banks, however, it is a widely held view that insolvency proceedings should commence at an earlier stage: by the time that a bank has actually failed to repay any deposit liabilities it will probably be too late for orderly resolution; on the other hand, the balance sheet may not provide a timely picture of the true depth of accumulated losses, because loan portfolios tend to deteriorate rapidly in bad times. Thus, a special, earlier trigger of bank insolvency may be more appropriate. National laws in many cases contain specific conditions for the placement of banks in insolvency proceedings. The legal criteria are, however, very different from country to country. Sometimes they go beyond financial considerations, to encompass violations of legal or regulatory requirements, or even the overall poor performance of a bank's management.[39] With regard to financial triggers, however, a balance-sheet near-insolvency test may be used. A good example is the 'critical undercapitalization' test of US law, whereby a bank is forcibly resolved once its risk-weighted capital-adequacy ratio has fallen under 2 per cent.[40]

Also in relation to the opening of proceedings, banking supervisors will frequently be in possession of unique information, enabling them to detect that a bank has crossed the insolvency threshold earlier than its creditors. This will be the case especially in systems using balance-sheet criteria or a special trigger, where insolvency does not depend on externally observable signs such as a failure to meet demands for the repayment of liabilities. Based on their informational advantage, supervisors may be in a position to initiate the forcible reorganization or liquidation of a financially unsound bank at a relatively early stage, when its economic value and goodwill have not been completely depleted, thus contributing both to the protection of the bank's depositors and to the stability of the broader financial system. It is, accordingly, essential that the rules provide for this possibility. In this context, many draw the conclusion that the supervisory assessment of bank insolvency is preferable to its judicial declaration. What is certain is that the procedural rules should give to the supervisory authority standing to petition the courts for an insolvency order.

In short, a separate insolvency framework for banks can circumvent the technical shortcomings of general corporate insolvency law and ensure consistency between the supervisory and insolvency processes. It must be asked, however, whether the technical limitations of the general system justify in all cases its replacement by a special banking regime, or simply call for a number of special banking rules.

At the end of the day, the optimal type of insolvency proceedings will be that which most effectively addresses a country's institutional, legal and practical realities. For choosing between alternative systems, the starting point should be an assessment of the quality of the general insolvency rules. A comparison of the institutional capacities of the judiciary and the supervisory authority in terms of their relative prestige, expertise, resources and integrity will also be indispensable. There might be significant differences in motivation, which should also be taken into consideration. For example, in some emerging economies, regulators may be younger, more influenced by market-based ideas and more committed to reform than the judges, who may also be influenced by deeply embedded pro-debtor attitudes. At the same time, it is generally accepted that regulators are often amenable to capture by the regulated industry and influenced by its interests. Regulatory decision-making may also be more politicized. Judges, by comparison, are more likely to be isolated from the political process and more focused on the 'fair' treatment of individual cases. Depending on the circumstances, these can be good or bad traits. Especially, a particularistic mode of thinking and a lack of familiarity with the banking sector and the financial economy may undermine the ability of judges to contribute meaningfully to a coherent bank resolution strategy.

There can be little doubt that in many jurisdictions general insolvency law is characterized by all sorts of inefficiencies: inadequate or perverse provisions, inexperienced courts, rigid procedures, inflexible or non-transparent administration of the estate, cumbersome disposal of assets. In this context, creating a special regime for banks and concentrating scarce administrative resources and skills to the task of dealing swiftly and effectively with banking failures, might appear beneficial, especially if one considers the importance of the financial sector for the performance of the broader national economy.

Nonetheless, it should be understood that it is not easy to build a coherent special system. Especially if this is of the administrative type, it will be very difficult to fall back on the standard private-law insolvency framework to close potential gaps in the special law; thus, complex legislative work will be required to ensure reasonable completeness of the rules and tolerable compatibility with the rest of the legal system. In a few jurisdictions, the termination of banks' normal corporate governance and the expulsion of their ownership and management by administrative fiat and without the protections of a judicial process may be resisted on grounds of basic legal principle or even for constitutional reasons relating to the protection of property rights. More generally, the operation of a separate system for banks may entail grave problems of scope. Banks come in many shapes and sizes, and in many countries their business activities overlap to a very considerable extent with those of non-bank financial institutions. Moreover, many banks belong to financial conglomerates or mixed-activity corporate groups. Thus, the existence of distinct insolvency regimes for banks, on the one hand, and their competitors and/or sister companies, on the other, can cause inconsistencies in the treatment of competing entities and lead to confusion and incoherence in the resolution of complex groups. It can also create considerable problems in the case of cross-border insolvencies, to the extent that administrative proceedings in one country may have to be recognized and reconciled with judicial proceedings in other countries where the insolvent bank had been active.

At the other extreme, where the economy is stable and the general insolvency system operates efficiently and flexibly, a small number of special rules of banking law may be all that is needed. This is, precisely, the approach followed by the UK, a country with a well-functioning – and characteristically pro-debtor – insolvency system, where the general framework applies to banks and other financial institutions, subject to minimal modifications. The system has operated well and without controversy over the years, and nobody argues for its replacement by an administrative system.

In regimes based on general insolvency law, some special banking rules may complement the main insolvency framework without directly affecting its operation. A characteristic example is that of rules relating to the establishment and operation of deposit insurance systems, including the determination of insured depositors' pay-off rights, which in most countries (but not in the USA) exercise their effect mostly outside the insolvency proceedings and in parallel to them.[41] The insolvency framework may, however, need specific adaptations, for the purpose of addressing certain peculiar aspects of bank insolvency. In particular, as explained above, it will be necessary to provide for the effective participation of supervisors in the initiation and conduct of proceedings. It might further be advisable to introduce special conditions for the declaration of a bank's insolvency (for example critical undercapitalization, as determined by the supervisor, as a substitute for balance-sheet insolvency), to make specific provision for the treatment of financial transactions and rights to financial collateral upon insolvency, to recognize netting arrangements in relation to orders entered in payment and settlement systems and so on. Furthermore, special rules might authorize the courts to delay the public announcement of proceedings relating to depository institutions, to excuse compliance with certain procedural strictures, to appoint the supervisory authority or persons nominated by that authority as administrators or liquidators and so on.[42]

11.5 Incentive structure of banking supervisors and their role in insolvency proceedings

As we have seen in the previous section, in jurisdictions where banks are included in the general corporate insolvency regime, the role of regulatory agencies (that is, the supervisory authority and/or the deposit insurance agency) in the insolvency can be quite limited; at an extreme, it may be confined to a simple right to initiate proceedings by applying for this purpose to the insolvency courts and/or to participate in various meetings and hearings. Evidently, regulators play a more intrusive role in the context of special proceedings. In some cases, the applicable rules exclude the common right of creditors to request the declaration of their debtor company's insolvency, but the final say remains with the courts, to which the supervisors must apply for this purpose. Where the special proceedings take the form of administrative (public-law) measures, the break with the normal practices of corporate insolvency law is even more pronounced and, typically, supervisors are allowed to exercise full control over the commencement and conduct of the proceedings, either directly or through administrators appointed by them.

The proponents of an administrative approach typically stress two key advantages that allegedly accrue when supervisors are placed in charge of the insolvency process: the increased flexibility, speed and finality of resolution in comparison to a court-based process; and the empowerment of supervisors to implement a structured policy in the public interest, combining strict and timely intervention with discretionary judgments concerning the choice of the most advantageous resolution technique for each case. In reality, however, the expected benefits may not be so easily attainable.

To start with, excluding the insolvency courts and placing supervisors in charge of the resolution process does not necessarily mean that the decisions of the latter are final and conclusive. In most cases, the supervisory actions will be subject to various rights of appeal conferred on certain parties (including the insolvent banks' ownership) and/or the general right of those affected by the decisions of the administration to apply for their invalidation by way of judicial review. These and similar mechanisms of legal redress seek to ensure that public officials stay within their mandate and do not abuse their powers.

Depending on a country's legal tradition, however, the effect of the judicial oversight of the supervisory decisions will sometimes be rather intrusive. Where the administrative courts follow a 'hard-look' approach to judicial review or are allowed to examine administrative decisions on their merits, they may be prepared to second-guess the supervisors and upset their decisions. In fact, in certain jurisdictions, the courts of private law tend to defer to the views of the administration more readily than the administrative courts. Paradoxically, then, in such jurisdictions the supervisory authority may be better able to achieve the implementation of its resolution plans by seeking their approval by the insolvency courts than by taking autonomous, but reviewable, action in its own name in public law.

In certain jurisdictions, the supervisors may find it within their power to assume provisional control of the management of a banking institution, but meet considerable legal resistance if they try to implement without judicial involvement measures which negatively affect the economic rights of creditors and/or shareholders. The supervisors will often prefer to utilize resolution techniques entailing the partial continuation of the banking business through an administrative allocation of past losses on shareholders and creditors and/or the forcible transfer of ownership to a solvent acquirer. However, it may be beyond their administrative powers to impose, based on their own appraisal of the financial situation, mandatory 'haircuts' or other prejudicial measures on creditors, or to violate the *pari passu* principle. At the same time, the aggressive exploration of recapitalization and third-party acquisition solutions may founder on the need to respect existing shareholders' property rights, which may preclude the administrative taking of measures which involve their forcible expulsion through the expropriation of their participation, the writing down of their shares' value or the issuance of new shares to a new controlling shareholder. It should be noted in this context that the question of shareholders' property rights will be especially thorny where bank insolvency is determined by a special trigger of banking law, allowing proceedings to commence while an institution still has positive net worth. To a certain extent, property rights may be protected by European, human rights or constitutional norms, which cannot be modified incidentally by the statutory legislation conferring administrative powers on supervisors. For instance, in the *Pafitis* case, the attempt of the Greek authorities to recapitalize an insolvent banking institution forcibly through an issuance of new capital, in which the existing shareholders were not given an opportunity to participate, was found by the European Court of Justice to be incompatible with European law. In so far as this was not a liquidation but a reorganization procedure, aimed at the rehabilitation of the institution as a legal entity, the protections for shareholders in the Second Company Directive continued to apply. It was contrary to the Directive, however, to increase the capital without giving an opportunity to existing shareholders to decide on the issue in a general meeting or to effectively participate in the subscription.[43] As a result of this decision, the Greek state was forced to pay hefty compensation to the shareholders.

Finally, in systems of the administrative type, the supervisory authority may be exposed to civil liability in the event of faulty performance of its resolution-related functions. In comparison, where the declaration of the insolvency and the approval of the resolution plans take place under the control of an insolvency court, the supervisory authority may be protected from civil actions, even though it has initiated the relevant actions itself. Thus, the conferral of full insolvency powers to the supervisory authority may produce a false appearance of supervisory omnipotence; but in reality, it may entail an equal, or even increased, level of legal risk and uncertainty of outcome.

As for the argument that an insolvency system based on special administrative powers is necessary to enable the supervisory authority to take prompt and decisive action, it does not seem particularly convincing. It is somewhat naïve to assume that supervisors can be blindly trusted to act resolutely in the desired direction and that the only thing that prevents them from doing so is a lack of full discretionary powers.

Many supervisors, when confronted with patent breaches of the substantive criteria for continuing authorization, tend to rely on negotiated remedial steps, and only contemplate unilateral formal action at a late stage – that is, when the regulated institution persistently fails to implement promised corrective measures and, especially, when its failure appears imminent. More specifically, where the statutory framework bestows on them sufficient discretionary powers to precipitate the early termination of undercapitalized or mismanaged financial institutions (whether by way of de-licensing or by initiating insolvency proceedings), they often prove reluctant to exercise these powers.[44]

The reasons for forbearance and laxity can be sought in the incentive structure for supervisors. In many cases, their aversion to aggressive enforcement is explicable by an eagerness to maintain cooperative relationships with their supervisees, thus facilitating the day-to-day performance of their function. The avoidance of legal disputes is another important incentive, especially in countries where the administrative courts are known for their readiness to overturn the decisions of the public administration. The prospect of political recriminations and negative reactions of the public opinion can also constitute a barrier to decisive action in conditions where this might appear to outsiders harsh, disproportionate or hasty. Moreover, regulators are likely to prefer corrective and enforcement options falling short of full-scale exit, because they want to avoid perceptions of malaise and crisis in their field of responsibility, but also because the *ex-post* recognition of problems of sufficient severity to justify the closure of a regulated institution reflects badly on their *ex-ante* supervisory performance.

As a result of the above, even in cases of deep undercapitalization or balance-sheet insolvency, as long as the banks concerned are still in position to meet current demands for the repayment of deposits, supervisory authorities occasionally refrain from opening insolvency proceedings, in the vain hope that a sudden turn of events will make the problem disappear. Supervisors are particularly likely to fall in a state of denial when the commencement of formal proceedings would lead to an immediate recognition of depositors' losses. For similar reasons, they tend to favour the reorganization of insolvent banks with public financial assistance to their closure and liquidation.

Of course, supervisors commonly invoke systemic risk as the reason for their reluctance to let insolvent banks die. This argument may carry particular force where the closure of one bank could lead to the recognition of financial problems in other institutions or if a systemic financial crisis has already erupted. But fears of systemic risk are frequently exaggerated.

In any case, rather than assuming that supervisors will always seek to implement the pre-announced priorities of bank resolution policy, a country should design its institutional framework for bank resolution based on a realistic assessment of their true incentives. This can have profound implications for the choice of type of insolvency proceedings, the exclusive or concurrent competence of supervisors to initiate proceedings, and the discretionary or mandatory nature of the relevant powers and decisions.

Even if a special insolvency regime for banks were chosen, to ensure prompt and decisive resolution it might still be necessary to circumscribe strictly the responsible authority's discretion both in law and in practice, by introducing quasi-automatic triggers and clear criteria for selection between resolution techniques. The US system, as it has developed following the enactment in 1991 of the Federal Deposit Insurance Corporation Improvement Act (FDICIA),[45] provides an example of this approach. In contrast, a nominally strict special administrative regime which leaves room for discretionary exceptions for banks which are deemed TBTF or whose failure may have 'systemic implications' could lead in reality to considerable laxity.

On the other hand, it should not be assumed that, in itself, the application to banks of general corporate insolvency law would necessarily lead to strict discipline, as reflected in an increase in insolvent liquidations. Other avenues may be open to the administration for ensuring the continuation of financially unsound banks: lending of last resort, public financial assistance or outright nationalization. From this perspective, the critical institutional issue is whether the decision regarding the possible use of public money is internalized in the supervisory authority or belongs to another agency. Where, for instance, the central bank is not itself responsible for banking supervision, it may be more reluctant to use its financial resources in a rescue operation under the guise of lending of last resort, because its own reputation is not at stake in the event of perceived supervisory failures. Moreover, the externalization of the spending decision increases the coordination problems involved in supervisors' attempts to organise the rescue of insolvent banks.[46]

A related issue concerns the procedural rights of creditors. Should they be able to initiate insolvency proceedings against banks? Where proceedings have been opened by the supervisory authority, should they have a right to be notified and be heard prior to the final decision on the resolution plan? Or should the supervisory authority be given full and exclusive control over these matters? The second solution might appear superior, in so far as it would prevent 'abusive' insolvency petitions by third parties and allow effective, expeditious and secretive resolution of banking institutions by the supervisory authority, acting also as insolvency official. However, it would create distortions in the economic operation of insolvency law across sectors. Furthermore, it would only be effective if the supervisory authority consistently lived up to its responsibilities, making wise and calculated use of its powers. Bitter experience shows that this is sometimes not the case – and the supervisors' incentive structure, as sketched above, may be an important part of the explanation. On balance, it appears preferable that creditors are not deprived of their right to initiate and participate in insolvency proceedings relating to banks. In this manner, the general fabric of insolvency law would be preserved, creditors' rights would remain enforceable at the instigation of their holders, and market discipline would be promoted.

Finally, bank insolvency proceedings are bound to involve conflicts between the interests of various groups of creditors, other 'stakeholders' (such as bank shareholders and employees), and even the state (which may have a financial stake in the form of recovery of deposit insurance payments, tax liabilities, administrative or criminal penalties, and so on). In particular, alternative methods of restructuring or liquidation will produce different effects in terms of the level and timing of satisfaction to be received by various classes of creditors (insured depositors, uninsured depositors and other creditors, subordinated debtholders, and even creditors by way of subrogation, such as the deposit insurance agency, as well as domestic as opposed to than foreign creditors), whose interests may not coincide. It is questionable whether the balancing of the conflicting interests should be left to regulatory agencies. The supervisory and deposit insurance agencies are not always neutral and disinterested parties, and this may be a strong reason for placing the proceedings under the control of the courts.[47] Additionally, the reputational costs for the regulators could be significant if they appeared to favour one group of creditors over another.

11.6 Bank resolution policies in European law

In the EU, bank resolution policy belongs in principle to the individual member states. European law contains a number of specific requirements, which constrain the national discretion in certain respects, but does not include a fully-fledged framework.

Thus, from a European perspective, the main question is whether bank resolution policy should stay in national hands or be transferred to the supranational level. In theory, the full Europeanization of official responses to bank failure might appear desirable in view of the proliferation of multinational banking groups and cross-border banking activities. Nonetheless, there are great impediments to such a shift. Generally speaking, the Europeanization of a policy field presupposes a modicum of agreement on the answers to be given to the basic policy dilemmas. This is a prerequisite both for measures relating to the harmonization of the national legislations and for the centralization of the relevant functions at the Union level. In the field under discussion, however, the huge disparity currently observed in national policies makes agreement on a common set of substantive rules particularly difficult, at the same time that it guarantees resistance to the centralization of the front-line decision-making procedures. Centralization would also be inconsistent with the current banking regulatory arrangements, whereby the European role is confined to the harmonization of the essential prudential norms, while responsibility for actual supervision is assigned, on a home-state basis, to the national competent authorities.[48] Besides, it is not clear, who might be a suitable candidate for performing resolution-related functions at the Union level: the ECB, the Commission, or a specially constituted insolvency tribunal? For these and other reasons, a single pan-European legal and administrative framework for bank resolution is still lacking – and unlikely to emerge in the foreseeable future.

Even so, the relevance of Union law is growing in this field too. Already, a number of European directives have a direct bearing on bank resolution policies. More specifically, these directives, which affect the treatment of credit institutions when these are already unable to meet their financial obligations and/or are subject to collective proceedings, constitute a fragmentary body of harmonized norms of special bank insolvency law.[49] Simultaneously, certain general norms of European competition and central banking law constrain the member state's ability to resolve troubled banks by way of rescue operations or other types of financial assistance.

The first directive dealing specifically with bank insolvency issues is the *Deposit Guarantee Directive*.[50] This instrument harmonizes the deposit insurance laws of member states, by setting out the minimum level of coverage that these must ensure in respect of all credit institutions for which they are responsible in their capacity as home states.

The Deposit Guarantee Directive requires member states to ensure that at least one deposit guarantee scheme is in operation in their territory. Credit institutions must be forced to participate in such a scheme in their home member state. National deposit guarantee schemes must offer protection not only in relation to domestic deposits, but also to deposits accepted by their members in branches set up elsewhere in the EU. The protection offered to depositors by a national scheme can be limited, but guaranteed payouts should cover at least 90 per cent of each depositor's total deposits with a failed member institution, regardless of the currency of the account, until the payment reaches the prescribed maximum amount of payment, which must be set at no less than €20,000 (Arts 3, 4(1) and 7–8). Where a European credit institution establishes a branch in a host member state whose deposit guarantee scheme offers to depositors coverage superior, in terms of its amount or scope, to that of the home-state scheme, it should be allowed to join the host-state scheme in order to bring the level of protection afforded to local depositors (i.e. depositors of the branch) up to the level guaranteed by that scheme ('topping-up' rule).[51] The Directive also includes procedural provisions requiring deposit guarantee schemes to pay out to the depositors of failed member banks the insured portion of their deposits as soon as possible after these have become unavailable. As a rule, payments of duly verified claims must take place within three months from the moment that the unavailability of the deposits has been officially recognized (Art. 10).

In short, the Deposit Guarantee Directive lays down a harmonized minimum level of protection to depositors once a bank's failure has already occurred. For this purpose, it includes substantive rules for the eventuality of cessation or suspension of payments. Although the relevant arrangements will generally operate in conjunction with bank insolvency proceedings of some sort, for the triggering of deposit insurance payments in observance of the Directive, it makes no difference whether the failed bank is legally insolvent or simply unable to repay its liabilities and whether it is protected by a moratorium following the opening of collective proceedings or not.[52] In this sense, the Directive sidesteps questions relating to the wider bank resolution policies of member states. The decision whether to rescue troubled banks or to allow them to fail remains a matter of national discretion; the same applies to the form and objectives of collective proceedings available in relation to banks whose insolvency has been formally recognized.

The more recent, and very important, *Winding-Up Directive*[53] harmonizes the rules of private international law applicable to bank collective proceedings with a view to ensuring the mutual recognition of the national measures relating to the reorganization and winding-up (that is, liquidation) of credit institutions in difficulty.[54] The Directive parallels in the banking field the European instrument governing general corporate insolvency law, the Insolvency Regulation,[55] which creates a single conflict-of-laws regime permitting the mutual recognition of collective proceedings relating to non-financial enterprises.[56] Both instruments cover issues of choice of forum, foreign recognition of the national proceedings and (to a certain extent) choice of law. In contrast, they do not affect the material (substantive) or procedural rules of domestic insolvency law. In particular, the rules on the order of priority of claims continue to be widely divergent across member states.

The draft text of the Winding-Up Directive was under discussion for fifteen years and only adopted in its final form in April 2001.[57] While the divergent views of member states on certain proposed provisions explain in part the huge delay in its adoption, severe drafting difficulties also arose from the fact that the general approach in the instrument departed in significant ways from that of the draft Bankruptcy Convention – the ancestor of the Insolvency Regulation, which was itself moving through various stages of preparatory work for almost 40 years, in the course of which its basic policies underwent substantial transformations.[58]

The main question of international insolvency law and policy, which the European instruments seek to address, is whether the collective proceedings relating to enterprises with activities in multiple jurisdictions should be governed by the principles of unity (in accordance with which, only a single set of proceedings, covering both the head office and its foreign operations, is available in relation to an insolvent enterprise) and universality (whereby national proceedings cover all foreign assets of, and all foreign claims against, the insolvent enterprise, and equivalent groups of creditors in different jurisdictions should be treated equally) or by their rival principles of plurality and territoriality.[59] Applied to credit institutions, the more specific question is whether all European branches of insolvent credit institutions should be treated as a single entity (one set of assets, one set of creditors) or as separate entities (one in each host state, with local or, possibly, world-wide assets made available for local depositors and other creditors).

Significantly, despite many similarities between the general policy approach of the Directive and that of the Insolvency Regulation, a major divide opens as a result of the recognition of 'secondary' territorial proceedings in the latter. There, the starting point is that of universal recognition of the main proceedings, which are opened in the member state where 'the centre of the debtor's main interests is situated'; this, for a legal person, is generally deemed to be the place of its registered office. However, territorial (secondary) collective proceedings, limited to the local assets, may also be opened in any other member state where the debtor possesses an establishment.[60] Once main proceedings have been opened, any secondary proceedings opened subsequently must be confined to liquidation (winding-up) (Art. 3(3)). Liquidators in other proceedings and foreign creditors can lodge claims in the main or the secondary proceedings.[61] Thus, the Regulation's system has rightly been characterized as a modified territorialist one, with universal cross-filing.[62]

In contrast, the Winding-Up Directive consistently applies the 'single entity' approach, which incorporates the principles of unity and – to a much more limited extent – universality.[63] The home member state is given exclusive competence both for the reorganization and for the winding-up of credit institutions.[64] Secondary proceedings are completely excluded.[65]

A technical difficulty resulting from the divergent approaches of the two instruments is that the Insolvency Regulation cannot be used to fill the gaps in the provisions of the Winding-Up Directive. This has necessitated the inclusion in the Directive of detailed provisions on the treatment of various categories of creditors' rights and claims (rights of employment law, secured rights, contractual claims relating to transactions on regulated markets, contractual rights of set-off governed by foreign law, lawsuits and so on). Nonetheless, the European legislator strove to reach solutions which are, to the extent possible, consistent with the treatment of similar issues in the Insolvency Regulation.[66] More substantially, the parallel operation of different regimes,[67] with discrepant procedural structures for credit institutions and other legal persons, raises the possibility of uneven treatment of similarly placed enterprises, but also creates problems with regard to conglomerates comprising both banks and non-bank financial institutions (insurance companies or securities firms).

On the other hand, the advantages of the Directive's approach include clear lines of responsibility, speed, simplicity and reduced costs, and the avoidance of lengthy litigation for the purpose of recognizing insolvency proceedings in other member states or participating in them. Moreover, the approach is fully consistent with the fundamental principle of home-state control, which underpins the European legislative framework for the organization, operation and regulation of financial institutions[68] – and, in particular, the so-called 'passport directives',[69] which allocate to the competent authorities of the home state responsibility for the prudential supervision of such institutions. The home-state principle was already enshrined in the rules relating to banks' authorization and prudential supervision[70] and deposit insurance,[71] and is now extended to bank insolvency law and practice. This is only reasonable, given the interconnection between ongoing prudential supervision and bank resolution, including by way of collective proceedings.

Specifically, where a European credit institution faces a crisis that places its solvency in question, the Winding-Up Directive recognizes the power of the competent authorities of the home member state to impose the necessary reorganization measures, applying their national law for this purpose (Art. 3). The European legislator is agnostic as to the legal form that the relevant proceedings should take. Accordingly, the Directive covers reorganization measures of any description, whether administrative or court-based, 'which are intended to preserve or restore the financial situation of a credit institution and which could affect third parties' pre-existing rights, including measures involving the possibility of a suspension of payments, suspension of enforcement measures or reduction of claims' (Art. 2, seventh indent). Such reorganization measures will now enjoy mutual recognition and will produce Union-wide effects,[72] even if the laws of the host member states do not make provision for equivalent measures (Art. 3(2)).

Where national law does not allow reorganization proceedings, or where reorganization measures are futile or inappropriate, or have been attempted, but failed to restore the insolvent institution to financial soundness, winding-up proceedings[73] may be opened by the relevant authorities of the home state (normally, the courts, but in some member states administrative authorities, including the competent supervisory authorities) (preamble, rec. (14) and Art. 9(1)).

The Winding-Up Directive makes clear that bank insolvency proceedings will be conducted in accordance with the national law of the home member state (which is also the law of the forum of the proceedings, or *lex concursus*).[74] This will determine the conditions for the opening of proceedings, and will govern their conduct, closure and effects – including, in appropriate cases, the scope and effect of the moratorium, the fate of contracts to which the insolvent bank is a party and, on liquidation, the order of priority of claims and manner of distribution of proceeds. However, since harmonization of the material rules of insolvency has proven impossible and the laws of the member states continue to diverge widely in terms of their treatment of certain rights and ranking of claims, the Directive contains a number of exceptions to the applicability of home-state law,[75] with a view to preserving rights established under the law of other member states, where the relevant legal relationships are more closely connected with these states.[76] This is, for instance, the case of netting arrangements, which in the context of bank insolvency proceedings continue to be governed by the proper law of the contract (*lex contractus* or *lex causae*). Concerning contractual rights relating to immovable property, or security rights, the Directive respects the principle of territoriality (*lex rei sitae* or *lex contractus*, depending on the case). The same applies to security rights relating to tangible or intangible assets (including fixed and floating charges, as well as transfers subject to a reservation of title) and contractual rights of set-off which might not be recognized under the law of the home state (*lex rei sitae* or *lex contractus*, depending on the case). The fate of transactions carried out on regulated markets must be decided according to the proper law of the contracts – which will usually be the law of the state where the markets are located.

Finally, it should be noted that the operation of the principles of unity and universality of insolvency proceedings in the Winding-Up Directive is limited both in geographical terms and in terms of the nationality of the persons covered. Thus, the relevant provisions only apply to the EU branches of European credit institutions, but not to their operations in third countries. Moreover, third-country institutions operating in Europe by way of branches are subject to separate insolvency proceedings in each host member state on a territorialist basis. In this case, the Directive requires no more than the exchange of information between host states and the coordination of their responses (Art. 19).

Two other directives lay down harmonized rules on certain technical issues of insolvency law impinging on the operation of banking and securities markets. These rules, which are in part substantive and in part of private international law, are largely, even though not exclusively, applicable to credit institutions and have major implications especially for the treatment of an insolvent bank's interbank obligations, as well as of the financial assets given as collateral in support of such obligations. In this sense, the directives can be said to introduce special rules of bank insolvency law.

The *Settlement Finality Directive*[77] applies to credit institutions, investment firms and public authorities participating in officially designated payment and securities settlement systems of the member states, as well as to the relevant central counterparties, settlement agents and clearing houses (Art. 2). The Directive is intended to eliminate certain legal risks with potential systemic implications, arising in connection with financial institutions' participation in wholesale net-settlement payment systems, and also in securities settlement systems, especially where these are closely connected to payment systems. It seeks to achieve this objective by ensuring the finality of settlement of transfer orders entered into a system and the enforceability of financial collateral given by the participants in support of their obligations.[78]

Specifically, the Settlement Finality Directive establishes that, with regard to rights and obligations relating to participation in a system, a direct participant's insolvency occurs at the moment when the administrative or judicial order opening insolvency proceedings is handed down, and the insolvency proceedings do not have retroactive effects; this excludes the operation of so-called 'zero hour' rule of certain national insolvency laws, whereby the effects of insolvency proceedings run back to the beginning of the relevant day, and, more generally, any rules leading to the reversal of transactions carried on during a suspect period (Arts 6–7). Furthermore, the Settlement Finality Directive stipulates that the rights and obligations arising from participation in the system be determined upon insolvency by reference to the law governing the system, not the *lex concursus* (Art. 8).

In substantive terms, the applicable law must recognize the validity and binding nature of all transfer orders and netting involving an insolvent participant, as long as the transfer orders have been entered into the system prior to the moment of opening the insolvency proceedings. The finality of transfer orders entered into the system and settled within the day, but after the moment, of the opening of the proceedings should also be recognized if the settlement agent, central counterparty or clearing house can prove that they were not aware of the insolvency order. In this context, the exact moment when an order is entered into the system is an issue to be determined with reference to the system's own rules. These rules seek to ensure that the revocation of a transfer order or the unwinding of a netting will never be allowed but do not affect any rights to recovery that another participant in the system or a third party may be able to exercise against the insolvent participant on the basis of the underlying transactions (preamble, rec. (13) and Art. 3).

Most importantly, member states are required to ensure the insulation of any collateral security supporting obligations in payment and securities settlement systems from the effects of the insolvency of the participant which provided this security. The same protection is afforded to the ECB and national central banks in relation to collateral security received from their counterparty banks in connection to their monetary and other operations. In relation to book-entry securities, the perfection of the security interest of the collateral taker (system participant or central bank) shall be governed by the law of the member state of the register or account (Art. 9). Moreover, the Directive grants a national discretion to the member state whose law governs a system to ring-fence the assets (funds or securities) on the settlement accounts of insolvent participants and to apply them for the fulfilment of existing obligations in the system, in preference to other claims (Art. 4).

The recently enacted *Collateral Directive*[79] seeks to create a common European regime for the bilateral provision of collateral in financial transactions, in situations where the collateral taker and/or collateral provider are public authorities, central banks or IFIs, financial institutions, including credit institutions, central counterparties in payment and settlement systems, settlement agents or clearing houses. Its provisions apply where both parties belong to the above categories, or where the other party is a non-financial enterprise, but not a private person (Art. 1(2)). The Directive sets out a number of substantive and conflict-of-laws rules in relation to security interests over cash and financial instruments, both in the form of a pledge or similar security interest and in the form of transfer of title, including repurchase agreements (repos). Specifically, it simplifies the formal requirements for the creation and perfection of the relevant security interests, as well as the conditions for their enforcement; requires the recognition by the member states of any contractual rights of use of the financial collateral by the collateral taker; and determines that issues relating to the validity, perfection and effect of security interests over book-entry securities shall be governed by the law of the country where the securities account is held (Arts 3–6, 9).

In relation to insolvency law, the Collateral Directive extends certain of the principles animating the Settlement Finality Directive by requiring the national legislation of the member states to recognize, with regard to transactions within its scope, close-out netting agreements and collateral arrangements, notwithstanding the commencement of insolvency proceedings in relation to any of the parties. In particular, financial collateral (including top-up and substitution collateral, where the collateral agreement provides for this possibility) granted prior to or within the day of the opening of the proceedings, but prior to the moment of the making of the relevant insolvency order (or even after that moment, if the collateral taker can prove that he was not aware of the order), cannot be invalidated or reversed (Arts 7–8). Provisions whereby the insolvency of one party is turned into an enforcement event (that is, event of default) must also take effect according to their terms (Art. 4(5)).

Even though the Directive allows member states to exclude transactions involving financial institutions, including credit institutions from the scope of application of their national implementing instruments (Art. 1(3)), its provisions are likely to apply in relation to the great majority of European banks. In this context, the true policy purpose of the new rules is to protect financial institutions acting as collateral takers (in other words, as secured lenders) against the insolvency of their counterparties. Generally, however, the Directive's significance as a measure of bank insolvency law will be felt in cases where an insolvent bank has acted as collateral provider, not collateral taker.[80] This is likely to be the case primarily in the context of interbank agreements. In situations of this type, the rights of the financial institutions acting as collateral takers will be protected in full, over and above any provisions of national law on the effect of the moratorium and/or the avoidance of transactions made during a suspect period. This can have a negative impact on the interests of depositors and other unsecured creditors but also, in the case of reorganization proceedings, on the prospects of survival of insolvent banks.

Moving from insolvency law to the broader array of bank resolution instruments, European law sets certain limits on the ability of member states to launch rescue operations or to provide financial assistance to insolvent banks. Two different types of constraints must be discussed in this context.

To start with, the unilateral use of public funds by a member state for the purpose of propping up a failing bank may be resisted on competition law grounds. National policy autonomy in this area is subject to the legal obligation to respect the EC Treaty provisions on competition and, especially, the rules on *state aids to industry*.[81] Thus, under Article 87(1) [ex Art. 92(1)], member states are not allowed to grant to commercial undertakings economic aid of any description out of state resources, if this is likely to distort competition and affect cross-border trade. Nonetheless, even where a state aid is *prima facie* incompatible with the prohibition, it may qualify for exemption under Article 87(2)–(3) [ex Art. 92(2)–(3)]. Thus, certain distortions of competition may be permitted in order to secure certain objectives recognized under EU law.[82] Aid may, in particular, be granted exceptionally in order to "remedy a serious disturbance in the economy of a Member State".[83] To benefit from an exemption, the member state concerned must notify the proposed aid to the Commission and refrain from putting it into effect until the latter has finally given its approval.[84] Nevertheless, the acceptability of any state aid depends on the 'common interest',[85] and not on the national interest, as defined by individual member states.[86]

In order to approve a state aid, the Commission must consider it necessary. The necessity of the aid is assessed in relation to the seriousness of the problems that the member state seeks to address and to the requirements of a solution to these problems. This criterion is related to the principle of proportionality. The Commission distinguishes between 'restructuring', 'rescue' and 'operating' aid to enterprises. Restructuring aid is defined as 'aid which forms part of a feasible, coherent and far-reaching plan to restore [the] long-term viability of the recipient enterprise'.[87] The Commission does not treat restructuring aid *per se* as contrary to the common interest.[88] Aid of this type may be authorized, if it facilitates development by re-establishing the competitiveness of the recipient[89] and remedying structural problems of a whole sector (rather than merely those of the recipient).[90] Rescue aid is temporary aid intended to keep in business a firm facing a substantial deterioration in its financial position, reflected in an acute liquidity crisis or technical insolvency, thus providing time for an analysis of the causes of the firm's difficulties and the devising of an appropriate plan to remedy the situation.[91] The Commission keeps such aid under strict control and requires that it be justified on sectoral grounds. Operating aid is the most objectionable type of aid from the perspective of competition policy. The European Court of Justice has defined operating aid as aid which is 'granted without any specific condition and solely by reference to the quantities [of the aided product] used',[92] and the Court of First Instance, as 'aid intended to relieve an undertaking of the expenses it would itself normally have had to bear in its day-to-day management or its usual activities'.[93] In its *Siemens* decision, the Court of First Instance ruled that such aid does not in principle fall within the scope of the exceptions potentially permissible under Article 87(3), because by its very nature it disorts competition without being capable of promoting the common interest.[94] It may be opposed, therefore, even if the result is closure of the prospective recipient.[95]

In principle, the prohibition on state aids could hinder governments seeking to bail out unsound institutions with public funds, so as to avoid the politically 'unpleasant' prospect of fully-fledged and openly recognized bank failure. Indeed, since the decision of the European Court of Justice in *Züchner*,[96] it is clearly established that the EC Treaty's provisions on competition are applicable to the banking industry on the same basis as to other sectors. This also means that the banking industry is not exempt from the restrictions on state aids to industry.

The first occasion on which the Commission addressed the issue of bank rescues directly involved the announcement, on 17 March 1995, by the French government of its decision to bail out the state-controlled Crédit Lyonnais, one of world's largest banks.[97] Following strong complaints by the bank's two largest private-sector competitors, Société Generale and Banque Nationale de Paris, who claimed that the planned rescue would gravely damage competition, the Commission launched an inquiry into the affair – possibly Europe's biggest state-aid case ever. The case shows that competition law can set strict limits on national authorities' ability to provide outright support to failed banks, by taking over their bad assets or indemnifying them for losses.

Specifically, in its decision on the matter,[98] the Commission concluded that the provision by the state of financial support to banks facing financial difficulties for the purpose of helping them to restore their solvency may indeed amount to state aid within the meaning of Article 87. When the private banking sector participates to a financially significant degree in a bank rescue on a non-obligatory basis, it may be assumed that no state aid is involved. If, on the other hand, the state provides all or most of the support, the Commission must evaluate the intervention, so as to establish whether it constitutes a prohibited aid to industry. The Commission must apply the 'principle of the private investor in a market economy' – that is, it must assess whether a comparable private investor, acting under the normal conditions of a market economy, would have undertaken a similar operation.

In the event of a systemic crisis, affecting the total banking system and attributable to reasons outside the control of banking institutions, the state could justifiably provide support to the banking sector as a whole but only in so far as this is necessary to restore the normal operation of the market. In principle, the difficulties of individual banks, especially when they are attributable to internal reasons, should not raise similar issues of systemic safety. Nonetheless, in certain cases the failure of a single large bank may put in jeopardy the survival of other banks, which are financially exposed or linked to the first bank. In this situation, state support may be justified, provided that: (i) it can restore the bank's financial soundness in reasonable time; (ii) it is proportional to the costs and benefits of the restructuring and does not go beyond what is strictly necessary; (iii) it causes the least possible distortions to competition and it places a significant part of the costs on the bank itself; and (iv) it is accompanied by countervailing measures, aimed at compensating to any extent possible for the anticompetitive consequences.

With regard to Crédit Lyonnais, the rescue plan contained important elements of state aid, with a potential cost to the state of FFr45 billion. Aid of such magnitude could have significant anticompetitive effects for the banking sector. Moreover, the bank's difficulties were the result of its own aggressive and ill-thought commercial policies. Nonetheless, the Commission exercised its discretion to exempt the rescue from the prohibition of Article 87(1). As the price for its consent, the Commission imposed strict conditions, setting limits to the bank's future ability to expand its activities or its branch network.[99]

A series of proceedings opened in relation to other credit institutions in recent years attests the Commission's commitment to a vigorous enforcement of the Treaty rules on state aids in the field of banking.[100] Relevant cases cover state aids both to solvent and to failing banks, whether these take the form of direct capital injections or state guarantees of the banks' liabilities. The investigations of the Commission in such cases have occasionally led to negative decisions.[101]

Nonetheless, a lot could depend on the concrete application of the general rules on state aids to particular bank rescues. There are reasons to doubt that the principles will be applied with full consistency and on a truly equal basis. The *Crédit Lyonnais* decision itself effectively recognized the TBTF doctrine as part of European competition policy, thus entrenching an important source of moral hazard. More ominously, the Federal Republic of Germany has successfully fought at the political level an attempt to apply the rules to a category of publicly-owned credit institutions set up by its Länder – the Landesbanken – benefiting from permanent and unlimited state guarantees, which substantially enhance their creditworthiness.[102] The politicization of enforcement, however, is likely to affect financial support to troubled banks more than any other type of state aid, due to the great resonance of banking crises in terms of public opinion. Finally, more tolerance may be shown in situations where state aids are granted in the context of formal bank insolvency proceedings, as a means for supporting the restructuring of failed banks. Such an approach, however, could result in long-winded reorganization efforts, involving considerable expense and potentially higher costs than the option of outright exit by way of liquidation, with no less serious implications for competition.

A related issue concerns the indirect rescuing of insolvent banks by way of *central bank refinancing*. The extension to insolvent institutions of central bank funds under the pretext of lending of last resort is a long-established – and politically more palatable – alternative to outright rescue operations. In this context, the formal decision-making responsibility will invariably belong to a member state's national central bank, subject possibly to the consent of the government in the case of loss-making operations. As a result of the Maastricht Treaty, however, the ability of central banks to engage in operations of this sort may be seriously constrained.[103]

Thus, the involvement of the ECB and the national central banks in refinancing activities depends on their legal capacity to apply their financial resources in this manner. The matter is now regulated by the conditions on lending operations in the Statute of the ESCB – even though it is not always clear whether the relevant operations are conducted under the authority and on account of the ESCB or by the individual national central banks acting as domestic institutions.

As might be expected, the Maastricht Treaty does not recognize explicitly the ESCB's role as lender of last resort, since this could create moral hazard. However, it gives to the ECB and the national central banks the power to conduct credit operations with credit institutions and other market participants as a means of furthering the ESCB's objectives.[104] The ECB is required to establish general principles for the credit operations conducted by itself or by the national central banks (Art. 18.2). Although such operations will in most cases constitute an instrument for achieving the ESCB's primary objective of price stability (monetary-policy instrument), they can also be relied upon for the purpose of supplying liquidity to the banking system and for the conduct of rescue operations (banking-policy instrument). However, a major constraint on the use of the instrument is that any lending must be based on adequate collateral. A strict insistence on high-quality collateral would in many cases prevent the exercise of the lender-of-last-resort function, because banks with a sufficient amount of high-quality, liquid collateral could sell it in the market and would not seek liquidity support from the central bank.[105] A relaxation of the rules of eligibility for paper used as collateral, on the other hand, beyond a certain point would constitute a breach of the EU Treaty by the ECB.

In short, the principles of an open-market economy with free competition, which animate the whole single-market structure, theoretically create a bias in bank resolution policy in favour of strict enforcement and set supranational limits on the ability of member states to bail out, whether directly or indirectly, banks in financial difficulty. In practice, however, it remains an open question whether the rules will exercise an actual binding effect or will, instead, succumb to circumvention and be mostly honoured in their effective breach.

Notes

* The author thanks Mr Jens Binder for numerous insightful suggestions, from which this paper has benefited greatly – and also for his unrelenting criticism of some of the original arguments, which has contributed to the conceptual clarification of the issues. In particular the emphasis placed in section 11.4 (pp. 294–5) on effects on third parties (creditors) as the distinguishing characteristic of insolvency proceedings is attributable to him.

1. Note that the term 'resolution' is used here to suggest any method for handling the problem of bank insolvency. Thus, resolution does not necessarily result in bank exit (that is, in the closure of the insolvent bank's business and/or its legal dissolution by means of liquidation proceedings), but can also lead to the complete or partial survival of the bank's operations, and even to its rehabilitation and continuation as a legal person.
2. Basel Accord.
3. Since the publication of the Basel Accord, the Basel Committee has produced many other papers for this purpose. More recently, the Committee's work has centred on the Basel Accord's replacement by a technically much more complex New Capital Accord.
4. For a very detailed survey of the literature relating to deposit insurance, see FDIC (2000).
5. See Goodhart and Illing (2002), esp. Part II (chs 8–13).
6. The public safety nets often take the form of nationalization or idiosyncratic refinancing operations. However, comprehensive deposit insurance schemes and central bank lending provide a more universal, stylized framework for the theoretical analysis of the dynamics and incentive implications of safety nets.
7. Basel Committee (2002), p. 3, n. 1. More generally, on the prevalence of financial sector problems and bank insolvencies across the world, see Lindgren *et al.* (1996, table 2) and Gup (1998).
8. The literature on bank resolution policies and insolvency law is still relatively small and of uneven quality. However, the academic interest is growing. See in particular: Asser (2001); Campbell and Cartwright (2002); Giovanoli and Heinrich (1999); Group of Thirty (1998); Hüpkes (2000); Lastra and Schiffman (1999); Oditah (1996); Ramsey and Head (2000).
9. On the concept of regulatory regimes, see Hood *et al.* (2001), chs 1–2, esp. pp. 9–14. The present discussion does not attempt to address all aspects of a bank resolution regime; instead, it focuses on the formal policy instruments, the allocation of official responsibilities and the objectives set out in the law.
10. For instance, in legal systems where banks are exempted from general insolvency law and their insolvency is dealt with through special administrative procedures under the control of the supervisory agency, the relevant procedures might be validly classified either as instances of regulatory enforcement or as types of insolvency proceedings, as is discussed later in this section.
11. The regulator can also provide informal guidance (or exercise so-called 'moral suasion') for the purpose of encouraging a bank's restructuring and recapitalization by means of voluntary private arrangements (or 'work-out' schemes). This presupposes, however, the willingness of the bank's ownership and management to cooperate.

12. In countries where the deposit insurance scheme is operated by a fully-fledged board or agency, the latter is sometimes given statutory powers to support the restructuring of failed banks by way of financial contributions, or even to take over such banks and recapitalize them under a regime of temporary nationalization. But this type of intervention forms part of the broader regular formal process for the recognition and resolution of bank insolvency and should be classified, accordingly, under the rubric of insolvency proceedings.
13. The main exception involves the actions of bank resolution agencies responsible for the restructuring of the whole banking system; typically, such agencies are created by emergency legislation following a generalized financial crisis.
14. An exact delineation of the sphere of insolvency proceedings is not always easy in such systems. For instance, HM Treasury (1994) 'Winding Up Directive: A Consultation Document Issued by HM Treasury', 1 June, paras 1.8–1.9, defines 'reorganisation measures' as 'measures taken, either administratively or by the courts, to change the financial position, structure or management of a credit institution to address prudential concerns and stave off potential liquidation', adding that these are 'effectively supervisory measures, albeit ones which would only be taken in particular circumstances'. See, however, the discussion in Section 11.3.
15. This is the term used in the World Bank's 'Principles and Guidelines for Effective Insolvency and Creditor Rights Systems' (April 2001), as well as in the European Winding-Up Directive; see infra, n. 72 and accompanying text. The equivalent term 'rehabilitation' is employed by the IMF's Legal Department (IMF LEG) in its report *Orderly and Effective Insolvency Procedures: Key Issues* (Washington, DC: International Monetary Fund, 1999). As a type of collective proceedings, the reorganization of insolvent enterprises is invariably contrasted to their liquidation or winding up; see IMF LEG, pp. 12–17. However, certain techniques of bank restructuring (usually employed in the context of special bank insolvency proceedings in administrative law) combine the partial economic reorganization of an insolvent bank's operations by means of their transfer to another institution with the liquidation of the residual part of its estate and the dissolution of its legal personality.
16. As access to the banking market is everywhere subject to strict regulatory controls, an existing bank's licence has significant economic value. This, together with any remaining goodwill, will be lost if the bank is closed down and placed in liquidation. Moreover, a bank's assets will usually include large amounts of non-tradeable financial claims in need of continuous servicing and, possibly, refinancing (or rolling over). Outright closure will reduce the value of such assets, thereby harming the interests of creditors. For this reason, keeping even fully insolvent banks open (maybe under new management) can potentially increase depositors' and other creditors' dividends. On the other hand, continuation of operations under the control of an administrator usually leads to rapid dissipation of assets and accumulation of further losses, which soon dwarf the supposed benefits.
17. Public resistance to strict enforcement will be particularly pronounced in relatively poor countries with limited or non-existent deposit insurance systems, where bank deposits may be the only form of financial assets for significant segments of the population.

18. In English insolvency law, the maximization of creditors' dividends has traditionally been the dominant consideration in insolvency proceedings, including in the field of banking – even though the situation became more nuanced following the introduction of the administration procedure, which provides greater flexibility and opportunities for rehabilitation. See Insolvency Act 1986, s. 8(3); and, more generally, 'Insolvency Law and Practice: Report of the Review Committee' (Cmnd 8558, June 1982) (the 'Cork Report'), esp. chs 4 and 9; the recently enacted Enterprise Act 2002, with its emphasis on rescuing insolvent firms reinforces this trend. Other nations, however, will have very different priorities.
19. For example, under English law, one of the statutory grounds for winding up a banking institution is that it is 'just and equitable' that the institution should be dissolved (Finch, 2002). The relevant provision, which was formerly set out in the Banking Act 1987, s. 92(1)(b), now appears in the Financial Services and Markets Act 2000 (FSMA), s. 367(3)(b). Liquidation on this public-interest ground is possible whether or not the institution is solvent, and even if it does not have any more outstanding deposit liabilities. It may be enough that, by carrying on deposit-taking activities in the past, the institution had shown disregard for the interests of its clients and engaged in illegal, unethical or unprofessional conduct. In this situation, the rationale for the petition is that '[b]y winding up the company the court would be expressing, in a meaningful way, its disapproval of the company's conduct. In addition to being a fitting outcome for the company itself, such a course [has] the further benefit of spelling out to others that the court would not hesitate to wind up companies whose standards of dealing with the investing public were unacceptable'. *Re Walter L. Jacob and Co. Ltd, The Times*, 29 Dec. 1988 (CA).
20. In *Re Walter L. Jacob*, the petition was made after the institution had already ceased trading.
21. Now in the form of a 'prohibition order' under s. 56 of the FSMA.
22. In Re Bank of Credit and Commerce International S.A. [1992] BCC 83; [1992] BCLC 570 (Ch.D), the court adjourned a decision on a petition by the Bank of England (at the time the banking regulator) for the winding-up of BCCI. The decision was based on the assumption that, even if the proposed restructuring were to succeed during the adjournment, the Bank of England could still renew its petition for the dissolution of the reformed bank and the court might exercise its discretion to make a winding-up order at that stage. This assumption was highly unrealistic, since the institution's potential acquirers would only agree to participate in its restructuring on the understanding that, if successful, this would absolve the bank from any past misconduct.
23. However, continuation of the business by way of purchase-and-assumption by another bank may still be possible, where this type of restructuring is legally available.
24. In England, a similar issue arose under the Banking Act 1987 in an appeal brought before the Banking Appeal Tribunal by the administrators of an insolvent institution, Mount Banking, against the decision of the Bank of England to limit its authorization to a very short period (three months); *Mount Banking Corporation Ltd. (in administration)* v. *The Governor and Company of the Bank of England*, 13 Oct. 1993, Banking Appeal Tribunal

(unreported), transcript of the decision, pp. 44–51. Mount Banking had been placed in administration following a petition presented by its owners and supported by the Bank of England itself. At the time, the existence of an administration order was a statutory ground for the revocation or restriction of a deposit-taking institution's licence; Banking Act 1987, s.11(8). Nonetheless, the Bank, having supported the administration order, did not subsequently use it as a basis for its decision to set the time limit; instead, it relied on past misconduct by the institution's owner-managers. The administrators unsuccessfully submitted that the bank should have taken into consideration the new situation that had emerged as a result of the administration regime – something that it had failed to do. For further discussion of the case, see Hadjiemmanuil (1996) pp. 275–6.

25. With regard to the production of policy guidelines, the Basel Committee has already published the report of a special task force on *Supervisory Guidance on Dealing with Weak Banks* (March 2002) (the Weak Banks Report); this is discussed extensively in this section and Section 6 of the Report is reproduced in full in Appendix 2 of this book. Moreover, the World Bank and the IMF have jointly launched a global initiative on the legal aspects of bank insolvency proceedings; the IMF is conducting work on the management of systemic crises; and the Financial Stability Forum has established a task force on deposit insurance. At the research level, the World Bank, the OECD, the EU Group de Contact and the Asia-Pacific Economic Cooperation (APEC) are all studying related issues, ranging from the causes of bank difficulties through practices for the resolution of individual banking institutions to systemic crisis management. See Basel Committee (2002, para. 7).
26. The title suggests that the Weak Banks report offers 'supervisory guidance'. In the text it is clarified that the report is not intended to be prescriptive, but merely to identify 'good practice' already in use. Presumably, this statement is included to distinguish the Weak Banks report from other pronouncements of the Basel Committee, such as the Basel Accord, which, despite the fact that they lack the attributes of hard, binding rules of international law, are supposed to necessitate compliance – and may be indirectly enforceable, for example, by means of IFI conditionality.
27. This is the term used most often in the report's main text.
28. Cf. *Century National Merchant Bank and Trust Co. Ltd.* v. *Davies* [1998] AC 628 (PC).
29. This distinction makes sense especially in the context of reorganization with public funds. In this case, legal closure, whereby the old shareholders are divested of their ownership rights, achieves one of the conditions of the proposed policy, that is, that shareholders internalize the costs of failure and be prevented from appropriating the capital injection. It is also important, however, in relation to the liquidation techniques applicable to banks: provided that the law enables the mandatory transfer of liabilities, a bank's estate could be wound up on a wholesale basis, not by merely selling pools of assets, but by transferring ongoing operations (branches, business lines or divisions of the insolvent bank) as a whole, including an appropriate amount of liabilities, as may currently happen in the USA in the case of purchase-and-assumption transactions.
30. Elsewhere, hybrid procedures are in force, requiring the cooperation of regulators and the courts. Generally speaking, bifurcated systems, with

concurrent administrative and court-based measures, generate additional jurisdictional problems and conflicts, for the avoidance of which a precise demarcation of responsibilities and/or appropriate mechanisms for the transfer of banks from one stream of proceedings to the other will be necessary.

31. See Hüpkes (2000).
32. 12 USC §1821o(h)(3).
33. Under the original provisions of the Federal Deposit Insurance Act 1950, the FDIC had almost unconstrained discretion regarding the choice of resolution technique. The available options included liquidation with pay-offs to insured depositors, refinancing or, most notably, purchase-and-assumption transactions, involving the subsidized sale of a problem bank's business as a going concern to another bank. The discretion of the FDIC has been reduced in recent years, as a result of a duty introduced by the Federal Deposit Insurance Corporation Improvement Act 1991 (FDICIA) to choose in each case the technique that is likely to result in lower costs to the FDIC itself (least-cost resolution). Pub.L. 102–242, 105 Stat. 2236 (1991) (12 U.S.C. §1831o). What is significant, however, is the existence of a special system of bank insolvency law, operated by the regulatory authorities, which enjoy extraordinarily wide powers in this respect.
34. FSMA, ss. 359 and 367–8, respectively.
35. FSMA, ss. 362 and 371, respectively.
36. In practice, the views of the FSA are likely to carry significant weight with the insolvency court; however, on at least one occasion the court has declined to follow the supervisors' submissions (BCCI) see note 22 above. It should be noted, however, that the FSA may exercise its regulatory discretion to de-license an institution while its reorganization is pursued under judicial supervision by way of administration proceedings. Thus, the possibility of conflicts between the regulatory process and the insolvency proceedings cannot be excluded.
37. See Christian Gavalda (ed.) (1995) *Les défaillances bancaires: Analyse des modalités de prévention et de traitement des difficultés des établissements de crédit* (Paris: Association d'Economie Financière), pp. 117–36; and Christian Gavalda and Jean Stoufflet (1999) *Droit Bancaire: Institutions – Comptes – Opérations – Services* (4th edn, Paris: Litec), pp. 67–70.
38. See also World Bank (n. 15 above), Principle 9C.
39. In the UK, the basic position remains that the general test of insolvency (that is, inability to pay debts as they fall due) applies to banks as to any other company. In addition, however, the FSA may petition the court for the winding-up of a financial institution on the ground that this is 'fair and equitable' (Insolvency Act, s. 123(1)(g)).
40. The concept of critical undercapitalization is part of the 'prompt corrective action' approach, introduced by FDICIA, to combat forbearance.
41. Of course, if the deposit insurance agency can be subrogated to the claims of insured depositors, this will have considerable implications for the conduct of the insolvency proceedings.
42. The banking authorities and the judiciary may be willing to cooperate, in order to ensure an appropriate result. For example, in the UK, administration orders ought usually to be made only after due consideration and after some time has been given for all parties concerned to make their voices heard. But

English courts have in appropriate cases entertained petitions *in camera*, thus avoiding observance of the pre-administration publicity requirements. Thus, in *Re Chancery Ltd.* [1991] BCC 171 (ChD), in circumstances where the directors of a deposit-taking institution had presented a petition for its placement in administration, the Bank of England (which, at that time, was still the supervisory authority) consented to a hearing at short notice. The judge, being satisfied that no third party was entitled to appoint an administrative receiver, heard the petition immediately *in camera*; the whole proceedings were completed within a few hours. One ground for the decision was that even an interval of a few days would have made it impossible for the directors to perform their duty effectively: the directors would have grave doubts about the propriety of continuing to receive deposits; there would be a serious risk of wrongful trading; and finally, extremely serious difficulties would be caused to the institution's customers. English courts have also been willing to use their residual power of direction to approve reorganization plans, for example, by way of sale of the insolvent institutions business as a whole, thus pre-empting creditors' meetings and preventing actions by creditors against the administrators' solutions under section 27 of the Insolvency Act. Although one might claim that this amounts to playing hard and fast with the normal statutory procedure, it can be necessary for the purpose of making the procedure fit the special needs of banks, without unduly jeopardizing creditor interests.

43. Case C-441/93, *Panagis Pafitis* v. *Trapeza Kentrikis Ellados AE* [1996] ECR I-1347.
44. In the immediate aftermath of the BCCI collapse, the Bank of England's then Governor, Robin Leigh-Pemberton, stated that it was 'the policy of the Bank of England as far as possible to preserve banking institutions in the interests of depositors.... [I]t must be right except in an overwhelming case to try to preserve rather than to try to terminate a banking institution' (Evidence to the Treasury and Civil Service Committee, Fourth Report: 'Banking Supervision and BCCI: International and National Regulation', H.C. (1991–92) 177, p. 104, q. 1). In the Bank's view, in situations where there was commitment to adequate remedial action on the part of an institution, it would be indefensible and contrary to its statutory mandate to terminate it outright if this would result in major losses to depositors. In the BCCI case, however, this approach had disastrous results. Faced with serious irregularities, the Bank of England deferred action, even though the corrective measures pursued by BCCI were neither adequate nor speedy; disregarded indications of misconduct and lack of probity on the part of the institution's management (as opposed to financial problems); and only acted when overwhelming evidence was brought together. See 'Inquiry into the Supervision of the Bank of Credit and Commerce International', H.C. (1991–92) 198 ('Bingham Report'). Given the final outcome, it is little wonder that its supervisory performance came under severe criticisms – possibly opening the way to the eventual transfer of its regulatory functions to the FSA six years later.
45. Pub. L. No. 102–242, 105 stat. 2236 (19 December, 1991).
46. In the UK, the supervisory functions formerly belonging to the Bank of England have been transferred to the FSA, while lender-of-last resort operations remain within the Bank's field of responsibility. This has led to the adoption of a trilateral MOU between the Bank, the FSA and the Treasury,

seeking to ensure their close cooperation with regard to lending of last resort (HM Treasury, Bank of England and FSA, 'Memorandum of Understanding between HM Treasury, the Bank of England and the Financial Services Authority' (28 October 1997)). It remains to be seen whether the new arrangements will make the Bank play a less decisive role in the organization of informal rescue operations than it did in the past. One also wonders whether the FSA will be able assume leadership in this context and what means it will use for this purpose. At the European level too, the separation of banking supervision (which is conducted at national level) from central banking (which, for countries participating in the Eurozone, has been centralized in the ESCB) raises questions both about the legal capacity of central banks to extend emergency liquidity support to ailing banks and about the practical arrangements that should be in place for this purpose. See infra, nn. 103–5 and accompanying text.

47. For instance, under English law, the FSA may act for the purpose of safeguarding the interests of domestic depositors, but the insolvency court will take into account the interests of all creditors, world-wide, trying to balance them against each other. See, for example, *Re Bank of Credit and Commerce International S.A.* [1992] BCC 83; [1992] BCLC 570 (ChD); the case illustrates the complexities facing an insolvency court (or, indeed, the regulators, where they are responsible for liquidating or administering failed banks) in such circumstances. Broadly analogous conflicts of interest between different classes of normal and subordinated creditors plagued the liquidation of Barings; *Re Barings Plc*, 2001 WL 676736 (ChD). Here too, it is doubtful whether a regulator could address the relevant issues more effectively than a court.
48. Cf. Communication of the Commission, 'Financial Services: Building a Framework for Action' (Jan. 1999, paras 34–7), which considers structured cooperation between national supervisory bodies, rather than the creation of new EU-level arrangements, to be sufficient to ensure financial stability and considers 'the adoption in Council of the winding-up and liquidation directives in banking and insurance [to be] a vital component of legal clarity in this area'.
49. See Clarotti (1997).
50. Directive 94/19/EC of the European Parliament and of the Council of 30 May 1994 on deposit guarantee schemes, OJ 1994 L 135/5. The Directive followed an earlier non-binding instrument, Commission Recommendation 87/63/EEC of 22 December 1986 concerning the introduction of deposit guarantee schemes in the Community. The Recommendation's approach, however, was very different from the policies eventually incorporated in the directive, in so far as it envisaged that deposit guarantee schemes should be organized on a host-state basis.
51. Deposit Guarantee Directive, Art. 4(2)–(4). The topping-up rule is included to avoid distortions of competition arising from the different levels of protection enjoyed by the local depositors of domestic and incoming institutions in particular national banking markets. The Deposit Guarantee Directive also included a provisional rule, whereby, if a credit institution had a branch in a host state whose local scheme provided a lower level of coverage than the institution's own home-state scheme, in the event of the institution's failure the branch's depositors could only receive compensation out

of the home-state scheme to the more limited extent determined by the host-state scheme – thus, preventing the 'exportation' of the home-state scheme's superior level of coverage ('no export' rule) (Art. 4(1)). This rule has now lapsed.

52. Recognition of the unavailability of deposits can take the form either of an administrative determination of the national supervisory authority, which the latter is required to make within 21 days from the moment that the inability of the bank to repay deposits became known to it, or of the judicial commencement of insolvency proceedings, if this has occurred earlier on (Deposit Guarantee Directive, Art. 1(3)).
53. Directive 2001/24/EC of the European Parliament and of the Council of 4 April 2001 on the reorganization and winding up of credit institutions, OJ 2001 L 125/15.
54. The national implementation of the Directive's provisions must be completed by 5 May 2004 at the latest (Winding-Up Directive, Art. 34).
55. Council Regulation (EC) No. 1346/2000 of 29 May 2000 on insolvency proceedings, OJ 2000 L 160/1. For detailed commentary, see Moss *et al.* (2002).
56. The Insolvency Regulation, Art. 1(2), excludes from its sphere of application financial institutions, including credit institutions, insurance undertakings, investment firms which provide services involving the holding of funds or securities for third parties, and undertakings for collective investments in transferable securities (UCITSs).
57. The Commission produced its first formal draft in 1986 (Proposal for a Council Directive concerning the reorganization and the winding-up of credit institutions and deposit-guarantee schemes, OJ 1985 C 356/55). A revised text was submitted two years later (Amended proposal for a Council Directive concerning the reorganization and the winding-up of credit institutions and deposit-guarantee schemes, COM(88) 4 final, OJ 1988 C 36/1). Discussions on this draft were discontinued in 1990 and only resumed in 1993, following the collapse of BCCI. Initially, the text included a draft article requiring member states to allow local branches of European credit institutions to join their national deposit insurance schemes on a host-state basis; this was made redundant as a result of the adoption of a separate Deposit Guarantee Directive, which operates, as explained above, on the basis of the home-state principle.
58. The draft European Union Convention on Insolvency Proceedings (commonly referred to as the 'Bankruptcy Convention') was negotiated under Art. 220(4) of the EC Treaty. The final text, which was the result of intermittent preparatory work starting in the 1960s, was opened for signature on 23 November 1995 for a limited period of six months, within which all fifteen member states should have acceded to the Convention. The period lapsed on 23 May 1996, with only the UK still holding out. See Michael Bogdan (1997), 'The EU Bankruptcy Convention', *INSOL International Insolvency Review,* vol. 6, p. 114. The project was revived in 1999 in the form of a Council Regulation. This came into effect two years after its final adoption, on 31 May 2002 in all participating member states (that is, all member states except Denmark, which, under the Maastricht Treaty, is exempted from the effects of legislation adopted under Part IV of the EC Treaty). The Insolvency Regulation replicates with few alterations the text of the

Bankruptcy Convention. On the exact relationship of the provisions of the two instruments, see I. F. Fletcher (2002), 'Historical Overview: The Drafting of the Regulation and its Precursors', in Moss *et al.* (2002), pp. 12–14.

59. On the principles of unity and universality and their rivals, plurality and territoriality, see Fletcher (1999), pp. 10–12.
60. Insolvency Regulation, Art. 3(2) and 16(2). The secondary proceedings only produce effects in relation to assets located in the member state where they have been opened. But within this limited scope they prevail over the main proceedings and are respected across the Community (Art. 17(2)).
61. Insolvency Regulation, Art. 32. In terms of the equal treatment of creditors, the possibility of cross-filings by all creditors and liquidators in all parallel proceedings makes this system a close functional substitute of the 'single entity' approach. In procedural terms, however, but also with regard to the applicable law, the differences from true universalism are very substantial.
62. J. L. Westbrook (1997), 'Universal Participation in Bankruptcies', in Cranston (ed.), *Making Commercial Law.*
63. Universality is respected in principle but numerous exceptions to the applicability of *Lex Concursus* in favour of host-state law significantly reduce its effective scope of operation; see infra, nn. 74–6 and accompanying text. On differences in the European treatment of general corporate insolvency in comparison to bank insolvency, see C. Chance's brochure, 'Risk, Default and the European Bankruptcy Convention and Winding-Up Directive' (March 1998), pp. 17–18; and D. Turing, 'The European Convention on Insolvency Proceedings' (1996) *Butterworths Journal of International Banking and Financial Law*, vol. 11, p. 56, p. 59. In addition to the recognition of secondary proceedings, other differences concern the sectoral scope of the respective instruments, their legal form, their territorial applicability and their impact on non-European institutions. In particular, in terms of territorial applicability, the Insolvency Regulation is a Community measure applicable to the member states, with the exception of Denmark, while the Winding-Up Directive is a text with EEA relevance.
64. Winding-Up Directive, preamble, rec. (6) and (16), and Arts 3(1) and 9(1).
65. Nevertheless, the puzzling provision of Art. 5 of the Winding-Up Directive refers to situations where 'the administrative or judicial authorities of the host Member State deem it necessary to implement within their territory one or more reorganisation measures'. In these circumstances, they must inform accordingly the supervisory authority of the home member state (not the authorities responsible for the opening of insolvency proceedings, if different). In view of the Directive's insistence on single proceedings, it is not evident what form the host-state authorities' determination should take (since it could not amount to the opening of secondary proceedings). The reference to measures 'within the territory' of the host state is also problematical, since Art. 3(2) makes clear that the reorganization measures adopted by the authorities of the home state are 'fully effective... throughout the Community'.
66. Winding-Up Directive, preamble, rec. (23)–(30), and Arts 20–32. Cf. Insolvency Regulation, Arts 5–15.
67. To be exact, there are four, not just two, separate regimes in operation in relation to cross-border insolvencies. The Insolvency Regulation excludes all

financial institutions, but the latter are treated in three different ways: credit institutions are covered by the Winding-Up Directive; insurance undertakings are subject to the provisions of Directive 2001/17/EC of the European Parliament and of the Council of 19 March 2001 on the reorganization and winding-up of insurance undertakings (the Insurance Insolvency Directive); and there is simply no European law on the insolvency of investment firms or UCITS, which must, accordingly, be decided in accordance with national private international law.

68. In contrast, the norms affecting financial institutions' conduct of business, contractual transactions and relationships with clients are largely based on the territorialist (host-state) principle.
69. Second Council Directive 89/646/EEC of 15 December 1989 on the coordination of laws, regulations and administrative provisions relating to the taking up and pursuit of the business of credit institutions and amending Directive 77/780/EEC (the Second Banking Directive, now replaced by Directive 2000/12/EC); Council Directive 93/22/EEC of 10 May 1993 on investment services in the securities field (the Investment Services Directive).
70. Now consolidated in Directive 2000/12/EC of the European Parliament and of the Council of 20 March 2000 relating to the taking up and pursuit of the business of credit institutions, OJ 2000 L 126/1.
71. Deposit Guarantee Directive. See the discussion at the beginning of this section.
72. Recognition means that the measures produce the same effects in any other member state as in the state where they were opened, without need for further formalities. In contrast to the Insolvency Regulation, Art. 26, the mutual recognition of bank reorganization or winding-up proceedings under the Winding-Up Directive is not subject to a public policy exception.
73. That is, collective proceedings aimed at 'realising assets under the supervision of [administrative or judicial] authorities'; Winding-Up Directive, Art. 2, ninth indent.
74. Winding-Up Directive, Arts 10. Cf. Insolvency Regulation, Art. 4.
75. Winding-Up Directive, preamble, rec. (23)–(30), and Arts 20–32. Cf. Insolvency Regulation, Arts 5–15.
76. Without harmonization, a more radical alternative to the full recognition of universal winding-up proceedings based on home-state national law would involve the creation of 'accounting sub-estates', whereby assets realized by the single liquidator in the context of a bank's pan-European winding-up would be attributed to the member state where they are located and distributed according to that state's order of priorities. The Directive's drafters preferred to retain the order of priorities of the home state. Nonetheless, they tried to ensure that the application of *lex concursus* does not render invalid or ineffectual contractual rights and security interests acquired under the law of another member state.
77. Directive 98/26/EC of the European Parliament and of the Council of 19 May 1998 on settlement finality in payment and securities settlement systems, OJ 1998 L 166/45.
78. Settlement Finality Directive, preamble, rec. (1)–(2) and (9). The Directive is intended to give effect to certain recommendations in the Lamfalussy Report.
79. Directive 2002/47/EC of the European Parliament and of the Council of 6 June 2002 on Financial Collateral Arrangements. Member states must implement the instrument by 27 December 2003 at the latest.

80. Even under current insolvency laws, the insolvency of collateral takers is unlikely to affect their security interests, since these involve rights, not liabilities, of the estate.
81. Treaty establishing the European Community, Part Three, Community policies, Title VI, Common rules on competition, taxation and approximation of laws, Chapter 1, Rules on competition, Section 2, Aids granted by States (Arts 87–89 [ex Arts 92–94]).
82. EC Commission, *Eighteenth Report on Competition Policy* (1989), p. 150, para. 169.
83. EC Treaty, Art. 87(3)(b) [ex Art. 92(3)(b)].
84. EC Treaty, Art. 88(3) [ex Art. 93(3)].
85. See AG Lenz in Case 234/84, *Belgium v. Commission*, [1986] ECR 2263, p. 2275. Equivalent expressions used in the practice of the Commission are, for example, 'common European interest', 'the Community's interest', or 'the interest of the Community as a whole'.
86. EC Commission, *Twelfth Report on Competition Policy* (1983), pp. 110–11, para. 160.
87. European Commission, Community Guidelines on State Aid for Rescuing and Restructuring Firms in Difficulty (1999/C 288/02), OJ 1999 C 288/2, para. 11 (definition originally contained in document 94/C 368/05, OJ 1994 C 368/12, para. 2.1).
88. C. D. Ehlermann (1995), 'State Aid Control in the European Union: Success or Failure?', *Fordham International Law Journal*, vol. 18, 1212–29.
89. Case C-301/87, *Boussac* [1990] ECR I-307, p. 336.
90. Case C-303/88, *ENI-Lanerossi* [1991] ECR I-1433, p. 1480.
91. This description is based on the 1994 Community Guidelines on State Aid for Rescuing and Restructuring Firms in Difficulty (94/C 368/05), OJ 1994 C 368/12, para. 2.1. See now the 1999 guidelines, OJ 1999 C 288/2, para. 10.
92. Case C-86/89, *Italy v. Commission Aid for use of grape must* [1990] ECR I-3891, p. 3909.
93. Case T-459/93, *Siemens v. Commission* [1995] ECR II-1675, p. 1696.
94. As no 93, pp. 1696–7.
95. Commission Decision 88/174 concerning aid which Baden-Wurttemberg had provided to BUG-Alutechnik GmbH, OJ 1988 L 79/29.
96. Case 172/80, *Gerhard Züchner* v. *Bayerische Vereinsbank A.G.* [1981] ECR 2021
97. At the end of 1993, Crédit Lyonnais was the largest European bank in terms of total balance sheet. See European Commission, *XXVth Report on Competition Policy, 1995* (1996), COM(96)126 final, p. 84, para. 197.
98. Commission Decision 95/547/EC of 26 July 1995 giving conditional approval to the aid granted by France to the bank Crédit Lyonnais, OJ 1995 L 308/92.
99. However, the real stringency of the conditions should be doubted. Indeed, subsequent to its original decision, the Commission approved a supplementary rescue package, involving so-called 'strictly interim protective measures', amounting to an additional FFr 3.9 billion. See Commission Decision 98/490/EC of 20 May 1998 concerning aid granted by France to the Crédit Lyonnais group, OJ 1998 L 221/28.
100. The cases included the granting of aid to Société Marseillaise de Crédit, Société de Banque Occidentale, Banco di Napoli, and, most notably, Westdeutsche Landesbank.

101. See, for example, Commission Decision 2000/392/EC of 8 July 1999 on a measure implemented by the Federal Republic of Germany for Westdeutsche Landesbank-Girozentrale (WestLB), OJ 2000 L 150/1. In Case C-209/00, *Commission* v. *Germany*, [2002] ECR I-11695, the ECJ declared that, by failing to implement promptly Decision 2000/392/EC, Germany was in violation of its Treaty obligations. Subsequently, however, the CFI annulled Decision 2000/392/EC on grounds of insufficient reasons. Joined Cases T-228/99 and T-233/99, *Westdeutsche Landesbank Girozentrale v. Commission*, [2003] ECR __, Court of First Instance, decision of 6 March 2003.
102. A non-binding declaration, allowing the continuation of this practice in so far as it affects the regional role of Landesbanken and, especially, their function as municipal savings banks, but not covering their international business, was adopted at the Amsterdam EU summit in June 1997. The German guarantees have now received conditional approval by the Commission (Aid No. E 10/2000, '*Anstaltslast* and *Gewährträgerhaftung* – State guarantees for public credit institutions in Germany', Commission Decision of 8 May 2001, SG(2001) D/2888482, OJ 2002 C 146/6; and Commission Decision of 27 March 2002, C(2002) 1286, OJ 2002 C 150/7).
103. Statute of the ECB and the ESCB, Art. 18. See Hadjiemmanuil (1996), pp. 142–3; C. Hadjiemmanuil, 'European Monetary Union, the European System of Central Banks, and Banking Supervision: A Neglected Aspect of the Maastricht Treaty', (1997) 5 *Tulane Journal of International and Comparative Law* 105; Tommaso Padoa-Schioppa, 'EMU and Banking Supervision', lecture at the Financial Markets Group, London School of Economics (24 February 1999), <http://www.ecb.int/key/sp990224.htm>, paras 21–31.
104. Statute of the ESCB, Art. 18.1, second indent.
105. Schoenmaker (1997) p. 429. In his opinion pp. 431–5, if the ECB were to devise rules or guidelines for emergency assistance, these might include collateral requirements for lending-of-last-resort operations and specification of eligible types of collateral, subject to overriding provisions for cases where the provision of liquidity appears necessary despite the absence of eligible collateral; clear allocation of responsibilities for the decision to provide or withhold support to each institution, possibly on the basis of home central bank responsibility; and methods for the coordination of the decisions and for taking into account the broader, supra-national implications of action or inaction. As the national central banks may be overzealous in assisting their domestic banking system, even when there is no direct systemic impact, Schoenmaker discusses the possibility of giving a power of veto to the ECB, although he accepts that, to the extent that the potential costs of the operations are borne by the lending national central bank only, a degree of rivalry between the national central banks is acceptable. However, the rescue of clearly insolvent banks would constitute a competitive distortion and should not be permitted.

Appendix 1 The Proposed Approach to Bank Insolvency Legislation

(Appendix 1 comprises chapters 8 and 9 of Mayes, Halme and Liuksila (2001).)

8 Robust Exit Policies to Underpin Market Discipline

Two main issues relate to the appropriate handling of problems and crises. The first relates to the incentives for banks to avoid getting into difficulties in the first place. The second relates to the authorities in running a system where such difficulties can be handled swiftly and smoothly without damaging the credibility of the financial system as a whole. However well run the banks and however vigilant the authorities, problems will still occur, as banking involves taking risks. Even with well-managed risks and good information about borrowers one can be unlucky. Financial accidents will occur, but their size and incidence can be reduced by robust exit policies. There is, indeed, a distinction between those general measures aimed at preventing bank failure in the first place, and the exit policies that address the problem of preventing further losses in the event of default or failure on the part of a bank. A role for government is warranted in minimising the costs to society and organising the means for a fair distribution of the loss.

The key incentive in setting out an exit policy in advance is that banks will run themselves in the knowledge of what will happen when they get into difficulty. The authorities face a classic time-consistency problem. To have a system that provides credible incentives for banks to avoid getting into difficulty the authorities need to precommit themselves to be very tough with any bank that encounters problems. However, should a bank get into difficulty, despite these threats, then there may very well be a smaller immediate cost to society from leniency in that specific case. A workout or bailout may be less costly than closure, taking that case on its own. In these circumstances the authorities feel they gain by reneging on their commitment. However, everybody knows that this temptation will exist, with the authorities ignoring the additional cost of encouraging other banks to run greater risks. Hence if the rules set in advance do not prevent the authorities from exercising leniency in the interest of systemic costs, the banks will be inclined to take more risks and hence generate potentially much bigger costs for society. The net benefit then disappears and society is not getting the more prudent behaviour it is seeking.

The system can never be completely credible because the government has the power to change the rules in the future. Nevertheless, making action compulsory and not discretionary for the banking supervisors and giving them the independence from political concerns to exercise it will increase believability. [...]

8.1 The need for efficient bank exit

In the current chapter we begin by exploring the need for exit policies to underpin market discipline. Removing unsuccessful banks from national banking systems requires treating banks differently from nonbank firms. Indeed, modern banking is not a free profession, but a highly regulated industry, which shares a range of public benefits and burdens.[1] There are many characteristics that make banks 'unique' but the key facets that underlie the changes in exit policies to complement market discipline, we recommend are:

- Any individual bank's financial condition is difficult to monitor.
- Though markets drive nonprofitable firms out, markets do not, for various institutional reasons, drive out weak banks in the same manner.
- Without adequate information, the failure of one bank can lead depositors to withdraw their funds from other banks as well (contagion), and may cause a run on a country similar to a bank run as investors, expecting other investors to sell off, cause a rapid and large scale sell off of assets (currency).
- Bank regulators supervise banks solely in the public interest, and, therefore, are called upon to withdraw authorisations to protect public confidence in the banking system as a whole, on occasion subordinating the rights of individual depositors and creditors of individual institutions to considerations of public policy.
- Historically, preventing a bank's failure and depositor losses by allowing it to continue operating when insolvent, encouraged excessive risk taking by that bank and other banks resulting in still larger losses down the line, which were ultimately paid for by the public treasury (taxpayers).
- Discouraging bank runs by guaranteeing all creditors of deposit-taking institutions has eliminated important market incentives for owners and uninsured creditors to monitor bank soundness, thus placing an unrealistic responsibility on regulators and supervisors, and, ultimately, on the taxpayer.
- The best way to preserve and enhance market discipline, while protecting the confidence of depositors on the soundness of banks, is for the regulators and supervisors to intervene early, while the problem bank still has sufficient assets to cover deposits, and to do so with such speed that depositors' access to funds is not seriously interrupted.

The characteristic strength of a bank should be an ability to manage risk. However, instead of reducing adverse selection and moral hazard in financial markets, a bank may easily become the problem itself. Usually, those firms that systematically act impulsively or underestimate the risks of investment are quickly replaced by those that calculate risks better. This kind of exit is less likely to occur with banks.

The owners and managers of low net worth and insolvent banks have a financial incentive to take excessive risks in the hope of restoring solvency (if they lose, their depositors, deposit insurance and/or the taxpayer bears the cost) (Kupiec and O'Brien, 1995). Typically, the outcome of excessively risky schemes is a growing net cumulative loss. This diverts deposits from other banks, which distorts the allocation of financial resources. Loss of confidence means shrinking the size and contribution of the banking sector in the overall economy.

If insolvent banks do not leave the industry there is a danger that other banks will take greater risks too, in order to be able to offer competitive rates to high quality customers. Spreads between deposit and lending rates will be greater than necessary and inefficient intermediation may slow the pace of economic growth. Ultimately bank insolvencies can create large fiscal costs in rescuing a range of institutions and may trigger capital flight. Furthermore, as national financial markets integrate, financial weaknesses in one country can more readily spill over to another.

8.2 Capital adequacy and market discipline

It is the vast mass of private decisions that is banking, and not the workings of the official apparatus that is engaged in a continuous review of private decisions under administrative and judicial systems of remedies and sanctions, and in continuous revision of the terms and conditions under which similar decisions will be made in the future. Generally, therefore, operating in the shadow of law and policy, it is for banks alone to work out their problems of capitalisation with other members of the public comprising their shareholders, borrowers and lenders, as well as any other third parties.

The maintenance of adequate bank capitalisation to meet the needs of business, market confidence and regulators is a continuous process of market based allocation of resources. It is thus a form of 'endogenous governance'. Market based allocation of resources presupposes competitive pricing by the market of the availability of legal capital (common or preferred stock), and of capital to meet regulatory requirements.[2] A bank's franchise is a tradable (and perishable) good. A bank's position, business policies, and prospects affect its value as a target for possible merger and acquisition by other banks.

In the event of a shortfall, regulatory capital requirements work like minimum (legal) capital requirements in that they require increased contributions from equity holders. Regulatory capital requirements also modify rankings among creditors, by shifting risks and costs to the holders of subordinated debt.[3] The depositor preference of the kind prevailing in the United States would be another way to reduce risks and costs of insolvency for depositors. Subordination occurs where creditors otherwise would rank equally. This axiomatically reduces risks and costs of insolvency to those ranking higher. Subordination, therefore, sharpens the incentives in the capital market compared to those for depositors.

Where banks capitalise themselves through the market, the market can drive a bank into inadequate capitalisation, providing a clear signal to the authorities of market perceptions regarding the condition of that bank. Where the market fails to provide a solution to the bank's problem it becomes an official concern because the impending outcome may have significant social and systemic risks and costs.

This raises the issue of the appropriate role for intervention by government, or by the administrative and judicial authorities (an exogenous process of governance), and of the form such intervention should take. Here we challenge the doctrine of constructive ambiguity. These issues cannot be resolved during a crisis but must be settled well beforehand.

8.2.1 Pricing of capital

In the foregoing discussion we have emphasised that for market discipline to be fully credible banks must expect that if they get into difficulties and need recapitalising, they will not be bailed out. The penalties will be progressive depending upon the scale of the problem. Under such circumstances, if the problem is limited, the banks in difficulty will either have to try to raise capital on the market, presumably at higher cost, as the problems will harm their credit rating, or through an injection of equity. Again the equity injection is likely to entail some costs, not just because it may dilute the position of the existing shareholders if they do not provide it but because the new shareholders may very well insist on management changes as a condition for providing the funds. In the case of a resort to capital markets, existing shareholders are also likely to insist on management changes. If the problem is more severe then so will be the resulting ownership change, leading to merger or takeover. Ultimately, the problem may be so bad that there are no willing providers of the necessary capital and the bank will have to be liquidated.

If the market system works well then the role of the authorities will be limited. They will need to ensure that the process is conducted under a set of rules that appear fair and they will need to be satisfied that the new capital and ownership structure complies with the rules for the registration of banks. The key issue here is likely to be speed. Banks in difficulty cannot continue trading long, as they will be faced with a run. Any protracted decision-making by the authorities will risk turning a resolvable difficulty into a crisis. The rules to be applied in these circumstances therefore need to be simple, clear and well known in advance by the market participants. In practice, this reduces the list of options quite sharply. New owners and managers need to be already acceptable to the authorities. New ownership structures need to be very transparent and the new capital needs to be clearly of adequate quality so there is no question about the viability of the new arrangements.

However, in a properly functioning market system, many banking problems are resolved well before a bank gets into real danger of failing to comply with regulatory capital requirements or exposure limits. If profitability and returns to shareholders begin to lag behind the banking sector as a whole then this will start to be reflected in the share price and the bank will become of increasing interest as a takeover candidate. At the same time, the bank itself will be looking for ways of restructuring in a manner that will be more attractive to the existing management. Action is therefore likely well before there is any need to involve the authorities. It is (almost by definition) only large shocks that are likely to cause unexpected problems for what appear to be sound banks. The exception will be problems that the management has succeeded in shielding from the information disclosed, particularly in the case of fraud.

If the market is not transparent, say, because the bank is privately owned, or state-owned or the market thin, then both the signals and the incentives may be weaker and difficulties may well become larger before the bank or its owners may feel obliged to act on them. As we have argued earlier, the authorities will wish to try to ensure that the opportunity for these incentives to be muted is as limited as possible. One such possibility was the requirement suggested by Calomiris (1999) that all banks should have to have a substantial amount of marketed subordinated debt so that the chance of signals coming through was greater and that there should be more real penalties for poor performance. Even so, private, savings, co-operative, government and 'post-office' banks are likely to face rather weaker pressures than traditional joint stock banks.

However effective the functioning of the market and however assiduous the authorities have been in trying to ensure efficiency by demanding substantial disclosure of information, deep markets and good assessments of both idiosyncratic and systemic risks, ultimately the authorities will face problems where they could or should act. Where that dividing line falls is open to debate. Some authorities fear that the market system may not operate well when a financial market participant is in difficulty and that they should at least act as a marriage broker, helping the parties get together and work out a quick solution involving only private funds. This was certainly the case with the intervention of the Federal Reserve in the case of Long Term Capital Management (LTCM) in the United States in 1999. It is more difficult to justify intervention if the 'market failure' would not result in any systemic problems. In the case of LTCM there were two main issues. On the one hand, a failure that perhaps could have led to LTCM filing for protection under Chapter 11 of the US Bankruptcy Code, would have had serious consequences because of the extent of the exposures. On the other the parties involved had both the resources and the self-interest to resolve the problem out of court provided that each of them could be sure that the others would provide their fair share of the total cost.

This latter is a classic prisoners' dilemma. If some partners can achieve lower costs by early exit (at the expense of the others), then all of them will opt for that outcome and incur higher costs than if the problem were resolved with all taking shares in the cost. Here the regulators and supervisors can play a role in ensuring both lower social costs and convincing the partners that all will participate. Unfortunately it is likely to be a judgement call for the authorities whether the market will 'work' well in any particular instance. They do not have the option of waiting to see whether the specific case works out, because, if it does not then it will be too late and distress will be turned into failure. Some authorities will be more predisposed to act than others, often depending upon how well the 'club' of bankers (if any) works. Of course, the more that market participants expect the authorities to take the lead then the less likely it is that the market will 'work' or a completely private sector solution emerge unaided.

We are predisposed towards the less interventionist end of the spectrum, primarily for a second reason, which is that the greater the active role of the public sector the greater is the chance that public funds may be called upon. However, the appropriate structure does depend upon the nature of the explicit obligations that exist. For example, if some deposits are insured the insurer becomes an interested party should there be a risk of bank failure and its having to pay out insured depositors. A capital injection to keep a bank trading might be a lower immediate cost than meeting the requirements to pay out to the depositors but the implications for greater risk-taking by banks in the *expectation* of this bailout still have to be taken into account.

We have not discussed in any detail who among the authorities should be involved in decisions over how to treat distress. Clearly the central bank will have an initial role to play as the ultimate provider of liquidity. It will have a further role if it is the guardian of systemic stability. Secondly the supervisory authority will have a role in validating whether any new proposed arrangements comply with the regulatory framework for operation as a bank – corporate structure, capitalisation, fit and proper persons, etc. However, if at any stage public money could be called upon, say, in case of an assisted merger, then it needs to be the government that can authorise the use of such money that needs to be involved. This could be the insurer, if like the FDIC it is an independent administrative agency and not a mere bank consortium. It could be the Ministry of Finance if the use of public funds is to be more direct.

The traditional argument (Goodhart *et al.*, 1998) is that there should be a clear distinction between supervisors and access to public funds. It is much more difficult when it comes to the judgement about systemic stability. It depends upon the regulations as to whether the central bank can use its own funds, even though it may judge that the appropriate response to ensure systemic stability is a capital injection. There is something to be said for a German style arrangement, where the use of such funds is at arms length and is much more like a form of insurance where more general agreement is required before action can take place. The more arms-length the arrangement then the less that prospective beneficiaries may believe it will be used and hence the greater the incentive to come to other arrangements.

The key step in the process is to try to encourage banks to act early and for difficulties to be resolved before they become serious, particularly before they threaten the system. On the whole market penalties encourage this because the penalty increases with the seriousness of the offence. A fixed penalty, such as loss of job, can encourage a go for broke strategy. If there is a small chance of avoiding the crisis by taking further risks but no greater cost to the risk taker from doing so then the chance of small problems being enlarged is much greater. In the same way, if there is a floor to the system because ultimately it is expected that the public sector will intervene financially then this may encourage an expansion of risks once difficulties set in. This is somewhat different from the standard moral hazard argument, that having any procedures that might imply a bailout, even if it is 'too big to fail', will tend to lead people to take higher risks more generally. The discipline of the market, in ensuring that people first of all start to lose remuneration if the bank under performs and ultimately their jobs, will argue against this even if the organisation can survive in some form. However, once job loss seems likely this progressive threat is largely removed, although re-employment prospects will be affected by the depth of the disaster that the manager has presided over, perhaps continuing the progressivity a little further.

The greater the lack of access to public funds then the more credible the authorities will be in the role of brokering purely private sector deals. If the private sector thinks that public money may be available then there may be a reluctance to incur costs. True, it makes sense for the private sector to let the public sector make the initial capital injection and organise the restructuring of the bank with taxpayers' money and then only step in when the public sector attempts to reprivatise or at least sell its share in the bank. In this way the risks and costs of the transaction are minimised for the private sector. However, public money should be used to fill residual finance gaps only on a last-in-first-out basis.

8.2.2 Forced exit policy

However, the theme of this chapter is not so much whether the public sector should intervene and how but that, given it does wish to act, does it have the necessary instruments or tools to do a good job? More importantly for market incentives to work well these processes must be believable to those who will be affected and include a very real possibility that the effects may be adverse. We argue in following chapters that in the European context, in particular, the national authorities may lack the necessary tools in three respects. There is a danger of them being insufficiently informed to be able to act early, let alone preempt some crises. Secondly, also because of the problem of 'home country control' they may be unable to act to resolve crises in banks that are primarily outside their jurisdiction, despite their systemic consequences. Lastly, even if the bank is totally within their jurisdiction, we argue that governments and administrative authorities lack the necessary powers to be able to resolve difficulties before they reach crisis proportions. The last point will be discussed in this chapter.

Bank regulators and supervisors can reduce moral hazard and adverse selection problems only if legislation lays down a legal basis for a robust exit policy for removing unprofitable banks from the industry, and, even more important, that government proceeds on that authority to take over and restructure institutions that do not have positive net worth. To be effective, this approach does not only require clear and efficient procedures for removing economically insolvent institutions from the industry, but also powers to take over and restructure them. Subject to notable exceptions, the latter powers have been missing in EEA countries.

In particular governments (and even less regulators and supervisors) have no effective legal powers to intervene if a bank becomes critically undercapitalised or its net worth turns negative. What is missing is a delegation of legislative authority to government or its designated agents to take over and restructure undercapitalised or insolvent banks. Findings by regulators and supervisors of a bank's failure to observe a prescribed financial benchmark should trigger the consideration of structural actions, remedies or sanctions. The triggering of such responses should not be dependent on conduct by the bank, which presupposes findings of fault. If another solution cannot be found the administrative authorities can only force it into judicial reorganisation or liquidation by withdrawing its banking licence, resulting in a lengthy administrative or judicial process. Ideally, administrative authorities would like to intervene before all shareholder value had disappeared and while routes to exit could be found that do not result in depositors having to take losses except in the sense of delays in payment due to temporary stays on individual legal actions that would force the insolvent bank to perform financial obligations on a 'first-come-first-served' basis.

8.2.3 Qualified applicability to banks of bankruptcy law qualifies market discipline

Experience in EEA countries shows that bankruptcy and other general insolvency proceedings are inadequate for the task of an expeditious, effective, and economic reorganisation or liquidation of insolvent banks (or of other deployment of their assets) in cases where the authorities are concerned about the wider costs to society or about unwelcome systemic consequences. Even where the authorities have no such concerns about an individual bank, there is the worry that procedures that are costly for those exposed, such as prolonged inability to access funds, may result in a lack of confidence in banking as a form of financial intermediation. Thus the rules themselves can be a systemic cost.

Where taxpayers have bailed out banks, the laws have failed the tests of expedition, efficiency and economy. It would appear that current laws do not wipe out the shareholders of an insolvent bank as a pre-requisite of a bailout by the taxpayer, as would happen if the bank had been liquidated as of the date of intervention. Indeed, the liquidation of an insolvent bank is unlikely in systemic cases. The authorities are likely to continue insolvent banks in legal personality and entity, at the expense of the taxpayer. With a bailout being a probability, there is little prospect of voluntary contributions from an insolvent bank's directors, managers and employees, or shareholders or other owners or indeed from its uninsured creditors, holders of its contingent liabilities, its landlords and so on. The chances that the government will rescue the bank are augmented for four intertwined reasons in EEA countries:

- The inability of government to proceed, without delegation of legislative authority, to seize the insolvent bank (that is, by 'taking' its worthless outstanding shares), in order to keep it open and operating for the time being (irrespective of whether it would be liquidated or reorganised later);
- The inability of the authorities to recapitalise an insolvent bank compulsorily without any approval by a general meeting of shareholders;
- In many EEA countries, banking laws place restrictions on the filing by the bank itself of voluntary petitions for reorganisation or liquidation, as well as on the filing by their depositors and other creditors of involuntary petitions for the opening of judicial insolvency proceedings contrary to the fundamental principles of access to judicial process to vindicate private rights and interests; and
- The availability of state aid for a bank's recapitalisation (at least) in the case of a bank of some size or in systemic cases, both to re-establish the solvency of the beneficiary of taxpayers' money, and even to recapitalise it to the point at which it would meet applicable legal and regulatory capital requirements.

Of course, the exposure of the taxpayer could be reduced, were the applicable law to reduce the insolvent bank's indebtedness to the point at which its assets would meet its liabilities, and to wipe out pre-existing shareholders' (worthless) interests to enable the private acquirers of the newly solvent bank to recapitalise according to applicable capital and solvency benchmarks. As a corollary, based on a hypothetical liquidation valuation of an insolvent bank's assets and liabilities, the law would preserve any liquidation rights and interests that existed as of the day of intervention by the authorities.[4] Ideally, a compulsory asset, debt and equity restructuring serves as a structural condition concurrent with any seizure, bailout or compulsory replenishment of capital the authorities may carry out.

There are powerful reasons to believe that there is a superior way to deploy bank assets than to rely on the opening of judicial proceedings as the only course of action. Generally, government intervention is necessary because courts are likely to fail to obtain individual assent by subject banks themselves, and their owners and creditors, to perform discretionary administrative functions. In law and reality, the court cannot take over and restructure an insolvent bank acting on the account of government, including the sale of equity or assets to new owners (e.g., through an 'assisted' merger). Discretionary powers, including the government's own financial powers to offer compensation to pre-existing owners, cannot be vested in judicial authorities, and, ultimately, in the hands of court-appointed individual accountants or lawyers acting under their supervision. Ideally, courts should be removed from the supervision of insolvent banks that are kept open and operating, and of the supervision of the liquidation of assets and liabilities of closed banks. Courts would be restricted to the performance of essentially judicial functions such as those pertaining to the resolution of disputes or issues involving adversary parties and matters appropriate for judicial determination, including (where required) review of any administrative decisions that affect, modify or annul private rights and obligations in restructuring.

8.3 Operation of capital and solvency requirements

Regulatory capital requirements may impose a higher level of capital adequacy on banks than they would have adopted in the absence of regulation. However, the Basel Committee has been wary of advocating any extreme form of rule-based regulation and supervision of capital requirements, such as the US approach. There regulators and supervisors are mandated to take prompt corrective action as the level of a bank's regulatory capital falls below the prescribed benchmark (2 percent of risk-weighted assets). However, the second pillar of the Basel Committee's new policy outlined in the 1999 Consultative Document, relating to 'supervisory review' is explicit in encouraging early action. Principle 4 reads '*Supervisors should seek to intervene at an early stage to prevent capital falling below prudent levels.*' Thus the Basel Committee recommends action *before* capital adequacy standards are breached.

It is a bit difficult to envisage quite how this might be done beyond exhortation and advice without effectively raising the limits themselves. It would not be easy to introduce a banking equivalent of prosecution for dangerous driving that did not involve substantial discretion for supervisors and rather soft ground for imposing any harsh remedies. Nevertheless it emphasises the point that the particular levels chosen by the Committee do not have any exact intrinsic merit but that lines have to be drawn somewhere. As capital gets lower so the remedies have to be increasingly drastic and the penalties for inadequate response increasingly severe.

The European Commission in its Consultation Document 'Regulatory Capital Requirements for EU Credit Institutions and Investment Firms' (18 November 1999) takes this even further and argues that supervisors should set capital ratios above the minimum for each individual bank based on a set of indicators, as a 'prudent level'. Pre-emptive action could thus be required above 8 percent. However, because banks cannot readily improve their capital position 'overnight', a degree of discretion is inevitable. After all the existence of the capital is to act as a buffer in the event of a shock, so that the shock only results in a problem not failure. It is therefore to be expected that banks will have to be given a reasonable opportunity to recapitalise after a shock but under a tight timetable. In the case of a generalised shock to the system too drastic a reaction would generate a credit crunch.

In the US case there is no authority for temporary deferment of the action in case of a bank that passes the intervention point, particularly if it is insolvent. At that point, a mandatory exit policy triggers the takeover by the authorities, placing the bank in conservatorship or receivership.[5]

A survey of existing law in EEA countries suggests a rather different position exists from that under Federal banking and bankruptcy laws in the US. An insolvent bank that continues payments can remain – practically or legally – immune both from administrative (forced) liquidation proceedings, as from the opening of judicial reorganisation and liquidation proceedings, for at least two institutional reasons. First, banking laws do not mandate regulators or supervisors to suspend or revoke authorisations of inadequately capitalised or even bankrupt banks forthwith. To protect the rights of individual depositors or other creditors they have discretion to defer making (or supporting) petitions for the opening of judicial proceedings by reason of their discretionary powers to pursue public interest over the rights of individual depositors or other creditors in case of systemic concerns. Insolvent banks may therefore remain open and operating. However, regulators have drawn up rules to compel action by banks in these circumstances. (As we argue in Chapter 5, the more transparent the regulator has to be the more difficult it is to do anything other than apply the rules diligently.)

The EEA approach is consistent with the objective of bank deregulation, which suggests the existence of a legislative preference for an enlarged freedom of action for banks to operate subject only to prescribed rules of conduct. As legal rules do not incorporate financial benchmarks directly (other than bankruptcy rules), the observance by banks of regulatory capital requirements is only a condition of continuing authorisation and hence normally a discretionary function performed by regulators and supervisors. By using a case-by-case approach, employing threats of withdrawal of authorisations, supervisors run the risk of micro management of the affairs of individual banks and their customers. In reality, where withdrawal of authorisation is the only remedy, the sanction may be but an empty threat, however intrusive the supervision may be.

In EEA countries, the idea of deregulation was to authorise the banks to carry out their business as financial market participants subject to general banking laws which in themselves are an expression of the stipulated purposes that fall within the public interest, without the banks having to run the risk that the laws themselves would be circumvented for other than prescribed purposes. Since 'deregulated' general banking laws now determine both the permissible range of private decision and the conditions under which the decisions are made (i.e., the sphere of private autonomy of each individual bank), regulation and supervision is significant in shaping the general character and direction of banking industry in EEA countries, as well as the characteristics of individual firms operating as banks within that industry. Legislatures have put strong emphasis on endogenous governance in EAA.

Under the regulatory theory, banks are deemed to be private firms first and foremost, like other private firms that are subject to general law, and to the jurisdiction of general courts. In the sphere of law, banks are treated on a par with nonbank legal entities. For example, as publicly held companies, banks are subject to a common body of European company law, including the permissible national variations of it. Remedies and sanctions that address the non-observance of legal capital requirements address the problem of limited liability of shareholders, as opposed to the regulatory capital requirements, which address the social or systemic risk, and costs of bank failure. For instance, capital increases and decreases require voting in shareholders' meetings: in the case of a publicly held corporation, general corporation law confers the powers of capitalisation directly on shareholders' meetings, and prohibit their delegation to any other corporate organ.[6] Government orders as such cannot increase capital.

Another example of the strong emphasis on private autonomy would have been the applicability of bankruptcy and other general insolvency laws to banks in distress. On paper, insolvency entails at least a loss of authorisation for the bank in question, and probably constitutes a compelling case for regulators and supervisors to turn it over to the protection of independent and impartial courts and tribunals. However, this discrepancy between law and reality is resolved almost invariably by a taxpayer bailout. Market discipline in respect of banks is highly qualified in a number of EEA countries on paper, too. It would appear that restrictive general banking and/or insolvency laws, may preclude – taken as a composite – private actions and petitions in respect of an economically insolvent bank in the following ways:

- Involuntary petitions by individual depositors and other creditors may be impermissible, with the law then reserving the right of initiative for regulators and supervisors.
- Voluntary petitions by banks themselves for the opening of insolvency proceedings (to obtain an automatic stay against actions by individual depositors and other creditors), may be impermissible.
- Privileges of voluntary liquidation to be carried out under the supervision of regulators may be restricted in the public interest.
- Powers of regulators and supervisors to carry out administrative (forced) liquidations of banks may be restricted to apparently solvent banks excluding, by necessary implication, insolvent banks subject to the operation of general insolvency laws.
- Where involuntary petitions by individual depositors and other creditors are permissible, insolvency proceedings are triggered by a default or failure (nonpayment or impending nonpayment), not by contentious net worth estimates.

In the case of banks of some size and in systemic cases, therefore, it is not surprising that banks in distress remain subject to the 'out of court' jurisdiction of regulators and supervisors. It is hard to identify any mandatory exit policies whereby regulators and supervisors relinquish jurisdiction by withdrawing authorisations in the face of an impending bailout. This would carry some assurance that judicial authorities would declare the bank insolvent or appointed a receiver if, in the end, no public money were made available. Mere economic insolvency does not serve as grounds for bankruptcy with the exception of Germany where courts are not permitted to second guess the supervisory authority on the question of observance by banks of a range of prescribed financial benchmarks (including just 'overindebtedness'). Having no authority to carry out takeovers, reorganisations or liquidations by administrative means instead, bank regulators and supervisors may do no more than appeal to government for a political decision.

8.4 Formulation and implementation of exit policy

Existing exit policies are generally predicated on the threat of denial or withdrawal of authorisations, and of the opening of judicial insolvency proceedings, in respect of banks, and not on placing them in public administration while in reorganisation or liquidation.

Traditionally, exit was the policy followed by the authorities in licensing institutions. General banking laws typically express the conditions of granting and withdrawal of authorisations in such a broad manner that they would appear to cover a range of financial benchmarks in that discretionary actions by regulators and supervisors are triggered by threats of capital impairment or insolvency. While withdrawals of authorisations serve as structural actions or sanctions, in themselves such decisions are mere status decisions. Typically, legal consequences such as an eventual takeover, reorganisation or liquidation attach to the subject bank. Of the familiar financial benchmarks, the legal solvency requirement is the only hard one because of its incorporation into bankruptcy and other general insolvency laws.

8.4.1 Binding and enforceable financial benchmarks

There seems to be no particular reason why a range of financial benchmarks could not be made hard by the formulation of appropriate exit rules whose execution would be triggered solely by their non-observance. This can be done in two ways.

- On the condition that the legal rule incorporating the specified benchmark includes precise or objective elements that are stated or defined in such a way that departure from them will be obvious to the subject bank and the authorities, the prescribed legal consequences could attach to subject banks quasi-automatically without the need for the exercise of judgement. Banks would then be assured that they would not be taken by surprise. Such a rule would be harsh like the bankruptcy, based on a debtor's absolute and unconditional obligation to pay debts, which does not treat errors of legal judgement on the side of the debtor as *bona fide* errors. It might not operate in the public interest in all cases, as wider consequences are not considered.
- In addition to precise or objective elements that are stated or defined in such a way that departure from them will be obvious, the rule could require the exercise by government of informed judgement to determine whether the legal consequences of its application would be within public interest. In the light of all the costs and benefits the rule would not so much impose a duty on banks but govern the performance by government of a discretionary (executive) function. If government acted on public interest grounds, therefore, creditors and owners would have maximum assurance that they would be compensated on an appropriate valuation of the bank's assets and liabilities as of the date of takeover (for manifest division and valuation errors, respectively). At worst, the depositors and other creditors would receive what they would have received in liquidation.

There are examples of the latter kinds of rules. In Greece under a special law enacted in 1951 and subsequent banking legislation, administrative authorities retained a power to order a bank to increase capital, and to set aside the legal effect of pre-existing shareholders' pre-emptive rights until 1996 when the law was held contrary to the Second Capital Directive.[7] In Norway, infringement upon legal capital requirements may trigger intervention by the authorities from 1985 when the 1961 law on Commercial Banks was amended to permit government to recapitalise a bank as and when shareholders did not proceed to do so and order it to decrease its capital to ensure the continued operation of the bank.[8] In Sweden from 1998 and as long as the universal deposit guarantee was in effect (it was withdrawn in 1995), government could, as and when regulatory capital fell below 2 percent of risk weighted assets, engage in a compulsory redemption of outstanding shares of a critically undercapitalised bank, or place it under compulsory administration. These techniques triggered the surrender of the outstanding shares of a corporate form bank to government, and the compulsory administration by the government of mutual savings banks.[9]

The opening by courts of bankruptcy and general insolvency proceedings gives rise to a drastic sanction, contingent on the withdrawal by regulators or supervisors of banking authorisations. However, no equivalent is available to governments, regulators and supervisors under the public law of banking. Indeed, in EEA countries, the role of regulators and supervisors is typically limited to withdrawal of authorisations, on the one hand, and to lodging a petition with the competent court to open judicial proceedings in respect of a bank in distress, on the other. Except in a few countries (including Sweden and the United Kingdom), the prescribed procedures preclude petitions by individual depositors and other creditors.

Market-based solutions are meant to substitute for official apparatus (substituting endogenous for exogenous governance), but for them to work banks would have to be completely 'privatised'. Making workouts successful probably entails the lifting of any vestiges of immunity that banks may enjoy from petitions lodged by individual depositors and other creditors. In the case of LTCM, which was cited above, the legal consequences of the failure to carry out the private workout were obvious from judicial practice under Chapter 11 of the US Bankruptcy Code. Nothing stood then between participants and the competent US Bankruptcy Court had LTCM or any individual creditor chosen to proceed. Analogous situations do not obtain in the field of banking in EEA countries, hence, any reliance on the competent court alone would be misplaced.

In contrast to cases of legal insolvency, which give rise to conduct based remedies and sanctions, the court cannot proceed on mere findings of negative net worth. Generally, the non-observance of benchmarks such as regulatory or legal capital requirements, or net worth requirements (economic insolvency), typically triggers no actions, remedies and sanction under general debtor–creditor, corporation, insolvency or other general laws. They may trigger actions by private parties (e.g., by individual shareholders) against directors, auditors or managers of the bank, but typically they do not give rise to conduct-related or structural actions by the authorities against the bank itself. Of course the administrative authorities will have a set of powers to require banks to act and restrict additional risk taking as the capital ratio falls but such powers alone are often not sufficient to prevent the slide into insolvency.

In EEA countries, banks are not subject to harsh breakdown actions in the case of criminal conduct. The law tends to criminalise conduct of members of organs of a corporation rather than the resulting conduct of the corporation itself making it liable for damages. Damages assessed on directors and managers may figure, however, if so determined by the court, as part of its general indebtedness. It is unique to the US law that criminal proceedings can be commenced against an insolvent bank engaged in criminal activity resulting in seizure and forfeiture of assets upsetting expectations about finality of transactions, and removing assets that would otherwise be distributed to creditors.

Therefore, it is probably safe to say that as long as an insolvent bank makes payments and transfers in keeping with its financial obligations, the jurisdiction over the bank is unlikely to shift for any non-observance of capital or maintenance of net worth requirements, to a court which could proceed with its reorganisation or liquidation. EEA banking laws do not mandate any prompt corrective action of regulators or supervisors as the financial condition of a subject bank deteriorates. Generally, insolvent or bankrupt banks have remained immune from legal proceedings as long as they retain their authorisation or licence. More specifically, existing legislation does not appear to lay down any mandatory exit policy of the kind that would place regulators or supervisors under duty to relinquish jurisdiction over subject banks in distress at a prespecified financial benchmark.

Relying on financial benchmarks typically involves highly technical assessments regarding the position of the subject bank. Hence, regulators and supervisors are equipped to deal with the flip side of capital adequacy, which is the pathology of capital inadequacy and negative net worth. Events such as (i) the critical undercapitalisation of a subject bank in terms of regulatory capital requirements; (ii) the incurrence by subject bank of losses of (legal) capital; and (iii) findings of negative net worth, do not in themselves manifest fault on the side of the bank, but, because of the threat they present, justify immediate action and give rise to further inquiries regarding the circumstances of the bank. The point is that financial benchmarks should not be formulated in a conduct-related manner because they may refer to events that are largely beyond the immediate control of a subject bank. For example, events such as critical undercapitalisation or negative net worth may be attributable to market developments, and nothing whatsoever turns upon the conduct of the bank or its directors or managers. Actions that take the form of remedies or sanctions presuppose a pre-existing duty to avoid certain financial results, and can never be applied without further administrative or judicial review to ascertain that there indeed was a failure by a subject bank to comply with an obligation incumbent upon it. In the event of a crisis, conduct-related rules afford no immediate recourse against auditors, directors, managers and employees. Indeed, authorities can never assume that because a person was under a duty to do a thing (or to refrain from doing it), he will be liable for doing (or not doing) it, but must await legal proceedings.

8.4.2 Specification of solvency (net worth) requirement as financial benchmark

It is unfortunate that courts do not test economic insolvency up-front upon the opening of insolvency proceedings in respect of banks, but do so only at the end following the distribution of proceeds of liquidation of assets. Judicial reluctance to carry out an up-front valuation to confirm a finding of fault in payments, in effect shifts the risk of initial valuation of the debtor bank's assets and liabilities, and of any subsequent changes in the value thereof to those holding claims and interests.

Hence, no revealed recovery rate can ever validate findings of legal insolvency to constitute findings of concurrent economic insolvency.[10] Negative net worth and other economic concepts of insolvency are not based on a finding of fault in payment but are predicated on a hypothetical liquidation valuation of subject bank's assets and liabilities. Indeed, as opposed to testing maturities of assets and liabilities (or the debtor's conduct when actually presented with a demand for payment), negative net worth concepts refer to a hypothetical liquidation valuation as of now of a subject bank's assets and liabilities. For example, administrative authorities may use such valuation to withdraw an authorisation. Any concurrent judicial finding of insolvency must come within the bankruptcy law meaning of insolvency, however.

Possible advantages attach to a use of administrative concepts of economic solvency, as opposed to the judicial testing of the nonpayment, or any impending nonpayment, of obligations of which the payment may demanded currently: under traditional jurical, a debtor bank would be insolvent if its available assets did not match liabilities that must be paid forthwith. The implications have been noted by Hadjiemmanuil (1996, p. 271):

> [T]he conception of solvency as an ability to settle immediately all debts currently due which was applied [by the UK court in *Re Goodwin Squires Securities Ltd. (1983)*] is unsatisfactory in the case of banking institutions, whose role as intermediaries depends on maturity transformation, i.e., the transformation of short-term deposit resources into long-term earning assets, whose immediate realisation may be economically or legally impossible. Essentially, banking involves the practical ability to meet repayment demands as they are actually made in normal circumstances, not the theoretical ability to repay the full deposit base of the institution immediately. Accordingly, the legal concept of insolvency should be confined to situations where an institution's net present economic value is negative or where the institution has been unable to repay debts which have been actually called for repayment.

Undoubtedly, an appropriate financial benchmark would cover those 'situations where an institution's net present economic value is negative', and its non-observance by the institution (debtor bank) could be sanctioned by structural actions such as takeover and restructuring or the withdrawal of its authorisation, the release of deposit insurance funds, and so forth. As a result of government having administrative powers, which are equivalent to those available under bankruptcy and other general insolvency laws, banks could be exempted from conduct-related actions, remedies and sanctions under general insolvency laws. The government could take over insolvent banks, as long as it offers compensation and its actions are warranted by purposes that are within the public interest, subject to review by an impartial and independent body (other than government) of requisite administrative actions that affect, modify or annul private rights and obligations.[11]

Notes

1. Benefits include privileges, including authorisation to take deposits from the public (unauthorised deposit taking from the public is a criminal offence), access to the central bank, and deposit insurance. Banking laws may give banks an immunity from bankruptcy petitions by individual depositors and other creditors, and limit competition between banks and nonbanks.
2. The problem of defining capital, net worth and legal insolvency has faced the drafters of laws and regulations world-wide, and the result has been a diversity of formulation. The adoption of differing concepts of insolvency has been largely in response to objectives of policy rather than the search for a single optimal definition. We have therefore opted for some simple generalisable definitions. The *regulatory capital requirements* placed on banks are typically expressed as a prescribed minimum ratio of equity acceptable for regulatory purposes (on the liability side of balance sheet) over the risk-weighted asset side of the balance sheet. This *regulatory equity* is capital (common stock, and preferred stock) that is treated as a liability by accounting convention, together with true liabilities such as certain subordinated debt (as deemed by regulators or supervisors to constitute equity).

   Legal capital requirements on the other hand pertain to requirements expressed as nominal capital, the quantum of which is determined in the light of general corporation laws. National legislation governing publicly-held limited liability companies follows EU capital directives defining legal capital as the sum of the par or accountable value of outstanding shares. Principles governing decreases and increases of capital are uniform within EEA countries. For example, profits cannot be distributed if net assets would thereby decline below the nominal capital plus reserves. Banking directives prescribe five million euros as minimum capital for authorised banks, whether they are publicly-held companies or not.

   Net worth maintenance requirements pertain to the observance of a positive ratio of assets over liabilities. Negative net worth denotes what we term *economic insolvency*, a situation that may give rise to withdrawal of authorisations.

   Legal solvency requirements are triggered by a default or failure in payment (nonpayment or impending nonpayment) on any undisputed debt that is due and payable by debtor bank, without awaiting any other enforcement action, which might take years. Debts, in contradistinction of other liabilities, mean absolute and unconditional obligations of which a default or failure in payment may trigger the opening by the court or tribunal of a compulsory reorganisation, liquidation or other insolvency proceeding.
3. Financial requirements and depositor preferences do combine in operation. For example, Federal banking laws in the US combine regulatory capital requirements with an unlimited preference for deposit liabilities (beyond the standard 100,000 dollars per insured depositor), including liabilities that may be owed to the FDIC as an eventual subrogee to the rights of depositors.
4. If a bank is apparently insolvent, the assets and liabilities of the debtor bank (by legal entity) must be determined by the general principles of property and contract law, the same way such law is applicable to any parties. In case of an

apparently insolvent bank, the principle of valuation is that of a hypothetical liquidation valuation of assets and liabilities.

Hypothetical liquidation valuation implies the application of rules and standards that would come into play in the liquidation of assets and liabilities, including the expenses of liquidation. Hence, the valuation of identified assets must be carried out on a break-up basis (as opposed to going concern basis), attaching market value to assets, and counting liabilities, including contingent liabilities, at net present values. Principles and methods of valuation applied in accounting are not apposite or relevant, and the authorities must proceed on estimates. For example, in order to augment assets, the court may set aside a range of transactions carried out over a prescribed period before the opening of proceedings. Future assets will be wiped out by termination of outstanding contracts by debtor bank, or by its counter parties. Counter parties may settle claims likely under water in respect of liabilities owed to them by negotiation as, in the case of reorganisation or liquidation, such liabilities could be wiped out in any event (including contingent liabilities).

5. Conservatorship may be reversible if supervisors are able to restore the bank to a sound and solvent condition.
6. The judgement of the European Court of Justice (ECJ) of March 12, 1996 in *Panagis Pafitis* v. *Trapetza Kentrikis Ellados, et al.* (C-441/93). In this case the ECJ gave judgement on the reference for a preliminary ruling, holding that an increase in the capital of a bank constituted in the form of a limited liability company by administrative measure was contrary to Article 25 of the Second Capital Directive on companies, which guaranteed each shareholder the right to vote on the issue. It also rejected the subject bank's new board of directors' argument that the applicants' civil action constituted an abuse of rights, declaring: 'the uniform application and full effect of Community law would be undermined if a shareholder relying on Article 25 § 1 of the Second [Capital] Directive were deemed to be abusing his rights merely because he was a minority shareholder of a company subject to reorganisation measures or had benefited from the reorganisation of the company. Since Article 25 § 1 applies without distinction to all shareholders, regardless of the outcome of any reorganisation procedure, to treat an action based on Article 25 § 1 as abusive for such reasons would be tantamount to altering the scope of that provision.'
7. See note 6 above.
8. Finans-og tolldepartementet, Ot. prp. nr. 10 [Proposed Parilamentary Bill no.10], *Om lov om endring I lov 24 mai 1961 nr. 2 om forretningsbanker mv* Chapters 1–5 (1991–1992) (containing the 1991 amendments to articles 5, 11 and 32 of the Law on Commercial Banks (Nor.).
9. Law on Government Support to Banks and Other Credit Institutions, SFS 1993: 765 of June 10.
10. In reorganisation cases, the parties proceed on their subjective assessment of the value of assets and liabilities as they vote on reorganisation plans that distribute losses and allocate entitlements. In liquidation cases, the declaration of insolvency or appointment of receiver sets into motion the liquidation of assets and the distribution of proceeds thereof.
11. Ibid. Additionally, an assessment of whether or not an institution's net present economic value is negative takes into account obligations undertaken by

the institution on its own account as well as any obligations incurred by related entities on their own account for which the institution may be liable, say, by virtue of cross guarantees and head office guarantees (including conventional and statutory guarantees). In a grouping, assets and property held by one legal entity may be available to discharge or meet liabilities, obligations, or losses incurred by other on their own account.

9 A New Approach to Orderly Bank Exit

There are two polar regimes for the enforcement of insolvency law in respect of banks. By comparing and contrasting their salient features, this chapter provides the basis for a new approach that requires the authorities to act early as banks get into difficulty and gives them the powers to do so. This requirement for early action should reduce the chance that taxpayers have to be called upon and sharpen the incentive for bank management themselves to act early to protect their own interests.

At one pole, the US system includes a range of powers for the deposit insurer to handle bank insolvencies and crises. At the other, the system in the EEA countries distributes the responsibility for handling bank insolvencies among the administrative and judicial authorities.[1] In EEA countries, functions of deposit insurers are limited to dispensing cash in the event of default or failure on the part of depository institution. The former is a general insolvency (private) law approach, while the latter is an administrative (public) law approach. The new scheme for bank reorganisation and liquidation, which is set out below, is based on public not private enforcement of the law.

9.1 Administrative and general insolvency law approaches

Bank insolvency laws in EEA countries are a part of general insolvency laws that are predicated on the principle of private autonomy. This presupposes the existence of impartial and independent courts or tribunals that decide upon the merits of each case on the basis of the record as established by the individual parties involved. States are not parties to bank insolvency proceedings. They do not, therefore, intervene as successors to an insolvent bank, or to its assets or liabilities, in insolvency proceedings before courts. (Although they may appear as interested non-parties, through having an exclusive right to file reorganisation or liquidation petitions, as in Germany.) As holders of claims and interests in respect of banks, governments intervene, like private shareholders and creditors, under private law. Private law distributes the losses and allocates the entitlements, according to the material general law (general property, contract and corporation laws), and the insolvency law (classified as civil procedure in some countries). The decision-making by which the process functions is carried out by courts, without review by governments.

In the United States, the government charters and terminates banks. Designated administrative agencies take over (seize) problem banks, and then, as successors in interest, liquidate their assets and liabilities for their own account (and not for the account of depositors and other creditors). Their successor liability is limited to the value of the 'receivership estate', a misnomer.[2] Under the prescribed rules of succession, they also succeed to the shareholders' interests, and to the creditors' claims with respect to the bank and its assets. Except to the extent the liabilities are supported by the hypothetical liquidation valuation of the seized bank's assets (including any amount available to the bank under the obligation that the FDIC owes to the insured institution), the law discharges as 'moot' any further liability that the government might have incurred as successor. These powers to carry out seizures of banks and their assets, to terminate the seized banks in legal personality and entity, and to limit successor liability *vis-à-vis* those divested of their property and assets, have not been successfully challenged, for example, on constitutional grounds.[3]

9.2 General insolvency (private) law approach

9.2.1 Constructive ambiguity

In EEA countries the authorities typically do not tie their hands regarding contingent events in the field of banking. Such 'constructive ambiguity' is normally justified on the grounds that, in the face of uncertainty, people will fear the worst and hence do their best to avoid ever getting into difficulty where they have to appeal to the state for help. The state can then afford to offset any systemic risks that may appear, because the event is rare. The drawback is that people appear to have placed exactly the opposite construction on the ambiguity and assumed that in the case of difficulty they will be bailed out. (The evidence suggests this belief is often correct.) In these circumstances ambiguity both increases the risk and the cost to the taxpayer. It is anything but constructive.

In cases of insolvency of banks of some size and in systemic cases where public interest comes into play, governments lack an discernible legal basis to take over, reorganise or liquidate them and are unable to predicate their performance of functions of lender (or investor) of last resort on mandatory restructuring and burden-sharing. As long as the observance by banks of applicable legal or regulatory capital requirements has not been made the absolute legal duty of subject banks, the authorities have no structural actions, remedies or sanctions to apply in the face of non-observance. It follows that situations in which a bank's net worth turns negative, are treated as questions of withdrawal of authorisation, or as fresh political questions.

Indeed, the lack of legal basis for structural actions (non-fault remedies and sanctions) in respect of insolvent banks is a constraint which leaves regulators and supervisors with the one option which is to remove case administration to judicial authorities to be carried out under bankruptcy and general insolvency laws. Almost invariably, however, regulators and supervisors have considered the latter course of action unrealistic and have not closed banks where they are large or there are systemic implications. Bailouts have been the only way to go.

In comparison, Federal banking and bankruptcy laws in the US contain far-reaching powers for bank regulators and supervisors to take over and resolve critically undercapitalised, insolvent banks in 'prompt corrective action' programmes under a comprehensive Federal *lex specialis*. The same is true of New Zealand where the law also contains powers for regulators and supervisors to apply structural sanctions such as the appointment of a statutory manager with powers in excess of a receiver in the event of non-observance of regulatory capital requirements.[4] In EEA countries, in contrast, supervisors and regulators have no like powers to engage in compulsory takeover, restructuring, or liquidation of insolvent banks.

Whether facing a banking crisis or not, government is dependent on the legislature for operating authority and budgets. According to the tripartite doctrine of checks and balances, the government, as well as government institutions and administrative agencies, which wish to set and enforce policy must await the delegation of powers, and operating authority and the authorisation and appropriation of resources from the legislature. Conversely, powers and resources not expressly conferred on government, administrative or judicial authorities, are vested in the legislature so that it can decide whether and to which organs to delegate the powers and transfer resources. Generally, legislatures can delegate any residual (unallocated) legislative powers to the government, except the power for government to review its own or other actions that affect, modify or annul private rights or obligations. Legislature can delegate such powers of review to administrative tribunals or courts.

Without authority for the valuation, takeover and restructuring of insolvent banks, there is no law for administrative authorities to apply as they investigate bank insolvencies in EEA countries. Although insolvency is sufficient grounds for revoking an authorisation forthwith on grounds of the deteriorating financial condition of a subject bank, the finding may not suffice for the court to open insolvency proceedings without further review.

Indeed, dormant legislative powers are exercisable solely by legislature, even in crises. Authorities in those EEA countries where there have been threats of large scale, system wide bank failures had to negotiate with banks in a legal vacuum. This experience shows that threats of withdrawal of authorisations and the opening of judicial insolvency proceedings, worked against governments rather than for them in such negotiations. Unable to substitute valid, legally binding orders for the missing individual assent from creditors and owners, the government could only bail out banks and their owners and creditors. Thus, the latter were treated better than they would have been had the bank in question been liquidated.

As in the United States, legislatures in EEA countries might have bypassed the government and delegated broad powers of administrative action and review in respect of banks to government and specialised administrative agencies (regulatory and supervisory authorities and central banks). In addition, to expedite the process of restructuring, they might have assigned the review of the decision-making to the extent private rights and obligations are affected to independent and impartial administrative tribunals (as opposed to courts). They might have centralised conduct-related and structural remedies and sanctions in government or specialised agencies (e.g., deposit insurers) and equipped them with appropriate financial powers.

9.2.2 Why did the courts remain unused in recent banking crises?

Bank insolvencies tend to fall in the cracks between two jurisdictions: (i) regulators and supervisors wish to retain jurisdiction over insolvent banks under general banking laws; and (ii) banks that are legally insolvent in the bankruptcy law sense fall under general insolvency laws, which prevent the voluntary or administrative (forced) liquidation.

Forbearance by regulators and supervisors can suffice to keep an insolvent bank open and operating. However, they cannot exercise jurisdiction over insolvent banks, as this belongs to the competent court under general insolvency laws. Only judicial authorities can act under general insolvency laws, which permit the carrying out by the court of a bank's reorganisation (without allowing its creditors to succeed to its assets) or the liquidation of its assets and liabilities, as the case may be. However, the courts cannot proceed on their own initiative.

General banking laws, and the bankruptcy and other general insolvency laws, are different legal systems for case administration, with no one to remove insolvent banks from the jurisdiction of regulators and supervisors in case of conflicts of jurisdiction between administrative and judicial authorities. The constructive ambiguity about the identity of the institution that might unlock an insolvent bank's access to the competent court, meant that the courts were available to declare banks insolvent and appoint receivers to administer their assets but this power was not called upon. The failure of legislatures to prescribe mandatory exit points may have turned bank insolvencies into political questions for governments to resolve with the legislature.

9.2.3 Problems of contingent and concurrent jurisdiction

Legislatures everywhere can delegate exit policy powers exclusively, contingently or concurrently. Experience shows that, due to the particular design and drafting of general banking laws, which assigned case administration to courts, general insolvency laws apply only contingently, as their applicability to banks is vested in the discretion and right of initiative of bank regulators and supervisors. Moreover, in case of a bank of some size as well as in systemic cases, the EC Commission has been prepared to approve state aid to keep them out of courts. Where things go badly wrong because of deadlocks caused by conflicts of jurisdiction, legislatures can change the delegation or distribution of powers as and when they see fit. So far, however, legislatures in EEA countries have not made any changes in the distribution or delegation of powers over banks in distress.

Artificial as it may be, the respective formulations of general banking and insolvency laws make a distinction between two legal situations. Bankruptcy and general insolvency laws are triggered in those cases in which insolvency is manifested by fault (nonpayment or impending nonpayment), whereas economic insolvency, which is demonstrated by opinions based on the valuation of assets and liabilities belonging to the debtor, does not constitute a default or failure by the debtor.[5] The distinction is not a mere quibble. In the former case of a bank that is insolvent and, nevertheless, continues trading by selling assets, the bank may well remain open and operating, as any insolvent firm can by discharging its demand liabilities on a first-come-first-served basis.

There are three reasons for this situation. First, general insolvency laws are conduct related, and require a showing of fault on the side of debtor in order to trigger the drastic remedies and sanctions, on the condition that individual depositors, creditors, or the authorities react by petitioning the court. Without such a finding of fault, the court cannot proceed. Second, the judicial reorganisation and liquidation powers do not necessarily involve undercapitalised or economically insolvent banks–that is, banks that have negative net worth. Third, in the event of bank insolvency of a bank of some size, as well as in instances with systemic implications, regulators and supervisors almost invariably want to retain control, and in that process of 'active' forbearance end up imposing enormous risks and costs on the taxpayer.

9.3 Administrative (public) law approach

9.3.1 Government role in case administration

As the apex of the executive branch, government is the appropriate organ to be charged with the formulation and enforcement of exit policies as well as with the performance of functions of lender or investor of last resort, with respect to insolvent banks.

Unless the government has requisite powers to take over, reorganise and liquidate insolvent banks, there can be no robust exit policy. The performance by government of financial functions on an *ad hoc* basis has imposed large losses on the taxpayer for lack of any pre-prescribed burden-sharing. Rules of restructuring should authorise debt and debt service reduction, as well as the wiping out of pre-existing shareholders, as a precedent or concurrent condition for the availability of public financial assistance in bailouts and approval by the EC Commission of state aid.

In their legal nature, structural actions, remedies and sanctions that may be imposed upon the economic insolvency of a bank, encompass actions to be taken by government in the public interest. These include individual measures such as the succession of the government to shareholders' interests in the bank, the taking or divestment by government of the property (assets) of the bank, and the taking or divestment by government of private property in the debt of the bank.

If the requisite actions are not those needed to ensure the succession of depositors and other creditors to the assets of an insolvent bank, they are necessarily expropriatory actions. The latter actions cannot be challenged, however, if carried out for purposes that are in the public interest, based on delegation of legislative authority for the purpose, and with the payment of appropriate compensation. Provided that the amount of compensation is subject to review by independent and impartial administrative or judicial authorities.

Unlike conduct-related remedies and sanctions, robust exit policies should be triggered by financial benchmarks, especially where they operate in conjunction with the performance by government of its functions of lender or investor of last resort.[6] Appropriately, therefore, the process by which the decision-making functions under robust exit policies belongs to government and not to administrative or judicial authorities, except as executing agencies. It is for government to decide upon any compulsory acquisition of private property, rights and interests (or liabilities relating to them) in the first place. For example, if valuation errors are made by regulators and supervisors, resulting in takeover of a bank that appears insolvent but is not (as it turns out), compensation must be paid to the previous owners.

Of course, there are risks and costs involved, in that government has no power to review any decisions that may affect, modify or annul private rights and obligations in individual cases. Imposing a duty on the part of government to compensate for private loss means that any delegation by legislature of robust exit policy powers is tantamount to the delegation of the power of the purse. Administrative and judicial authorities cannot enter on their own account into transactions that commit the State to pay compensation, as determined by the competent court or tribunal. As bailouts are not entitlements belonging to insolvent or bankrupt banks, bailouts can hardly constitute nondiscretionary expenditure under the budget.

The key decision involved in the takeover and restructuring of a bank is the valuation of its assets and liabilities, which tells whether the condition of insolvency is fulfilled. Lawyers always argue that there is no such thing as 'final' insolvency until the termination of a debtor because future 'enrichment' cannot be excluded as long as the debtor continues in legal personality and entity. However, legislature may confer the power to make the determination of insolvency on, say, an executive agency. Based on its determination, government may proceed, keeping in mind that any review of actions taken by government or administrative authorities belongs to independent and impartial administrative tribunals and judicial courts.

Legislatures may attach automatic legal consequences to administrative findings of economic insolvency based on a hypothetical liquidation valuation of a bank's assets and liabilities. Negative net worth, as such, implies no fault, which precludes the application of conduct-related remedies and sanctions. Law need not treat situations of negative net worth as transitory conditions, but may dispose of the case on such a finding. Here, the US courts have solved the problem of finality of determination of insolvency, in two ways under the FDI Act:

(1) owners of banks cannot complain of confiscation because they should have read the law that says that the FDIC would step into their shoes if things go badly wrong (e.g., the bank becomes insolvent);
(2) creditors of banks cannot complain of confiscation because of the 'prudential mootness doctrine'.[7]

Maximum liability of the FDIC in its receivership capacity on creditors' claims is limited to what would have been received in liquidation. Thus, as the court has stated, the FDIC 'will never have any [other] assets with which to satisfy unsecured claims'. Therefore, such a determination establishes the 'impossibility of any effective relief' by courts (ibid., pp. 426–9). All litigation thereafter by owners or creditors typically stops on summary judgment. In other words, the determination of insolvency may become final solely because of the legal consequences that are attached to the finding itself.

Bank insolvency that threatens the stability of financial markets permits the legislature to construct a legal theory for compulsory taking and restructuring by government of insolvent banks, without even having to attach to banks any conduct-related duty to avoid insolvency. Although individual depositors and other creditors of an insolvent bank are not at fault, the law may cancel their claims above the point at which its assets equal its liabilities on hypothetical liquidation valuation. As has been noted above, this 'solvency point' can be determined by way of official hypothetical liquidation valuation.

Indeed, technically, the solvency point determines the loss of creditors in the takeover, reorganisation and liquidation of the subject bank. An appropriate principle and method eliminates any negative net worth by way of debt restructuring. In equity restructuring nothing whatsoever turns upon any conduct of shareholders, which is the same point that applies in debt restructuring, where nothing turns upon conduct of individual depositors or other creditors. In most cases banks become insolvent without, and almost certainly against, the will of shareholders or creditors.

The liability of shareholders for loss of their interests would flow immediately from the threats that insolvency poses. Similarly, the liability of junior creditors would flow immediately from the mootness of their claims on a hypothetical liquidation valuation of the bank's assets and liabilities, as of the day of its takeover. The protection of public interest is a necessary and sufficient ground for this and may serve as an outright legal basis for the takeover and restructuring of an insolvent bank.

Omitting to impose any duty on a bank to avoid insolvency has advantages. We can say directly that a bank, if determined to be insolvent by regulators and supervisors on a hypothetical liquidation valuation of its assets and liabilities, becomes liable for prescribed structural actions, remedies and sanctions by government. Otherwise, the government would have to show breach of duty making the bank liable for insolvency. Instead, the question of liability of government in taking over and restructuring of the bank turns to the conduct of the government. Here the public law of expropriation places at least a general hypothetical duty on the state not willfully to take and convert private property, or to divest ownership of private property, except for appropriate compensation and for purposes that are within public interest.

Under the public law of expropriation, acting in the public interest, government may proceed with a takeover, reorganisation, or liquidation without having to await the commencement of insolvency proceedings by the court. Such structural sanctions can be distinguished in that they serve purposes that are within public interests.

Nothing whatever turns upon any conduct of the owner. All that is needed is that the government has legislative approval, and compensates the divested party on the basis of appropriate valuation by the government of the object (as reviewed by competent courts or tribunals). Delegation by the legislature of authority for the government for this constitutes necessary and sufficient legislative approval.

9.3.2 How might it work

Economic efficiency and depositor confidence suggest that intervention takes place immediately upon the event of 'economic insolvency', in order to maximise the value of the assets of the bank (i.e., minimising losses to all creditors). The opacity of valuation of bank assets means that the decision over what constitutes this idea of economic insolvency can be generated by particular levels of financial indicators. Restoring the depositors' access to funds calls for the distribution of losses at the very beginning of the intervention, through an up-front restructuring of an insolvent bank. The distribution of losses (as of that date) and the allocation of entitlements would be concurrent under a reorganisation plan, listing the restructured creditors' rights and assigning pre-existing shareholders' interests to new owners.

Clearly, a solution to the problem of an up-front distribution of losses is to make the subject bank solvent again. Examples are:

- augmentation of its assets through the usual legal techniques that are there to swell assets of bank debtor in reorganisation or liquidation ('asset restructuring');
- reduction of its debt and debt service to the point at which its liabilities equal its assets ('debt restructuring' or 'haircut reorganisation'), and
- carrying out of a forced acquisition of its outstanding shares that are worthless without compensation (equity restructuring).

Generally, continuing a bank in legal personality and entity, under new ownership and management, is a solution to the problem of closing and liquidating the bank piecemeal. The latter option of closure and liquidation can be only a solution of last resort, rarely a practical option for all but the smallest banks. The re-establishment of solvency is, of course, a prerequisite for continuing a bank as a legal entity for the time being.

The ability of the government to seize an insolvent bank, succeeding to its shareholders' interests or to its assets, would represent a fundamental change in the legal nature of exit policies in many countries. Having an option to transfer the ownership of the bank from its shareholders to government, or to a designated specialised agency, allows the authorities a free hand to dispose of the shares and assets attached to the bank to the greatest advantage (i.e., to maximise their value and to recoup the expenses of the rescue).

Of course, the government incurs an obligation to compensate those divested of their rights and interests, based on a hypothetical liquidation valuation of the subject bank's assets and liabilities as of the date of intervention. Taking by government of title to the subject bank, as well as any divestment by government of any depositors and other creditors of their rights of succession to the bank's assets, is inconsistent with bankruptcy and general insolvency laws, and, thus, requires exemption from the provisions of the bankruptcy and other general insolvency laws, which do not authorise such conversions of ownership in reorganisation or liquidation process.

An asset, debt and equity restructuring is necessary since seized banks would generally be deeply insolvent, making it impossible to sell them at a positive price. If such a restructuring is not carried out up front at the point of takeover, the government may become liable as successor for the losses of the subject bank, which would undo the advantages of the proposed scheme.

In order to pass title to the bank to the eventual new owners (whether through public offering or private placement), the authorities must be able to take title to the bank's outstanding shares. Its shares would be sold to an acquirer that is able and willing to recapitalise the newly solvent bank up to the applicable legal and regulatory requirements. Since banking supervisors have no particular expertise in running or administering banks, the bank will need to be sold (in whole or in part) very quickly in a newly solvent condition.

The designated agency could also dispose of the bank through a sale of the whole bank as an economic entity. This can be done by selling its assets and liabilities. The executing agency may also arrange for a purchase and assumption of a substantial part of the bank and liquidation of the rest. Thus it is necessary for the agency to acquire title on its own account to the bank.

Thus, the bank would remain in public ownership and administration during only a short period from the date of takeover. Takeover would therefore preclude the operation of traditional bankruptcy procedures, which froze the pre-petition claims of depositors and other creditors (by imposing an 'automatic stay'), and subordinated them to post-petition claims that permitted reorganisers and liquidators to operate the bank at the expense of pre-petition creditors.

If financial assistance is needed (whether from the government budget, deposit insurance fund, or reductions in the claims of creditors) to make the sale possible, it would be inappropriate (both in terms of fairness and economic incentives) for the owners of the insolvent bank to benefit from such assistance. Any reliance on the budget as a source of such assistance would also be inappropriate, both in terms of taxpayer acceptance and market discipline. For both these reasons, the insolvent bank, if continued in legal personality and entity, presupposes comprehensive restructuring.

In order to carry out a forced acquisition, the designated agency must be able to determine the hypothetical liquidation value of the subject bank's assets and liabilities in a manner that disposes of the case without any second-guessing by administrative tribunals or judicial courts. The role assigned to the latter would be confined to determining compensation for private parties for manifest valuation errors, without having any power to reverse decisions based on the initial determination of the value of assets and liabilities. Annulment would not be a pre-requisite for compensation awards (if any).

The problem of valuation is heightened in court-conducted corporate reorganisations. No objective figure is available in judicial proceedings under general insolvency laws for the value of the firm that is subject to reorganisation, and such laws consign the determination of the size of the 'reorganisation value' to bargaining and litigation among classes of creditors (including even shareholders). This may take years, usually involves costs of litigation, and almost invariably produces an inefficient capital structure for the reorganised form. There the value of the assets and liabilities of subject firm is revealed at the end of the process as of the date of voting by creditors (and shareholders) of a reorganisation plan.[8] The courts generally approve (confirm) a plan if the prescribed majorities of all classes approve it.

In contrast to judicial reorganisation models under which the reorganisation value of a firm is subject to bargaining and litigation, our proposed scheme presupposes that the reorganisation value is determined, in terms of monetary value, up-front as a subject bank is determined to be economically insolvent. Using the same rankings of claims and interests that apply in judicial process, we can arrive at a division of the cake that is perfectly consistent with participants' entitlements, based on any remaining private property, rights and interests in the subject bank or its assets. Claimants will receive what they would have received had the bank been liquidated as of the date of take over. Conversely, those debt- and equity holders determined to be under water by official valuation would receive nothing.

The takeover by government of an insolvent bank is really just a fictional 'forced' sale of the bank to the government at the price prescribed by the government. Somewhat analogously, in judicial reorganisations there is a fictional sale of the debtor company to its creditors, except that the court can provide neither an objective, indisputable figure, nor any other figure, for the value of the assets and liabilities in question. Generally, in judicial reorganisation proceedings there is no official estimate for parties to work on, but each and every creditor (or shareholder) votes on his or her subjective estimates which, due to strategic manipulation, are pitched up by those who rank lower (shareholders, subordinated creditors, general creditors), and down by those who rank higher. Shareholders, whose shares are worthless in case of an insolvent company, even so hope to inflate asset values to support their continuing participation, a flaw of the bargaining model.

Moreover, it is unrealistic to think that judicial reorganisation models would permit a bank to continue trading the same way as nonbanks can continue trading. While suppliers and other creditors of a manufacturer may tolerate debt and debt service reduction and the suspension of repayments while profitable production continues, a bank's business is the taking of deposits repayable in currency, at par and on demand. The vast numbers of depositors and shareholders of a bank of some size would not be interested in bargaining and litigating to keep a bank open and operating. They are unlikely to be able to make bargaining and litigating decisions by arriving at any informed subjective estimates of the bank's reorganisation value. They would protest for having to await access to deposits for long periods of time. The banks' assets would diminish, and its liabilities would increase, and its reorganisation value would probably fall below what its liquidation value would have been had its assets and liabilities been liquidated up-front as of the day of the opening of the proceedings (perhaps, years earlier).

Under our scheme, the process of establishing the value of assets and liabilities of a subject bank and, derivatively, the value of each claim supported by the assets can be completed later, as of the date of takeover. The process is pure arithmetic if the authorities follow the absolute priority principle. The valuation provides a key to the selection of claims and interests for cancellation. In addition to the ratable reduction of liabilities (haircuts), the privilege of cancellation would extend to contingent liabilities and to the selective repudiation of the bank's future liability on a range of possible claims (including repudiation of outstanding labour and rental contracts) as well.

The legal provisions for the seizure of an insolvent bank, its financial restructuring up-front, and its sale to new owners must be carefully designed and drafted to ensure that they are not confiscatory of private property of its owners or creditors. The law must ensure due process in settling claims, in case, for example, the apparently insolvent bank is not, in truth, insolvent, as of the date of intervention. In the event of any under valuation of assets or overvaluation of liabilities, the law could provide that the net profit remaining in the agency's books after administrative expenses could be returned to those divested of their rights or interests.

The requisite legal issues differ from country to country because there is no uniform bank insolvency law. The fact that some countries follow civil law and others follow common law complicates the analysis. The next sections examine these problems and propose an approach that would appear to be legally sound and economically efficient.

9.4 Outline of the new scheme

The objective of the scheme is to provide the legal means for taking an insolvent bank from its owners, financially restructuring it (up front and without significant interruption in the access of depositors to their funds) if needed in order to sell it or its assets to new owners. Such a process would improve the prospect for prompt action by the supervisory authorities, thereby reducing the moral hazard and ultimate cost to the taxpayer of forbearance and bailouts.

Under the new scheme the administrative authorities would remain in control of the legal consequences that licence revocation or other similar intervention bears on the depositors and other creditors of an insolvent bank. Thus, in lieu of simply revoking the licence of an insolvent bank (and, indeed, remaining indifferent to litigational outcomes), the authorities would carry out a seizure and restructuring. Their succession to the ownership of the subject bank would ensure a speedy conversion of the ownership of the bank in reorganisation from pre-existing shareholders to new owners. Alternatively, their succession to the ownership of the assets of the bank would ensure their speedy conversion into cash to satisfy the claims of its depositors or other creditors. The latter option would be always available if the authorities wish to skip finding a new owner, and, hence, proceed to an outright liquidation of assets.

In other words, the seizure of ownership of the bank (as opposed to a seizure of its assets) under the new scheme, implies that the bank continues in legal personality and entity, and does not change its status from a bank to a nonbank. Compare this with the seizure of assets from the insolvent bank, which removes, by the operation of law, the bank's competence to dispose of them. In the latter case, the bank may well survive as a corporation under EEA-type general corporation laws, which may continue its existence, for the time being, in legal personality and entity as an empty legal shell. Under the US banking laws, having been placed in receivership, the insolvent bank cannot continue. Although the government succeeds – by the operation of law – to its shareholders' interests, the mandatory pulling of its charter terminates it in legal personality and entity forthwith. As a result, the US law, unlike the new scheme precludes bank reorganisations.

Moreover, the purpose of a new system is not to underwrite the losses incurred by an insolvent bank. A concurrent asset, debt and equity restructuring of an insolvent bank upon its seizure would limit its indebtedness to what is supported by its assets, on a hypothetical liquidation valuation carried out as of the date of intervention (that is, as if the bank had been liquidated on that date). Such a restructuring, which would be carried out by the operation of law, as of the date of intervention, would re-establish the solvency of the bank. Thus, upon its seizure by the government, the bank's net assets would be zero, limiting the bank's and the government's successor liability (if any) to meeting the post-seizure losses arising during the agency's ownership of the bank. Any successor liability of the State would be limited accordingly.

Unlike the US scheme, the new scheme offers the option of keeping a bank alive (if it is worth more alive than dead), which means continuing it in legal personality and entity. This cures the defect of the FDI Act, which is the categorical requirement that each and every bank must be resolved upon seizure. This would not be a realistic move where the costs and risks of converting an insolvent bank's assets into cash through judicial insolvency proceedings would be exorbitant, especially if the deposit insurance covers only small claims or a fraction of all claims. Outright policy reasons may disqualify buyers, say, to prevent the largest bank from absorbing all others. Normally, a bank's assets are worth much more if sold as a going concern to other banks than if sold piecemeal to nonbanks, where there are few or even no nonbank buyers with both accurate information about the quality of assets and sufficient resources to acquire them. In consequence of its inability to reorganise banks, the FDIC must unnecessarily create 'new' or 'bridge' successor banks (as asset managers) whenever bids come in too low.

The proposed new scheme allows for the exercise by Government of expediency, efficiency and economy in carrying out of the diverse mandate of regulator and lender or investor of last resort in the event of bank insolvency. The scheme seeks to eliminate

(1) the costs and risks that the taxpayer might otherwise incur in the event of bank insolvency;
(2) the moral hazard that always attaches to extending state aid to insolvent banks; and
(3) the undue delay that causes losses of bank assets which typifies negotiations with banks in distress and any of the rather (theoretical) alternative judicial reorganisation and liquidation proceedings.

These objectives can be realised through the following six key features that make the proposed scheme preferable to most existing systems of private or public enforcement:

1. It authorises the government to take over an insolvent bank, as and when the government determines that the bank is economically insolvent or, in other words, has negative net worth. As a bank's financial condition deteriorates compared to the prescribed minimum regulatory capital standards, so it becomes less relevant to value its assets and liabilities on the basis of its continuing as a going concern. The appropriate basis becomes that which would be used in a liquidation.
2. The seized bank would retain its franchise to conduct banking business and may be kept open and operating through the process. By becoming an owner of the bank, the government will have plenary competence to control the bank and to dispose of its interests in the bank. Acting on its own account, it would carry out a merger, sale or other disposition of the bank as a going concern.
3. It is self-financing in the sense that each insolvent bank that comes under the scheme is restructured up-front, as of the date of takeover, through asset, debt and equity restructuring (including the wiping out of the interests of pre-existing shareholders and subordinated debt-holders). In reverse order of priority the claims of subordinated debt-holders and other junior creditors are eliminated up to the point that claims equal the value of the subject bank's assets as determined by the hypothetical liquidation valuation of its assets and liabilities.
4. The remaining depositor and other creditor claims are then fixed and guaranteed by the government. Thus the division of the cake among claimants, follows the 'absolute priority principle', which is pure arithmetic, for the

purposes of the distribution of losses and, conversely for the allocation of guaranteed entitlements. This way the scheme avoids collective proceedings or out of court bargaining among creditors and shareholders. Hence the newly solvent bank can be continued by government in legal personality and entity, ensuring the prompt settlement of claims held by depositors and other creditors to the extent supported by assets.

5. The revaluation of the assets and liabilities of a subject bank eliminates the Government's successor liability through the imposition of the cutoff or 'solvency point' (under (3) above) in respect of all liabilities (including contingent, nonbook and undiscovered liabilities). This is subject to the exception that if the valuation erroneously wipes out debt or equity that turns out to have positive value as of the date of takeover the government must pay compensation to those divested of valuable rights and interests. The residual exposure of the government is limited to solvency support after the date of takeover during the prescribed short period while the subject bank remains in public administration pending disposition.
6. If the newly solvent bank cannot be disposed on terms and conditions acceptable to the government in transaction with a third party able and willing to recapitalise it to meet legal and regulatory capital requirements within the prescribed maximum holding period, its assets and liabilities would have to be liquidated by the government. Here again, government would be acting for its own account, which may involve a gain or loss.

9.5 Conclusions

The preceding sections provide a comparative examination of current national legislation in the United States and in the EEA countries pertaining to (i) the distribution of losses and, conversely, the allocation of remaining entitlements in the reorganisation and liquidation of insolvent banks, and (ii) the administrative and judicial decision-making by which the process functions. The question is whether or not there are overriding or hard legal constraints that prevent the adoption of more expeditious, effective and economic bank insolvency laws than the existing laws. We conclude that the answer is no.

The European Human Rights Convention (EHRC) requires no judicial review of administrative acts that affect, modify or annul civil (or common law) rights and obligations.[9] Indeed, case law under the Convention shows that the requirement can be met by setting up a dispute settlement body inside an administrative agency, or a separate administrative tribunal. The Convention imposes no maximum speed for the conduct of insolvency or like proceedings before a dispute settlement body, on the condition that the body is impartial and independent, and that its decisions are final and binding (i.e., they cannot be reviewed by the government).

It appears that no hard legal constraints prevent the delegation of legislative authority for bank reorganisation and liquidation to government or a specialised agency, although there lingers a perception that the supervision of insolvent banks belongs to courts. No such constraint can be identified in EEA countries. In the US, however, their seizure belongs to an administrative agency that settles, in its capacity as successor to their assets, any claims for its own account under a *lex specialis*. The US Constitution does permit the agency to settle debt disputes by entering conclusive factual and legal findings. The agency is 'no more an adjudicator than an insurance company authorised to disallow any claim not proven to its satisfaction...'[10] By assigning the settlement of claims to an administrative agency and the settlement of disputes thereof to courts, the US banking laws greatly gain in speed and efficiency.

Moreover the chapter is concerned with the principles of hypothetical liquidation valuation of an insolvent bank's assets and liabilities and the relative and absolute priority principles which come into play in the allocation of entitlements during bank reorganisations (e.g., debt and equity instruments). The latter determine the multilateral burden-sharing (if any) between the public treasury (as it may be claiming reimbursement of costs and indemnity for risks), and the shareholders, depositors, and other creditors. We show that current law does not extract mandatory concessions from the latter, or require the assignment of an insolvent bank's future earnings to the public treasury as a prerequisite of a bailout. Asymmetric rules apply to the 'who gets what, how much, and in which order' in the distribution of the proceeds of reorganisation, as opposed to the priority that creditors should have over shareholders in the liquidation of the assets of an insolvent bank.

The chapter is also concerned with the scope and content of the administrative and judicial decision-making by which the process of bank reorganisation and liquidation functions. What is it that the owners and uninsured creditors of an insolvent bank have in the back of their minds as they turn into potential free riders and holdouts? The answer is that they know that bailouts by the government do not generate legal consequences for them except by their own assent (e.g., in collective proceedings). The government cannot (unless it can show intentional wrongdoing) make pre-existing shareholders discharge any of the obligations of the subject bank, or make them meet the losses incurred by it. For example, the EU Commission's approval policy regarding state aid for problem banks does not condition its approvals of infusions of public money on the making of prior concessions by pre-existing shareholders or creditors.[11]

The state aid provisions of the EU Treaty do not preclude permanent legislation that wipes out pre-existing shareholders of insolvent banks, re-establishes the solvency of the bank by debt or debt service reduction, or authorises the State to recapitalise the newly solvent bank. According to the private investor principle, the State may subscribe to share issues on the same basis as any investor.

In conclusion, efficiency, expedition and economy speak for taking insolvent banks out of the supervision of courts and vesting the decision-making by which the process functions in the administrative authorities under a public law *lex specialis*. Appropriate procedures for the seizure, reorganisation or liquidation of insolvent banks could be put in place.

Notes

1. In generalising about the regime in the EEA countries, we are in some cases ignoring the details of the particular, especially for the UK and Ireland, in order to discuss the polar approach. (Here as elsewhere the European Economic Area includes the current membership of the 15 EU countries plus Norway, Iceland and Liechstenstein.)

2. The FDIC is not appointed as conservator or receiver by a court but by the US Comptroller of Currency, or even by itself in certain cases. More appropriately, therefore, the FDIC could be referred to as an administratively appointed receiver (forming an administrative receivership), as opposed to a court-appointed receiver that takes his or her instructions from the court (judicial receivership).
3. There are a number of cases on the point. See *California Housing Securities*, 959 F.2d. The Court in *California Housing Securities* held that the appointment of the U.S. Resolution Trust Corporation as conservator and receiver of *Saratoga Savings and Loan Association* did not violate the Fifth Amendment of the US Constitution that states that 'private property [shall not] be taken for public use without just compensation.' U.S.C.A. Const. Amend. 5; 5 U.S.C.A. § 706(2)(A).
4. These powers include taking on those of a general meeting of the existing shareholders, being able to continue the business of the bank or reforming it into a new recapitalised entity.
5. See chapter 8 for a definition of these terms.
6. As mentioned earlier the financial benchmark that we use in most of the discussion, 'economic insolvency', is only one among several levels of undercapitalisation that could be used to trigger intervention. Its use makes the discussion a little simpler, as shareholder value is effectively zero even without withdrawal of the licence. At higher intervention levels the shareholders will be entitled to some compensation.
7. See McNeily v. US, 839 F. Supp. 426, 429–430 (N.D. Tex 1992). See also, The Federal Insurance Act ('FDI Act'), U.S.C. § 1821(c)(2)(A)(ii).
8. No similar problem exists in the judicial liquidation of the assets of a debtor firm, where an actual sale of the assets of the firm to third parties takes place. The liquidation results in an exchange of the assets for cash, with the receiver starting to pay creditors (and shareholders), according to the relative ranking or priorities assigned by law to their rights and interests, until no money is left, based on the value of assets realised on the date of sale. No bargaining among stakeholders is necessary.
9. Article 6 § 1 of the European Convention on Human Rights, 3 September 1953/18 provides that, in the determination of his civil rights and obligations, everyone is entitled to a fair and public hearing within a reasonable time by an independent and impartial court or tribunal established by law. Accordingly, Article 13 of the First European Banking Directive provides that member states shall ensure that decisions taken in respect of a credit institution in pursuance to laws, regulations and administrative provisions adopted in accordance with the Directive may be subject to the right to apply to the courts, and that the same shall apply where no decision is taken within six months of its submission in respect of an application for authorisation which contains all the information required under the provisions in force.
10. *Morrison-Knudsen Co.* v. *CHG Infl Inc.*, 811 F.2d 1209 (9th Cir. 1987). The holding in *Knudsen* was reviewed in *Coit*, which confirmed that administrative agencies cannot be empowered to resolve disputes with the force of law. They can only notify the claimants of their claims and wait for a reasonable time before filing suit while the agency decided whether to pay, settle or

disallow the claim. *Coit Indep. Joint Venture* v. *Federal Savings and Loan Ins. Corp.*, 489 US 561, 109 S.Ct. 1361 (1989).

11. In contrast, the FDIC's approval authority for 'open-bank' financial assistance is subject to conditions *inter alia* regarding concessions by bank shareholders and creditors. Section 13(c) of the FDI Act (12 U.S.C. § 1823(c)), governs the authority of the FDIC to provide open-bank assistance (i) to prevent the default of insured institutions, or closed bank assistance to facilitate the acquisition of insured institutions that are in danger of default by another institution or company; or (ii) if severe financial conditions exist that threaten the stability of a significant number of insured institutions or of insured institutions possessing significant financial resources, to lessen the risk to the FDIC posed by such insured institutions under such threat of instability. It provides that FDIC assistance must be provided by the least-costly resolution method and that the FDIC may not acquire voting or common stock; otherwise, Section 13(c) does not limit FDIC discretion to structure transactions. It also contains certain additional requirements for open-bank assistance added by the Federal Deposit Insurance Corporation Improvement Act of 1991 (FDICIA).

    As a matter of policy, the FDIC's standards for 'open bank' assistance were revised on December 8, 1992 to accord with the statutory requirements added to Section 13(c) by FDICIA. See FDIC Statement of Policy on Assistance to Operating Insured Depository Institutions, 57 FR 60203 (December 18, 1992). Under those standards, such an assistance proposal was evaluated pursuant to a number of primarily financial criteria such as:

    (1) The cost of the proposal to the FDIC must be determined to be the least-costly alternative available. In order to ensure that a proposal for open assistance is the least-costly alternative, the FDIC, in many cases, also seek proposals for resolving the institution on a closed basis.
    (2) The amount of the assistance and the new capital injected from outside must provide for a reasonable assurance of the future viability of the institution.
    (3) The FDIC will consider on a case-by-case basis whether the proposal shall provide the FDIC with an equity or other financial interest in the resulting institution.
    (4) Preexisting shareholders and debtors of the assisted insured institution shall make substantial concessions. In general, any remaining ownership interest of preexisting shareholders shall be subordinate to the FDIC's right to receive reimbursement for any assistance provided.

The above-referenced FDIC 'open-bank' policy was allowed to lapse in 1998, pending further review. A proposed revision of this policy was submitted for comments in 1996, but has not been subsequently adopted.

Appendix 2 The Basel Committee Guidance on Weak Banks

Appendix 2 reproduces an excerpt from Basel Committee on Banking Supervision: *Supervisory Guidance on Dealing with Weak Banks*

6 Resolution issues and exit

133. This section sets out general principles for dealing with banks that encounter major difficulties, the various resolution techniques when failure is imminent, and closure of the bank in event of failure. Resolution techniques require specialised and legal skills. Supervisors that do not possess the required skills may need to hire experts to assist them.

6.1 Guiding principles for banks resolution policy

134. The principles for dealing with weak banks, as set out in section 2.2, are elaborated upon below to guide supervisors in bank resolution policy and the choice of the appropriate technique. It is recognised that, in some circumstances, not all of these principles can be achieved simultaneously:

Bank failures are a part of risk-taking in a competitive environment. Supervision cannot, and should not, provide an absolute assurance that banks will not fail. The objectives of protecting the financial system and the interests of depositors are not incompatible with individual bank failures. The occasional bank exit may help provide the right incentive balance. To deal with these, there should be well-defined criteria for determining when a bank requires intervention or closure (legal or economic). When such criteria are met, the supervisor should take action promptly.

Private sector solutions are best. A private sector solution – one that does not impose a cost on taxpayers and introduces the least distortions in the banking sector – is in line with the least cost criterion. This usually entails the takeover by a healthy institution that finds ownership of the bank attractive. The supervisor has a role to play, if necessary, to encourage a private sector solution. Public funds are only for exceptional circumstances.

Expedient [sic] resolution process. Weak banks should be rehabilitated or resolved quickly and banking assets from failed institutions should be returned to the market promptly, in order to minimise the eventual costs to depositors, creditors and taxpayers. The longer a bank or banking asset is held by an administrator, the more value it will lose. Experience has shown that if left unchecked, the resolution of weak banks may drag on for a long time.

Preserving competitiveness. In case of resolution by merger, acquisition or purchase-and-assumption transaction, the selection of an acquiring bank should be done on a competitive basis. An additional factor to consider is whether competition for banking services would be adversely affected. Any sweetener to facilitate deals should not distort competition and penalise the more efficient banks.

Minimise disruption to market participants. A bank closure may disrupt the intermediation of funds between lenders and borrowers, with potential negative effects on the economy. Borrowers may find it difficult to establish a relationship with a new bank and may find existing projects threatened if expected bank credits are not forthcoming. It may take the deposit insurer some time to determine who are the insured depositors, to close their accounts and pay them off.[1] In the absence of a deposit insurer, the delay to depositors – if they are entitled to receive any monies back – will be even longer as liquidation procedures can be protracted. In any case, the choice of resolution measures, and the choice between resolution and closure, should be made with the aim of minimising market disruption.

6.2 Resolution techniques

135. The distinction between a legal closure and economic closure of the bank is important. In a legal closure, the licence of the bank is withdrawn and the legal entity ceases to exist. In an economic closure, there is interruption or cessation of the operations of the bank which may often lead to severe disruption and possibly losses for the bank's customers. The art of resolving bank problems often entails achieving a "legal closure" while avoiding an "economic closure".

6.2.1 Restructuring plans

136. While a weak bank may be required to reorganise its operations as a corrective action, if insolvency is imminent, the bank may be required to carry out a radical restructuring. Such a strategy is only worth adopting if there is a real chance of getting the business back on a sound footing in the short term. Far-reaching restructuring may be the only solution for large and complex institutions that are unlikely to find partners with the financial resources to carry through a merger or acquisition.

137. On top of operational and organisational restructuring, there can be financial restructuring. Where the bank has issued capital instruments under Basel Committee rules that count as regulatory capital, the holders of these instruments must be available to absorb losses. The absorption of losses, by way of write-down or conversion into equity (after eliminating existing shareholders' claims) must be triggered prior to failure of the bank. In addition, the supervisor or other relevant authorities should pursue whether there can be conversion of subordinated debt into preferential or new equity where the supervisor or other authorities have the required legal means.

138. When the Board of Directors, management or controlling shareholders are reluctant to take timely action, supervisors should consider the appointment of an administrator to draw up the restructuring plan and implement its initial phases. In such cases, the administrator should replace the management and take over running of the company and have all the functions and powers of the ex-directors. Some curtailing of shareholders' powers could also be necessary.

6.2.2 Mergers and acquisitions

139. When a bank cannot on its own resolve its weaknesses, it should consider a merger with, or acquisition by, a healthy bank. This is a private sector resolution technique. Banks (even those that fail) are attractive targets to investors, especially financial institutions, because of their intrinsic franchise value.[2]

140. Arrangements for a merger or acquisition (M&A) should take place early before assets dissipate in value. In some cases, owners and certain creditors may have to make concessions to attract acquirers. Acquirers should have sufficient capital to meet the costs of the new bank and a management capable of projecting and implementing a reorganisation programme. Where the acquirer is a foreign bank, the supervisor needs to pay attention to additional aspects such as the laws and regulations of the relevant foreign jurisdictions. The supervisor will also need to liaise closely with foreign supervisors to inform itself about the acquirer and its related activities.

141. Supervisors should keep in mind that M&As are, even in good times, not easy undertakings for the institutions. This stems from different corporate cultures, incompatibility of IT systems, need for personnel layoffs, etc. Integration of staff and information systems has to be very carefully thought through in any merger plan.

142. The interested bank should have a clear understanding of the underlying causes and problems of the weak bank. Full and accurate information should be provided by the weak bank to all potential acquirers, although this may have to provided sequentially and under strict confidentiality agreements. In countries where the law permits, this could be done in cooperation with the supervisors. Restricting access to information will discourage potential acquirers, leading them to demand more concessions from the regulators or acquired bank. It is possible that full information may result in the interested bank deciding to abort the planned M&A. But this is better than an ill-considered takeover that may result in serious subsequent difficulties for the acquiring bank itself. The supervisor must be careful to ensure that in solving one problem, the strategy does not create another (larger) problem at some stage in the future.

143. Where the controlling shareholders of a weak bank are reluctant to sell their holdings and yield control of the bank and thus delay the M&A, the authorities may consider appointing an administrator having all the powers of the former management. Some pressure to persuade the weak bank's shareholders to accept the M&A may be necessary – even up to the expropriation of the majority stake. All the above will be subject to the appropriate legislation, which should also provide for fair treatment of the disenfranchised shareholders. A key issue is how, when and with what authority the supervisor can write down the value of shares.

144. There are other considerations. Owners of a weak bank who are trying to sell their stake to reduce their own personal losses will generally not attach great importance to the identity of the prospective buyers. In these circumstances, there is a risk that some potential buyers will be less interested in the banking operations of the bank than in its legal title and registration. Shareholders who are not fit and proper may wish to misuse the bank for dubious purposes (e.g. money laundering) or other business interests that may jeopardise the bank's continuing existence. In accordance with the Core Principles, supervisors are obliged to check the reliability of any new shareholder and have the power to reject applicants. Supervisors should use these powers uncompromisingly.

145. The advantages of an M&A type solution are that it:

- maintains the failing bank as a going concern and preserves the value of the assets (thereby reducing the cost to the government or deposit insurer);
- minimises the impact on markets as there are no disruptions in banking services to customers of the failing bank; and

- all assets are transferred in an M&A and all depositors and creditors are fully protected.

146. In a resolution by M&A, the supervisor should continue actively to monitor the problems in the acquired bank and take steps to ensure that they will be adequately addressed by the management of the resultant bank.

6.2.3 Purchase-and-assumption transactions

147. If a private sector M&A is not forthcoming or cannot be arranged, a purchase and assumption (P&A) transaction may be considered. A P&A transaction is one where a healthy institution or private investor(s) purchases some or all of the assets and assumes some or all of the liabilities of a failed bank. P&A transactions in most countries require withdrawal of the bank licence and the commencement of resolution proceedings by the liquidator. The acquiring bank purchases assets of the failed bank but not its charter.

148. A P&A transaction may be structured in many different ways, depending on the objectives and requirements of the deposit insurer[3] or the government, as well as of the acquirer. The transaction may be structured so that the acquirer purchases all assets and assumes all deposits. As with a M&A, this type of P&A transaction can be attractive to an acquirer – because of the intangibles – even when the bank is insolvent. However, such situations are rare. More often than not, to make the bank attractive for potential acquirers, a financial inducement may be necessary. Incentives may take the form of cash injections by the deposit insurer,[4] or in exceptional cases, by the government. This form of assistance must be justified as the least cost alternative.

149. A P&A transaction may be arranged so that the acquirer purchases only a portion of assets and assumes a portion of the deposits. For example, the liquidator may assign to the acquirer performing loans and other good-quality assets for an amount corresponding to the insured deposits it will assume.[5] A clean bank P&A transaction occurs when the acquiring institution assumes the deposit liabilities and purchases the cash and cash equivalent assets, the "good" loans and other high quality assets of the bank.[6] Assets not sold to the acquirer at resolution are passed on to the liquidator for disposal.

150. If non-performing loans and other risky investments are to be assigned to the acquirer, some arrangement will be needed to mitigate the consequent risk. This may take the form of a loss-sharing agreement or a put-back provision that allows the acquirer to return assets that become impaired within specified periods. In the sale of such assets, the acquirer must not be indemnified for all losses, otherwise there is no incentive for the acquirer to manage the bad loans to minimise losses, leading to a higher resolution cost. Alternatively, the acquirer could be hired, with appropriate incentives, to manage the nonperforming loans but not take them onto its own balance sheet.

151. A P&A transaction should be completed as quickly as possible. This will avoid the interruption of business so as to preserve the value of the bank and reduce the resolution cost.

152. As with M&A, the acquirer should have the financial and organisational capability to combine with the failed undertaking. If there is more than one eligible acquirer, a winner could be decided by competitive bidding so that the best price is obtained for the net assets of the failed bank.

153. Closing the bank as a legal entity implies that the shareholders lose their investment and the management are removed. From this standpoint a P&A transaction is compatible with minimising moral hazard.
154. The P&A type solution has the following benefits:

- it saves the value of the assets of the failed bank (thereby reducing the resolution cost);
- it minimises the impact on the market by returning assets and deposits to normal banking operations with the acquiring bank quickly. It can typically be completed over a weekend; and
- customers with insured deposits suffer no loss in service and have immediate access to their funds at the acquiring bank if the P&A transaction can be completed over the weekend.

6.2.4 Bridge bank

155. A bridge bank is a resolution technique that allows a bank to continue its operations until a permanent solution can be found. The weak bank is closed by the licensing authority and placed under liquidation. A new bank, referred to as a bridge bank, is licensed and controlled by the liquidator. The liquidator has discretion in determining which assets and liabilities are transferred to the bridge bank. Those assets and liabilities that are not transferred to the bridge bank remain with the liquidator. A bridge bank is designed to "bridge" the gap between the failure of a bank and the time when the liquidator can evaluate and market the bank in such a manner that allows for a satisfactory acquisition by a third party. It also allows potential purchasers the time necessary to assess the bank's condition in order to submit their offers while at the same time permitting uninterrupted service to bank customers.
156. A bridge bank transaction is most commonly used when the failed institution is unusually large or complex or when the deposit insurer or the government believes there is value to be realised or costs minimised, but does not have a ready solution other than a payoff. It has the advantage of gaining time to find another bank willing to step in and prepare the terms of the operation. However, it should not be used to postpone a permanent solution, nor should the arrangement be allowed to remain in place for any significant length of time as the bank will lose value if customers withdraw.

6.3 Use of public sector monies in a resolution

157. Public funds are only for exceptional circumstances. Public funds for the resolution of weak banks may be considered in potentially systemic situations, including the risk of loss or disruption of credit and payment services to a large number of customers. An intervention of this nature should be preceded by a cost assessment of the alternatives, including the indirect cost to the economy.
158. Government support may take the form of financial inducements to facilitate a resolution measure discussed in section 6.2.
159. Alternatively, the government may offer solvency support to a weak bank to allow it to remain open for business. "Open bank assistance" may take the form of a direct capital injection; loans provided by the government to the bank; or the

purchase of troubled assets by asset management companies created expressly for this purpose or other institutions and whose losses are covered by the government.

160. As the provision of solvency support puts taxpayers' money clearly at risk, the decision to do so should always be taken and funded by the government and the legislative body, and not by the central bank. The central bank is often required to advance the funding until legal changes have been made or budgetary appropriations have been approved. Close cooperation and information sharing between the central bank and the government is necessary.

161. The provision of solvency support is not a resolution measure in the sense of providing a lasting solution to the underlying weaknesses of the bank. The disbursement of public monies should be made dependent on the implementation of an action plan, approved by the supervisor, including measures to restore profitability and sound and prudent management. The government should always retain the option of getting its money repaid if the resolution of the bank so allows.

162. If public monies are used, shareholders of the weak bank should be made to bear the cost of the resolution via a dilution or even elimination of their shareholding interests. One principal difficulty of arranging such transactions is the time required to get shareholder approval for a significant reduction of their interests. When shareholders realise that government assistance may be forthcoming, negotiations can be complex and lengthy.

163. By rescuing a troubled bank, the government may find itself as the majority or sole owner, i.e. the bank is in practice nationalised. This should be a temporary solution, and the government should actively seek interested buyers in order to divest its holding. In the meantime, the government should operate the bank on market-oriented terms and with professional staff. The government should also make its intentions very clear to other market participants and to the general public.

6.4 Closure of the bank: depositor pay-off

164. If no investor is willing to step in to rescue the bank, the repayment of depositors and the liquidation of the bank's assets are unavoidable. In countries with a deposit insurance scheme, closure of the bank and depositor pay-off is also the right decision where a depositor pay-off is less costly than other resolution measures. The costs of a depositor pay-off will fall in the first instance on the other banks if the insurance scheme is privately funded or on the government otherwise.

165. The liquidators will proceed with the direct realisation of the assets in order to pay creditors under the rules governing general insolvency proceedings or bank-specific insolvency proceedings, depending on the institutional framework in place. Where depositors are protected by deposit guarantee schemes, the schemes usually acquire creditor status after making payment and participate in the liquidation allotments in place of the depositors.

6.5 Management of impaired assets

166. In all resolution techniques, unless all of the assets of a weak bank are acquired by another institution, there will be a large amount of impaired loans and other bad assets that needs to be managed. This occurs both for open bank assistance as well as resolution techniques that result in a closed bank. Asset

recovery should aim to be economic, fair and expeditious, with a view to maximising the recoveries on a net present value basis. Recovery of impaired assets can be done through direct collection (foreclosure of assets of debtors, especially from large debtors) or sales of assets to third parties, or by handling the assets (e.g. through debt work-outs) to prepare them for later sales.

167. Where the portfolio of assets is dismembered and sold individually to different acquirers at different times, a strategy that balances the risks and advantages of holding and managing the assets instead of rapidly selling them should be defined. Adverse economic effects from a strategy of rapid recoveries of non-performing loans should also be considered. The choice also depends on the capability and skills available for active management of the assets.

168. Different methods are available for selling the assets, such as sales en bloc, "portfolio" sales, asset-by-asset sales, securitisation or sales to a restructuring agency. The choice of method depends on the quality of the assets, overall economic and financial market conditions, interested domestic and foreign investors, and the available resources.

169. Experience has shown that there are several reasons to separate the handling of the bad assets from the rest of the bank:

- Once removed, the balance sheet is improved, thus making the bank more attractive.
- Bank management can focus on steering the bank through its present problems and on its strategic development rather than having to spend a large part of its scarce time on problem assets.
- Specialists may be hired with the aim of maximising the recovery of the impaired assets, for instance by adapting the assets to make them more attractive for investors.

170. The separation of assets can take different forms. They include a division in the bank, a subsidiary, or a separate asset management company, funded and managed by private investors or by the government.

171. Where all non-performing and other sub-quality assets are sold at market values to a separate company specially set up for this purpose, the resolution technique is called a "good bank–bad bank" separation. The asset management company – referred to as a "bad bank" – will need to be capitalised by the government or deposit insurer since typically no private investor is available or interested, at least initially, in acquiring the sub-quality assets. The company has the objective of managing the assets to maximise cash inflows. Transparency, expertise, sound management and appropriate incentives are essential for the maximisation of recoveries of this company. The remaining part of the bank is referred to as the "good bank". Recapitalisation will be needed if no share capital remains. The good bank should now focus on correcting operational weakness and its ongoing banking activities. Alternatively, the good bank can be offered for sale. A "good bank–bad bank" solution should be considered only if there is franchise value in the "good bank".

6.6 Public disclosure of problems

172. An important issue is whether, and at what point, the bank, the supervisor, central bank or perhaps the government, should comment publicly on

problems faced by a weak bank.[7] As a general rule, disclosure should be favoured to the extent legally permissible and required. Both the timing and content of any disclosure are important, bearing in mind that delays in disclosure could result in winners and losers (in particular new depositors) depending on whether they have access to the privileged information. The overriding consideration in the choice of timing and content of the disclosure must be how they contribute to resolving the weak bank, while maintaining overall confidence and systemic stability.

173. If there are already persistent rumours about the bank's problems, giving publicity to the remedial action being taken by the bank may help maintain or boost confidence in the bank. The bank should be encouraged to declare the situation and the prospects of returning to normal activity ahead of the supervisor's announcement. If the senior management of the bank are to be dismissed as a result of a supervisory decision, the supervisor should be the first to disseminate the information and set it in the right context. Information, at least the initial set presented by the supervisor, should be succinct and clear, and should contain only the content of the decision taken, a brief description of reasons why and the goals being pursued by the supervisor. Comments such as "depositors have no cause for alarm" or similar may be interpreted as implying endorsement of, or support for, the bank and the supervisor may feel morally obliged to bail out the bank subsequently.

174. If the problems of the bank are not yet in the public domain, the supervisor should consider whether it is less costly and disruptive to disclose a bank's problems after remedial actions have started. If the bank's problems are severe, premature disclosure may result in a bank run.

175. In all cases, the bank has to be mindful of any statutory or regulatory obligations to make disclosures. For example, if the bank's shares are listed on the stock exchange, certain disclosures may be required by the listing rules. The supervisor may also have obligations, formal or informal, to keep other parties informed such as other domestic supervisors, and overseas supervisors if the bank has overseas presences.

176. A related issue is whether formal supervisory action taken against the bank should always be disclosed. The same considerations apply. In some countries, all enforcement actions taken are made public in the interest of transparency.

177. In any case, whenever there is a decision on disclosure, it is essential that there is close co-ordination between the bank, the supervisory authority and other interested parties such as the central bank, the deposit insurer and the government. The co-ordination applies to both the timing and content of the disclosures. Experience has shown that when banks and authorities have made inconsistent or discordant disclosures, this has led to confusion and has made the resolution efforts more difficult.

Notes

1. The law or regulations must ensure that the deposit insurer has access to bank information early on in the process and that such information is accurate and relatively complete. Staff of the deposit insurer should also have adequate expertise to respond quickly and put money in the hands of the depositors.

2. Intangible benefits may include instant access to a particular market segment, acquisition of a desirable deposit pool and a vast financial distribution system with a minimum investment.
3. The role of the deposit insurer in a resolution is mentioned here in a narrow context. In some countries, the deposit insurer plays a much bigger role, including providing financial support, assisting with capital restructuring, and facilitating mergers with other institutions.
4. In some countries, the deposit insurance agency is restricted to paying out depositors only. This resolution technique will still be considered a private sector solution if the financial inducement is provided by a privately funded guarantee scheme.
5. The deposit insurer should give to the liquidator cash for an amount equivalent to the insured deposits, whose protection is ensured through the assignment. The uninsured depositors will jointly share with the deposit insurer the allotments that the liquidator will distribute using the cash given by the deposit insurer and the recoveries obtained from the disposal of the poor-quality assets.
6. This is one way of implementing a good bank–bad bank separation (section 6.5).
7. The discussion on public disclosure refers to all weak banks, whether under corrective action (section 5) or under resolution measures (section 6).

References

Aghion, P., Hart, O. and Moore, J. (1992) 'The Economics of Bankruptcy Reform', *Journal of Law, Economics and Organization*, vol. 8, pp. 523–46.

Allen, L. and Rai, A. (1996) 'Bank Charter Values and Capital Levels: An International Comparison', *Journal of Economics and Business*, vol. 48, pp. 269–84.

Andrews, D., Prescott, C., Moss, J. E., Marshall, D. and Rawcliffe, G. (2002) *Bank Support in the Developed World*, New York: Fitch Ratings Ltd.

Armour, J. and Deakin, S. (2000) 'Norms in Private Insolvency: The "London Approach" to the Resolution of Financial Distress', ESRC Centre for Business Research Working Paper 173, September.

Ashmead, J. (1994) 're Colonial Realty Co', *Brooklyn Law Review*, vol. 60, pp. 517, 519.

Asser, T. M. C. (2001) *Legal Aspects of Regulatory Treatment of Banks in Distress*, Washington DC: International Monetary Fund.

Bank for International Settlements (2002) 'Report of the Contact Group on the Legal and Institutional Underpinnings of the International Financial System: Insolvency Arrangements and Contract Enforceability'.

Barth, J. R., Caprio, G. Jr and Levine, R. (2003) 'Bank Regulation and Supervision: What Works Best?', *Journal of Financial Intermediation* (forthcoming).

Basel Committee on Banking Supervision (2002) *Supervisory Guidance on Dealing with Weak Banks*, Report of the Task Force Dealing with Weak Banks, March, Basel: Bank for International Settlements.

Basset, B. and Brady, T. (2001) 'The Economic Performance of Small Banks 1985–2000', *Federal Reserve Bulletin*, pp. 719–28.

Baumann, U. and Nier, E. (2002) 'Market Discipline, Disclosure and Moral Hazard in Banking', Bank of England Working Paper.

Bebchuk, L. A. (1988) 'A New Approach to Corporate Reorganizations', *Harvard Law Review*, vol. 101, pp. 775–804.

Beck, T. (2002) 'Deposit Insurance as Private Club: Is Germany a Model?', *Quarterly Review of Economics and Finance*, vol. 42, pp. 701–19.

Benston, G. J. (1995) 'Safety Nets and Moral Hazards in Banking', in K. Sawamoto, Z. Nakajma and H. Taguchi (eds), *Financial Stability in a Changing Environment*.

Benston, G. J. and Kaufman, G. G. (1997) 'FDICIA After Five Years', *Journal of Economic Perspectives*, vol. 11 (Summer), pp. 139–58.

Berger, A. N., King, K. K. and O'Brien, J. M. (1991) 'The Limitations of Market Value Accounting and a More Realistic Alternative', *Journal of Banking and Finance*, vol. 15 (September), pp. 753–83.

Berkowitz, J. and White, M. J. (2002) 'Bankruptcy and Small Firms Access to Credit', NBER Working Paper No. 9010, June.

Bliss, R. and Flannery, M. (2001) 'Market Discipline in the Governance of US Bank Holding Companies: Monitoring vs. Influencing', Federal Reserve Bank of Chicago, March.

Blowers, B. (2002) 'The Economics of Insolvency Law: Conference Summary', *Financial Stability Review*, December, pp. 153–6.

Bonin, J. and Wachtel, P. (2002) 'Financial Sector Development in Transition Economies: Lessons from the First Decade', Helsinki, BOFIT Discussion Papers 2002, no. 9, Bank of Finland, Institute for Economies in Transition.

Boot, A. W. A. and Thakor, A. V. (1993) 'Self-interested Bank Regulation', *American Economic Review*, vol. 83, pp. 206–12.

Bordo, M., Eichengreen, B., Klingebiel, D. and Martinez-Peria, M. S. (2001) 'Is the Crisis Problem Growing More Severe?', *Economic Policy*, vol. 32, pp. 51–82.

Bovenzi, J. F. and Spaid, M. (1998) 'The FDIC's Role as Receiver', in Federal Deposit Insurance Corporation, *Managing the Crisis: The FDIC and RTC Experience 1980–1994*, p. 211.

Boyd, J. H., Kwak, S. and Smith, B. (2002) 'The Real Output Losses Associated with Modern Banking Crises, or "The Good the Bad and the Ugly"', mimeo, University of Minnesota.

Brierley, P. and Vlieghe, G. (1999) 'Corporate Workouts; the London Approach and Financial Stability', *Financial Stability Review*, November, pp. 168–83.

Brown, D. (2000) 'The Term Structure of Credit Spread Innovations: Theory and Evidence', NISA Investment Advisors, LLC.

Bryis, E. and de Varenne, F. (1997) 'Valuing Risky Fixed Debt: An Extension', *Journal of Financial and Quantitative Analysis*, vol. 32, pp. 239–48.

Calomiris, C. W. (1989) 'Deposit Insurance: Lessons from the Record', *Economic Perspectives* (Federal Reserve Bank of Chicago), May/June, pp. 10–30.

Calomiris, C. W. (1990) 'Is Deposit Insurance Necessary? A Historical Perspective', *Journal of Economic History*, vol. 50, pp. 283–95.

Calomiris, C. W. (1997) 'The Postmodern Bank Safety Net: Lessons from Developed and Developing Economies', American Enterprise Institute, Washington DC.

Calomiris, C. W. (1999) 'Building an Incentive-compatible Safety Net', *Journal of Banking and Finance*, vol. 23, pp. 1499–519.

Calomiris, C. W. and Powell, A. (2000) 'Can Emerging Market Bank Regulators Establish Credit Discipline? The Case of Argentina', NBER Working Paper 7715.

Campbell, A. and Cartwright, P. (2002) *Banks in Crisis: The Legal Response*, Aldershot: Ashgate.

Carletti, E. and Hartmann, P. (2002) 'Competition and Stability: What's Special About Banking?', ECB Working Paper 146.

Chakravarty, S. and Molyneux, P. (1996) 'The Single European Market in Financial Services', *European Business Review*, vol. 5, pp. 43–53.

Clarotti, P. (1997) 'Bank Insolvency Legislation in the European Union', *Yearbook of International Financial and Economic Law*, 27.

Clementi, D. (2001) 'Debt Workouts for Corporates, Banks and Countries: Some Common Themes', *Financial Stability Review*, December, pp. 203–10.

Collin-Dufresne, P., Goldstein, R. and Martin, J. (2001) 'The Determinants of Credit Spread Changes', *Journal of Finance*, vol. 56, pp. 2177–207.

Contact Group on the Legal and Institutional Underpinnings of the International Financial System (2002) *Insolvency Arrangements and Contract Enforceability*, Basel: BIS.

Cordella, T. and Yeyati, E. L. (2002) 'Financial Opening, Deposit Insurance and Risk in a Model of Banking Competition', *European Economic Review*, vol. 46(3), pp. 471–86.

Cranston, R. (ed.) (1997) *Making Commercial Law: Essays in Honour of Roy Goode*, Oxford: Clarendon Press.

Cull, R., Senbet, L. W. and Sorge, M. (2001) 'Deposit Insurance and Financial Development', World Bank Policy Research Working Paper 2682.

Daniel, J. A. (1997) 'Fiscal Aspects of Bank Restructuring', IMF Working Paper 97/52.

Daniel, J. A., Davis, J. M. and Wolfe, A. M. (1997) 'Fiscal Accounting of Bank Restructuring', IMF Paper on Policy Analysis and Assessment 97/5.

De Bandt, O. and Hartmann, P. (2000) 'Systemic Risk: A Survey', ECB Working Paper 35.

De Juan, A. (undated) 'Dealing with Problem Banks: The Case of Spain', mimeo.

de la Torre, A. (2000) 'Resolving Bank Failures in Argentina: Recent Developments and Issues', World Bank Policy Research Working Paper 2295.

Demirgüç-Kunt, A. and Detragiache, E. (2003) 'Does Deposit Insurance Increase Banking System Stability?', *Journal of Monetary Economics*, forthcoming.

Demirgüç-Kunt, A. and Huizinga, H. (1999) 'Market Discipline and Financial Safety Net Design', World Bank Policy Research Working Paper 2183.

Demirgüç-Kunt, A. and Kane, E. (2002) 'Deposit Insurance Around the Globe: Where Does it Work?', *Journal of Economic Literature*, vol. 60, pp. 175–95.

Demirgüç-Kunt, A. and Sobaci, T. (2001) 'Deposit Insurance Around the World: a Data Base', *World Bank Economic Review*, vol. 15, pp. 481–90.

Dewenter, K. and Hess, A. (1998) 'An International Comparison of Banks' Equity Returns', *Journal of Money, Credit and Banking*, vol. 30, pp. 472–92.

di Martino, P. (2002) 'Approaching Disaster: A Comparison between Personal Bankruptcy Legislation in Italy and England (1880–1930)', mimeo, Bristol University.

Dialynas, C. and Edington, D. (1992) 'Bond Yield Spreads: A Post-Modern View', *Journal of Portfolio Management*, vol. 19, pp. 68–75.

Diamond, D. W. and Dybvig, P. H. (1983) 'Bank Runs, Liquidity and Deposit Insurance', *Journal of Political Economy*, vol. 91(3), pp. 401–19.

Dugger, R. H. (1984) 'Testimony of Subcommittee Deputy Staff Director, Accompanied by Gary Bowser, Senior Auditor, General Accounting Office'. Hearings Before the Subcommittee on Financial Institutions, Supervision, Regulation and Insurance of the House Committee on Banking Finance and Urban Affairs, September 18, 19 and October 4.

ECB (2002) *Report on Financial Structures*, Frankfurt, October.

Edwards, F. R. and Scott, J. (1976) 'Regulating the Solvency of Depository Institutions: A Perspective for Reform', mimeo, Columbia University.

Eisenbeis, R. A. and Wall, L. D. (2002) 'The Major Supervisory Initiatives Post FDICIA: Are they Based on the Goals of PCA? Should They Be?', Federal Reserve Bank of Atlanta Working Paper 2002-31.

English, W. B. (1993) 'The Decline of Private Deposit Insurance in the United States', Carnegie-Rochester Conference Series on Public Policy, vol. 38, pp. 57–128.

Evanoff, D. and Wall, L. (2002) 'Subordinated Debt and Prompt Corrective Regulatory Action', Federal Reserve Bank of Atlanta Working Paper 2002-18.

Fama, E. and French, K. (1989) 'Business Conditions and Expected Returns on Stocks and Bonds', *Journal of Financial Economics*, vol. 25, pp. 23–49.

Fan, W. and White, M. J. (2002) 'Personal Bankruptcy and the Level of Entrepreneurial Activity', NBER Working Paper No. 9340.

FDIC (2000) *Deposit Insurance: An Annotated Bibliography, 1989–1999*, Washington, DC: Federal Deposit Insurance Corporation.
Feldman, R. J. and Rolnick A. J. (1998) 'Fixing FDICIA: A Plan to Address the Too-Big-To-Fail Problem', *Federal Reserve Bank of Minneapolis Annual Report*, March.
Fernandez de Lis, S., Martinez Pages, J. and Saurina, J. (2000) 'Credit Growth, Problem Loans and Credit Provisioning in Spain', *Bank of Spain Working Paper*, 18, October.
Financial Stability Forum (2001) FSF Report Guidance for Developing Effective Deposit Insurance Systems, September, available via the Internet at http://cdic.ca/international/docs/1_FSF_Final_Report.pdf.
Finch, V. (2002) 'Public Interest Liquidation: PIL or Place-bo?', *Insolvency Lawyer*, vol. 5, p. 157.
Fletcher, I. F. (1999) *Insolvency in Private International Law: National and International Approaches*, Oxford: Clarendon Press.
Franks, J., Nyborg, K. and Torous, W. (1996) 'A Comparison of US, UK and German Insolvency Codes', *Financial Management*, Autumn.
Franks, J. and Sussman, O. (2002) 'Financial Distress and Bank Restructuring of Small to Medium Size UK Companies', mimeo, London Business School, June.
Freixas, X., Giannini, C., Hoggarth, G. and Soussa, F. (2000) 'Lender of Last Resort: What Have We Learned Since Bagehot?' *Journal of Financial Services Research*, vol. 18, pp. 63–84.
Frydl, E. J. and Quintyn, M. (2000) 'The Benefits and Costs of Intervening in Banking Crises', IMF Working Paper 00/147.
Garcia, G. G. H. (2000) Deposit Insurance Actual and Good Practice, International Monetary Fund Occasional Paper 197.
General Accounting Office (1984) 'Statement for the Record by the Comptroller General of the United States Concerning the Federal Rescue of Continental Illinois National Bank', submitted to the House Committee on Banking, Finance, and Urban Affairs, December 14.
General Accounting Office (1989) 'Thrift Failures: Costly Failures Resulted from Regulatory Violations and Unsafe Practices', AFMD-89-62.
George, E. A. J. (1994) 'The Pursuit of Financial Stability', *Bank of England Quarterly Bulletin*, February, pp. 113–18.
Giovanoli, M. and Heinrich, G. (eds) (1999) *International Bank Insolvencies, A Central Bank Perspective*, The Hague: Kluwer Law International.
Glaessner, T. and Mas, I. (1995) 'Incentives and the Resolution of Bank Distress', *World Bank Research Observer*, vol. 10, pp. 53–73.
Goodhart, C., Hartmann, P., Llewellyn, D., Rojas-Suarez, L. and Weisbrod, S. (1998) *Financial Regulation: Why, How and Where Now*, London: Routledge.
Goodhart, C. and Illing, G. (eds) (2002) *Financial Crises, Contagion, and the Lender of Last Resort: A Reader*, Oxford: Oxford University Press.
Gorton, G. (1988) 'Banking Panics and Business Cycles', *Oxford Economic Papers*, vol. 40(4), pp. 751–81.
Gottschalk, A. (1988) Der Stimmrechtseinfluß der Banken in den Aktionärsversammlungen der Großunternehmen, WSI Mitteilungen, vol. 41, pp. 294–304.
Granlund, P. (2002) 'Bank Exit Legislation in US, EU and Japanese Financial Centres', *Bank of Finland Discussion Paper*, no. 25/2002.

Granlund, P. (2003) 'Economic Evaluation of Bank Exit Regimes in US, EU and Japanese Financial Centres', *Bank of Finland Discussion Paper*, no. 5/2003.

Greenspan, A. (2001) 'The Financial Safety Net', in Proceedings of the Federal Reserve Bank of Chicago's 37th Annual Conference on Bank Structure and Competition, May.

Gropp, R. and Vesala, J. (2001) 'Deposit Insurance and Moral Hazard: Does the Counterfactual Matter?', ECB Working Paper 47.

Group of Thirty (1998) *International Insolvencies in the Financial Sector*, Washington DC.

Gup, B. E. (1998) *Bank Failures in the Major Trading Countries of the World: Causes and Remedies*, Westport, CT and London: Quorum Books.

Guttentag, J. and Herring, R. (1983) 'The Lender of Last Resort in an International Context', Princeton Essays in International Finance no. 151.

Hadjiemmanuil, C. (1996) *Banking Regulation and the Bank of England*, London: LLP.

Halme, L., Hawkesby, C., Healey, J., Saapar, I. and Soussa, F. (2000) *Financial Stability and Central Banks: Selected Issues for Financial Safety Nets and Market Discipline*, London: Bank of England, Centre for Central Banking Studies.

Hart, O. (1999) 'Different Approaches to Bankruptcy', presented at Annual World Bank Conference on Development Economics, Paris, June.

Hoggarth, G., Reidhill, J. and Sinclair, P. (2002) 'Resolution of Banking Crises: Theory and Evidence', mimeo, Bank of England.

Hoggarth, G. and Saporta, V. (2001) 'Costs of Banking System Instability: Some Empirical Evidence', *Financial Stability Review*, no. 10, pp. 148–65, Bank of England.

Hoggarth, G. and Soussa, F. (2001) 'Crisis Management, lender of the Last Resort and the Changing Nature of the Banking Industry', in *Financial Stability and Central Banks: A Global Perspective*, Routledge.

Honohan, P. and Klingebiel, D. (2000) 'Controlling Fiscal Costs of Banking Crises', World Bank Working Paper No. 2441.

Hood, C., Rothstein, H. and Baldwin, R. (2001) *The Government of Risk: Understanding Risk Regulation Regimes*, Oxford: Oxford University Press.

Hovakimian, A., Kane, E. and Laeven, L. (2002) 'How Country and Safety-net Characteristics Affect Bank-risk Shifting', World Bank mimeo.

Hüpkes, E. (2000) *The Legal Aspects of Bank Insolvency*, The Hague: Kluwer Law International.

Hüpkes, E. (2002) 'Dealing with Distressed Banks – Some Insights from Switzerland', *Journal of International Banking Law*, vol. 17, pp. 153–60.

IMF LEG (1999) *Orderly and Effective Insolvency Procedures: Key Issues*, Washington, DC: IMF.

Ingves S. and Lind G. (1996) 'The Management of the Bank Crisis in Retrospect', *Quarterly Review*, no. 1, Sveriges Riksbank, pp. 5–18.

Inquiry into Continental Illinois Corp. and Continental Illinois National Bank (1984) Hearings Before the Subcommittee on Financial Institutions, Supervision, Regulation and Insurance of the House Committee on Banking Finance and Urban Affairs, 18, 19 September and 4 October.

INSOL (2000) 'Statement of Principles for a Global Approach to Multi-Creditor Workouts', INSOL International, International Federation of Insolvency Professionals.

Jackson, P. (1996) 'Deposit Protection and Bank Failures in the United Kingdom, *Financial Stability Review*, no. 1, Autumn, pp. 38–43.
Jackson, T. H. (1982) 'Bankruptcy, Non-Bankruptcy Entitlements, and the Creditors' Bargain', *Yale Law Review*, pp. 857–907.
James, C. (1991) 'The Losses Realised in Bank Failures', *Journal of Finance*, vol. 46 (September), pp. 1223–42.
Jokivuolle, E. and Peura, S. (2001) 'A Value at Risk Approach to Banks' Capital Buffers: An Application of the New Basel Accord', *Bank of Finland Discussion Paper* 15/2001.
Jokivuolle, E. and Peura, S. (2003) 'Simulation-based Stress Testing of Banks' Regulatory Capital Adequacy', *Bank of Finland Discussion Paper* 4/2003.
Jonung, L. and Hagberg, T. (2002) 'How Costly Was the Crisis of the 1990s? A Comparison of Finland and Sweden's Deepest Crises', paper presented at 'Sweden and Finland: Economic Interaction, Processes and Comparisons', Työväen Akatemia, Kauniainen, September.
Kane, E. (1989) *The S&L Insurance Mess: How Did it Happen?* Washington, DC: Urban Institute Press.
Kane, E. (2000) 'Designing Financial Safety Nets to Fit Country Circumstances', World Bank Policy Research Working Paper 2453.
Kaufman, G. C. (1986) 'Bank Runs: Causes, Benefits and Costs', *Cato Journal*, vol. 7(3), pp. 589–94.
Kaufman, G. C. (1996) 'Bank Failures, Systemic Risk, and Bank Regulation', *Cato Journal*, vol. 16, p. 17.
Kaufman, G. C. (1997a) 'FDICIA After Five Years', in Kaufman (1997b).
Kaufman, G. C. (1997b) *FDICIA: Bank Reform Five Years Later and Five Years Ahead*, Amsterdam: JAI Press.
Kaufman, G. C. (2002) 'Too Big to Fail in US Banking: Quo Vadis?', mimeo, Chicago, October.
Klingebiel, D. (2000) 'The Use of Asset Management Companies in the Resolution of Banking Crises: Cross-Country Experience', World Bank Policy Research WP No. 2284.
Kupiec, P. H. and O'Brien, J. M. (1995) 'Recent Developments in Bank Capital Regulation of Market Risks', Federal Reserve Board, November.
La Porta, R., Lopez-de Silanes, F. and Schleifer, A. (1999) 'Corporate Ownership Around the World', *Journal of Finance*, vol. 54, pp. 473–517.
La Porta, R., Lopez-de-Silanes, F., Schleifer, A. and Vishny, R. (1997) 'Legal Determinants of External Finance', *Journal of Finance*, vol. 52, pp. 1131–50.
La Porta, R., Lopez-de-Silanes, F., Schleifer, A. and Vishny, R. (1998) 'Law and Finance', *Journal of Political Economy*, vol. 106, pp. 1113–55.
Laeven, L. (2002a) 'Bank Risk and Deposit Insurance', *World Bank Economic Review*, vol. 16, pp. 109–37.
Laeven, L. (2002b) 'Pricing of Deposit Insurance', World Bank, mimeo.
Lastra, R. M. and Schiffman, H. N. (eds) (1999) *Bank Failures and Bank Insolvency Law in Economies in Transition*, The Hague: Kluwer Law International.
Lehnert, A. and Maki, D. (2002) 'Consumption, Debt and Portfolio Choice: Testing the Effect of Bankruptcy Law', mimeo, Federal Reserve Board, October.
Lindgren, C.-J., Garcia, G. and Saal, M. (1996) *Bank Soundness and Macroeconomic Policy*, Washington, DC: International Monetary Fund.

Llewellyn, D. T. (1994) 'Secular Trends in Banking', Financial Integration in Western Europe – Structural and Regulatory Consequences, Occasional Paper 10 (Emil Ems, ed.), Stockholm: Sveriges Riksbank.

Llewellyn, D. (1999) 'Alternative Approaches to Financial Regulation', Institute of Economic Affairs, Financial Regulation Lecture, October.

Lundberg, E. (1999) 'Saneamento do sistema financeiro – a experiência Brasileira dos últimos 25 anos', in J. Saddi (ed.) 'Intervenção e liquidação extrajudicial no sistema financeiro nacional – 25 anos da Lei 6.024', Textnovo, São Paulo, pp. 53–70.

Lybeck, J. A. (1992) 'Finansiella kriser förr och nu', Stockholm: SNS Förlag.

Marino, J. and Shibut, L. (2002) 'Resolution Strategies for Large US Commercial Banks', presented at CCBS workshop on Crisis Resolution.

Mayes, D. G. (1997) 'A Market Based Approach to Maintaining Systemic Stability', *Bank of Finland Discussion Paper* 18/97.

Mayes, D. G., Halme, L. and Liuksila, A. (2001) *Improving Banking Supervision*, Basingstoke: Palgrave.

Merton, R. (1974) 'On the Pricing of Corporate Debt: the Risk Structure of Interest Rates', *Journal of Finance*, vol. 29, pp. 449–70.

Milhaupt, C. (1999) 'Japan's Experience with Deposit Insurance and Failing Banks: Implications for Financial Regulatory Design?', DP 99-E-8, IMES, Bank of Japan.

Ministry of Economic Affairs (1994) *Den Danske Pengeinstitutsektor* (The Danish Banking Sector), Copenhagen.

Ministry of Economic Affairs (1995a) *Finanstilsynets kontrol med de danske penge-institutter* (The Quality of Supervision of Danish Banks), expert group report, chaired by Professor Mogens Koktvedgaard, University of Copenhagen, Copenhagen.

Ministry of Economic Affairs (1995b) *Redning af pengeinstitutter since 1984* (Rescue of Banks since 1984), Copenhagen.

Ministry of Economic Affairs (1997) *Håndtering af pengeinstitutkriser* (The Procedure Applied in Banking Crises), Copenhagen.

Ministry of Economic Affairs (1999) *The Financial Sector after Year 2000*, Copenhagen.

Mishkin, F. S. (1997) 'Evaluating FDICIA', in G. C. Kaufman (ed.), *Research in Financial Services: Private and Public Policy*, Amsterdam: JAI Press.

Mishkin, F. S. (2000) 'Lessons from the Tequila Crisis', *Journal of Banking and Finance*, vol. 23, pp. 1521–33.

Moss, G., Fletcher, I. F. and Isaacs, S. (2002) *The EC Regulation on Insolvency Proceedings: A Commentary and Annotated Guide*, Oxford: Oxford University Press.

Nivorozhkin, E. (2003) 'The Information Content of Subordinated Debt and Equity Prices in the Presence of Bankruptcy Costs', Gothenburg University.

Oditah, F. (ed.) (1996) *Insolvency of Banks: Managing the Risks*, London: FT Law and Tax.

Peek, J. and Rosengren, E. S. (1997) 'Will Legislated Early Intervention Prevent the Next Banking Crisis?', *Southern Economic Journal*, vol. 64(1), p. 268.

Perotti, E. C. and Suarez, J. (2002) 'Last Bank Standing: What Do I Gain if You Fail?', *European Economic Review*, vol. 46(9), pp. 1599–622.

Quintyn, M. and Taylor, M. W. (2002) 'Regulatory and Supervisory Independence and Financial Stability', IMF Working Paper 02/46.

Ramsey, R. L. and Head, J. W. (2000) *Preventing Financial Chaos: An International Guide to Legal Rules and Operational Procedures for Handling Insolvent Banks*, The Hague: Kluwer Law International.

Rolnick, A. and Weber, W. E. (1986) 'Inherent Instability in Banking: The Free Banking Experience', *Cato Journal*, vol. 5(3), pp. 877–90.

Sandal, K. (2002) 'The Nordic Banking Crisis in the Early 1990s – Resolution Methods and Fiscal Costs', presented at CCBS workshop on Crisis Resolution.

Schoenmaker, D. (1997) 'Banking Supervision and Lender-of-Last-Resort in EMU', in M. Andenas, L. Gomley, C. Hadjiemmanueil and I. Harden (eds.), *European Economic and Monetary Union: The Institutional Framework*, The Hague: Kluwer Law International.

Schwartz, A. (1994) 'Systemic Risk and the Macroeconomy', conference on 'Banking, Financial Markets and Systemic Risk', Washington DC: Comptroller of the Currency.

Seidman, L. W. (1991) Testimony on 'The Implications of Too Big to Fail' before the Subcommittee on Economic Stabilization, Committee on Banking, Finance and Urban Affairs, United States House of Representatives, May 9. Serial 102-32: pp. 69–101.

Senate Report 97-536 (1982) US Code Congressional and Administrative News, Vol. 3, 97th Congress, Second Session.

Sigurðsson, J. (1995) 'Nordens banker och Europa', Helsinki, Nordic Investment Bank, paper presented at a conference of the Nordic Association of Bank Lawyers, Akureyri, 21 June.

Sigurðsson, J. (2002) 'The Future of Classical Banking', Helsinki, Nordic Investment Bank, paper presented at a conference of the European Banking and Financial Forum, Prague, 24 March.

Soussa, F. (2000) 'Too Big to Fail: Moral Hazard and Unfair Competition?', pp. 5–31 in Halme *et al.* (2000).

Stern, G. and Feldman, R. (2003) *Too Big to Fail: The Hazards of Big Bank Bailouts*, Washington: Brookings Institution.

van der Zwet A. (2003) *The Blurring of Distinctions between Financial Sectors: Fact or Fiction?* Occasional Studies, De Nederlandsche Bank, vol. 1, no. 2.

Wall, L. D. (1993) 'Too-Big-to-Fail After FDICIA', *Federal Reserve Bank of Atlanta Economic Review*, January/February, pp. 1–14.

Werlauff, W. (1998) *Lovmæssige hindringer for fusion og virksomhedskøb mellem virksomheder i de nordiske lande*, Copenhagen: Report to the Nordic Council of Ministers, December.

Wheelock, D. C. and Kumbhakar, S. (1994) ' "The Slack Banker Dances": Deposit Insurance and Risk-Taking in the Banking Collapse of the 1920s', *Explorations in Economic History*, vol. 31, pp. 357–75.

Wheelock, D. C. and Kumbhakar, S. (1995) 'Which Banks Choose Deposit Insurance? Evidence of Adverse Selection and Moral Hazard in a Voluntary Insurance System', *Journal of Money, Credit and Banking*, vol. 27(1), pp. 186–201.

Wilkinson, A. J. O. and Turing, D. (1996) 'Regulation and Insolvent Banks', ch. 1 in Oditah (1996).

Wood, G. E. (2003) 'Too Much Regulation?', mimeo, City University Business School.

World Bank (2002) *Building Trust: Developing the Russian Financial Sector*, Washington, DC.

Index